Uganda's Economic Reforms

Uganda's Economic Reforms

Insider Accounts

Edited by
Florence Kuteesa, Emmanuel Tumusiime-Mutebile,
Alan Whitworth, and Tim Williamson

OXFORD
UNIVERSITY PRESS

OXFORD

UNIVERSITY PRESS

Great Clarendon Street, Oxford ox2 6DP

Oxford University Press is a department of the University of Oxford.
It furthers the University's objective of excellence in research, scholarship,
and education by publishing worldwide in

Oxford New York

Auckland Cape Town Dar es Salaam Hong Kong Karachi
Kuala Lumpur Madrid Melbourne Mexico City Nairobi
New Delhi Shanghai Taipei Toronto

With offices in

Argentina Austria Brazil Chile Czech Republic France Greece
Guatemala Hungary Italy Japan Poland Portugal Singapore
South Korea Switzerland Thailand Turkey Ukraine Vietnam

Oxford is a registered trade mark of Oxford University Press
in the UK and in certain other countries

Published in the United States
by Oxford University Press Inc., New York

© Oxford University Press 2010

The moral rights of the authors have been asserted
Database right Oxford University Press (maker)

First published 2010

British Library Cataloguing in Publication Data
Data available

Library of Congress Cataloging in Publication Data
Data available

Typeset by SPI Publisher Services, Pondicherry, India
Printed in Great Britain
on acid-free paper by Clays Ltd., St Ives Plc

ISBN 978–0–19–955622–9 (Hbk.)

1 3 5 7 9 10 8 6 4 2

Dedication

To Martha, Betty, Jamilah, Kyom, and to all our former colleagues in the Ministry of Finance, Planning and Economic Development.

Preface

The fifteen years of political violence and economic mismanagement that followed Idi Amin's coup in 1971 left the Ugandan economy in ruins. In 1986 peace and political stability were established in most of the country, although North Uganda continued to experience insecurity. Between 1986/87 and 2006/07 GDP growth averaged 6.9 per cent per annum—making Uganda's one of the fastest growing economies in Africa. This was accompanied by a substantial reduction in poverty levels, from 56 per cent in 1992 to 31 per cent in 2006.

Not surprisingly, Uganda's economic success has attracted considerable international attention. The 2005 Paris Declaration on Aid Effectiveness, the Heavily Indebted Poor Countries (HIPC) debt relief initiative, and the growth of budget support have all been strongly influenced by Ugandan experience and thinking. Ugandan innovations such as Poverty Reduction Strategies, Public Expenditure Tracking Surveys, Virtual Poverty Funds, and Participatory Poverty Assessments have been widely adopted elsewhere—often promoted by the World Bank and other donors—as other countries sought to emulate Uganda's success. Kampala has become a popular destination for study tours.

Transplanting reform measures that have worked well in one environment to a different environment may fail (or disappoint) if critical factors underlying their success are absent. The purpose of this book is to contribute to improved understanding of the reforms that have underpinned Uganda's economic success since 1986 and to draw out key lessons, both for Uganda and for other developing countries. The focus is on economic reforms undertaken by central government—particularly the Ministry of Finance, Planning and Economic Development, but also the Bank of Uganda and the Ministries of Public Service and Local Government. While political developments, policy reforms at the sector level, and the battle against HIV and AIDS were also crucial, they are beyond the scope of this volume.

The following chapters discuss in detail the reforms undertaken since the late 1980s across a wide range of areas of economic policy for which central government is responsible. They are insider accounts; the authors are practitioners, not academics. Each author was centrally involved inside the Uganda government in implementing the reforms he or she describes; many were also responsible for their design. While authors have attempted to be as objective as possible, none is a totally disinterested observer. Hopefully, any shortfall in objectivity is outweighed by authenticity.

All but two of the authors work, or have worked, for the Ministry of Finance, Planning and Economic Development. The book is very much a team product, which has benefited from the help of numerous colleagues in the Ministry, both directly in the form of comments and help with data, and indirectly in the implementation of the reforms discussed here. However, it should be stressed that each author writes in his or her personal capacity and *not* on behalf of the Uganda government.

The editors are grateful to former colleagues Tim Lamont, Mary Muduuli, and Jamilah Whitworth for helpful comments and suggestions. They are particularly grateful to James Sheppard for providing an outsider's perspective on the text and for strengthening its structure and format.

Finally, the book could not have been produced without financial support from the UK Department for International Development. We are grateful to Jonathan Beynon, Gwyneth Lee, Mercy Mayebo, and Peter Oumo of DFID Uganda for their help and encouragement. The views or opinions in this book of co-author Alan Whitworth are entirely his own and do not represent those of DFID, where Alan has worked for several years.

Florence Kuteesa, Emmanuel Tumusiime-Mutebile, Alan Whitworth, and Tim Williamson

Contents

Contents

Contents

List of Figures

List of Tables

List of Tables

List of Boxes

List of Abbreviations

ADF	African Development Fund
APIR	Annual PEAP Implementation Review
APPERD	Action Plan for Public Enterprise Reform and Divestiture
ASYCUDA	Automated System for Customs Data
ASU	Anti Smuggling Unit
BFP	Budget Framework Paper
BoP	Balance of Payments
BoU	Bank of Uganda
CDF	Comprehensive Development Framework
CMB	Coffee Marketing Board
COMESA	Common Market for Eastern and Southern Africa
CPI	Consumer Price Index
CSO	Civil Society Organisation
CST	Coffee Stabilization Tax
CTL	Commercial Transactions Levy
DAC	Development Assistance Committee
DFID	Department for International Development (UK)
DHS	Demographic and Health Survey
DRIC	Divestiture and Reform Implementation Committee
EAC	East African Community
EACSO	East African Common Services Organisation
EASD	East African Statistical Department
EFAG	Education Funding Agencies Group
FDS	Fiscal Decentralization Strategy
GBS	General Budget Support
GoU	Government of Uganda
GDP	Gross Domestic Product
HBS	Household Budget Survey
HIPC	Heavily Indebted Poor Country

HIV/AIDS	Human Immunodeficiency Virus/Acquired Immunodeficiency Syndrome
IDA	International Development Association (World Bank)
IFMS	Integrated Financial Management System
IMF	International Monetary Fund
IPO	Initial Public Offering
LG	Local Government
LGBFP	Local Government Budget Framework Paper
LGDP	Local Government Development Programme
LGFC	Local Government Finance Commission
LTD	Large Taxpayer Department
MDA	Ministries, Departments, and Agencies
MDF	Multilateral Debt Fund
MDG	Millennium Development Goal
MDRI	Multilateral Debt Relief Initiative
M&E	Monitoring and Evaluation
MIGA	Multilateral Investment Guarantee Agency
MoES	Ministry of Education and Sports
MoF	Ministry of Finance (until 1992 and 1996–1998)
MoFEP	Ministry of Finance and Economic Planning (1992–1996)
MoFPED	Ministry of Finance, Planning and Economic Development (since 1998)
MoPED	Ministry of Planning and Economic Development (until 1992 and 1996–1998)
MoLG	Ministry of Local Government
MoPS	Ministry of Public Service
MTEF	Medium Term Expenditure Framework
NDF	Net Domestic Financing
NDP	National Development Plan
NGO	Non-Government Organization
NIMES	National Integrated Monitoring and Evaluation Strategy
NPA	National Planning Authority
NPV	Net Present Value
NRA	National Resistance Army
NRM	National Resistance Movement
NTE	Non-Traditional Exports
NWSC	National Water and Sewerage Corporation
ODI	Overseas Development Institute

OECD	Organisation for Economic Cooperation and Development
OPM	Office of the Prime Minister
PAF	Poverty Action Fund
PE	Public Enterprise
PEAP	Poverty Eradication Action Plan
PEC	Presidential Economic Council
PER	Public Expenditure Review
PERD	Public Enterprise Reform and Divestiture
PETS	Public Expenditure Tracking Survey
PEWG	Poverty Eradication Working Group
PFM	Public Financial Management
PIP	Public Investment Plan
PIU	Project Implementation Unit
PMAU	Poverty Monitoring and Analysis Unit
PMES	Poverty Monitoring and Evaluation Strategy
PMU	Parastatal Monitoring Unit
PPA	Participatory Poverty Assessment
PPG	Public and Publicly Guaranteed (Debt)
PRGF	Poverty Reduction and Growth Facility (IMF)
PRSC	Poverty Reduction Support Credit (World Bank)
PRSP	Poverty Reduction Strategy Paper
PSRRC	Public Service Review and Re-organisation Commission
RDP	Rehabilitation and Development Plan
REER	Real Effective Exchange Rate
RSDP	Road Sector Development Plan
SDA	Social Dimensions of Adjustment
SRPS	Special Revenue Police Service
SWAp	Sector Wide Approach
SWG	Sector Working Group
TA	Technical Assistance
TIN	Taxpayer Identification Number
ToT	Terms of Trade
UBI	Uganda Business Inquiry
UBoS	Uganda Bureau of Statistics
UCB	Uganda Commercial Bank
UCF	Uganda Consolidated Fund
UCS	Uganda Computer Services

UDC	Uganda Development Corporation
UEB	Uganda Electricity Board
UEDC	Uganda Electricity Distribution Company Ltd
UEGC	Uganda Electricity Generation Company Ltd
UETC	Uganda Electricity Transmission Company Ltd
UGX	Uganda Shilling
UIA	Uganda Investment Authority
UMA	Uganda Manufacturers' Association
UNDP	United Nations Development Programme
UNHS	Uganda National Household Surveys
UPE	Universal Primary Education
URA	Uganda Revenue Authority
URC	Uganda Railways Corporation
USD	United States Dollar
USE	Uganda Stock Exchange
UTL	Uganda Telecom Ltd
VAT	Value Added Tax
WTO	World Trade Organization

Notes on Contributors

Martin Brownbridge is a consultant on macroeconomics and fiscal policy. From 1998 to 2004 he was Macroeconomic Advisor in the Ugandan Ministry of Finance, Planning and Economic Development. He has also worked as macroeconomic advisor to the Ministry of Finance in The Gambia, as a long-term consultant in Ghana and Tajikistan, and as macro-fiscal advisor for the East Africa Regional Technical Assistance Centre of the International Monetary Fund.

Gustavio Bwoch has been the Accountant General of Uganda since 2003. He joined the Ministry of Finance, Planning and Economic Development as Commissioner, Treasury Office of Accounts in 1998 and served as Director of Accounts in 2002. He previously worked as Deputy Financial Manager with the Water and Sewerage Authority of Lesotho and as a Financial Accountant with Transocean (Uganda) Ltd.

Charles Byaruhanga is the Budget Advisor in the Ugandan Ministry of Finance, Planning and Economic Development. Between 1992 and 1999 he worked as a senior economist in the Economic Analysis Unit and the Macroeconomic Policy Department of the Ministry, and served as Commissioner for Macroeconomic Policy. In 1999 he left to undertake public sector consulting assignments for a number of development agencies, including the World Bank, before returning to the Ministry in 2005.

Gerry Cawley is an independent economic consultant based in Nairobi, Kenya. From 1994 to 2000 he was Tax Policy Adviser in the Ugandan Ministry of Finance, Planning and Economic Development, Kampala. He worked for twelve years as an economist in Ireland's Department of Finance and for fourteen years as an economist/tax adviser for the governments of Lesotho and Botswana.

Giulio Federico is a Senior Consultant at CRA International and a Research Fellow at IESE Business School in Barcelona. From 2001 to 2003 he worked as a Senior Economist in the Budget Policy Department of the Ugandan Ministry of Finance, Planning and Economic Development, with responsibility for the management and execution of the Medium Term Expenditure Framework.

Mark Henstridge is Director, Group Economics at BP, London. From 1988 to 1990 he was an Economist in the Ugandan Ministry of Planning and Economic

Development, as an ODI Fellow. From 1994 to 1996 he was the Advisor on Macroeconomic Policy in the Ministry of Finance and Economic Planning. From 1997 to 2001 he was an Economist at the International Monetary Fund, Washington, DC.

Margaret Kakande is Head of the Budget Monitoring and Accountability Unit in the Ugandan Ministry of Finance, Planning and Economic Development, and chair of the Advisory Group to the International Chronic Poverty Centre, Manchester University. From 1996 to 2008 she was the Poverty Analyst and Head of the Poverty Monitoring and Analysis Unit that led the formulation of the first Poverty Eradication Action Plan and the Participatory Poverty Assessments. Prior to joining government she lectured in statistics at Makerere University.

Louis Kasekende is Chief Economist of the African Development Bank. Prior to joining the Bank, he worked for seventeen years in the Bank of Uganda in several capacities, including as Deputy Governor, Executive Director for Research and Policy, and Director of the Research Department. From 2002 to 2004 he was Executive Director, representing twenty-two African countries, on the Executive Board of the World Bank. He has also lectured in economics at Makerere University.

Damoni Kitabire is a Lead Economist in the Fragile States Unit of the African Development Bank. He held several senior positions in the Ugandan Ministry of Finance, Planning and Economic Development, including Commissioner Macroeconomic Policy (1993–97), Director Budget (1997–98), Director Economic Affairs (1998–99), and Macroeconomic Advisor (2004–07). From 1999 to 2003 he was a Senior Economist in the Policy Development and Review Department of the International Monetary Fund, Washington, DC.

Florence Kuteesa is an Independent Public Expenditure Management Consultant based in Kampala. From 1983 to 2004, she woked for the Ugandan Ministry of Finance, Planning and Economic Development, rising from the level of Economist to Budget Director. She was a Senior Manager in Pricewaterhouse-Coopers, Nairobi, from 2005 to 2006. Between 2007 and 2009 she was a Public Expenditure Management Advisor in the East Africa Regional Technical Assistance Centre of the International Monetary Fund, Dar es Salaam.

Ishmael Magona has been the Commissioner for Infrastructure and Social Services in the Ugandan Ministry of Finance, Planning and Economic Development since 2005. His government career began in 1988 as an Economist in the Manpower Planning Department of the Ministry of Planning and Economic Development. He was Commissioner, Budget Policy and Evaluation, between 2003 and 2005.

Kenneth Mugambe has been the Commissioner, Budget Policy and Evaluation, in the Ugandan Ministry of Finance, Planning and Economic Development since 2005. He started as an Economist in the Ministry of Planning and Economic Development in 1992. From 1999 to 2004 he was Assistant Commissioner, Economic Development Policy and Research, where he was a leader of the team that formulated the Poverty Eradication Action Plan 2004.

Robert Muwanga is a Public Expenditure Management Advisor with the United Nations Development Programme in Sudan. Prior to this he was project coordinator for the Financial Accountability Programme (2006–07) and the Economic and Financial Management Project (1999–2006) in the Ugandan Ministry of Finance, Planning and Economic Development, Kampala. Between 1988 and 1998 he worked as a systems analyst/programmer, supporting the budget and accounting system in the same Ministry.

E. S. K. Muwanga-Zake is the Chairman of the Board of Directors of the Uganda Bureau of Statistics. Between 1994 and 1998 he was the Commissioner for Statistics, Statistics Department, Ministry of Finance and Economic Planning. He led the process of converting the Statistics Department into the Bureau of Statistics. He taught statistics at the Institute of Statistics and Applied Economics, Makerere University between 1978 and 1988. He has also worked at the Bank of Uganda for ten years.

Emmanuel Nyirinkindi is the Manager for Africa Region in the Infrastructure Advisory Department of the International Finance Corporation, Johannesburg. From 1989 to 2006 he worked in various positions with the privatization and parastatal reform programme—including as a Director from 1996—of the Ugandan Ministry of Finance, Planning and Economic Development. Prior to joining the Ministry, he worked for Esso Standard (Uganda) Ltd and as a Graduate Research Fellow in the Faculty of Commerce at Makerere University.

Michael Opagi is a Senior Investment Officer with the International Finance Corporation in Johannesburg. From 1989 to 2007 he worked in various positions with the privatization and parastatal reform programme—including as the Director of the Privatization Unit from 1996—of the Ugandan Ministry of Finance, Planning and Economic Development. He also worked as a privatization expert on short term contracts to the World Bank in Ethiopia and Zambia. He has served on several boards of directors.

Mary Goretti Sendyona is an Assistant Commissioner in the Ugandan Ministry of Public Service. Since 1992 she has been involved in implementing the Public Service Reform Programme, working on pay reform, wage bill management, payroll management, retrenchment, and voluntary retirement.

Emmanuel Tumusiime-Mutebile has been Governor of the Bank of Uganda since January 2001. His previous appointments include: Permanent Secretary/

Secretary to the Treasury, Ministry of Finance, Planning and Economic Development, 1998 to 2000; Secretary to the Treasury, Ministry of Finance, 1996 to 1998; Permanent Secretary/Secretary to the Treasury, Ministry of Finance and Economic Planning, 1992 to 1996; Permanent Secretary, Ministry of Planning and Economic Development, 1986 to 1992. While President of the Makerere University Students' Guild he was forced to flee from the Idi Amin regime in 1972, completing his education in the UK. After lecturing at the University of Dar es Salaam he returned to Uganda in 1979, working at State House before joining the Ministry of Planning and Economic Development in 1981.

Alan Whitworth is an Economic Adviser in the Zambia office of the British government's Department for International Development. From 1990 to 1995 he was Development Adviser in the Ugandan Ministry of Finance and Economic Planning. As well as working for DFID in the UK, South Africa, and Malawi, he has lectured at Glasgow University and spent twelve years working as an economist for the governments of Tanzania, Papua New Guinea, Nigeria, and Jamaica.

Tim Williamson is an independent economic consultant based in Kampala, and a Research Associate with the Overseas Development Institute, London. He worked at the Ugandan Ministry of Finance, Planning and Economic Development between 1998 and 2002, first as an ODI Fellow, then as an advisor on the Poverty Action Fund and on Fiscal Decentralization. He continues to work regularly with the Ministry on aspects of budgetary reform and public financial management.

Justin Zake is Advisor in the Fiscal Affairs Department's Revenue Administration Division of the International Monetary Fund, Washington, DC. From 1991 to 2004 he worked in various senior management positions in the Uganda Revenue Authority, including Deputy Commissioner General (Revenue). He lectured at Makerere University from 1982 to 1991 and also headed the Economic Analysis Unit in the Ministry of Finance. He was a member of several IMF missions before being posted to the IMF East Africa Regional Technical Assistance Centre, Dar es Salaam, from 2004 to 2006.

1

Overview of Ugandan Economic Reform since 1986

Alan Whitworth and Tim Williamson[1]

1. Introduction

Following Idi Amin's coup in 1971, Uganda suffered fifteen years of brutality, war, and civil war, which turned one of Africa's more prosperous economies into one of the poorest.

When the NRM Government assumed power in January 1986, it inherited a nation torn apart by ethnic and religious conflicts, and an economy shattered by years of civil war, political instability and physical insecurity. Severe macroeconomic imbalances fuelled inflation and contributed to acute foreign exchange scarcity. Revenues had dropped to 7.4 per cent of GDP. Industrial enterprises lay abandoned. Even the remarkably resilient agricultural sector had been disrupted as farmers fled their farms in search of refuge. Uganda's once impressive economic and social infrastructure lay devastated by war and lack of maintenance. Its skilled personnel and experienced administrators, terrorized by successive repressive regimes, had fled to safer pastures. Those who remained were deeply demoralized by physical insecurity and declining real incomes.[2] (World Bank 1991: 2)

Despite continuing insecurity, being landlocked, and having (until the recent discovery of oil) few mineral resources, over the last twenty years Uganda has had one of the fastest growing economies in sub-Saharan Africa (see Figures 1.1 and 1.2). This has contributed to a substantial reduction in poverty levels, from 56 per cent in 1992 to 31 per cent in 2006.

The purpose of this book is to contribute to improved understanding of the economic reforms which have underpinned Uganda's economic success since

---

[1] Helpful comments from Martin Brownbridge and Louis Kasekende are gratefully acknowledged.

[2] A conspicuous omission from this litany of woes is that Uganda was one of the countries worst affected by the HIV and AIDS pandemic during the 1980s. This had a particularly severe impact on the urban population and the public service.

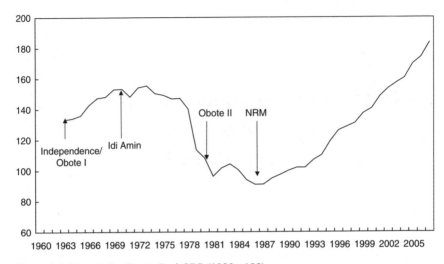

Figure 1.1 Uganda Per Capita Real GDP (1990=100)

Source: Selassie (2008), based on Penn World Tables and Uganda Bureau of Statistics.

1986 and to draw out key lessons, both for Uganda and for other poor countries. The focus is on economic reforms undertaken by central government. This synthesis chapter attempts to pull together the key features and lessons from the individual chapters into a consolidated (loosely chronological) account of these reforms. It also includes material that fell between the cracks of the individual chapters. The chapter focuses on reforms to the core economic activities of the Ministry of Finance, Planning and Economic Development (MoFPED),[3] namely macroeconomic, revenue and public expenditure management.

The development of economic policy since 1986 can be divided into four distinct phases.

1) 1986 to 1990
This can be characterized as the 'Pre-Reform' period during which the NRM agonized over the direction economic policy should take—dirigisme or liberalization.

2) 1990 to 1995
This was the period when the most fundamental economic reforms were undertaken, irrevocably setting Uganda on the road to a liberal market economy. Three milestones stand out: (i) the legalization of the parallel

---

[3] The title of the ministry has changed three times since 1992. Between 1992 and 1996 the title was the Ministry of Finance and Economic Planning. In 1996 it was split into the Ministry of Finance and the Ministry of Planning and Economic Development, before being re-merged under the present title in 1998 (see Chapter 2).

foreign exchange market in March 1990 (which marked the start of the reform programme); (ii) liberalization of coffee marketing in 1991 (see Box 1.1); and (iii) the merger of the Ministry of Finance and the Ministry of Planning and Economic Development in March 1992 and the achievement of macroeconomic stability.

3) 1995 to 2002

During this period the fundamental reforms initiated in the early 1990s were taken forward and built upon through developments such as decentralization, the Poverty Eradication Action Plan, and the Medium Term Expenditure Framework. The focus of policy was on poverty reduction and expanded provision of public services.

4) 2002 onwards

The period since 2002 has been one of consolidation and adjusting to political and personnel changes. The emphasis of economic policy has shifted from poverty eradication to economic growth, with a somewhat more interventionist role for government.

2. The pre-reform period: 1986 to 1990 (see Chapters 2 and 3)

The National Resistance Army fought its way to power in 1986 following a bitter bush war against the Obote II regime. Few political movements take up arms in the cause of capitalism and building capitalism did not feature in Yoweri Museveni's speech when he was first sworn in as President. Yet Uganda today has a thriving liberal capitalist economy. This book attempts to show how Uganda got from there to here.

The National Resistance Movement (NRM) government's instinctive approach to economic policy was dirigiste. Museveni had studied at the University of Dar es Salaam, where it was taken for granted that the state should play a direct role in driving development through planning and through ownership of utilities, marketing, and industrial enterprises. The National Resistance Army's military victory owed much to its discipline and it was implicitly assumed that economic agents would respect the basic requirement of military discipline to obey orders.

In 1986 a group sponsored by the International Development Research Centre of Canada was charged with developing a strategy for economic recovery. A minority within the group favoured the revaluation of the exchange rate and administered prices, believing that devaluation would fuel inflation and slow recovery by raising the cost of imported inputs. Despite being the minority, a number of their recommendations were adopted and the governor of the central bank was appointed from the minority. The most significant measure was the revaluation of the official exchange rate in nominal terms in August 1986. However, the economy did not respond favourably and inflation accelerated from 120 per cent in May 1986 to 240 per cent in May 1987.

In response an agreement was reached with the International Monetary Fund (IMF) and the World Bank in 1987 on a package of reforms that included a currency reform and a large nominal devaluation of the exchange rate. Although the decision to seek donor assistance was made with the support of President Museveni, the debate over the exchange rate continued for another three years. There was no consensus regarding the importance of price stability, or how to achieve it. Inflation remained high, fuelled by loose control of the budget and by rapid growth in credit to the monopoly marketing boards (mainly the Coffee Marketing Board) to finance the purchase of export crops. The official exchange rate was occasionally devalued to recover the ground lost to inflation. However, no consistent direction on exchange rate policy was established until 1990.

Two developments influenced the exchange rate debate. First, a high profile government seminar in 1989 brought together academics, politicians, and officials formally to discuss economic reform for the first time. The seminar was useful in sensitizing all participants about the key issues—including the role of the parallel foreign exchange market in everyone's lives. Second, the Presidential Economic Council (see Chapter 2) provided a forum for debate between the President, ministers holding economic portfolios, and senior officials. Officials from the Ministry of Planning and Economic Development (MoPED) led the argument for macroeconomic stabilization and liberalization. They recommended prudent budgeting to control inflation, the promotion of exports through legalization of the parallel market, and devaluation of the official exchange rate to a competitive level.

3. The technocratic era: 1990 to 1995

After four years of agonizing over the direction of macroeconomic policy, in 1990 the government started turning its back on the interventionist policies followed since Independence. Between 1990 and 1993 a series of fundamental reforms were initiated which set Uganda irrevocably on the road to a liberal, capitalist economy where the private sector was the engine of growth. Although it was not expressed this way at the time, government's role was to facilitate private investment—through developing an attractive economic environment and investing in infrastructure—and to provide social services.

The reforms during this period can be grouped under four headings:

1. 'Getting prices right';
2. The establishment of macroeconomic stability;
3. Strengthening revenue and public expenditure management; and
4. Private sector promotion.

This section looks at the main reforms in the above sequence.

4

3.1 'Getting prices right'

EXCHANGE RATE REFORM (SEE CHAPTER 3)

The start of Uganda's economic reform programme can be dated with precision to March 1990, when MoPED persuaded the Presidential Economic Council that the parallel exchange rate should be legalized and the official and parallel exchange rates unified. Like many African countries at the time, Uganda had a dual exchange rate. The official exchange rate bore little relation to economic fundamentals and was maintained by the Bank of Uganda at an artificially strong level, ostensibly to support access to foreign exchange by manufacturers and importers of 'essential' goods. Meanwhile, most unofficial transactions took place in the 'black' or 'parallel' market.

MoPED analysis showed that this arrangement was distorting economic incentives and demonstrated that a devaluation of the official rate would help the government implement a budget consistent with low inflation, without leading to an offsetting depreciation of the parallel rate. Another persuasive argument for legalization was the widespread observation that, in reality, everyone used and needed the parallel market—and that this fact should be legally recognized.

The legalization of the parallel market was announced in the 1990 budget, along with a sharp depreciation in the official exchange rate. It was a bold reform, going well beyond the conditionality agreed with the IMF. It triggered a rapid expansion of non-coffee exports, from about USD25 million in 1990 to around USD125 million four years later. Importantly, it laid the foundation for the liberalization of coffee exports.

TRADE REFORM (SEE CHAPTER 5)

In 1986 the NRM government inherited a trade regime, which had been in place since the 1970s, characterized by high export taxes and extensive non-tariff barriers. All exports apart from coffee had collapsed in response to export taxes. Coffee represented 70–80 per cent of total exports in the late 1980s and export duty on coffee contributed as much as 50 per cent of total domestic revenue. Coffee smuggling was rife.

Recognizing that this regime was a major deterrent to export production and an impediment to growth, the government embarked upon a unilateral liberalization programme in the early 1990s designed to reduce anti-export bias and encourage increased international trade. Non-tariff barriers were gradually removed following the introduction in 1991 of automatic licensing under an import certification scheme. The coffee export tax was abolished and replaced with import tariffs (Collier and Reinikka 2001: 32). Initially, import tariffs ranged as high as 350 per cent, making them the largest single contributor to total revenue. Meanwhile, as much as 40 per cent of the value of imports was subject to exemptions (mainly for international organizations, holders of

---

Box 1.1 LIBERALIZATION OF COFFEE MARKETING

The 1969 Coffee Act gave the parastatal Coffee Marketing Board (CMB) a total monopoly in the coffee export market. During the 1980s coffee represented 70–80 per cent of exports and contributed 25–50 per cent of government revenue. The government kept producer prices low in order to reduce crop financing requirements, the budget deficit, and inflation. Between 1986 and 1989 producer prices fell by more than 50 per cent in real terms, dramatically reducing production incentives and making the system untenable.

Coffee marketing reforms were a condition of a World Bank Structural Adjustment Programme. CMB's monopoly over exports ended in 1991 when it was turned into a limited liability company and four cooperative unions were allowed to export coffee. The Uganda Coffee Development Authority was set up at the same time to monitor and regulate the industry and advise on policy. The Bank of Uganda was relieved of responsibility for crop financing and commercial banks began providing financing.

The market was liberalized progressively between 1990 and 1995 through a series of measures: dropping the dual exchange rate system; lifting the coffee export tax; permitting pre-financing arrangements and the formation of joint ventures; lifting the requirement that coffee be transported by train; and abolishing the mandatory floor export price. Gradually private firms were allowed to export and, along with the cooperative unions, soon began to handle almost all coffee exports. The government's powers were reduced and private sector representation on the Coffee Development Authority board increased.

Adapted from Akiyama (2001: 96–103)

---

investment licences, and materials used by specified industries). Both import tariffs and exemptions were gradually scaled down; by the end of the decade the highest import duty rate had been reduced to 20 per cent and the duty rate regime greatly simplified. Uganda now has one of the most liberal tariff regimes in Africa.

Trade liberalization had an immediate and dramatic impact. Table 5.3 shows that merchandise exports more than tripled—and imports doubled—in US Dollar terms between 1991 and 1995. While much of this was initially attributable to the 1994/95 coffee boom, these increases were sustained up to 2006/07.

3.2 *Merger of the finance and planning ministries and achievement of macroeconomic stability (see Chapter 3)*

Today it is widely recognized that macroeconomic stability is a necessary condition for sustained economic growth. However, this was not the case in the 1980s. In much of English speaking Africa the terms 'fiscal discipline' and 'macroeconomic stability' were viewed with suspicion, as part of IMF ideology.

Uganda did not achieve macroeconomic stability until 1992, following a fiscal crisis. Although commitment to macroeconomic stability was part of the adjustment programme agreed to with the IMF and the World Bank from 1987 onward, continued loose control of budget implementation resulted in larger than planned fiscal deficits. Borrowing from the central bank financed these and the resulting monetary expansion led to an average annual inflation rate of 191 per cent between 1986 and 1989.

While the degree of commitment to fiscal discipline can be questioned, fiscal management at the time was particularly challenging. Tax revenue averaged just 5.8 per cent of GDP between 1985 and 1990, a third of the African norm. Domestic revenue was largely committed to the public service wage bill and debt service, both of which were inflexible in the short term. Foreign aid financed some 50 per cent of public expenditure, but this was mainly in the form of projects and was highly unpredictable.

Budget implementation closely followed the approved budget in 1989/90, which helped inflation drop significantly. However, the following year was characterized by a renewed loss of fiscal control, a consequent expansion in credit to the government, and increased inflation. Two shocks in the first half of 1991/92 drove inflation up further. First, a drought led to sharply increased food prices. Second, there was a shortfall in both tax revenues and programme aid inflows. By December 1991 only one fifth of the programme aid budgeted for the fiscal year (July to June) had been received. Despite this shortfall in re-sources, no offsetting adjustment was made to expenditures, which were fi-nanced by an increase in credit to the government equivalent to 40 per cent of the money stock. Inflation surged to a peak monthly rate of 10.6 per cent in April 1992 (equivalent to an annualized rate of more than 200 per cent).

The surge in inflation and the resulting fall in the exchange rate brought home to the President the significance of fiscal discipline. He blamed the management of the Ministry of Finance (MoF) for the crisis and responded by merging it with the Ministry of Planning and Economic Development in March 1992. The new management, largely from MoPED, then cut expenditure in the fourth quarter of 1991/92 by the equivalent of 1.8 per cent of GDP. This drastic measure stopped the increase in credit to government, the expansion of the money supply, and the rise in inflation within just three months. With the introduction of strict cash management of the budget inflation was brought down to single figures where, except for occasional blips (usually caused by food shortages), it remained for the next fifteen years.

The key lesson to be drawn from this episode is that political support is critical for macroeconomic stability. Previous attempts to control expenditure had been thwarted by behind the scenes pressures from spending ministries and ministers to obtain additional resources. Slashing expenditure in 1991/92 was extremely disruptive, particularly for capital projects. Despite this, because the President had explicitly and publicly mandated the new Ministry of Finance and Economic Planning (MoFEP) to control inflation, ministries recognized that lobbying would no longer be effective. Enforcing fiscal discipline is technically straightforward; simplifying somewhat, once budget lines are exhausted no more funds are released. Once the merged ministry was authorized to impose a cash budget mechanism strictly limiting expenditure to the resources available, government borrowing, the money supply, and inflation all dropped automatically—and virtually overnight.

3.3 Strengthening revenue and public expenditure management

Having established macroeconomic stability and removed the worst price distortions relatively quickly, the government was now able to concentrate on the much more difficult long term tasks of rebuilding government capacity, mobilizing additional resources, and utilizing them effectively to repair the war damage and provide basic public services. This had to take place in an environment where:

- Tax revenue had collapsed and foreign aid was funding half of public expenditure;
- Most government systems had effectively collapsed;
- The public service was bloated, inefficient, and corrupt;
- Aid was fragmented, donor driven, and not being used effectively; and
- Foreign debt had reached an unsustainable level.

REVENUE REFORM (SEE CHAPTER 5)

Clearly, little could be done without additional resources. An obvious policy priority, therefore, was to increase tax revenue so as to reduce dependence on aid. The main problem was the collapse of systems for collecting tax, rather than tax rates. MoF was responsible for tax collection, through its inland revenue, income tax, and customs and excise departments. However, the erosion of public service salaries and morale meant there was little prospect of rapid improvement in tax collection under existing institutional arrangements. In 1991, therefore, responsibility for tax administration was transferred to a new, semi-autonomous organization: the Uganda Revenue Authority (URA). This was to be operated along similar lines to the Ghana Revenue Authority, which had achieved impressive results in Ghana.[4] URA employees were to be paid salaries that were competitive with the private sector in order to retain staff and reduce the danger of corruption.

URA was given the target of increasing tax revenue by 1 per cent of GDP every year to bring Uganda up to regional norms. Over the next fifteen years URA established itself as a fairly robust and effective institution. Its greatest challenge was the introduction of Value Added Tax in 1996, which provoked a rebellion by traders before eventually taking root. Over the course of the

---

[4] The revenue authority model was subsequently adopted in most former British colonies in Africa.

1990s Uganda's extremely distorted tax structure, which strongly discouraged production for export, was replaced by a stable, liberal regime, broadly in line with international best practice. Reduced reliance on taxing international trade was accompanied by increased taxation of consumption, income, and profits.

Total domestic revenue increased from 6.8 per cent of GDP in 1991/92 to 13.0 per cent in 2006/07 (see Table 1.1); with substantial growth in GDP over the period, the real value of collections increased dramatically. Nevertheless, this was still well below government's original target and the sub-Saharan African average of 18 per cent of GDP. URA's failure to catch up with its neighbours has been attributed to a number of factors including the collapse of the tax compliance culture during the period of civil disorder, the structure of the economy, low political commitment to tax enforcement, and corruption in revenue administration. The incentive to raise additional domestic revenue may also have been reduced by Uganda's success in attracting increased foreign aid.

AID MANAGEMENT AND EXPENDITURE REFORM (SEE CHAPTER 6)

Revenue reform was a long term project and was never going to be sufficient to meet government's short to medium term rehabilitation needs. In order to mobilize the necessary resources government needed to:

- Ensure that existing domestic resources were more effectively utilized (e.g. through public service reform, see Box 1.2);
- Attract additional aid; and
- Channel aid to the highest priority uses.

This required central government to play a much more assertive role in public expenditure management than hitherto. The merger of MoF and MoPED was critical here. The period following the merger and the establishment of fiscal discipline in 1992 saw a number of reforms designed to establish central oversight and control over public resources (local and foreign). During this period, with strong Presidential backing, MoFEP became the most powerful ministry within government and began to establish an international reputation as one of the strongest finance ministries in Africa.

The focus of the reforms initially was on attracting and better utilizing project aid. Whatever progress was made by URA, and in improving the efficiency of existing resources, with most government resources pre-committed to wages and debt service the only way to increase resources significantly in the medium term was to attract additional aid. While the public rhetoric was that government wanted to reduce its aid dependency, the main focus of reform in the early 1990s was on creating the right conditions to enable Uganda to attract additional aid flows and to use aid more effectively in pursuit of government priorities.

Box 1.2 PUBLIC SERVICE REFORM (SEE CHAPTER 4)

Uganda's public service in 1986 was bloated, corrupt, and inefficient. With the collapse of government revenue, the public service wage bill was just 2.3 per cent of GDP in 1991/92. A graduate entry officer and a permanent secretary earned the equivalent of USD7 and USD23 a month respectively. Public servants were forced to survive on allowances, by moonlighting, or through corruption. Recognizing that it was impossible to retain and motivate public servants on such salaries, government embarked on a reform programme —with strong support from the President—designed to reduce the role of the public service and the number of public servants, and to pay a 'minimum living wage'.

In 1991 the number of ministries was cut from thirty-eight to twenty-one. The number of public servants was cut dramatically from 320,000 in 1991 to 157,000 in 1995 through a combination of eliminating 'ghost' workers, retrenchment, voluntary retirement schemes (with generous donor-funded severance packages), a six year recruitment freeze, and divesture of non-core government functions. Most allowances were monetized. With an improving fiscal position, the wage bill increased steadily, peaking at 5.6 per cent of GDP in 2002.

The commitment to increase public services in the 1997 Poverty Eradication Action Plan (see below) implied recruitment of significant numbers of teachers, health workers, etc. The recruitment freeze was lifted in 1998, therefore, and public service numbers increased steadily to 228,000 by 2005.

The reform momentum has slowed since the late 1990s, with the President appearing to lose interest. The wage bill has stagnated at about 5.5 per cent of GDP since 2001, well below the sub-Saharan African average of 6.5 per cent. While wages have increased, the target of a 'living wage' was not achieved. Plans to introduce results oriented management made little progress. Recent growth in the 'political bureaucracy', and in the number of ministers and districts, combined with a stagnant wage bill, call into question the commitment to further pay reform (Robinson 2006).

The government faced two main constraints. First, much aid received at the time was ineffectively used. The policy vacuum and the absence of central aid coordination in the late 1980s meant that most donors were 'doing their own thing', with little guidance from government. Inevitably, therefore, donors designed projects themselves together with line ministries. They were effectively presented to MoF or MoPED as a *fait accompli*.

Second, many donors required government to provide 'counterpart funding' of their projects. Managing these obligations and providing funds in a timely manner was beyond the capacity of government at the time and the lack of counterpart funding was seen as the single most important bottleneck to project implementation. Since failure to implement existing projects undermined the case for additional aid, managing counterpart funds became a key priority.

If government was to ensure both that aid was used in support of its, and not donors', policy priorities and that counterpart funds were properly managed, it needed to incorporate aid into the planning and budgeting systems. Since

Independence government priorities for public investment had been set out in five-year plans. These had little impact because they comprised mainly project 'wish lists' produced by the planning ministry. They were not linked to the budget, which was controlled by MoF, and they ignored most aid even though most public investment was funded by aid.

MoPED initiated a number of reforms to the planning system in 1991 designed to address these weaknesses. The Plan was turned into a three-year 'rolling' plan integrated with the budget. It was to be updated annually, with year-one expenditure estimates for projects constituting the Development Budget for that year.[5] The principle was established that *all* resources, whether local or from donors, should be allocated through the planning and budgeting system. This, in turn, meant that all project aid of any size should henceforth be included in both the Plan and the Development Budget.

An important element of the reform was the formation of the Development Committee by MoPED in 1991 to:

- Vet all new project proposals prior to their inclusion in the Plan;
- Oversee preparation of both Plan and Development Budget expenditure and funding estimates, ensuring consistency of aggregate expenditure with anticipated resources, and of sectoral allocations with policy priorities;
- Manage the government's counterpart funding commitments; and
- Advise on general (sectoral) policy issues.

Prior to the Committee's formation there was no central oversight or coordination of the preparation of the Plan or the Budget within MoPED or MoF. Responsibilities for planning, preparing the recurrent and development budgets, and aid management were split across the two ministries, which were suspicious of each other. Yet effective public expenditure management clearly required close cooperation.

The reforms therefore received a major boost in 1992 with the merger of the two ministries. Of particular significance was the bringing together of MoPED sector economists and finance officers from the MoF budget office in the new Budget Directorate. This created a critical mass of professional staff, which enabled the Directorate to develop sufficient technical competence and experience in sectoral issues to engage meaningfully with both ministries and donors on sector policy and budgets—i.e. to undertake what is now termed the 'challenge function'. A key factor in developing sector expertise was that each sector unit was made responsible for all aspects of sector policy within central government and for the entire budget cycle.

---

[5] The Ugandan budget is in two parts, recurrent and development. The Development Budget covers expenditure on investment and comprises a list of capital projects.

Following the merger, the Development Committee's membership was expanded to include the key economic divisions (Budget, Macro, and Aid Management) of the new Ministry. It was chaired by the Budget Director and was increasingly able to look at expenditure as a whole, not just at projects. Working within expenditure limits provided by the Macro Directorate, it attempted to ensure new projects and budget allocations were consistent with policy. A releases sub-committee was formed to minimize the damage of within-year cuts and protect 'pro-poor' budget lines. The Committee also took on responsibility for managing counterpart funds and aid generally.

In the three years following the restoration of macroeconomic stability in 1992 MoFEP succeeded in establishing a planning and development budgeting system (see Box 1.3) which for the first time captured nearly all public resources, both from government and donors. This enabled MoFEP to slow the accumulation of new counterpart funding commitments and to honour most existing ones. Counterpart funding had largely been brought under control by 1995. This was an important factor in the steady increase in project aid from USD136 million to USD400 million between 1991/92 and 1996/97 (see Table 13.2).

By the mid 1990s budget credibility had been established. Government resources were increasingly being allocated through proper budget systems in accordance with policy priorities. Counterpart funding and funding generally were now much more reliable. This, in turn, encouraged increased commitment and disbursement of aid. While public expenditure was still very much donor driven, government influence over donor spending decisions was increasing and a number of aid offers were now being turned down.

Box 1.3 PROJECT PLANNING SYSTEM

From 1991 all projects approved by government, whether locally or donor funded, had to be included in the Public Investment Plan (PIP). The MoFEP Development Committee was the 'gatekeeper', responsible for appraising new projects, ensuring consistency with government policy, managing counterpart funding commitments, and allocating government funding.

The PIP essentially comprised a database of projects. For each project, estimates of both expenditure and funding (distinguishing between local and donor) for the next three years were updated annually as part of the budget process. Actual historic data was also recorded.

The year one PIP estimates constituted the Development Budget for that year. The Development Committee allocated government funds between PIP projects within the Development Budget ceiling, with priority given to counterpart funding commitments.

By 1994 the PIP represented a fairly comprehensive database of project expenditure and aid funding and most counterpart funding commitments were being honoured.

3.4 *Private sector promotion*

While MoFEP saw the establishment of macroeconomic stability as the key factor in promoting private investment, a number of proactive measures were also undertaken. For example, in 1991 Parliament passed the Investment Code. This established the Uganda Investment Authority (UIA) as an independent agency to promote private investment. The Authority was intended to be a 'one stop shop' for issuing investment licences and approving applications for investment incentives—exemptions from various taxes and import duties. The initial incentives were over-generous and undermined efforts to increase tax revenue; most were phased out between 1995 and 1997 (see Chapter 5). Despite this, UIA licensed over 2,000 projects between 1991 and 2003, with the potential to employ up to 190,000 people, 'realising about half of these projects as actual investments'; UIA is 'now viewed in many respects as a model in Africa' (MIGA 2005: 49).

While much of this investment would probably have taken place with or without UIA, the privatization programme which commenced in 1993 had a substantial impact on the role of the private sector in the economy (see Chapter 16). In 1986 there were 129 public enterprises, with some 45,000 employees. They were engaged in virtually all sectors of the economy and generated about 10 per cent of GDP. 'The performance of these enterprises was characterized by low productivity, high losses, and rising debts, which placed a considerable burden on the banking system, public finances, and the balance of payments' (Collier and Reinikka 2001: 37).

Despite political controversy, by 2008 most of these enterprises had been either privatized or closed down under the privatization programme. Such significant economic entities as the telecommunications utility and Uganda Commercial Bank were divested, while the assets of the electricity utility and the railways were leased out on long-term concessions (see Chapter 16). A 2005 impact assessment found that the main beneficiary had been the national treasury—in the form of increased tax and lower subsidies, rather than sales proceeds. The programme had also promoted competition and encouraged foreign direct investment, though without creating significant employment (Adam Smith International et al. 2005).

Arguably, the most effective demonstration of government commitment to private sector development (and to the rule of law) was the return during the early 1990s of most of the properties which had been expropriated following Idi Amin's expulsion of most of the Asian community in 1972 (see Box 16.2). This was a politically brave measure because 'it involved handing back assets to an emigrant ethnic minority, and sometimes required expelling people currently living in properties' (Collier and Reinikka 2001: 29).

4. The poverty eradication period: 1995 to 2002

Figure 1.1 shows that the combined result of political and macroeconomic stability, improved public expenditure management, and trade and exchange rate liberalization was a rapid acceleration in economic growth. The announcement in the 1995/96 budget speech that GDP growth had reached double digits in 1994 signalled that Uganda's economic recovery was well underway. By 1995 the economic ship had been steadied. The establishment of macroeconomic stability and a credible budget system was largely attributable to the merger of the finance and planning ministries and the ruthless imposition of measures to enforce fiscal discipline and establish central control over resource allocation. Progress was rapid because, with strong backing from the President, MoFEP economists were able to impose the necessary measures with little regard to the views of line ministries or politicians. This had made the period from 1992 a 'dream' period for technocrats.

The adoption of a new democratic Constitution in 1995 marked the beginning of the end of the technocratic era. The need to fight elections meant that the President became increasingly sensitive to public and political opinion. While the maintenance of macroeconomic stability remained the paramount objective of economic policy, a number of significant changes were made to public expenditure management from the mid 1990s. Some, such as the Medium Term Expenditure Framework and an increased role for ministries in sector budgets, had been on MoFEP's agenda for some time and represented further development and elaboration of the (technical) reforms undertaken since 1991.

Others were political in origin. Two political initiatives in particular—the Poverty Eradication Action Plan (with free Universal Primary Education as its centrepiece) and decentralization—had profound implications for expenditure management and for attracting aid. This section discusses the impact of these developments. It then goes on to look at Uganda's role in the HIPC debt relief initiative and in persuading donors to move from project aid to direct budget support, and at the implications of increased aid for macroeconomic management.

4.1 *Poverty Eradication Action Plan (see Chapter 7)*

Figure 1.2 below shows that, following fifteen years of decline, GDP rebounded when the NRM government came to power and growth accelerated during the 1990s. Despite this, by 1995 mounting public concern that the benefits of rapid economic growth were bypassing the poor led the President to demand an overhaul of the planning system and a switch in emphasis from growth to poverty reduction. With public expenditure now under control, expenditure allocations were henceforth to be determined by their impact on the poor.

In 1996 a National Task Force on Poverty Eradication was established to review policy across the spectrum of government activity and to recommend changes in the allocation of public expenditure to better meet the needs of the poor. It represented a watershed in public expenditure management because, following the centralization of the resource allocation process within MoFEP in the first half of the 1990s, the process was progressively opened up not only to line ministries but also to districts, civil society, the private sector, and donors. Sector Working Groups (with members drawn from these constituencies) were set up to review policies for individual sectors, prepare sector action plans, and recommend changes in public expenditure allocations. These groups subsequently became institutionalized with an important formal role in the annual planning and budget processes (see below).

The end product of this exercise was the Poverty Eradication Action Plan (PEAP), which was launched in 1997. It set out government's strategy for reducing poverty in the form of detailed sector plans and policies. Henceforth these were to be the basis for expenditure allocations. The PEAP was essentially a much more detailed, thorough and consultative version of the Public Investment Plan. An important part of this exercise was a review of the projects in the PIP, which now became Volume 2 of the PEAP. Projects were categorized and prioritized on the basis of their expected impact on poverty reduction.

Arguably, the centrepiece of the PEAP was the introduction of free Universal Primary Education (UPE) from 1997/98. In the lead up to the 1996 elections President Museveni announced that he would introduce free UPE if re-elected. With its obvious benefits for the poor and its substantial budgetary implications,[6] more than any other measure UPE underlined the government's commitment to poverty reduction and the credibility of the PEAP document.

The World Bank and other donors were impressed by the PEAP's explicit focus on poverty reduction as well as its technical strength and the extensive public consultation process, which ensured a high degree of public 'ownership'. As a result, preparation of a Poverty Reduction Strategy Paper (PRSP)—explicitly modelled upon the PEAP—was made a central requirement for countries wanting to receive debt relief under the Heavily Indebted Poor Countries Initiative.[7]

---

[6] Primary enrolment doubled from 2.6 million to 5.2 million between 1997 and 1998, while government expenditure on UPE increased from 1.5 per cent of GDP in 1997/98 to 2.7 per cent in 2001/02 (see Table 9.1).

[7] However, these were rarely as effective as in Uganda for the simple reason that PRSPs were a foreign transplant. One of the authors observed the PRSP process in Malawi, where the PRSP was effectively just a hoop to be gone through in order to access debt relief and other donor support. Substantial resources were devoted to producing the PRSP, and to public consultation, but it played no discernible role in resource allocation.

Revised versions of the PEAP were published in 2000 and 2004 following increasingly extensive consultation processes.

4.2 Medium Term Expenditure Framework (see Chapter 8)

Uganda was one of the first developing countries to introduce a Medium Term Expenditure Framework (MTEF) and its system is one of the most highly regarded. An MTEF is a tool to help budget planners improve the allocative efficiency of scarce budget funds while maintaining macroeconomic stability. It aims to provide 'hard budget constraints' for budget planners so that they have incentives to prioritize expenditures within these constraints. A medium term perspective gives budget planners more scope and incentive to reallocate resources towards strategic priorities. Planners at the sector level are typically required to identify priorities and to draw up medium term sector expenditure plans to deliver these priorities. This helps counter the common problem with annual budgets of only being able to make incremental changes.

Uganda's MTEF was introduced gradually, starting with the preparation of an annual Budget Framework Paper from 1992. This focused on the macro/fiscal framework and on allocations to major budget categories such as the wage bill, non-wage recurrent, 'priority programme areas', and the PIP. With the extreme uncertainty of both domestic and foreign revenue at the time, there was little scope for looking more than one year ahead. The only attempt to look further ahead was the PIP, which included three-year expenditure estimates for individual projects.

As macroeconomic stability became established and budgeting was strengthened, the scope for medium term planning steadily improved. Since 1997/98 the budget documents have included an MTEF table (see Appendix 8.2) which presents the budget framework for the next three years, divided into sectors corresponding to broad functional expenditure classifications (health, education, etc.) and within sectors by central budget agency and local government grant; it is also broken down by the major economic classifications (wage, non wage recurrent, and development). The MTEF comprises all expenditure by central government and transfers to local governments.[8] It is integrated into the annual budget process; allocations in year one of the MTEF are consistent with the annual budget estimates presented to Parliament. *Ex ante* estimates of donor project expenditures are also presented.

The introduction of the MTEF table as the link between the planning and budgeting systems provided an opportunity to realign resources towards PEAP priorities. The table allowed all stakeholders in the budget to understand how the government planned to allocate its budget resource envelope among the

---

[8] Excluding taxes and arrears payments.

major sectors over the coming three years. Budget allocations were now clearly linked to the expenditure priorities outlined in the PEAP. The 1997/98 MTEF foreshadowed large increases in allocations to priority poverty reducing activities, most prominently the introduction of free UPE that year.

4.3 *Sector Working Groups and Sector Wide Approaches (see Chapter 9)*

As noted above, the initial measures to strengthen budgetary management involved centralizing responsibility for budget allocation decisions in the Development Committee. Budget submissions from line ministries were reviewed and presented to the Committee by sector desk officers and decisions were made with little opportunity for ministries to argue their case. While the system was effective in building sector technical capacity within the Budget Directorate, MoFPED recognized that responsibility for determining expenditure priorities *within* sectors must rest largely with the sectors themselves, with MoFPED performing the 'challenge function'.

By 1997/98, with macro stability firmly established, the downsizing of the public service largely complete, and *inter*-sectoral budgetary allocations clearly set out in the MTEF table, MoFPED felt sufficiently confident to relax its grip over *intra*-sectoral allocations. Impressed by the success of the consultation process in winning broad public support for the PEAP, MoFPED encouraged the establishment of Sector Working Groups (SWGs) to review sector policies, investment plans, and budget allocations. Such groups had already been set up in sectors such as roads and education in response to political pressure to develop sector policies and investment programmes in a coordinated way. The lead line ministry in the sector chaired these groups, while the sector desk officer from the Budget Directorate in MoFPED served as secretary.

SWGs had two radical features. First, for the first time, institutions outside MoFPED were given a formal role in determining intra-sectoral budget allocations through the preparation of sector Budget Framework Papers—medium term budget strategy documents. Second, the consultation process included not just sector ministries but also a broad range of stakeholders, including civil society and donors. Showing budget proposals to donors prior to the budget speech, let alone allowing them to participate in discussions on sector priorities, was unheard of in Africa at the time. MoFPED's willingness to involve donors in the budget process reflected its confidence in the budget system, recognition that much of the limited sector technical expertise in the country was based in donor organizations, and acknowledgement that since donors were financing half of the government budget they were legitimate stakeholders. It also reflected the commitment to consultation and transparency and the general lack of 'hang ups' about foreigners that distinguished the Uganda government from much of Africa in the 1990s.

A number of parallel processes developed at the sector level which collectively came to be known as the Sector Wide Approach (SWAp). These included sector investment plans, which were developed first in the roads and education sectors and provided a focal point for intra-sectoral resource allocations in the MTEF (and for donor funding), and regular sector review meetings. What set Uganda's SWAp experience apart from other countries was the emphasis on strengthening government systems for service delivery, rather than creating parallel systems through projects or basket funds. This was facilitated by the use of sector and general budget support (see below). SWAps were developed in all the sectors that saw a rapid expansion in service delivery from 1997. While much of this expansion was a consequence of political decisions (e.g. UPE and the abolition of health user fees), SWAps became important instruments in planning and managing the expansion of services. Policy-making, planning, implementation, monitoring, and evaluation at the sector level all improved as a result. The approach evolved differently in different sectors, which fostered a process of learning.

4.4 Decentralization (see Chapter 14)

As noted above, the establishment of strong budgetary management and macroeconomic stability was achieved through the fairly ruthless centralization of financial decision making within MoFEP from 1992. This was dictated not only by technical factors, but also by the extremely low levels of capacity at all levels of government. However, there was a tension between MoFEP's technocratic urge to centralize and the NRM's political instincts. A key factor in the NRA's military victory was the establishment of 'Resistance Councils', an informal system of local participatory democracy, which established strong grass roots support for the NRA in much of the country. One of the NRM's first moves upon assuming power was to legalize the Resistance Councils in 1987.

In 1993 a new decentralization policy was announced by the President; the provision of public services was to be progressively decentralized to district governments and local councils. MoFEP officials were (silently) appalled. The problems of building capacity at line ministry headquarters level appeared daunting enough; decentralizing resource management to the local level was a project for the long term. However, the President's experience in the bush had convinced him that decentralization was the best way of ensuring public service provision at the local level. He was not prepared to wait for capacity to be built at the centre first. Even though macroeconomic stability and budget systems were still very fragile, MoFEP was faced with the challenge of how to decentralize resources to local governments and—even more challenging—ensure their effective use.

Implementation of the reforms started in 1994, with elements of administrative and fiscal decentralization being phased in over a three-year period. The legal framework was embedded in the 1995 Constitution and elaborated upon in the 1997 Local Government Act. The major services mandated to be delivered by local governments were primary and pre-primary education, district hospital services and primary health care, district and community roads, rural and urban water and sanitation, as well as agricultural extension and advisory services. The system of grants from central government originally envisaged a high degree of discretion, with most service delivery being funded through unconditional grants, supplemented by equalization grants, and conditional grants for jointly agreed programmes funded by central government. Central government ministries maintained responsibility for setting service delivery policies and standards, and for monitoring their implementation.

However, contrary to the original plans, decisions on the allocation of resources by local governments were driven largely by the central government policy agenda, spearheaded by MoFPED and sector ministries, to expand basic service delivery in the priority areas for poverty reduction laid out in the PEAP. From 1998, conditional grants earmarked for those services were used as the main channel for funding this expansion. They were attractive to MoFPED, line ministries, and donors supporting those sectors, as they provided channels through which they could earmark funding towards the achievement of their policy objectives. However, especially with the decline and subsequent abolition of the Graduated Tax (the main locally generated source of tax revenue), this severely limited local government fiscal autonomy.

Despite MoFEP's and line ministries' initial misgivings, significant capacity has been gradually built up in local government and fiscal decentralization facilitated a dramatic expansion in public services at the local level. The President's instinct that local service provision required meaningful decentralization was largely vindicated. Uganda's decentralization experience is regarded as one of the most successful in Africa.

4.5 Debt relief (see Chapter 12)

Uganda's debt stock had grown rapidly between 1986 and 1991 as the government sought to rebuild public infrastructure. In 1990 there was a debt crisis when government ran out of foreign exchange to service its external debt obligations, following a sharp decline in the terms of trade. In 1991 a number of measures were taken to try and bring external debt under control. These succeeded in cutting the external debt to GDP ratio from 83 per cent in 1991 to 64 per cent in 1995. Most of the reduction was in bilateral debt.

Despite this reduction, debt service still accounted for 14.2 per cent of government expenditure in 1995/96 (see Table 12.1). Moreover, multilateral debt now represented 75 per cent of the debt stock. Since multilateral debt could not be rescheduled, there was little scope for further reductions. In 1995/96 a Government–Donor Debt Committee was set up which met quarterly to review

Uganda's economic performance and debt reduction efforts. The government used this forum to demonstrate to the international community: (a) that debt service was crowding out expenditure on social services and PEAP priorities; and (b) that little could be done about it without multilateral debt relief. The forum was later expanded to include civil society organizations, which were proving increasingly effective in lobbying for debt relief (through their international networks and governments) and for pro-poor expenditure. The Committee played a critical role in what eventually became the Heavily Indebted Poor Countries (HIPC) Initiative.

Uganda became the 'poster boy' for the international debt relief campaign which led to the HIPC Initiative. It was ideally qualified for this role because it had:

- A track record of macroeconomic stability and sound public expenditure management;
- Established clear priorities for tackling poverty in the PEAP following a consultative process;
- Translated PEAP priorities into public expenditure allocations through the MTEF and the budget; and
- Adopted a responsible debt strategy designed to minimize debt service.

In other words, Uganda had done all that it could reasonably be expected to do to manage its debt and increase pro-poor expenditure. Further progress was not possible without debt relief on multilateral debt.

Uganda was the first country to benefit from the HIPC Initiative, reaching 'decision point' in 1998. To cement its case for multilateral debt relief the government proposed an innovation, which has been widely adopted elsewhere. The Poverty Action Fund (PAF, see Chapter 13) was set up in 1998/99 to demonstrate that debt relief provided under the HIPC Initiative would only be used to increase expenditures on public services that directly contribute to poverty reduction.[9]

PAF funds were only used to fund budget lines which were of particular benefit to the poor, such as primary education, primary health care, water and sanitation, and rural feeder roads. The aggregate level of these expenditures in 1997/98 (the year before the PAF was set up) was used as a base from which to determine future spending levels for PAF budget lines. Resources from HIPC debt relief and from the Nordic donors were added to this base to determine the minimum level of PAF expenditures. The PAF was a virtual fund in that PAF expenditures were an integral part of the budget; however, they were protected from within year budget cuts. The creation of the PAF contributed to major increases in expenditure on pro-poor areas, which increased from 1.8 per cent

---

[9] A secondary motive was to provide a vehicle for Nordic donors to continue giving programme aid (originally provided to help meet multilateral debt service payments) after Uganda's debt service became 'sustainable' under HIPC.

of GDP in 1997/98 to 5.6 per cent in 2001/02 (see Table 1.1). While it began as a vehicle for HIPC debt relief, over time the reassurance it provided to donors that aid would directly benefit the poor helped to mobilize additional budget support over and above debt relief savings.

Table 12.1 shows that Uganda saved over USD1 billion in debt service payments as a result of various debt relief schemes between 1995/96 and 2006/07. Not surprisingly in view of its leading role in illustrating the case for multilateral debt relief, the HIPC institutional architecture was strongly influenced by Uganda. In particular, as noted above, preparation of a Poverty Reduction Strategy Paper—explicitly modelled on the PEAP—was made a requirement for accessing the scheme.

4.6 Budget support (see Chapter 13)

As noted above, once macroeconomic stability had been established, the main motivation behind many of the reforms of the early 1990s was to increase the overall level of resources (from both tax and aid) available for public expenditure and to increase the proportion that was used in support of government priorities. Initially, project aid was the dominant aid modality; in the chaos of the late 1980s donors understandably had no confidence in government's capacity to manage aid itself. The focus of reform initially, therefore, was on developing coherent policy priorities, bringing projects within the planning and budgeting systems (in order to exercise some government influence over donor allocations), and strengthening the management of counterpart funds (so as to improve project implementation).

The increase in project aid from USD136 million in 1991/92 to USD400 million in 1996/97 (see Table 13.2) suggests that the reforms were highly successful in attracting increased volumes of project aid. However, while government influence over donor allocations was increasing, for as long as project aid remained the dominant aid modality the allocation of much public expenditure would remain essentially 'donor driven'. From the mid 1990s, therefore, MoFPED started pressing donors to switch their funding away from projects and towards programme aid.

Programme aid had traditionally been provided in support of structural adjustment, and as balance of payments support. Now that Uganda had established macroeconomic stability, programme aid could no longer be justified on structural adjustment grounds. A new form of programme aid was therefore required. The term 'budget support' was coined to meet this need. It referred to programme aid that explicitly supported government expenditure through the budget. Budget support is channelled through the government budget. It avoids many of the problems associated with project aid such as the costs of tying aid, duplicate management and reporting arrangements, the bias towards capital expenditure, and counterpart funds.

Budget support was provided in two main forms. 'Sector Budget Support' (SBS) was provided to support specific sectors from 1998/99. MoFPED guaranteed that SBS resources would result in equivalent increases in sector budget allocations. From 2000/01 donors also provided un-earmarked 'General Budget Support' (GBS). GBS contributed to the pool of resources available to fund all government expenditures, and was, by definition, used to finance government's highest priorities.

Table 13.2 shows that the campaign to persuade donors to shift their aid towards budget support was successful. While project aid declined in real terms (and from 6.3 per cent to 4.0 per cent of GDP) between 1996/97 and 2004/05, GBS increased from USD165 million (2.6 per cent of GDP) to USD477 million (5.2 per cent of GDP) over the period. 'Uganda's public revenues and expenditures have increased in real terms by 240% over the last ten years. [Budget support] funding has contributed 31% of the real increase in public expenditures between 1997/98 and 2003/04' (OECD 2006).

At the same time that it was serving as poster boy for the international debt relief campaign, Uganda was also in the vanguard of the movement to persuade donors to switch from project aid to budget support. The move to GBS was one of the most profound developments in the aid business in recent years (OECD 2006). Just as it was the first country to qualify for HIPC debt relief, Uganda was one of the first and largest recipients of GBS from the late 1990s.[10] There is a common explanation.

By the late 1990s the government had established a solid track record of macroeconomic and public expenditure management. Donors were increasingly preoccupied with poverty during this period. The combined effect of decentralization, the adoption of the PEAP following widespread consultation, and the explicit translation of PEAP priorities (which most donors endorsed) into budget allocations through the MTEF, was to give Uganda's commitment to poverty reduction real credibility in donor eyes. Essentially, the government had demonstrated that it could be trusted to spend donors' money effectively and on the right things. Moreover, donors (and the public) were routinely consulted on allocations through SWGs and the annual Public Expenditure Review. In this context, much of the case for project aid had evaporated. While accounting for public expenditure remained a weak area, government undertook to strengthen public financial management (see Chapter 15). This would be easier in a context where aid was increasingly being channelled through government systems and where donor projects were no longer poaching government accountants.

[10] The World Bank piloted its budget support lending instrument, the Poverty Reduction Support Credit, in Uganda.

4.7 Problems of managing increased aid (see Chapter 13)

The reforms introduced from the early 1990s aimed at attracting increased aid proved highly successful. Table 13.2 shows that gross aid increased from USD253 million in 1991/92 to USD841 million in 2004/05.[11] Moreover, aid was much better aligned with government priorities, with the proportion of programme aid increasing from 46 per cent to 57 per cent over the period and with closer scrutiny of project aid.

The resource gap was so large in the early 1990s that it was implicitly assumed that any additional aid could be readily absorbed and added to total public expenditure. However, by the turn of the century the scale of the increase in aid was such that it was causing problems for macroeconomic management. Government expenditure was relatively stable at about 17 per cent of GDP until 1998/99. The sharp increase in aid from 1999/2000, mainly in the form of budget support, facilitated a commensurate increase in expenditure, peaking at 24.5 per cent of GDP in 2001/02. The budget deficit excluding grants widened from 6.3 per cent of GDP in 1997/98 to 11.6 per cent of GDP in 2001/02 (see Table 13.1). This created problems for two areas of macroeconomic management: monetary policy and the exchange rate.

Since most of the increased expenditure was in domestic currency (such as teachers' wages following UPE) there was a corresponding increase in fiscal liquidity creation, from less than 1 per cent of GDP in the mid 1990s to nearly 7 per cent of GDP in 2001/02. To meet its base money target and keep inflation in check, the Bank of Uganda had to sterilize this increased liquidity through sales of either domestic securities or foreign exchange. This proved difficult because both the domestic money and the foreign exchange markets were shallow. To avoid discouraging exports through exchange rate appreciation the Bank focused on sales of government securities, which rose from 0.6 per cent of GDP in 1997/98 to 2.6 per cent of GDP in 2001/02. Since government securities competed with private sector credit for the resources available for lending by commercial banks, (aid fuelled) fiscal expansion effectively crowded out private sector credit even though government's domestic borrowing requirement was small. Moreover, as the bulk of government expenditure consisted of non-traded goods, the fiscal expansion also threatened to drive up the real effective exchange rate—leading to 'Dutch disease' and damaging export competitiveness.

---

[11] Most of the increase occurred in two bursts, between 1991/92 and 1994/95 and between 1999/2000 and 2003/04. The latter was largely explained by greatly increased budget support.

5. 2002 onwards

The sheer pace of economic reform in Uganda during the 1990s meant that there was bound to be a loss of momentum at some stage and a need for consolidation. The record of reform since 2002 has been much less dramatic and less smooth, as the earlier reforms needed to be consolidated in a changing institutional and political environment. There has been some slight backtracking from decentralization. Economic policy has also become somewhat more interventionist. Yet important progress has been made in several—arguably more difficult—areas.

POLITICAL AND INSTITUTIONAL CHANGE

The early reform period was characterized by particularly strong political and technical leadership of the reform agenda. Inevitably, there were changes over time. The long-standing Permanent Secretary and Secretary to the Treasury[12] was appointed as Governor of the Bank of Uganda in 2001. A number of other technocrats who had spearheaded reforms during the 1990s also left MoFPED over the next few years. A new Minister of Finance, Planning and Economic Development was appointed in 2002.

This represented a test of the depth of institutional capacity in MoFPED. Although the pace of reform slowed after these personnel changes, MoFPED has remained a capable institution. Previously weak areas, such as the Office of the Accountant General, have been strengthened significantly since 2002. A new National Planning Authority was established, in line with the 1995 Constitution. While MoFPED delayed its establishment for as long as it could, Parliament ensured it became an institutional reality.

At the political level, the fact that the President ceased chairing Cabinet regularly meant that the finance minister received less protection from his colleagues. However, while there have been some slippages in budget discipline, aggregate fiscal discipline has broadly been maintained and the budget remains a reliable guide to actual spending. Following the 2001 Budget Act, a Parliamentary Budget Office was established to provide technical support to MPs. Parliamentary committees, such as the Budget and the Public Accounts Committees, have become much more active and effective, especially since the return of multi-party politics in 2006.

In response to local demands, the government created a large number of new districts in the lead up to the 2006 elections. This spread capacity more thinly, and added to administrative costs. Meanwhile the main local revenue source, Graduated Tax, was suspended and various administrative changes were made, which reduced local government autonomy and independence from the centre.

---

[12] The head of MoFPED.

There has been a gradual change of emphasis in economic policy since 2002, with somewhat less emphasis on poverty reduction. Table 1.1 shows that expenditure on PEAP priority areas peaked (as a share of GDP) in 2002/03, following debt relief and the jump in budget support. There was growing political frustration that economic growth was not being translated into structural change in the economy, such as increased industrialization and formal sector job creation. Following a decade of state withdrawal from direct economic activity, government has adopted a somewhat more interventionist stance since 2002. This has taken the form, *inter alia*, of budget funding for supporting productive activities (such as energy investments) and 'strategic exports', and the revival of ad hoc investment tax incentives.

The changes since 2002 are perhaps best encapsulated in the decision to replace the PEAP with the National Development Plan and to transfer responsibility for its drafting from MoFPED to the National Planning Authority. It is too early to assess the value added by the Authority and whether this (re-)separation of planning from expenditure management will undermine the progress made during the 1990s in directing public expenditure towards political priorities.

MACROECONOMIC MANAGEMENT

As noted above, MoFPED and the Bank of Uganda became increasingly concerned that aid-fuelled increases in public spending on pro-poor services around the turn of the century were crowding out private sector growth and threatening export competitiveness. A new medium term strategy of fiscal consolidation was adopted, therefore, in 2002. Its objective was to cut the fiscal deficit before grants, which had reached 11.6 per cent of GDP in 2001/02, in order to ease the pressures on monetary policy. Previously, budgeted aggregate expenditure was determined by the maximum amount of resources (domestic and foreign) that could be mobilized, adjusted for the domestic borrowing target. The new strategy involved a phased reduction in the fiscal deficit before grants to 6.5 per cent of GDP by 2008/09, or reductions of about 0.7 per cent of GDP a year. In drawing up the fiscal framework for the MTEF during the budget process, if projected aid disbursements exceeded the level needed to fund the budget—given the deficit target—government would save the excess resources; the additional aid would be added to foreign exchange reserves.

The strategy succeeded in scaling back the deficit to 6.8 per cent of GDP by 2005/06. The amount of domestic liquidity created by fiscal operations was cut by 65 per cent over four years, allowing net issues of securities to be reduced. This created room for a rapid recovery in bank lending to the private sector (see Table 13.4) and an acceleration in private investment (UBOS 2008).

However, the new strategy put a brake on the rapid increases in public expenditure of recent years. There was no longer a guarantee that increased sector budget support would lead to additional expenditure in a sector—which concerned spending agencies and donors alike. MoFPED struggled to enforce spending agencies' expenditure ceilings when they knew that increased sector budget support was on offer. Meanwhile, new policy demands from the President and Cabinet continued to emerge.

PUBLIC FINANCIAL MANAGEMENT (SEE CHAPTER 15)

Macroeconomic stability and rapid growth were achieved in the 1990s despite very weak financial management and accountability systems; strong public financial management was clearly not a necessary condition for *starting* growth. Public financial management reform only began to be taken seriously after the turn of the century—well after the main economic reforms—as its importance for *sustaining* growth was recognized. It was driven by a number of factors. First, entrenching reforms to the budget process required the establishment of formal systems. Second, effective political and public oversight of budget implementation was dependent upon accurate and up to date accounts. Third, donors would only continue to provide budget support if they had confidence in government's ability to manage and account for their funds.

The main public financial management reforms include: the 2003 Public Finance and Accountability Act, which provided the legal framework for reform; the 2003 Public Procurement and Disposal of Public Assets Act, which decentralized the procurement function to spending agencies and local government; and the introduction of an Integrated Financial Management System, also in 2003. These were accompanied by the establishment of the Office of the Accountant General and a major effort to expand and professionalize the accounting cadre within government through large amounts of training and technical support and improved conditions of service. However, these reforms have yet to translate into significant improvements in public financial management outcomes.

AID AND GOVERNMENT–DONOR RELATIONSHIPS

Following a highly positive and productive relationship during the 1990s, which saw a substantial increase in the quantity and quality of aid received by Uganda, government–donor relations deteriorated in the 2000s. After the shift to General Budget Support, donors became increasingly concerned with issues of governance, in particular the political environment and corruption. The relationship between donors and government became less constructive and more confrontational, especially in the lead up to the 2006 Presidential elections.

MoFPED had anticipated that the shift to budget support would be permanent. However, there was a resurgence of project aid from 2003/04. This was partly due to the deteriorating relationship between donors and government, but also to changes in the international aid environment, particularly the arrival of global health initiatives such as the Global Fund for HIV and AIDS. In addition, the above change in fiscal policy provided an incentive for donors to provide aid off budget. Many provided support directly to line ministries without going through MoFPED processes. The Development Committee and associated project aid management structures within MoFPED had become lax.

Since the 2006 elections donor–government relations have improved, and an arguably more pragmatic and responsible framework for that relationship is emerging. The government has become more cautious in its dialogue, whilst donors are more realistic about what to expect from government. MoFPED recognizes that project aid is here to stay, and has begun to examine ways of better integrating it into the budget process. However, it has yet to be seen whether lessons have been learnt from the difficult period of government–donor relations.

6. Impact of economic reforms

6.1 Growth

Table 1.1 and Figures 1.1 and 1.2 show that Uganda has enjoyed two decades of sustained economic growth since the NRM took over government in 1986, averaging 6.9 per cent per annum between 1986/87 and 2006/07. Real per capita GDP reached the level of 1973 (its previous peak) in 2003. Growth has consistently exceeded that of sub-Saharan Africa, and of landlocked countries in particular, since 1986.[13] There was a marked acceleration following the major reforms of the early 1990s. This book makes no attempt to quantify the contribution of the individual economic reforms discussed here to Uganda's growth performance. However, it can be asserted with confidence that—along with the crucial precondition of the establishment of peace and security in most of the country[14]—the combined reforms played a major role in accelerating and sustaining growth.

The impact of reforms on growth can be divided into two broad categories: those that facilitated economic activity by the private sector and improved provision of public services by government itself. The key facilitating reforms were the liberalization of the foreign exchange market in 1990, the liberalization of coffee marketing in 1991, the establishment of fiscal discipline and macro stability (and the taming of inflation) in 1992, and the rationalization

---

[13] Growth has been accompanied by significant structural changes in the economy. Agriculture's share of GDP declined from 53.2 per cent in 1986/87 to 36.3 per cent in 2004/05. The shares of Industry and Services increased from 11.0 per cent to 20.4 per cent and from 35.7 per cent to 43.3 per cent respectively over the same period (Kitabire and Oumo 2005).

[14] The growth performance is all the more impressive considering that northern Uganda suffered continuous insecurity throughout the period.

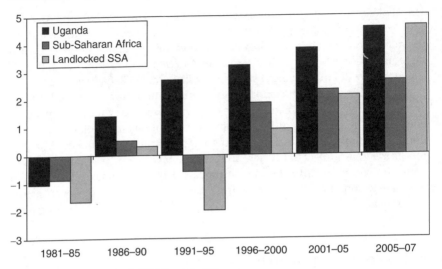

Figure 1.2 Per Capita Real GDP Growth (%)

Source: Selassie (2008), based on Penn World Tables, Uganda Bureau of Statistics, and IMF World Economic Outlook.

of the tax and trade regimes. The combined result was to turn Uganda from one of the most distorted economies in Africa into one of the most liberal and least distorted. The above—essentially 'price'—reforms were supplemented by a number of pro-active measures to promote private investment, in particular the 1991 Investment Code, the privatization programme, and the return of 'departed Asian' properties.

The combined impact of the above reforms is illustrated in Table 1.1. In the 1990s GDP growth was achieved despite limited investment; gross investment averaged only 16.7 per cent of GDP between 1990/01 and 1999/2000. Growth was driven by a combination of increased capacity utilization, rehabilitation of existing capacity, and some limited new investment; this was made possible by the increased availability of foreign exchange and increased private sector confidence, following the restoration of macroeconomic stability and measures such as the privatization programme. This is a pattern of economic recovery that has occurred in many countries which have suffered steep economic contractions but then managed to restore macroeconomic stability.[15]

---

[15] As Collier and Reinikka observe, post conflict economies have certain advantages over peaceful countries with regard to growth, such as the opportunities presented by the flight of private capital during periods of disorder. By 1991, 67 per cent of Ugandan private wealth was held abroad. This represented a substantial potential source of investment. Between 1993 and 1997 some USD650 million (17 per cent) was repatriated in response to the improving economic climate (Collier and Reinikka 2001: 30).

Table 1.1 Selected Fiscal Indicators (% GDP), 1991/92–2006/07

	1991/92	1992/93	1993/94	1994/95	1995/96	1996/97	1997/98	1998/99
Domestic Revenue	6.8	7.3	8.3	9.8	10.2	10.9	10.2	11.3
Gross Aid (grants & loans)	11.0	13.8	10.7	9.8	8.1	8.9	8.5	8.4
Budget Support	5.1	6.1	4.9	3.8	2.2	2.6	3.1	3.0
Project Aid	6.0	7.7	5.8	6.0	5.8	6.3	5.4	5.4
Expenditure & Net Lending	21.6	16.8	15.5	16.9	16.4	18.3	16.5	18.8
PEAP Priorities							1.8	2.8
Gross Fixed Capital Formation (at market prices)	16.2	15.6	15.3	16.5	17.0	16.9	15.6	19.1
Real GDP Growth (at market prices), %	4.0	8.0	6.4	10.9	9.9	4.9	4.8	7.8

	1999/2000	2000/01	2001/02	2002/03	2003/04	2004/05	2005/06	2006/07
Domestic Revenue	10.9	10.5	11.5	11.5	11.9	11.9	12.7	13.0
Gross Aid (grants & loans)	9.3	11.1	11.4	10.7	11.3	9.1	7.5	10.5
Budget Support	3.4	5.0	6.5	6.6	6.2	5.2	3.1	5.7
Project Aid	5.9	6.1	4.9	4.2	5.0	4.0	4.4	4.7
Expenditure & Net Lending	21.5	20.4	23.1	21.4	21.4	20.4	19.5	21.0
PEAP Priorities	3.3	4.3	5.6	5.6	5.3	5.1	5.0	5.3
Gross Fixed Capital Formation (at market prices)	19.5	19.3	20.1	21.0	22.1	22.4	21.2	23.7
Real GDP Growth (at market prices), %	5.4	5.2	8.6	6.6	6.8	6.3	10.8	7.9

Note: In 2008 Uganda Bureau of Statistics published revised estimates of GDP for the period since 2000/01, using a new base year and an improved methodology. Estimates for earlier years have not been revised.

Sources: Tables 13.1, 13.2, and 9.1, Uganda Bureau of Statistics (2008).

The above pattern of growth was starting to run out of steam by the end of the 1990s, partly because most of the useable capacity had been brought back into production and partly because of a decline in the external terms of trade. To sustain growth increased investment was needed. Table 1.1 shows that the average investment/GDP ratio in the early 2000s increased to 21 per cent, reaching 23.7 per cent in 2006/07. Particularly striking is the increase in private investment. Private gross fixed capital formation, which had dropped as low as 6 per cent of GDP in the late 1980s, increased to about 17 per cent of GDP in the mid 2000s (UBoS 2008: Table 4.1.L). Private investment accelerated following the fiscal consolidation from 2002/03, which facilitated a rapid increase in private sector credit, and increasing foreign direct investment. Investment also benefited from growth in remittances from overseas. The Bank of Uganda estimates that remittances averaged USD340 million annually between 2000 and 2007.

Public expenditure has also been a major contributor to economic growth. Table 1.1 shows total expenditure and net lending increasing from the range 15–17 per cent of GDP between 1992/93 and 1995/96 to 19–23 per cent of—rapidly expanding—GDP since the turn of the century. As noted above, public expenditure increased by 240 per cent in real terms between 1994/95 and 2003/04. This was financed from a steady increase in domestic revenue following tax policy and administration reforms (6.2 per cent of GDP between 1991/92 and 2006/07, see Table 1.1) and increased budget support and debt relief since 2000. Increased expenditure contributed to growth both directly and indirectly. For example, the increase in primary education expenditure from 1.5 per cent to 2.7 per cent of GDP between 1997/98 and 2001/02 (see Table 9.1) directly increased the incomes of teachers while also improving the (future) productivity of the labour force.

6.2 *Poverty reduction (see Chapter 10)*

Between 1997 and 2006 the explicit overall objective of government policy was poverty eradication. Table 10.1 shows that Uganda's sustained economic growth since the late 1980s has been translated into broad-based growth of consumption. While there have been marked variations between regions and over time (and an increase in income inequality), the proportion of the total population below the national poverty line declined from 56 per cent in 1992 to 31 per cent in 2006. This is one of the largest and fastest reductions in income poverty ever recorded. The finding that coffee growing districts contributed more to poverty reduction than non-coffee districts suggests that liberalization of coffee marketing and the exchange rate was particularly significant for poverty reduction.

The progress in reducing income poverty is mirrored in most non-financial dimensions of poverty. Given the substantial increase in public expenditure on basic social services (see Table 9.1) from the late 1990s, significant improvements in social indicators would be expected. A review of Uganda's progress towards meeting the United Nations' Millennium Development Goals confirmed that there has been significant progress in the areas of primary education, literacy, maternal health, HIV and AIDS, and safe water, although progress in reducing infant and under five mortality was slow and these targets are unlikely to be achieved (UNDP 2007).

6.3 Reform failures

Perhaps inevitably, this chapter (and this book) focuses on those areas of reform which have successfully contributed to economic growth and poverty reduction in Uganda. In the interests of balance, it is appropriate to highlight a number of areas where progress has been disappointing. Despite rapid economic growth, there are a number of concerns relating to the state of the economy:

- The limited diversification of the economy.
- The lack of formal job creation despite rapid growth.
- The failure to attract large scale private investment in industry.
- The weak state of the indigenous private business sector.
- The delay in commissioning new electricity generation capacity and the persistence of load shedding throughout the 1990s and 2000s.
- The slow pace of financial deepening and broadening, especially the virtual absence of medium to long term financing, largely as a result of delay in reforming the pension system.

Despite substantial progress in public expenditure management, there have also been a number of failures:

- The quality of government services and public infrastructure is generally poor. The rapid expansion of services in the health, education, water, and road sectors came at the expense of investment in quality and sustainability. There has been inadequate budgeting for maintenance of infrastructure, particularly roads.
- Expenditure on administering the public sector has increased rapidly, both at the centre and at local government level (due to the creation of new districts). This has been at the expense of the quality of public services.
- Corruption has spread alongside the rapid increase in public expenditure.
- An important factor in all the above is the failure to pay public servants a 'living wage'.

7. Conclusions

Since 1986 Uganda's economy has been transformed from a state of collapse into one of the fastest growing, most vibrant economies in Africa. Economic growth has, in turn, led to substantial reductions in poverty. In attempting to summarize how this has been achieved it is important to highlight the interplay between 'technical' economic reforms and political forces.

7.1 Technical reforms

While the economic reform programme of the 1990s was very much Ugandan designed and some of the individual reforms were highly innovative, it was initially a conventional programme that differed little in its basic principles from conventional World Bank and IMF 'structural adjustment' programmes. The early emphasis was on 'getting prices right' (e.g. exchange rate, tariff, and tax reform) and helping markets operate (e.g. trade reform, particularly coffee market liberalization), on the one hand, combined with establishing fiscal discipline and macroeconomic stability on the other. The emphasis on the private sector as the 'engine of growth' reflected the pragmatic recognition that public sector capacity to operate public enterprises had collapsed, rather than ideological conviction. Measures to promote private investment, such as the Investment Code and privatization, were again conventional.

The overall conclusion from the above is that these policies worked pretty well. The most powerful lesson was that little progress can be made towards growth without macroeconomic stability. The shock measures adopted to enforce fiscal discipline and macro stability in 1992 were highly effective and established a platform on which all subsequent reforms were built. Today the importance of macro stability is recognized across most of Africa. In 1992 it was a revelation, at least in Uganda.

Only after fiscal discipline was imposed did distinctively Ugandan features of economic management (such as the PEAP, MTEF, PAF, and SWGs) begin to emerge.

Maintaining fiscal discipline requires a strong finance ministry, both technically and politically. The merger of the finance and planning ministries in 1992 was a watershed in economic management. For the first time, the allocation of all public resources was considered together by a single institution in an integrated planning and budgeting process. The consolidation of responsibility for all aspects of sector policy and expenditure within central government in the Budget Directorate was a key element of this. The merged ministry was able to build real technical capacity by pooling the scarce manpower resources of the two ministries, establishing sound management, maintaining stability in senior positions, and making effective use of technical assistance (see Box 2.2). Always in control of its own reform programme, MoFPED established itself as the undisputed custodian of economic policy and one of the few African finance ministries to effectively discharge its 'challenge function'.

Uganda was a pioneer in aid management. Despite the public rhetoric about reducing aid dependence, it was recognized within government that rehabilitating the economy could not wait for revenue reform to bear fruit. Substantially increased aid needed to be attracted and channelled to priority areas. Uganda has been highly successful in both respects. It is useful to identify the key steps in the process. The main bottleneck in utilizing project aid in the early 1990s was the availability of counterpart funding. This was overcome by bringing most aid into the PIP system and by active management of counterpart funding.

Having broken this bottleneck, MoFPED turned its attention to the allocation of aid. The elaboration of sector policies during the early 1990s culminated in the publication of the PEAP in 1997. With donors increasingly preoccupied with poverty reduction, the launch of the PEAP was timed perfectly from the point of view of attracting increased aid. The wide consultation process enabled the government to present the PEAP as a public consensus on the priorities for reducing poverty in Uganda—and to demand that donors fund implementation of the PEAP instead of continuing to develop their own projects. Given that most donors largely endorsed the PEAP priorities, it was hard for them to argue. The credibility of the PEAP and of government's commitment to poverty reduction was greatly enhanced by the decentralization process and by the announcement of free UPE, which was clearly pro-poor. The significant reallocation of funds towards UPE in the 1997/98 MTEF table demonstrated that government was 'putting its money where its mouth was'.

The PEAP greatly strengthened the case for donors to both increase aid to Uganda and to entrust the funds to government. This was reinforced by two further innovations. First, the decentralization of decision making over sector policy and budget allocations to SWGs, on which donors were represented, gave donors a direct say in those allocations. Second, the establishment of the PAF in 1998/99 reassured donors that debt relief and other aid would be used for pro-poor expenditure. Along with efforts underway to strengthen public financial management (see Chapter 15), these measures combined to make a compelling case that the government could be trusted with donors' money and that donors should therefore switch their support from project aid to budget support. As noted above, the donors were convinced; general budget support increased from USD165 million to USD477 million between 1996/97 and 2004/05.

7.2 The political dimension

The above technocratic account of Uganda's reforms would be seriously incomplete without considering the political dimension. Adoption of many of the key reforms would have been impossible without political support, while others were a response to political initiatives. 'Political' here refers largely to one man—President Museveni. Throughout the 1990s he took a close interest in economic management and played a highly significant—and largely positive—role in the policies discussed here.

Between the NRM take over of government in 1986 and the adoption of the new Constitution in 1995 Uganda was effectively a 'benign dictatorship'; the President's word was law. A pivotal moment for economic reform was the fiscal crisis of 1992. Up to that point the President had listened to economic advice from a number of directions. However, he was shocked by the rapid acceleration in inflation in 1992; once he was persuaded by the MoPED permanent secretary that it was a direct result of fiscal indiscipline, he merged the finance and planning ministries and mandated the new ministry to establish fiscal discipline and bring inflation under control. Presidential backing was crucial for the drastic expenditure cuts made following the merger and the successful battle with inflation. The next few years were a technocrat's dream. As long as the minister and permanent secretary were convinced of the case for a reform, since they were known to have strong Presidential support, there was little need to persuade anyone else.

Other controversial reforms that could not have proceeded without Presidential support include the legalization of the parallel foreign exchange market, the liberalization of coffee marketing, the halving of the size of the public service between 1991 and 1995, the privatization programme, and the implementation of Value Added Tax. As well as backing such proposals from technocrats, the President instigated a number of initiatives himself which had major implications for economic management. In 1993 he announced that most public services would be decentralized to local governments. The PEAP was produced in response to the President's complaint (in 1995) that the PIP paid insufficient attention to poverty reduction. In 1996 the centrepiece of the President's election campaign was a pledge to introduce free UPE. While some MoFPED officials had misgivings about decentralization and UPE, both initiatives were largely successful in increasing service delivery to the poor. This, and the fact that the PEAP was a Presidential initiative, gave high credibility in donor eyes to the PEAP and the government commitment to poverty reduction.

This chapter has provided an overview of Uganda's economic reforms since 1986. The interplay of the political and technical dimensions of reform was crucial in their success, and is the focus of the next chapter. Subsequent chapters delve more deeply into the technical reforms discussed in this chapter. Together, they have contributed to the transformation of the Ugandan economy.

2

Institutional and Political Dimensions of Economic Reform

Emmanuel Tumusiime-Mutebile

1. Background: the economy before 1986

At independence in 1962 Uganda's economy was one of the most promising in sub-Saharan Africa. Fertile soils, an equable climate and an industrious population made the country self-sufficient in food. The agricultural economy provided inputs for a relatively well-developed manufacturing sector as well as export earnings that were more than adequate to finance imports and normally resulted in a current account surplus. Fiscal and monetary management was sound and a relatively liberal trade and payments system existed. By 1970 Uganda's GDP per capita (USD512 in 1980 prices) was the fifth highest in Eastern and Southern Africa, after South Africa, Rhodesia, Mauritius, and Zambia. Inflation was never above 5 per cent and the fiscal deficit was typically about 2.5 per cent of GDP.

The onset of the Idi Amin regime in January 1971 reversed all this progress. Gross economic mismanagement and state inspired violence destroyed the economy. Although Amin was overthrown in 1979, the successive governments that came to power after his overthrow failed to implement an effective recovery programme.

When the National Resistance Movement (NRM) took power in 1986 the economy was in ruins. In the previous fifteen years per capita output had fallen by 42 per cent (see Figure 1.1). Not only had the size of the economy shrunk, there had been retrograde structural changes; between 1970 and 1986 the share of manufacturing fell from 9 per cent of GDP to 4 per cent while the shares of agriculture and the non-monetary sector rose from 47 per cent to 62 per cent and from 30 per cent to 40 per cent of GDP respectively. The collapse of the formal sector meant that the government's tax base also collapsed. By the mid 1980s tax revenues had fallen to only 6 per cent of GDP (see Chapter 5), down from 15 per cent in 1970. As a result, the government could no longer afford to provide the most basic public services and physical infrastructure had fallen apart for lack of maintenance funds.

Why did the economy collapse in the 1970s? The main reason was the disastrous economic policies pursued during this period. Government expenditure was out of control, and the central bank was forced to print money to finance its fiscal deficits, leading to rampant inflation. With the exchange rate fixed at an artificially determined level and high inflation, the exchange rate became massively overvalued. Coffee farmers saw the real value of the farm gate price of their coffee fall dramatically because of the overvalued exchange rate, destroying the incentive to produce coffee. As a result, coffee production volumes fell by 26 per cent between 1970 and 1986.

The economy was also enmeshed in a web of administrative controls over imports, access to foreign exchange, the prices of exports and consumer goods, and interest rates. These controls severely distorted incentives for productive activity. The viability of a business became dependent upon the whims of government officials who controlled access to vital inputs. As a result, many businesses ground to a halt because of shortages of imported inputs or spare parts. The shortages of vital inputs, combined with the high rates of inflation, made long term business planning almost impossible, with the consequence that private investment in the Ugandan economy had virtually ceased by the mid 1980s.

The first attempt at introducing economic reforms was made during Milton Obote's second government (Obote II) which lasted from January 1981 to May 1985. The reforms were championed by the Presidential Economic Advisory Council, which was formed in 1981. It was a powerful body, with direct access to the President, who also held the portfolio of Minister of Finance. Ambassador Plenipotentiary, representing State House, chaired the Council. Other members included the Governor of the central bank and his deputy, the Permanent Secretary and the Chief Planning Economist of the Ministry of Planning and Economic Development, the Secretary to the Treasury, and the Chairman/Managing Director of Uganda Commercial Bank. The Council's mandate included coordination of economic management, seeking and negotiating aid, and fostering economic cooperation with multilateral institutions. The informality of the body became a major strength. Regular access to the Head of State coupled with intensive preparation meant that the Council had the authority and respect to recommend fundamental changes.

In his 1981 budget speech, President Obote announced fiscal and monetary policy reforms as well as trade and external payments reforms. These included the first ever floating of the Uganda Shilling on foreign exchange markets; the Shilling immediately depreciated from UGX7.8 to UGX78 to the US Dollar. There was also a reduction in government's recourse to the banking system to finance the budget deficit, the dismantling of a wide range of price controls, the rationalization of tariff rates, and a reform of the structure of tariffs.

The Obote II government introduced further reforms in subsequent budgets. These included the introduction of a dual exchange rate. Window I, the less depreciated exchange rate, was used for 'essential' imports (such as raw materials and petroleum), and for debt service. All other foreign exchange needs were met at Window II, the more depreciated rate, which was determined through a foreign exchange auction. The two windows were meant to be a transition mechanism to a more depreciated but unified exchange rate at some point in the future. Further tariff and trade reforms were also introduced including the dismantling of remaining price controls.

These reforms at first delivered impressive results, arresting economic decline and reducing inflation. For example, GDP growth increased from about minus 3 per cent in 1981 to about 7 per cent in 1982 and about 6 per cent in 1983, while inflation fell from 104 per cent in 1979 to an average of about 30 per cent between 1981 and 1983. However, as the war waged by the National Resistance Army in the Luwero Triangle intensified from 1983, military expenditure increased and expansionary monetary policies resumed—undermining the economic reforms. GDP growth fell to minus 5 per cent in 1984, while inflation increased to 62 per cent in 1984 and 144 per cent in 1985. In 1985 Obote was removed from power by his army and by the time the National Resistance Army overthrew that army in January 1986 hardly any of the reforms survived apart from the foreign exchange auction.

2. Institutions inherited by the NRM government

There were four main institutions responsible for economic policy and management when the NRM government took power. These were the Ministry of Finance, the Ministry of Planning and Economic Development, the Bank of Uganda, and the Presidential Economic Council. These institutions were inherited from the Obote II era and, initially at least, there was little attempt by the new government to reform the way they operated.

The Ministry of Finance (MoF) was basically responsible for public finances and the annual government budget. It was responsible for setting tax rates and tax collection, as well as for setting public expenditure priorities and controlling public accounts. In addition to fiscal policy, MoF was in charge of public external borrowing and monetary policy. It was also responsible for licensing commercial banks and insurance companies. All parastatal companies came under MoF, along with the Central Purchasing Corporation, the Central Tender Board, and the Departed Asian Custodian Board (responsible for the assets of Asians expelled by Idi Amin). In keeping with its broad remit, MoF staff were drawn from a range of disciplines, including economics, commerce, and accountancy. However, specialists in macroeconomics were very scarce.

The Ministry of Planning and Economic Development (MoPED), which was established in the 1960s, was primarily responsible for producing the National Development Plans. These were renamed Rehabilitation and Development Plans from 1986, reflecting the urgent need to rehabilitate the economy. MoPED also had responsibility for macroeconomic planning, manpower planning, grant aid, national accounts and statistics, and coordination of the National Research Council. MoPED was mainly staffed by macroeconomists, micro/sector economists and statisticians. MoPED staff increasingly became the 'champions' of macroeconomic reform under the NRM government.

The Bank of Uganda (BoU) was established in the mid 1960s with the traditional functions of a central bank. These included the issuing of bank notes and coins, the prudential supervision of commercial banks, the management of external reserves, external public debt management, and the setting of short-term interest rates. However, the legislation at the time stipulated that in the area of monetary policy the Bank was an adviser to the Minister of Finance whose decisions were handed to the Bank to implement. Also, while the Bank was responsible for administering exchange controls, it shared with MoF the role of setting the exchange rate. The licensing of commercial banks was also the responsibility of MoF, not BoU.

The Obote II Presidential Economic Advisory Council was renamed the Presidential Economic Council (PEC) because, unlike Obote, President Museveni chaired it himself. This Council was responsible for making decisions on the major economic issues of the day. It acted like a Cabinet sub-committee, although non-ministers and senior civil servants in attendance could express their views freely. This latter quality ensured that the voice of non-political 'constituencies' was heard at PEC meetings, which was to prove helpful in advising President Museveni on economic reforms.

3. January 1986 to mid-1987: starting out

Born in 1944, Yoweri Museveni had been politically active since secondary school. He studied at the University of Dar es Salaam, where he majored in political science but also took courses in law and economics. His reading of Marx, Lenin, Mao, Fanon, and Rodney, shaped his intellectual and political outlook. He was also influenced by President Nyerere's attempt to build his brand of socialism and central economic planning in Tanzania. So it is fair to say that when he became President of Uganda, his instincts were not for developing a market economy.

Indeed, several months after he came to power, when a Cabinet Memorandum recommended the continuation of some of the IMF/World Bank supported economic stabilization measures initiated under Obote II, President Museveni was furious. He said that he could not be expected to implement the very policies that he had criticized in the Ten Point Programme, which he had written to guide the NRM in the struggle to overthrow Obote. Instead, he imposed administrative rationing of consumer goods and foreign exchange and used the Bank of Uganda to finance the government budget. This was essentially a return to the old control regime introduced in the late 1970s, by Amin and then again under Obote II. The President's advisors argued that Bank financing of the deficit would not be inflationary because the spending would elicit a supply response, which would dampen inflationary pressure.

The NRM government's instinctive approach to economic policy was dirigiste. It was implicitly assumed that economic agents would respect the basic requirement of military discipline to obey orders. However, President Museveni appeared to have sufficient intellectual self-confidence to allow an open debate on economic policy. (Henstridge and Kasekende 2001: 50)

As part of this debate, in May 1986 President Museveni invited the International Development Research Centre (IDRC) of Canada to commission a study team to review the state of the economy and to advise government on the way forward. He knew of a number of academics associated with the IDRC who had worked in Tanzania and had reputations as liberal economists. The IDRC commissioned a team of international and Ugandan economists for this purpose.

The IDRC team could not reach agreement on all the points of the reform package. A minority of the team recommended a 'control model' for economic adjustment, which would attempt to bring down prices by taking administrative control over economic imbalances and revaluing the Shilling to make imports less expensive. Since this was basically the model that the government chose to pursue when it re-imposed price controls and revalued the Shilling in 1986, it is instructive to quote at length the majority view on the 'control model':

There are margins of error in any form of projection modeling. On the basis of common assumptions with other scenarios, however, the control model failed miserably as a strategy for balancing either the balance of payments, or the budget—the two key problems which need to be addressed. In all variants [of the control model] the most implausible assumption was that the rate of inflation fell to minus 25% per year and stayed there for three years. In no other country in the world over the past thirty five years has inflation fallen to this extent, even for one year. Even then, the balance of payments remains in deficit each year and import levels remain at their current inadequate levels. The budget is also grossly out of balance in each year and there is no adjustment in civil servant salaries except through the negative inflation assumptions. Neither can the development budget expand. The majority of the team felt that these results speak for themselves. The control option is a dangerous one for Uganda which could bring immeasurable harm. In its professional judgement, the majority advises against implementing any variant of it. (IDRC 1986: 115)

This advice was rejected initially. A new governor of the central bank was appointed from the minority. The official exchange rate was then revalued in nominal terms. The economy did not respond favourably. With inflation accelerating from 120 per cent in May 1986 to 240 per cent in May 1987, the real appreciation of the official exchange rate reached around 380 per cent over the same period (see Chapter 3).

4. Mid-1987 to 1992: early reforms

Following the revaluation episode, the government revised its economic policies and initiated further monetary, fiscal, and exchange rate reforms. These sought to restore domestic and external stability and to stimulate economic recovery. To achieve the twin objectives of growth and stabilization, the government followed a two-pronged strategy of structural reform and financial stabilization. Stability was to be restored through fiscal and monetary restraint and through increased exports.

In May 1987 a number of currency reform measures were taken, including removing two zeros from the Shilling, an instantaneous devaluation of 60 per cent, and imposition of a currency conversion tax of 30 per cent. A number of measures to broaden the tax base were also introduced. These focused particularly on export taxes, where additional government revenues amounting to 4 per cent of GDP were collected as a result—mainly from coffee. However the external situation became difficult and balance of payments support from the IMF and the World Bank was required.

There was considerable uncertainty and disagreement within government about how to respond to the economic problems. Central planning rhetoric continued. The Ministry of Finance was not entirely committed to macroeconomic stabilization and structural adjustment. Revenues were extremely limited as a result of the collapsed economy, yet the government's expenditure requirements were massive. Increased inflation was the inevitable result. Somewhat ironically, it was the Ministry of Planning and Economic Development (not the Ministry of Finance) that emphasized the need for fiscal discipline and macroeconomic stability; however, during this period MoPED had virtually no control over public expenditure.

Continued rapid inflation (averaging 191 per cent per annum between 1986 and 1989) necessitated frequent devaluations of the Shilling. Given the government's dependence on export taxes, mainly on coffee, devaluing the currency became an important source of government revenue. However, in 1989 there was strong support in the National Resistance Council (the legislature) for a resolution rejecting any further official devaluation of the Shilling. This alerted President Museveni to the precariousness of the situation. Since when did the legislature vote on exchange rates?

The exchange rate debate was influenced by two key developments. First, the government organized a seminar in September 1989, which brought together academics, politicians, and civil servants formally to discuss economic reform for the first time. The seminar was useful in providing open debate and sensitizing all participants about the key issues in macroeconomic stabilization and structural adjustment—including the role of the parallel foreign exchange market in everyone's lives.

Second, as discussed in Chapter 3, the issue was hotly debated between ministers holding economic portfolios and senior officials in PEC meetings. MoPED officials led the argument for macroeconomic stabilization and liberalization in a statement of macroeconomic strategy called 'The Way Forward I'[1] (Government of Uganda 1992). In this discussion paper, MoPED recommended prudent budgeting to control inflation, promotion of exports through legalization of the parallel market, and devaluation of the official exchange rate to a competitive level. The strategy was approved by PEC in March 1990 and the legalization of the parallel market was announced in the 1990 budget. This was one of the most significant milestones in Uganda's economic history and marked the start in earnest of the reform programme. The impact of exchange rate liberalization is discussed in Chapter 3.

While liberalization of the foreign exchange market was implemented immediately, progress on macroeconomic stabilization was much slower. MoF was not convinced of the need for fiscal discipline and was subjected to constant pressure from line ministries for additional resources. Total expenditure and fiscal deficit outturns exceeded the approved budget by wide margins. The gap was plugged by borrowing from BoU. Inflation, therefore, remained high and the Shilling continued to slide—albeit with the rate now determined largely by the market. Early in 1991/92, failure by the Ministry of Finance to cut expenditure in response to fiscal shocks led to a fiscal crisis, a huge increase in borrowing, and a surge in inflation.

5. 1992 to 1995: establishment of fiscal discipline

President Museveni was becoming increasingly frustrated at receiving conflicting advice (from MoF and MoPED) on budget matters and by the fact that the national budget bore little or no relation to the Rehabilitation and Development Plans produced by MoPED. In March 1992, following the surge in inflation and in response to the fiscal crisis, he made two related decisions which had profound consequences for economic management. Firstly, he decided to merge the Ministry of Finance and the Ministry of Planning and Economic Development. The former Minister and Permanent Secretary of

---

[1] Two more discussion papers were produced by MoPED on structural adjustment issues called 'The Way Forward II' and 'The Way Forward III'.

MoPED took over the leadership of the new Ministry of Finance and Economic Planning (MoFEP).

The second decision was to put fiscal discipline at the heart of economic policy. MoPED officials succeeded in persuading the President that inflation resulted from a lack of fiscal discipline, which was analogous to military indiscipline. This resonated well with a former military leader whose victory over the Obote regime owed much to the strong discipline of the National Resistance Army. Addressing the National Resistance Council immediately after the Minister of Finance and Economic Planning had presented his Budget for 1992/93, President Museveni declared 'There will be no inflation. Inflation is indiscipline.' He instructed MoFEP to do whatever was necessary to bring inflation down. With little scope to increase revenue in the short term, this meant drastic cuts in expenditure. As discussed in Chapter 3, the combined MoFEP was able to cut expenditure (by 1.8 per cent of GDP in the fourth quarter of 1991/92 alone) through the ruthless imposition of cash budgeting. Initially the rule was very simple—January's expenditure was capped by December's revenue. Inflation was reduced from over 200 per cent in April 1992 to single digits within a few months. Except for occasional price hikes due to drought, inflation remained in single figures until the external shocks of 2008.

It is hard to over-state the significance of President Museveni's conversion to the cause of fiscal discipline. Until that point, he himself and many others in government were deeply ambivalent about the need for fiscal discipline—a concept associated in many minds with the IMF and 'neo-colonialism'. Without political support MoF was unable to withstand spending pressures from ministries and there was little prospect of inflation being controlled. Following the merger of MoF and MoPED, line ministers were furious at the expenditure cuts imposed by MoFEP and at being told to live within their approved budgets. However, it soon became clear that MoFEP had the President's full authority to do whatever was necessary to contain inflation. The economic technocrats had taken over. If ministers were unhappy they could complain to the President. 'At the time that these economic reforms were implemented, they were not popular and required unwavering political will' (Museveni 2008). While cash budgeting was gradually relaxed as macroeconomic stability was established, the commitment to budget discipline has been sustained ever since.

The merger of MoF and MoPED was crucial to the success of shock therapy in controlling inflation and establishing macroeconomic stability. While technical capacity for macroeconomics was largely concentrated in MoPED, it was MoF that controlled the national budget. The merger not only put economists in charge of economic management, it also removed at a stroke the duplication of three key functions. First, responsibility for short and medium term macroeconomic planning and management was now combined under one department. Second, instead of MoF managing the recurrent budget and MoPED having responsibility for the development (i.e. capital) budget, responsibility for all sector policy and expenditure planning and execution was assigned to the Budget Office of the new ministry. This was critical for aligning policy and resources and for the efficiency of public expenditure. Third, responsibility for all aid, both grants and loans, was now consolidated in a single aid management office. The performance of the combined ministry was also greatly enhanced by the introduction of 'incentive' payments to staff (see Box 2.1) and a number of measures designed to strengthen its technical capacity (see Box 2.2).

Box 2.1 SALARY SUPPLEMENTS OR 'INCENTIVES'

When I told DFID colleagues in late 1989 that I was moving to Uganda to work for MoPED, a common response from colleagues who had visited Kampala recently was that I would have the office to myself. MoPED officers had a reputation for 'moonlighting'—only visiting the office to use the telephone. Since few public servants received a salary in excess of USD20 a month—well below a living wage—this was hardly surprising.

However, the predictions were wrong. I found office attendance no worse than elsewhere. Indeed, weekend working was more common than at DFID. The explanation for the transformation was that in October 1989 the UNDP 'Assistance to Economic Planning' project started paying salary supplements to most MoPED staff. Professionals received USD130 a month and support staff USD70—essentially for being at their desks. The scheme was policed by the project's four expatriates. Deductions were made for unexplained absences or overseas trips (where *per diems* were payable), but there were no reporting or output requirements. A similar scheme was introduced soon after by two World Bank projects supporting the Statistics Department (which reported to MoPED).

The 'incentive' scheme was revolutionary at the time. While donors funded capital projects and technical assistance, governments were expected to fund all recurrent costs. Donor funding of public service salaries was taboo. However, the project manager's argument that there was little point MoPED introducing reforms when there were no members of staff to implement them eventually overcame donor scruples.

The impact was dramatic. Virtually overnight, MoPED was transformed into a 'full time' ministry. The incentives meant that it was the only ministry whose staff could live adequately on their (supplemented) salary and work full time, without the need to moonlight. Yet until the merger of MoPED and MoF in 1992 the total cost of the scheme to UNDP was less than that of a single expatriate technical assistant! Given that most of the key economic reforms discussed in this book were initiated by MoPED, the incentive scheme was surely one of the most cost-effective donor interventions in Ugandan history?

When MoPED merged with the (much larger) Ministry of Finance the coverage of the scheme was extended to staff of the combined ministry. The World Bank picked up most of the additional cost.

It was recognized from the outset that donor supplementation of public servants' salaries was unsustainable (and was resented in the rest of government). It was emphasized, therefore, that the incentive scheme was temporary and would end once progress had been made in improving general public service salaries. While salaries had increased significantly by the time the scheme ended in 1996, MoFPED staff nevertheless experienced a sharp cut in take home pay as a result. However, fears of a mass exodus of staff proved unfounded.

(Alan Whitworth)

Coordination between MoFEP and the Bank of Uganda was also strengthened. Various committees, with representatives from both MoFEP and BoU, were formed to ensure consistent macroeconomic management:

- The Economic and Financial Policy Committee, chaired by the Minister of Finance and Economic Planning, addressed policy issues. Members included the BoU Governor, the Permanent Secretary/Secretary to the Treasury, and senior MoFEP officials;
- Technical committees such as the Macroeconomic Committee, the Debt Management Committee, and the Balance of Payments Working Group;
- Initially, while the entire government was operating on a cash budget, a Cash Flow Management Committee met weekly.

In parallel with the strengthening of fiscal management, a number of reforms were undertaken aimed at strengthening monetary policy and the financial sector. In particular, the role of the Bank of Uganda was strengthened through two pieces of legislation. First, the 1993 Bank of Uganda Statute delegated full authority for monetary policy to the central bank. Second, the 1993 Financial Institutions Statute strengthened BoU's powers to regulate and supervise banks and other financial institutions (see Chapter 3).

The 1995 Constitution granted BoU increased independence. 'In performing its functions, the Bank of Uganda shall conform to this Constitution but shall not be subject to the direction or control of any person or authority' (Government of Uganda 1995: Article 162 (2)).

Box 2.2 BUILDING ECONOMIC MANAGEMENT CAPACITY

Today MoFPED is one of the best regarded finance ministries in Africa. Yet in the late 1980s the (separate) finance and planning ministries were among the very weakest. Systems and salaries had collapsed (graduates earned just USD7 a month—see Chapter 4) and, with the HIV and AIDS pandemic exacting a heavy toll, there were only a handful of competent—but demoralized—staff. How was this transformation achieved? It began with the introduction of the incentive scheme in 1989, which dramatically improved staff motivation (see Box 2.1). The 1992 merger of the ministries also helped rationalize the deployment of scarce economic skills.

Mallaby (2004) emphasizes the role that expatriate technical assistance played. The MoPED Permanent Secretary recognized that, with so little local capacity, undertaking reform and building economic management capability was only possible with outside support. Throughout the 1990s a number of (mainly British) expatriate economists worked alongside MoFPED staff in designing and implementing the technical aspects of the reform programme and in developing skills. They were a combination of conventional technical assistants and young economists, filling public service positions, recruited through the Overseas Development Institute in London. In a country notorious for Amin's expulsion of the Asians, the absence of 'racial hang-ups' was remarkable and enabled MoFPED to make particularly effective use of technical assistance (Mallaby 2004: 220).

> Equally significant was the way MoFPED made the best use of its own resources. With many senior staff having died or left for greener pastures, the most able officers were often quite young. If normal public service procedures had been followed it would have taken many years for them to rise through the ranks. In order to make the best use of limited resources, the Permanent Secretary (sometimes using technical assistants as 'talent spotters') had no qualms about appointing able young officers to management positions over the heads of longer serving officers.
>
> By appointing a few talented officers to strategic positions throughout the ministry, often supported initially by technical assistants, MoFPED was able to effectively manage the reform programme despite limited resources. Crucially, by keeping them in post for several years, the ministry experienced unprecedented stability in both personnel and policy. With the parallel improvement in salaries and the lifting of the freeze on public service recruitment in 1998 (see Chapter 4), MoFPED was increasingly able to recruit and retain skills through conventional channels and to dispense with technical assistance.
>
> (Alan Whitworth)

6. 1995 to 2002: the poverty agenda

By 1995 there was growing dissatisfaction with the way economic reforms were going. While the economy had been stabilized and economic growth appeared healthy, the public perception was that poverty was increasing. Partly reflecting these concerns, President Museveni made a key speech in 1995 at a forum on poverty in which he directed MoFEP to redirect the allocation of resources in the Public Investment Plan and the budget towards activities that would directly benefit the poor. This led MoFEP to begin preparation of the first Poverty Eradication Action Plan (PEAP, see Chapter 7).

Government expenditure allocations in the Budget needed to be reassessed in terms of their impact on poverty. The PEAP was first drawn up in 1997 after nearly two years of consultation with civil society and other stakeholders. MoFEP understood the need for 'buy-in' by stakeholders long before widespread stakeholder consultation by government came into vogue in the development aid 'industry'. In this sense, it can justly be said that Uganda's PEAP is 'domestically owned'. The PEAP, which was revised in 2000 and 2004, set out a comprehensive strategy for eradicating mass poverty in Uganda by the year 2017, based on four pillars:

- Creating a framework for economic growth and transformation;
- Ensuring good governance and security;
- Directly increasing the ability of the poor to raise their incomes;
- Directly increasing the quality of life of the poor.

The PEAP has been particularly important as a tool for shaping public policy and building political support for the policies which reduce poverty in three crucial aspects. First, the PEAP identified the key sectors of the government budget which can make the greatest contribution to poverty reduction, such as the provision of universal primary education, primary health care, water and sanitation, rural roads and agricultural extension; and it provided the impetus for prioritizing these sectors in budgetary allocations.

Second, the PEAP brought into focus the imperative of modernizing the smallholder food crop agricultural sector, where the vast majority of the poor earn their livelihoods. This stimulated the development by government of the Plan for the Modernization of Agriculture (see below), which focused on the need to enhance the natural resource based livelihoods of peasant farmers.

Third, the PEAP forced government to confront the hard choices which must be made between competing claims on government resources and to evaluate these policies in terms of their impact on poverty. The challenge for policy makers was to understand the inter-relationship between all the different aspects of poverty in order to devise a mix of policies which maximizes progress towards poverty reduction, but which is also feasible within the 'hard budget constraint'. Living within this resource envelope and avoiding excessively expansionary fiscal policies is especially important for the poor because the poor have only a limited range of financial assets and are, therefore, more likely to hold their financial savings in cash—if they have any savings at all. The poor, therefore, would bear a disproportionate burden of any inflation tax. Living within the resource envelope requires policy makers to make choices. Not all policies that are thought to have a poverty reducing impact can be implemented in a given budget year.

The PEAP provided a powerful basis for further reforms:

- Sector Working Groups (SWGs, see Chapter 9) were formed, working within the guidelines of the PEAP. These subsequently became important instruments for 'cascading' the macroeconomic resource envelope to the various sectors in the Medium Term Expenditure Framework (MTEF, see Chapter 8).
- The PEAP was a deliberately long-term document, with the MTEF the vehicle for its implementation, and the annual budget just a 'slice' of the MTEF.
- The expenditure ceiling for each sector remained paramount and was the constraint within which Sector Working Groups were required to prepare their MTEF and budget submissions.

In order to assess progress towards poverty eradication, a Poverty Monitoring Unit was set up in MoFEP, which supplements information collected by the Uganda Bureau of Statistics and the Uganda Participatory Poverty Assessment Process (see Chapter 10). Among other activities, these institutions conduct regular household surveys and a Poverty Status Report is prepared on a biannual basis; together these provide high quality estimates of poverty trends. Monitoring progress is essential in order to inform regularly the key policy makers involved and to allow implementation strategies to be continually modified to build on what works and to avoid repeating mistakes.

The Poverty Action Fund (PAF, see Chapter 13) was created by the government in 1998 to ring fence the financial resources saved as a result of debt relief under the Highly Indebted Poor Countries initiative. Uganda voluntarily earmarked all the savings from debt relief for spending in PEAP priority areas. This has allowed the government to show, in a transparent manner, that new expenditure arising from additional resources is being fully disbursed to the social sectors.

The PEAP provides a framework for sector-wide plans and investment programmes, which in turn are translated into actual budgets in the MTEF. Consultation and the delegation of responsibility in PEAP preparation, sector planning, and budgeting to sectors and line ministries was important. Through Sector Working Groups, stakeholders were allowed to come up with their own priorities, provided they fitted within the framework and objectives of the PEAP, and the principle of the aggregate resource constraint. Sector economists from the Ministry of Finance, Planning and Economic Development (MoFPED)[2] Budget Directorate were crucial in this, as they served as the secretariat for the SWGs. They were given real authority when dealing with sectors and, because they were relatively senior, more experienced and well motivated, they were able to play this function well.

However, as these processes matured, ministries began to be wary of the PEAP, MTEF, and SWGs. The agriculture sector was a case in point. The Ministry of Agriculture prepared a 'Plan for the Modernization of Agriculture', which focused on developing the progressive farmer, without reference to the SWG or the PEAP. This advocated substantial government investment in agriculture, without explaining why government should be involved in production. MoFPED convinced the President that this programme was inconsistent with the PEAP, and produced a new document for which the President wrote the preface. The revised Plan took a cross-sectoral livelihoods based approach to developing agriculture, focusing on modernizing peasant agriculture. It was developed alongside the first version of the PEAP and was consistent with the PEAP approach.

7. Attachment to planning

An intriguing phenomenon in Uganda is the continuing yearning of its politicians for long term planning, despite the fact that the country has experienced twenty years of rapid economic growth without such plans. A series of

---

[2] This has been the title of the combined ministry since 1998.

five-year National Development Plans were produced by MoPED during the 1960s. The NRM government revived these under the name Rehabilitation and Development Plans. However, since they comprised essentially unconstrained project 'wish lists' and the resources required to finance them were controlled by either MoF or donors, they had negligible influence on public expenditure (see Chapter 6).

The 1992 merger of MoF and MoPED brought responsibility for planning and budgeting under one roof for the first time. This greatly improved the prospects of plans actually being implemented—as long as they were consistent with the 'resource envelope' and adopted a more realistic medium term perspective. Having established fiscal discipline through short term 'shock therapy' in 1992, MoFEP progressively developed an integrated system of medium term planning and budgeting based on the Public Investment Plan, the PEAP, and the MTEF (see Chapters 6, 7, and 8 respectively). As illustrated in Chapter 3, this facilitated both macroeconomic stability and accelerated economic growth.

This progress went largely unnoticed by politicians. 'Where is the government's plan?' was a common complaint from MPs. As far as they were concerned, no plan had been produced by the merged planning and finance ministry; there was too much focus on macroeconomic stability at the expense of 'real' planning. This concern led to two major developments. First, the Constituent Assembly felt that Uganda needed a separate institution responsible for delivering long term plans. The 1995 Constitution therefore provided for a National Planning Authority (NPA) to produce comprehensive and integrated development plans for the country (Government of Uganda 1995).

Second, despite the commencement of the PEAP process in 1995, in July 1996 the President split MoFEP into separate finance and planning ministries. He had been attracted to the idea of long term planning since his student days in Tanzania. The new Minister of Planning and Economic Development had persuaded him that increasing the pace of industrialization through increased investment required a ministry focused on long term planning.

The arrangement failed. Although MoPED embarked on a parallel, long term planning initiative promoted by UNDP, called Vision 2025, it took a long time in gestation and never enjoyed much policy traction. Meanwhile the Ministry of Finance remained the custodian of the PEAP, which was published in 1997. The PEAP was signed by the President and enjoyed significant ownership as it talked to the NRM policy agenda. It increasingly dawned on the political leadership that implementation of whatever plans MoPED formulated would require financing—and, therefore, an interface with the Ministry of Finance. The perceived gains from creating a separate planning ministry were hardly visible. With increasing conflict between the political leadership of the two ministries, they were merged for a second time in May 1998 to form the Ministry of Finance, Planning and Economic Development (MoFPED).

MoFPED took a long time to establish the NPA, as it felt the PEAP and sector planning were sufficient for the time being while macroeconomic stability was being nurtured. It was only after pressure from the Parliamentary Committee on Finance that the National Planning Authority Bill was enacted in 2002 (Government of Uganda 2002). The Authority was inaugurated in 2003. By 2008 preparation of the NPA's first National Development Plan, the successor to the PEAP, was well underway, with public debate of background papers.

8. Impact of democracy

Between 1986 and 1995 the legislature took the form of the National Resistance Council. The membership was initially appointed by the President, although elections were subsequently held in 1989. Democracy was reinstated following the promulgation of the 1995 Constitution. The first full presidential and parliamentary elections were held in 1996, under the movement no-party system of governance. The 2001 elections were also held under this system. The first multi-party elections were held in 2006.

Prior to 1996 the President made economic decisions largely on his own. In many ways, this was a technocrat's dream. As long as the MoFEP minister and permanent secretary were convinced of the case for reform, since they were known to have strong Presidential backing, there was little need to persuade anyone else. Since 1996 the President has increasingly needed to take account of the views of Parliament.

Parliament has become increasingly engaged in economic and budgetary issues. For example, the 2001 Budget Act resulted from a private member's bill, which arose out of Parliament's concern that it was not being involved early enough in the budget process. Ironically, this resulted in a number of technocratic budget reforms initiated by MoFPED (such as the MTEF and budget framework papers) being incorporated in legislation. It also involved the establishment of a Parliamentary Budget Committee and a Parliamentary Budget Office to provide technical support to MPs in the early stages of the budget process. As a result, Parliament's scrutiny of the budget has improved, although capacity building is needed. The Public Accounts Committee has also become increasingly active, and the legislature's role in holding the executive to account for the use of public funds is taken more seriously. The advent of multi-party democracy in 2006 has added vigour to these processes.

9. Uganda Commercial Bank

Parliamentary interventions have not always been comfortable for the executive. A case in point was Parliament's opposition to the sale of the state owned

Uganda Commercial Bank (UCB) by the central bank in 2001, which forced the President to intervene. By 1998 UCB had become insolvent, despite government recapitalization. Under the Financial Institutions Statute, the central bank was empowered to intervene when banks failed, and sell them on once they had been made solvent. The Bank of Uganda intervened in UCB in November 1998 and appointed new managers, who returned the bank to solvency. In 2001 BoU wanted to remove itself from the management of the bank, and 'resolve UCB'. It advertised the sale of UCB, received and evaluated bids, and selected the South African Bank, Stanbic, as the successful bidder.

Parliament objected to this, and tried to block the sale, claiming that it was a privatization which had not been conducted in line with the legal framework for privatization. There were also claims that the sale had been corrupt. There were, however, other motives; one of the factors behind the insolvency of UCB was that for a long time it had been used for political purposes. Yet, having intervened in a failed bank, it would create moral hazard for the Bank of Uganda if it were to hand the bank back to its majority shareholder—the government, in this case—which had made it insolvent.

The President intervened in support of BoU, arguing that Parliament could not stop the central bank from selling UCB as it was not a privatization, but a resolution of BoU's intervention in UCB. To calm the political storm, the President summoned the leaders of the committees of Parliament to a meeting. He also directed MoFPED to request DFID to finance a team to investigate the allegations. Eventually, the team found there was no substance to the allegations: 'We consider that this transaction was concluded entirely absent of any corruption' (GBRW Limited and Denton Wilde Sapte 2002).

10. Conclusions: the role of President Museveni

When President Museveni came to power, he rejected the previous regime's feeble attempt at financial stabilization and structural adjustment as imperialism inspired. He revalued the exchange rate massively, reimposed price controls and the administrative allocation of consumer goods, and abandoned the foreign exchange auction in favour of allocation by a committee of officials.

Within a year the economy was about to collapse again. Exporters suffered from an over-valued exchange rate that was used to translate their export earnings into Shillings, inflation jumped to triple digits and the parallel foreign exchange market became ubiquitous, with the exchange rate premium ten times the official rate. In this situation only the elite with access to scarce foreign exchange benefited.

In his search for a new Jerusalem, President Museveni went to the precipice, peered over the edge and did not like what he saw; it was scary. That is why he will never dare to go back; that is why he decreed that the government must never spend money it does not have; that is why in 1992 a monthly cash budget rule was enforced which enabled the government to run a domestic fiscal surplus; that is why Uganda has achieved an enviable record of rapid economic growth with low inflation. The President's firmness in maintaining fiscal discipline has underpinned the discipline in economic management since 1992. His insistence on discipline and his chairing of Cabinet meant that ministers were forced to toe the line and live within the fiscal constraints. The President also gave MoFEP/MoFPED the space to establish and maintain fiscal discipline, backing the finance minister in Cabinet.

A number of other key reforms discussed in this volume emanated from State House. The 1993 decision to decentralize government had a profound impact on service provision at the local level (see Chapter 14). As noted above, in 1995 the President directed MoFEP to reorient expenditure towards the poor, starting the process which led to the development of the PEAP. Arguably, the political initiative that had the single greatest impact on the allocation of public expenditure was the 1996 election commitment to provide free universal primary education (see Chapter 9). While MoFEP officials were apprehensive over some of these decisions at the time, few question them today. Uganda's progress in sustaining rapid economic growth and poverty reduction since 1986 is largely due to the combination of sound economics and the President's political instincts.

3

Exchange Rate, Fiscal, and Monetary Policy

Charles Byaruhanga, Mark Henstridge, and Louis Kasekende[1]

1. Introduction

Between 1992 and 2008 Uganda's economy grew by an average of 7.5 per cent a year, while the number of people living in poverty fell from 56 per cent in 1992 to 31 per cent in 2006 (see Chapter 10). Sustained economic growth and poverty reduction were founded on two big reforms: the legalization of the parallel market in foreign exchange in 1990, and the achievement of low inflation in 1992.

These two reforms laid secure foundations for subsequent reforms. The legalization of the parallel market supported the liberalization of exports. In particular, the liberalization of coffee marketing made possible a substantial reduction in poverty by ensuring that the benefits of the 1994–95 coffee boom went directly to coffee-growing households. In the first section of this chapter we explain how these reforms happened. It is also significant that these reforms were not driven by donor conditions, but arose from vigorous debate within Uganda.

The second section shows how macroeconomic stability was sustained during the mid-1990s. Keeping budget implementation on track was difficult, especially during a coffee boom. It was made possible by the 'Cashflow' of the Ministry of Finance. The Cashflow was a simple spreadsheet that tracked the outturns for revenue, aid flows, debt payments, and spending as the fiscal year unfolded, so as to strengthen budget implementation. The strict monitoring helped to sustain low inflation despite fiscal surprises and economic shocks which threatened to de-rail implementation of the budget.

[1] This chapter is a substantially revised and updated version of Henstridge and Kasekende (2001). We are grateful to the World Bank for permission to reproduce some of that material here.

The third section of this chapter focuses on developments since the turn of the century. Deeper financial markets allowed conventional instruments of monetary policy to become more effective. This section discusses the persistence of challenges to fiscal management, and changes in the way that macroeconomic stability was sustained. On a foundation of fiscal consolidation and cautious budget implementation, sales of government securities and foreign exchange were increasingly used to sustain low inflation.

2. The two big reforms of the early 1990s

On winning power in 1986, the National Resistance Movement (NRM) government's approach to economic policy was *dirigiste*. It was assumed that the economy would obey orders—a requirement of military discipline—an attitude melded in the guerrilla campaign. But the top leadership of the NRM had sufficient intellectual self-confidence to be open to a debate, supported by sound evidence, on economic policy. Ultimately, a reasoned consensus on policy evolved: from the revaluation of the official exchange rate in 1986, through increased inflation, and an ineffectual IMF programme from 1987, until the achievement of path-breaking reform in 1990.

In 1986 a working group[2] sponsored by the International Development Research Centre of Canada was charged with establishing a strategy for economic recovery in pursuit of an 'independent, integrated, self-sustaining economy'. This was a strategic objective of the NRM's 'Ten-Point Programme' drawn up in the bush when fighting the second Obote government. A minority within the group favoured a revaluation of the exchange rate and a set of officially administered prices to amend the old control regime centred upon a fixed official exchange rate, but little attention to fiscal discipline. They believed devaluation would fuel inflation and slow the country's economic recovery by raising the cost of imported inputs. There was an appreciation of the nominal official exchange rate in August 1986 and, subsequently, the Governor of the Bank of Uganda was appointed from this minority. However, the lack of fiscal discipline led to an acceleration of inflation from 120 per cent in May 1986 to 240 per cent in May 1987. This, in turn, caused a real appreciation of the official exchange rate of around 380 per cent over the same period.

With macroeconomic balances worsening, and foreign support needed to fund rehabilitation, an agreement with the IMF and the World Bank was concluded in 1987, which included a currency reform and a large nominal devaluation of the official exchange rate. Although the decision to seek donor

---

[2] The working group consisted of a mix of NRM officials, and Ugandan and international experts and academics.

assistance was made with the support of President Museveni, the debate over the exchange rate continued.

While there was little political consensus on the importance of price stability, or how to achieve it, inflation remained high. It was fuelled by central bank credit to government to finance a loose budget and rapid growth in credit to the monopoly marketing boards to buy export crops, the largest of which was coffee. The official exchange rate was devalued occasionally to recover ground lost to inflation. Despite the IMF programme, a consistent direction on macro-economic stabilization was absent.

The debate over the exchange rate was then influenced by two developments. First, a government seminar in 1989 under the theme: 'A critical look at Uganda's policy under the NRM government' brought together academics, politicians, and officials to talk about economic reform for the first time on a formal basis. The discussions were open, and addressed key issues—including the reality that the parallel market in foreign exchange (or *kibanda*) played an important role in the real economy.

Second, the Presidential Economic Council (PEC) provided a forum for a focused discussion between ministers holding economic portfolios and senior officials. Officials from the Ministry of Planning and Economic Development (MoPED) led the argument for macroeconomic stabilization and liberalization in a statement of macroeconomic strategy called 'Way Forward I' (Republic of Uganda 1992). This recommended prudent budget implementation to control inflation, and export promotion through the legalization of the parallel market, and devaluation of the official exchange rate to a competitive level.

2.1 Legalizing the parallel market exchange rate

The prevailing wisdom was that a depreciation of the official exchange rate just imported more inflation; which led to a depreciation of the parallel market rate, and so re-established a premium between the parallel and official rates. This view was reflected in a strand of academic economics literature derived largely from the Latin American experience of untangling import-substituting control regimes. It suggested that devaluation or floating the official exchange rate could be dangerous.[3] If the local currency equivalent of (net) foreign currency payments—say, for debt service—is financed by increased central bank credit to government, which is monetized, then the ensuing inflation would depreciate the parallel market and re-establish a premium.

However, analysis within MoPED found the opposite result would hold for Uganda: a devaluation of the official rate would both help the government implement a budget consistent with low inflation, and would not lead to an

---

[3] See Kharas and Pinto (1989), Pinto (1988, 1989), and Lizondo (1987).

offsetting depreciation of the parallel exchange rate. Two MoPED discussion papers (Morris 1989a, 1989b) presented the analysis. The first paper showed that changes in the parallel market exchange rate quickly pushed up prices. The common cause of both parallel market exchange rate depreciation and inflation was increased money supply, which in turn was mainly a result of the growth in credit to government used to finance the budget deficit—essentially, printing money. On the other hand, the parallel market rate could be stabilized by sales of foreign exchange by the central bank to importers of consumer goods.

The second paper focused on the consequences of official exchange rate devaluation. It showed that the official exchange rate did not directly determine any component of the official balance of payments. The impact of an official exchange rate devaluation on the government budget was as an accounting price. As the government was a net seller of foreign exchange—courtesy of donor support—devaluation of the official exchange rate increased the Uganda Shilling (UGX) value of foreign exchange receipts more than it increased the Shilling value of foreign exchange payments. This was the key difference from the more Latin American-focused analysis. This net effect remained even when adjustments to the official retail prices for petroleum products and the official producer price of coffee were taken into account. For a constant nominal Shilling level of other expenditures, a devaluation of the official exchange rate therefore would lead to a reduction in the budget deficit, and reduced financing from central bank credit to government. Printing less money both lowered inflation and slowed the rate of depreciation of the parallel market exchange rate.[4] These arguments were subsequently formalized in Morris (1995).

Backed by this analysis, the strategy presented in the Way Forward I was approved by the PEC. An additional and persuasive argument for the legalization of the parallel rate was the widely shared observation that, *de facto*, everyone used and needed that market, and that this should be recognized *de jure*.

The legalization of the parallel market was announced in the 1990 Budget Speech, together with a sharp depreciation of the official exchange rate. The only transactions remaining at the official rate were government transactions, financing the importation of 'essential goods', and the sale of coffee export proceeds. All other export proceeds could be sold at the prevailing market rate. The legalization of *kibanda* was unexpected and bold. It was not a result of donor conditionality, but was born of vigorous debate within Uganda.

The results included a rapid expansion in non-coffee exports, from about USD25 million in 1990 to around USD125 million four years later; easier current transfers; and reduced rationing in imported consumer goods. The reform also laid the foundation for the liberalization of coffee exports which, in turn, ensured that the bulk of the windfall from the 1994–95 coffee boom

---

[4] Kasekende and Ssemogerere (1994) concluded that domestic prices and the parallel exchange rate were both driven by monetary expansion due to slack fiscal policy between 1987 and 1992.

went to coffee-growing households, making possible one of the single biggest reductions in poverty in Uganda (Appleton 2001).

2.2 The achievement of macroeconomic stability

Despite the adjustment programmes agreed with the IMF and the World Bank from 1987 and the approval of the Way Forward I in 1990, macroeconomic stability was not achieved until 1992.

The Way Forward I recommended prudent budgeting as well as the legalization of the foreign exchange market. The problem, however, was loose control of budget *implementation*. No matter how carefully programmed the budget, a combination of revenue shortfalls, volatile donor disbursements of 'import support' (or 'programme aid'), and persistent demands for supplementary expenditures resulted in larger than planned fiscal deficits. While the deficits were financed by borrowing from the Bank of Uganda (BoU), the resulting monetary expansion fuelled inflation. Inflation averaged 191 per cent a year between 1986 and 1989. While inflation briefly dropped to just over 30 per cent in June 1990, a renewed loss of fiscal control led to a further expansion in government credit and re-emergence of inflation.

Two shocks during the first half of 1991/92 contributed to the increase in inflation. First, a drought led to sharply increased food prices. Second, there was a shortfall in both revenue and programme aid inflows. The revenue shortfall was a result of an overly optimistic budget. Aid inflows fell short of projections in part because some donors waited for a foreign exchange auction to start in January 1992 before disbursing, but also because others did not deliver on pledged support. By December 1991, only one-fifth of the programme aid budgeted for the fiscal year had been received. But despite this shortfall in resources, there was no offsetting cut in spending. The widening deficit was financed by an increase in credit to government from BoU, equivalent to 40 per cent of the money stock. This led to a surge in inflation to a peak monthly rate of 10.6 per cent in April 1992, equivalent to an annualized rate of over 200 per cent.

In response to the accelerating crisis, in March 1992 the Ministry of Finance and the Ministry of Planning and Economic Development were merged into a new ministry, largely under the management of the latter. The key policy decision was simply to cut expenditure in the fourth quarter of 1991/92 by the equivalent of 1.8 per cent of GDP.[5] This stopped the increase in credit to government, which then stopped the expansion of the money supply. Prices essentially stopped rising within three months.

---

[5] This is an understatement of the decisiveness of this adjustment, being only the amount by which the expenditure outturn for that fiscal year was less than the original budget, and so does not count those budgeted expenditures that were cut to accommodate demands for additional spending made during the year.

Table 3.1 Before and After Stability

	Before	After	
	Average	Average	Average
	1986/87–1991/92	1992/93–1996/97	1997/98–2007/08
Domestic financing of the budget (% of GDP)	1.2	–1.4	–1.0
Growth in average money M2 (% per year)	105.5	28.6	17.0
Average end-period inflation (% per year)	107.6	6.6	5.1
Growth of GDP (% per year)	5.7	8.0	7.3
Money M2 (% of GDP)	6.3	9.4	13.1

Sources: *Background to the Budget*, 1996/97, 1997/98, 2004/05, 2006/07, 2007/08. Ministry of Finance, Planning and Economic Development; *2007* and *2008 Statistical Abstract*, Uganda Bureau of Statistics; Bank of Uganda *Quarterly Economic Report* (various issues).

The stabilization in the last quarter of 1991/92 marked the beginning of both broad macroeconomic stability and accelerated growth. From July 1992 until June 2008, annual inflation averaged 5.3 per cent and GDP growth averaged 7.5 per cent. Table 3.1 shows the shift in key macroeconomic indicators after stability was achieved. Of course, accelerated growth was not solely the consequence of macroeconomic stability; however, it would have been much harder to sustain if inflation had remained persistently in double figures.

3. Sustaining reform during the 1990s

Sustaining macroeconomic stability during the 1990s required continued careful implementation of the budget as each fiscal year progressed. This section shows how, in the face of shocks, the 'Cashflow' helped implement the budget. The objective of the Cashflow, as a fiscal instrument, was low inflation: in essence, this was an inflation-targeting regime. This section also shows how the unified exchange rate was managed.

3.1 *Sustaining fiscal discipline*

Keeping inflation low is more a matter of sustaining a process for sound management, than the drama of debate, crisis, and big reform. Maintaining fiscal discipline nonetheless needs political authority. The management of the newly created Ministry of Finance and Economic Planning (MoFEP) was tasked by the

President with keeping inflation low by matching spending to resources. In a statement following the 1992 budget speech, President Museveni said: 'There will be no inflation. Inflation is indiscipline. If there is no money then we will close down some ministries and walk.' Uganda's main newspaper, *New Vision*, reported:

On inflation, the President blamed the old team at the helm of the Finance Ministry for mismanagement. He said, 'You just can't print money because the World Bank has not given you money in time'. He observed that the act had undermined the country's currency. (Obbo and Waswa 1992)

After 1992 the main instrument of fiscal control was the monthly release of cash from MoFEP to line ministries. This was set by the MoFEP Macroeconomic Policy Department in the monthly Cashflow Committee meeting, attended by representatives of the main institutions involved in monitoring macro-economic policy.[6] The Committee's main tool was a spreadsheet containing information on budget implementation on a month-by-month basis. This allowed the government's evolving fiscal position, the corresponding path of net credit to government from BoU, and inflation to be tracked and monthly cash releases to be adjusted accordingly.

The data and mechanics of the Cashflow spreadsheet are discussed in Box 3.1. The process is illustrated in Table 3.2: it shows when data became available, when the Cashflow was updated, the sequencing of data on price and monetary conditions, and when the Cashflow Committee met.

The Cashflow was not a cash budget. A cash budget, such as had been operated in Tanzania and Zambia, typically sets one month's expenditures based on the previous month's revenues, or an alternative rule to achieve a zero cash balance every month. In Zambia, for example, the monthly cash budget limited recurrent expenditure (including domestic interest payments) to recurrent revenue excluding grants (Adam and Bevan 1997). However, matching expenditures with available revenues on a monthly basis is not necessarily desirable, and it prevents smoothing between (often lumpy) receipts and expenditures. By comparison, the Uganda Cashflow was flexible. It did not demand a zero cash balance each month, and it did not renounce smoothing.[7] The Cashflow helped ensure that, in the face of shocks within the fiscal year, fiscal policy remained consistent with the objective of low inflation.

---

[6] The committee included representatives from MoFEP responsible for revenue mobilization and expenditure management, and Bank of Uganda officials responsible for tracking government's foreign receipts and payments, and for monetary policy.

[7] Dinh et al. (2002) study the impact of Zambia's cash budget on poverty reduction, with a comparison of fiscal management in Tanzania and Uganda. Stasavage and Moyo (1999) compare Uganda's Cashflow with the operation of a cash budget in Zambia.

Box 3.1 THE CASHFLOW

The Cashflow tracked fiscal operations every month. As the fiscal year proceeded, data on actual monthly outturns replaced the projections originally based on the annual budget. The Ugandan Revenue Authority (URA) recorded data, available with a lag of ten days. Non-URA revenue (appropriations-in-aid) was recorded (also with a lag) by the Treasury Office of Accounts. Budget support was initially recorded by the BoU Foreign Exchange Operations (FEO) department when disbursed by the donor. Foreign grants were shown as receipts 'above the line' and loan disbursements as positive foreign financing 'below the line'. Expenditures were recorded either as releases (which constituted authorization to spend), or as the value of cheques printed and issued, or as the value of cheques presented to the BoU and paid. Expenditure was shown broken down into interest on both domestic and foreign debt, wages and salaries, and other recurrent and local development spending. Once district administrations were decentralized, the transfers to districts were shown separately. Foreign financing was the sum of loan disbursements and amortization. BoU financing was the sum of changes in government accounts (sometimes referred to as changes in the 'ways and means' account) and the change in BoU holdings of treasury bills. Commercial bank financing was the sum of changes in government-owned accounts at commercial banks and changes in the banks' holdings of government securities, which could include promissory notes as well as treasury bills. Non-bank financing was primarily changes in the non-bank holdings of treasury bills (though in 1996/97 a large quantity of promissory notes was also issued).

There were differences in timing and valuation in the records of some components of the government accounts. For example, although revenue was, initially, recorded as collections by the URA, the accounts of the BoU showed revenue when it was received from a transfer from the URA revenue accounts at the Uganda Commercial Bank (UCB). However, it was the sum of deposits in the government accounts held by the BoU that determined the financing of the budget. As a result, if URA data were to be used as the record of revenue, an adjustment for the difference between revenue received by the revenue account at UCB and the revenue transferred from UCB into the consolidated fund at the BoU had to be made. This was also the case for differences between donor funds received by FEO and those credited to the government accounts, and between the value of releases, cheques printed, and of cheques paid and debited from the government accounts. Alternative sources of data were used for presentations on a *commitments* basis and on a *cash* basis, with the differences reflected as an *adjustment to cash*. The magnitude of the differences between data on the same flow, but monitored at different points, was largely a function of the slowness with which the accounts at BoU were compiled, but could also have been caused by different valuation dates for foreign transactions. Taken together, the timing differences from different data sources, possible valuation differences, and the potential difficulties in the classification of government accounts help explain the existence of a residual at the bottom of the Cashflow spreadsheet, if not its fluctuations or magnitude (see Table 3.2).

Table 3.2 shows the relationships between the various data lags for the compilation of the Cashflow and for the data on money and prices on the one hand, and the timing of the decisions on releases taken by the monthly Cashflow committee on the other. The committee usually met in the third week of each month, when some provisional data (though not from BoU accounts) would be available on the outturn of the previous month. Actual fiscal data for month t would not be available until month $t+2$, along with base money and a provisional figure for currency in circulation. Data on broad money for month t would not be finalized until month $t+3$, although price statistics were usually available for each month with minimal lags.

Table 3.2 Information Lags, Cashflow Compilation, and Short-Term Macroeconomic Management

End-Month t	Month t+1				Month t+2				Month t+3			
Weeks:	1	2	3	4	5	6	7	8	9	10	11	12
Fiscal data	URA revenue collections		Prov. revenue receipts Prog. grants receipts		Non-URA revenue collections and receipts		Actual revenue receipts Actual grant receipts					
Non-project expenditure releases	Cheques printed		Prov. cheques paid			Actual cheques paid						
Debt authorizations			Debt payments T-bill sales & stocks Prov. foreign financing Prov. BoU financing Prov. T-bill financing			Actual BoU financing Actual T-bill financing					Actual commerical bank financing	
Monetary data Exchange rates (daily)			Initial estimates of base money		Provisional base money		Actual base money and provisional M0		Provisional monetary survey and bank liquidity indicators		Actual monetary survey (including broad money)	
Real economy			Month t prices & inflation		Month t+1 prices & inflation				Month t+2 prices & inflation	Month t's stance starts to appear in price & inflation data	Index of key industrial production	
			Cashflow meeting for month t+1				**Cashflow meeting for month t+2**				**Cashflow meeting for month t+3**	

Source: Henstridge (1997).

Table 3.3 Actual Budget and Cashflow Outturn, 1991/92–1996/97[1]

	1991/92		1992/93		1993/94		1994/95		1995/96		1996/97	
	Programme	Outturn	Rev. budget	Outturn	Budget	Outturn	Programme	Outturn	Budget	Outturn	Budget	Outturn
	(As a percentage of GDP, except where otherwise indicated)											
Revenue & grants	15.3	9.4	11.2	11.2	11.7	12.1	10.6	12.3	12.5	13.2	14.4	13.6
Revenue	9.4	7.2	7.6	8.1	9.8	9.9	9.7	11.0	11.3	11.7	13.4	11.8
Grants	5.9	2.2	3.6	3.1	1.9	2.2	1.0	1.4	1.2	1.5	1.0	1.9
Expenditures & net lending	14.7	10.9	9.6	9.3	11.1	10.8	10.4	11.2	11.3	11.6	12.8	12.0
Recurrent	11.5	9.1	8.0	8.3	9.7	9.1	8.9	9.3	9.9	9.9	10.5	10.1
Domestic development	3.2	1.7	1.6	1.0	1.4	1.7	1.4	1.8	1.4	1.7	2.4	1.9
Overall balance	0.6	-1.5	1.6	1.9	0.6	1.3	0.3	1.1	1.1	1.6	1.5	1.7
Other, arrears & cheque float	-1.3	-1.4	-1.7	-1.9	-1.6	-2.1	-0.9	-0.9	-1.0	-0.3	-2.4	-0.4
Overall balance (cash)	-0.6	-2.9	-0.1	-0.1	-1.0	-0.7	-0.6	0.2	0.1	1.4	-0.9	1.3
Financing	0.6	2.9	0.1	0.1	1.0	0.7	0.6	-0.2	-0.1	-1.4	0.9	-1.3
External	2.6	1.3	0.7	0.4	1.3	1.3	1.6	0.7	1.1	0.0	0.5	-0.1
Domestic	-1.9	1.6	-0.6	-0.4	-0.3	-0.9	-0.9	-0.6	-1.2	-0.7	-1.2	-0.7
Of which: Bank of Uganda	-2.3	1.4	-0.9	-0.6	0.0	-1.5	-0.9	-1.2	-1.0	-1.2	-1.4	-1.5
residual	*0.0*	*0.0*	*0.0*	*0.1*	*0.0*	*0.3*	*0.0*	*-0.3*	*-0.1*	*-0.7*	*1.5*	*-0.5*
Memorandum Items:												
GDP (at current market prices, UGX bn.)[2]	2,182	2,588	3,766	3,626	3,924	4,036	4,953	4,828	5,428	5,521	6,230	6,307
Domestic financing (UGX bn.)	-42.4	42.4	-22.4	-15.5	-13.4	-35.0	-46.6	-26.8	-64.1	-39.3	-75.0	-42.1
Of which: Bank of Uganda	-49.4	35.3	-32.4	-21.7	0.0	-61.7	-46.6	-57.2	-51.6	-67.0	-85.0	-92.5
Underlying inflation (period average, %)		42		26		9.9		7.5		10.9		4.4
Annual inflation (period average, %)		42		30		6.5		6.1		7.5		7.8
Annual inflation (end-period, %)		66		-2.4		16.1		3.4		5.4		10.4

[1] Data mainly on a 'cash' basis, excluding donor-financed projects; fiscal years from July 1st to June 30th.

[2] GDP data for budgets are as used in original projections, where available; the estimates shown for outturns are from the series in use in the 1990s, as reported in Henstridge and Kasekende (2001), and so do not reflect subsequent re-estimates of the national accounts.

Sources: Ministry of Finance, Planning and Economic Development; Bank of Uganda; Uganda Bureau of Statistics.

Table 3.3 shows the budget and the outturn recorded by the Cashflow between 1991/92 and 1996/97 expressed as a percentage of GDP, with the outturn on inflation shown at the bottom of the table.[8]

In 1991/92—before the Cashflow was introduced—the outturn for domestic financing was 3.5 per cent of GDP higher than budgeted, mostly accommodated by increased credit from the Bank of Uganda. This is where the early 1992 burst of inflation came from. By contrast, an outturn tighter than budgeted was achieved for every year between 1991/92 and 1996/97. Overall, Table 3.3 shows that the *planned* fiscal stance in the budget was consistent with stability, but the fact that the *outturn* was usually less than programmed implies that the achievement of low inflation depended on how the budget was implemented.

Getting the implementation of fiscal policy right depended on being able to make adjustments to spending through the course of the year in the face of shocks. Here we show the response to three shocks: a shortfall in revenues, supplementary expenditure requests, and the coffee boom of the mid 1990s.

3.2 Revenue shortfall

After 1992 there was no shortfall in donor resources—although there were continued difficulties in predicting the timing of disbursements. There was a small shortfall of revenue in 1993/94, but it was not until 1996/97 that actual receipts were significantly less than projected, in this case by the equivalent of 1.4 per cent of GDP.[9] The monitoring of budget implementation through the Cashflow enabled the government to cut expenditures (on a cash basis) by 0.76 per cent of GDP, with the remaining gap more than offset by increased foreign grants. At the same time, however, higher commitments to spend were financed by increased domestic arrears. The adjustments made to cash expenditure in 1996/97 delivered low underlying inflation of 2 per cent despite lower than projected revenue.[10] This achievement is in contrast to the underlying inflation of 50 per cent that followed the failure to adjust to a revenue shock in 1991/92. The Cashflow made it much easier to keep inflation low in the face of a shock to resources. The accumulation of arrears was a result of tight control of cash releases but limited ability to restrain commitments. This proved to be a persistent problem.

---

[8] Donor-financed projects are excluded because there were difficulties in compiling accurate outturn data and because they could not be controlled using the Cashflow.

[9] Revenues were UGX90 billion less than projected, owing to sluggish imports and difficulties in implementing the new Value Added Tax (see Chapter 5).

[10] The underlying inflation index excluded food crop prices (but included processed food) and was not, therefore, sensitive to the possibility of bad weather pushing up food crop prices.

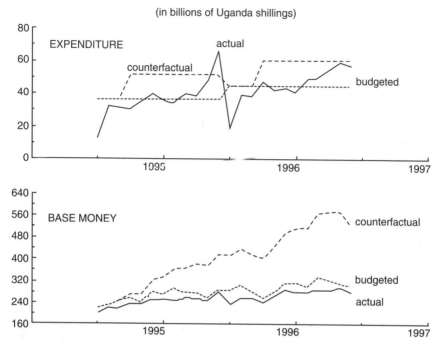

Figure 3.1 Actual and Counterfactual Government Budgetary Operations, 1994/95–1995/96

3.3 Supplementary expenditure

Since 1992 there have been persistent demands from within government to increase spending during each fiscal year. The top graph in Figure 3.1 shows actual expenditure, the monthly average of budgeted expenditure, and counterfactual spending for 1994/95 and 1995/96. Spending above the budget required a 'supplementary appropriation'. The line for counterfactual spending shows what would have happened if all of the 'supplementaries' approved by Parliament were spent evenly over the last nine months of each fiscal year, with no offsetting adjustment to other expenditures.[11] Had all else remained the same, the supplementaries would have been financed by increased credit to government, raising base money, as shown in the bottom graph of Figure 3.1. This counterfactual estimate of base money peaks at UGX560 billion, which is

---

[11] The amounts finally approved by Parliament in 1994/95 and 1995/96 were much smaller than those originally requested by spending ministries. In Figure 3.1 they were allocated over the last nine months of the fiscal year because parliamentary approval was not forthcoming until three months into the year.

about twice both the actual and budgeted levels. Assuming that prices would have increased in proportion to the excess increase in the supply of money, inflation would have risen to an annual rate of at least 25 per cent. This is actually an understatement of the consequences of such monetary expansion: annual rates of inflation above about 10 per cent are likely to lead to a sharp reduction in the private sector's demand for real money balances. So as inflation crept higher the velocity of money would have gone up, and inflation would have increased by rather more than implied by the counterfactual series on base money. Chapter 8 also discusses the impact of supplementaries on the outturn for the budget.

3.4 Coffee boom

There was a boom in coffee prices between 1994 and 1996, because of a frost in Brazil in 1994. At the same time there were significant inflows of foreign capital, mainly owing to progress on the return of property confiscated by the Amin regime from the Asian population in 1972, which led to an increase in private transfers for reinvestment in those assets. Both threatened an appreciation of the exchange rate. The Bank of Uganda intervened, buying foreign exchange to dampen nominal exchange rate appreciation (see below). These increases in the net foreign assets of the Bank of Uganda would have raised the growth of the money supply unless offset by lower net domestic assets—which required lower net credit to government. This implied a tighter fiscal policy.[12]

The coffee boom was a temporary trade shock; theory and experience both suggest that such a temporary shock leads to real exchange rate appreciation.[13] The appropriate fiscal response to a temporary trade shock, and to increased inflows of foreign capital, is to increase public savings, as reflected in the negative central bank financing from 1993/94 onward (see Table 3.3). These reductions in central bank credit to the government were in part due to a tight budget, but were actually achieved through the Cashflow.[14]

Figure 3.2 illustrates the impact of the coffee boom and the policy response. The top graph shows that the increase in the terms of trade was followed by an increase in the producer price of coffee, with a lag of one quarter. With a lag of another quarter, there is a sustained increase in a weighted average of the quarterly underlying inflation index.[15] The bottom graph shows the increased

---

[12] Bevan (1998) concludes that the impact on the exchange rate of additional inflows is at worst ambiguous, at best benign.

[13] See Bevan et al. (1989, 1990), and Collier and Gunning (1996).

[14] In addition, the government also imposed a coffee stabilization tax, which was a hotly debated topic in Uganda at the time. The arguments for and against the coffee tax are presented in Henstridge and Kasekende (2001: Boxes 2 and 3).

[15] The means and ranges of these series have been adjusted to maximize visual correlation, and the left-hand scale is therefore that of the terms of trade index.

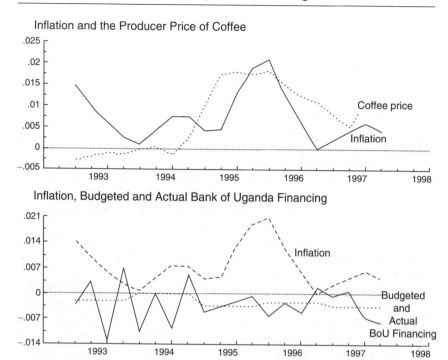

Inflation and the Producer Price of Coffee

Inflation, Budgeted and Actual Bank of Uganda Financing

Figure 3.2 Short Term Fiscal Response to Increased Inflation, 1992/93–1997/98

Sources: MoFPED, and Bank of Uganda. The producer price of coffee, and budgeted and actual Bank of Uganda financing have been rescaled to match the inflation scale on the left hand axis.

underlying inflation during 1995 and a change in the relationship between the planned budget and the implemented fiscal stance, as proxied by the budgeted and actual change in credit to government. Between the second quarter of 1994 and the first quarter of 1996 government savings with the Bank of Uganda increased each quarter as the Cashflow enabled the government to implement a tighter-than-budgeted fiscal policy in response to the increase in inflation. The short-term fiscal response can also be seen in the reduction in the volatility of actual central bank financing relative to the budget. In addition, from the beginning of 1994 there was an appreciation of the nominal exchange rate, which was partially countered by intervention in the foreign exchange market. Reductions in net domestic assets through the tightening of fiscal policy were intended to offset the monetary impact of increased net foreign assets.

Having reviewed three examples of the Cashflow being used to sustain reasonably low and stable inflation in the wake of the achievement of price stability in 1992, we next review the challenges in sustaining a market-determined exchange rate through the development of the market in foreign exchange following the legalization of the *kibanda* market.

3.5 *Exchange rate unification*

Following legalization of the *kibanda* market in 1990, the market exchange rate operated through registered foreign exchange bureaux, with the official exchange rate periodically devalued to lower the premium. BoU instituted an auction for foreign exchange in early 1992. The clearing price at each auction set the official exchange rate for official transactions. The auction was well-funded with donor import support. Total bids were greater than the amounts offered in only two out of the first ten auctions. Despite the auction clearing, a premium between the parallel and official rates persisted. Kasekende and Malik (1994) discuss the reasons for this persistent premium. Perhaps most important was that imports financed from foreign exchange bought from the BoU at the official exchange rate were more thoroughly assessed for import taxes compared to those financed through the foreign exchange market. The evidence was the compression of the premium in March 1992, following the requirement that all shipments be cleared by customs centrally rather than at the border; this made it harder to evade import duties.

An inter-bank market replaced the auction in November 1993. This unified the exchange rates as well as the transaction costs—particularly in terms of the likelihood of being taxed—for both markets. As a result, the market rates appreciated toward the (former) official rate, rather than converging on the relatively depreciated bureaux exchange rate.

Figure 3.3 shows both the convergence of the official and market exchange rates for the period 1985 to 1997 and the surge and then elimination of the premium of the market rate over the official rate. From 1990 depreciation of the official rate rapidly closes the premium until 1992. During the auction in 1992–93, the premium diminishes, but persists until the new inter-bank rate in November 1993 eliminates it. The figure also shows a sharp appreciation in the exchange rate from late 1993 through 1994.

During this period the coffee boom and increased capital inflows raised new problems for the management of the exchange rate. With coffee marketing and export now liberalized, the increase in export sales and subsequent repatriation of proceeds led to a significant increase in the supply of foreign exchange to the market. This, in turn, led to episodes of sharp exchange rate appreciation early in 1994, and problems associated with large foreign exchange inflows.[16]

The first intervention in the foreign exchange market was in December 1993, shortly after the start of the inter-bank market. When the Bank of Uganda saw the exchange rate strengthen, it sought to slow the appreciation.

---

[16] The management of foreign exchange inflows is discussed in more detail in Kasekende et al. (1996), Brownbridge and Tumusiime-Mutebile (2006), and Chapter 13.

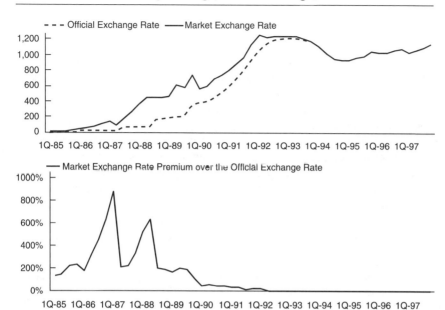

Figure 3.3 UGX/USD Exchange Rates

Sources: Ministry of Finance, Planning and Economic Development; and Research Department, Bank of Uganda.

In early 1994 there were sharp appreciations. Since the earlier intervention had had relatively little effect, the possibility of targeting a particular exchange rate was clearly limited. But there was justification for intervention to promote market stability, and stop the market becoming disorderly. In the early days of 1994 some banks had refused to quote for the purchase of foreign exchange. As events unfolded in the market, government policy remained that the authorities would not take a view on the level of the exchange rate, but would intervene to maintain orderly market conduct, a position held through the 2000s.

3.6 Inflation targeting through short-term fiscal policy

Operating fiscal policy through the Cashflow in pursuit of an inflation target raises a number of questions: Why target inflation rather than the monetary aggregates used in financial programming? Why emphasize short-term fiscal adjustment rather than a more active use of monetary policy? What were the costs of short-term fiscal adjustments in terms of reduced quality of public spending?

INFLATION TARGETING

Inflation was targeted directly because data on prices and inflation were available quickly while monetary data were slow and erratic. With flexible prices that responded quickly to changes in monetary conditions, combined with a three-month lag in the compilation of the monetary survey, changes in monetary conditions showed up in inflation data at about the same time that they appeared in the statistics for broad money.[17] In other words, monetary data did not offer a leading indicator for inflation. Looking directly at the price data also sidestepped the difficulties of separating signal from noise in the monetary data, especially the unpredictable short-run changes in money demand that are characteristic of a remonetizing economy. As a result, the 'money multiplier'—the ratio of broad money to base money—was unstable. Trying to follow a short-term monetary programme would have meant trying to work out why there was price stability when the programme appeared to be 'off-track'.

SUSTAINING LOW INFLATION: SHORT-TERM FISCAL ADJUSTMENT VERSUS CONVENTIONAL MONETARY POLICY

There were two main reasons for retaining tight control of monthly cash releases each month. First, the lesson of the late 1980s and 1991/92 was that it was the loss of control of budget implementation which led to inflation; second, conventional monetary instruments did not have a big enough impact.

Two monetary policy instruments were available in the 1990s: changing reserve requirements of commercial banks and issuing treasury bills.[18] Changing the banks' reserve requirements would, in principle, reduce lending at the margin, and hence lower net domestic assets and money in the economy. But in the mid 1990s, the central bank was unwilling to change reserve requirements because several of the smaller commercial banks were too fragile to comply without being bankrupted, which neutered one instrument of monetary policy.

What remained was the treasury bill. However, in the 1990s the government's judgment was that a short-term fiscal adjustment provided more monetary bite—both through a reduction in base money and a reduction in aggregate demand—than did increased issues of treasury bills. Nonetheless, the volume of sales of Treasury Bills in the primary auction managed by BoU was not determined by the financing requirements of the government: since June 1992 the government had set budgets with no planned increase in domestic

---

[17] Table 3.2 shows the rolling timetable for the compilation of the Cashflow and the information lags involved in tracking the implementation of the budget and the evolution of the economy.

[18] In addition, the BoU retained control of the rediscount rate when interest rates were liberalized. However, in an uncompetitive, segmented commercial banking sector with excess liquidity, changes in the rediscount rate had little bite.

borrowing./The main reason for these sales was to develop a capital market, specifically a secondary market in treasury bills, within which BoU could conduct open market operations. However, in the 1990s there was virtually no secondary trading of treasury bills. Banks held the bulk of outstanding bills (83 per cent of a total of UGX88 billion in June 1997), so the role of the treasury bill as an instrument of monetary policy was limited to its influence on the composition of the banking system's assets. Many commercial banks held large cash reserves because they were under-lent and had a strong liquidity preference. The net effect of additional sales of treasury bills on banks' liquidity depended on whether any of these excess reserves would have gone into increased lending instead of the additional treasury bills./If so, then there was some dampening of liquidity. This was unlikely, however, because the reasons why banks had excess reserves in the first place—they were under-lent—had not changed. From a commercial bank's perspective, lending to the private sector in the 1990s was much like an equity investment because audits had little credibility, making systematic risk assessment hard, and foreclosure or loan recovery through the courts was difficult if not impossible. If, for these reasons, additional treasury bills did not substitute for lending, then sales in the primary auction served as substitutes for otherwise unremunerated excess reserves, and so had no impact on monetary conditions, and correspondingly no impact on inflation.

The banks also held excess reserves because of a strong liquidity preference in the absence of an inter-bank or overnight market. Beyond the point where additional treasury bills served to remunerate excess reserves, banks required sharply higher interest rates to compensate for the increased risk of reduced liquidity. As a result, increased primary issues of treasury bills beyond the point where they started to have a monetary impact led to a sharply higher interest cost for the government budget. In the government's view short-term fiscal adjustments were more effective than increased issues of treasury bills, and were the preferred instrument of short-term management.

SUPPLEMENTARIES: BUDGET ALLOCATIONS VERSUS CONTROL OF BUDGET AGGREGATES

Within-year adjustment to the release of funds clearly disrupts original spending plans, partly through increasing volatility but also through weakening the budget as the institution for the allocation of public resources. However, the use of the Cashflow for macroeconomic management was not to blame. Two thirds of the difference between the budgeted and actual allocations for each ministry between 1992 and 1997 was due to one ministry's budget being cut to accommodate extra spending by another so as to keep total expenditure under control (Moon 1997). The Cashflow was not responsible for persistent demands for supplementary spending—indeed, Stasavage and Moyo (1999) argue that this was at least as rampant prior to the adoption of the Cashflow. Rather, it was essential for containing the damage. The composition of the public spending programme suffered from unexpected cuts mostly because supplementary expenditures were approved, rather than because the Cashflow was being used to keep total spending under control.

In any case, the calculation of costs and benefits needs to take into account the likely counter-factual outcome for the economy as a whole from accommodating demands for supplementaries, rather than just the costs suffered by the spending programme. When one allows for the broad economic costs of higher inflation, the trade-off is more firmly in favour of retaining control of aggregate expenditures. As an illustration, the indicators in Table 3.1 imply that the costs of inflation would have been large. In addition, efforts were made to minimize the impact on spending on programmes important for reducing poverty, such as health and education, by designating them 'priority programme areas', which were not to be cut (see Chapter 8). In effect, this was equivalent to a contingent decision on which items would be hit if, or in most years when, budget discipline broke down.

COMMITMENTS AND ARREARS

Controlling cash does not prevent an accumulation of commitments to spend. If, in the face of a commitment to spend, the cash for payment is not released, the spending has not actually been cut; it has instead been financed by the accumulation of arrears. As well as distorting the allocation of public resources, the accumulation of arrears can also be associated with inflated contracts, as suppliers factor into their prices the likely delay in payment, as well as a premium for the risk of not being paid at all.

An initial attempt to address this problem through a system of local 'letters of credit' was set up to prevent suppliers from contracting to deliver, or actually delivering, goods and services unless the means of payment had been earmarked in a government account at the Bank of Uganda. However, this did not prevent arrears from accumulating to a total of about UGX260 billion by 1999 (28 per cent of domestic revenue), partly because the system was cumbersome but also because suppliers appeared willing to risk delayed payment.

A new system of commitment control was implemented in 1999/2000 across central government spending agencies for non-wage expenditure. As a result, over-commitments were somewhat reduced. It was estimated that during the first two quarters of 1999/2000 over-commitments totalled only UGX6.4 billion, compared with an annual average accumulation of domestic arrears of over UGX100 billion over the previous three years. However, the challenge of maintaining control over cash spending while still preventing the accumulation of arrears remained (the outcome for the remainder of 1999/2000 was UGX45 billion—discussed below), along with the persistent problem of revisions to spending through supplementary budgets.

Efforts to improve fiscal management, and the evolution of the instruments of macroeconomic stability since 2000, are addressed in the next section.

4. The evolution of macroeconomic policy during the 2000s

Macroeconomic management in the 1990s was characterized by two elements: short-term fiscal adjustment in pursuit of an inflation target; and a unified floating exchange rate with limited BoU intervention to smooth market operations. Although a somewhat unconventional configuration of policy instruments, this was a sensible way to sustain macroeconomic stability in the face of shocks. However, control of total spending was at the expense of the composition of public spending, because meeting demands for supplementary expenditures during the course of implementing the budget meant that some spending that had been part of the original budget was cut.

Sustained economic growth has changed the economy since the 1990s, and government policy has evolved towards a more conventional configuration of instruments. This section reviews the main changes in the economy, including the reform of the financial sector, before reviewing the implementation of the budget. We argue that progress in strengthening the budget process has been undermined by persistent demands for within-year supplementary spending and the accumulation of domestic arrears. We then look at the development of monetary policy and review the trade-offs between the use of open market operations and foreign exchange interventions in the pursuit of low inflation.

4.1 Changes in the real economy

Table 3.4 highlights the changes in Uganda's macroeconomy since the late 1990s. At market exchange rates Uganda was a USD15 billion economy in 2008—compared with less than USD4 billion in 1993. During the 1990s economic growth was driven by a combination of post-conflict rehabilitation and increasing capacity utilization, as well as the coffee boom. Since 2000 these effects had faded: the rehabilitation of infrastructure was largely complete, capacity utilization had increased, and coffee prices had come down. To sustain growth, investment had to be increased. Private investment grew from an average of just under 10 per cent of GDP in the period 1992/93–1996/97, to an average of 19 per cent between 2003/04 and 2007/08, reaching 24 per cent of monetary GDP[19] in 2007/08 (UBoS 2008).

---

[19] Total GDP includes estimates for non-monetary, 'own consumption' or 'subsistence' economic activity, while monetary GDP excludes these.

Table 3.4 Macroeconomic Indicators, 1997/98–2007/08

	1997/98	1998/99	1999/00	2000/01	2001/02	2002/03	2003/04	2004/05	2005/06	2006/07	2007/08
	(in billions of Uganda Shillings at end-period, except where otherwise indicated)										
Government Financing											
Change in Bank of Uganda claims on government (as % beginning of period money, M2)	−103	24	470	−42	−190	−207	−168	−471	−136	−743	−609
	−15%	3%	49%	−4%	−16%	−14%	−10%	−24%	−6%	−29%	−20%
Outstanding Treasury Bills and Treasury Bonds (% GDP)	2%	3%	4%	6%	9%	10%	10%	11%	10%	11%	12%
Domestic financing of the Budget (% GDP)	−2.0%	−1.9%	5.1%	−2.4%	−5.3%	−1.5%	−0.5%	−0.7%	0.1%	−2.7%	−1.1%
Monetary Conditions											
Bank of Uganda foreign reserves (US$ million)	750	748	719	773	869	964	1,133	1,326	1,407	2,154	2,684
Change in reserves (as % beginning of period money, M2)	...	0%	−5%	9%	14%	13%	18%	17%	7%	48%	28%
Growth of money, M2 (end-period, %)	24%	9%	15%	15%	25%	17%	10%	12%	19%	17%	30%
M2/base money (the 'money multiplier' ratio)	2.34	2.21	2.36	2.16	2.35	2.70	2.35	2.33	2.50	2.47	2.48
M2/GDP (%)	11%	11%	12%	12%	14%	14%	14%	13%	14%	14%	16%
Commercial banks' credit to the private sector (% GDP)	5%	6%	6%	6%	6%	7%	7%	8%	8%	9%	12%
Outcome for the Real Economy											
Real GDP growth	4.8%	7.8%	5.4%	5.2%	8.6%	6.6%	6.8%	6.3%	10.8%	7.9%	9.8%
Inflation (end-period)	−1.6%	5.2%	1.9%	5.9%	−2.5%	10.1%	0.9%	10.7%	7.4%	5.9%	12.5%

Sources: Ministry of Finance, Planning and Economic Development; Bank of Uganda; IMF.

Uganda has also become a more monetized economy, with a deeper financial sector. In other words, the use of money, bank accounts, and credit, have all grown by more than the growth in economic activity. For example, in June 2008 the M2 measure of broad money supply was equivalent to 16 per cent of GDP, compared to 11 per cent in June 1998. The outstanding stock of government securities as well as commercial banks' credit to the private sector were both equivalent to 12 per cent of GDP (roughly USD1.8 billion) in June 2008, both significantly higher than ten years earlier. Deeper monetization reduced the sensitivity of the price level to monetary shocks in the 2000s compared to the volatility and flexibility of prices in the 1990s.

The drivers of monetization are illustrated in Figure 3.4 (which uses data from Table 3.4). The steady reduction in the net credit to government from BoU has offset expanding foreign reserves to contain growth in broad money, M2, while still accommodating growth in private sector credit. At the same time, the expansion of outstanding government securities has allowed for a more orthodox approach to monetary management.

4.2 Financial sector reform

Increased monetization was supported by a combination of macroeconomic stability, improvements in financial oversight and bank supervision, and more sophisticated financial markets. This was a transformation from the situation at

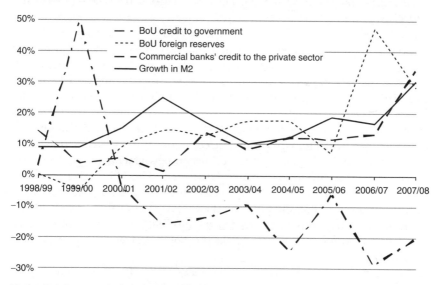

Figure 3.4 Drivers of Monetary Conditions

Sources: Ministry of Finance, Planning and Economic Development; and Research Department, Bank of Uganda.

the end of the 1980s, when Uganda's financial sector was shallow and highly segmented, and had no significant financial intermediation. A state controlled bank, Uganda Commercial Bank (UCB), dominated the commercial banking sector with a market share close to 80 per cent. It was inefficient, insolvent, and its overbearing market presence stifled competition. The inter-bank money market was characterized more by liquidity support from the central bank to the commercial banking system than credit activities between commercial banks. Efforts to reduce inflation through fiscal restraint were undermined by the liquidity support to the banking system.

Reforms in the 1990s were aimed at restructuring and strengthening the financial sector, promoting competition and efficiency, while strengthening BoU's role as the monetary and supervisory authority. The Bank of Uganda Statute of 1993 delegated monetary authority to BoU to take decisions on the conduct of monetary policy without influence or direction from any other authority. Moreover, the Financial Institutions Statute 1993, which replaced the 1969 Banking Act, strengthened BoU powers to fulfill its regulatory and supervisory functions in relation to banks and other depository institutions. While BoU had strengthened authority over licensing or closure of banks it still had to consult the finance minister on any revision to the minimum capital requirements or closure of insolvent institutions. Nevertheless, with these new powers, BoU increased the minimum capital requirements to UGX1 billion and UGX500 million for foreign and local banks respectively.

This was a compromise following a protracted debate between reformers and advocates of continued state control. The latter feared that: (i) liberalization of interest rates would crowd out strategic investments that they considered deserving of subsidized interest rates, particularly by the state marketing boards; (ii) strengthening banks through capital increases would mean foreign dominance of the banking sector; (iii) the changes would erode the developmental role of the state (i.e. directing credit to 'strategic sectors'); and (iv) banking services to the poor would suffer.

The initial reforms failed to provide BoU with sufficient authority to superintend the financial sector effectively. The compromise capital requirements for local and foreign banks had the effect of sustaining segmentation in the sector. Implementing reforms in the commercial sector and BoU in parallel presented the Bank with a role it was ill equipped to handle. As the number of licensed institutions swelled, BoU did not have the capacity to supervise effectively the many small banks. Further, the shared responsibility of the finance ministry and BoU on closure of insolvent banks inevitably delayed prompt action on weak banks.

These compromise reforms sowed the seeds of the 1997/98 banking crisis which represented a turning point in resolving the debate between reformers and supporters of state activism in the financial sector. By the end of the crisis, four commercial banks had been closed and BoU had intervened in UCB. All four closed banks were characterized by imprudent banking practices and a lack of sound internal governance. To address problems of insolvency in the banking system, a statutory instrument was issued in 2000 to increase minimum unimpaired capital requirements. All banks and credit institutions were required to maintain minimum unimpaired capital of UGX2 billion and UGX1 billion, respectively.

In the aftermath of the banking crisis, it was decided to strengthen further the role of the central bank as the supervisory authority, with minimal shared responsibilities. The 1993 Statute was replaced by the Financial Institutions Act 2004, which included provisions on corporate governance and mandatory corrective action by BoU to take action promptly before banks become insolvent. BoU also published an intervention policy stipulating that no weak bank would be propped up and that there would be immediate intervention in any bank that failed to comply with statutory requirements. The minimum unimpaired capital was raised to UGX4 billion for banks while shareholding of any one person, family, or group was limited to a maximum of 49 per cent of total equity in a bank. Insider lending was severely curtailed. The Microfinance Deposit Taking Institutions Act 2003 governed microfinance deposit-taking business. The requirement for the minister to approve changes to minimum capital requirements was retained to protect local investors.

The next landmark in the restructuring of the financial sector was the sale of UCB. The process leading up to the sale was characterized by an acrimonious debate involving the Presidency, parliament and the public, again focused on the issues of foreign ownership, the instruments of a developmental state, and outreach. In addition, the legal powers of BoU to resolve an intervention in a state owned bank using the Financial Institutions Statute—rather than the privatization legislation—was challenged. Following a prolonged process and debate, the Bank ended its intervention in UCB in 2002 by selling it to a reputable international bank.

These reforms have eliminated segmentation; the sector now comprises well-managed and solvent institutions. The inter-bank market in both local and foreign exchange has expanded, while the credibility of the regulators has been greatly enhanced. Fears that closure of insolvent institutions would undermine public confidence in the financial sector and cause a systemic crisis have proved unfounded. If anything, weeding out weak institutions has strengthened public confidence in the sector and enhanced financial intermediation.

The reforms also provided the institutional framework necessary for the conduct of market based monetary policy, with equivalent development in capital markets. In the 1990s treasury bills took the form of Bearer Certificates. Because they were owned by whoever held them, the security risks involved in moving them around discouraged secondary trade. In 1999 the Bank of Uganda introduced an electronic registry of investors in government securities called the book-entry Central Depository System. This system solved the problem of transferring ownership of securities. However, the law was worded such that a security had to be in paper form; the courts did not recognize electronic securities. The Financial Accountability Act of 2003 gave the Minister of Finance, Planning and Economic Development power to issue securities both in paper and electronic form, and paper treasury bills were discontinued.

The Repurchase Agreements (repo) Market was introduced in 2002 by the Bank of Uganda as a mechanism to manage liquidity in the banking system in the interval between auctions of treasury bills. The vertical repo market reflects transactions between primary dealer commercial banks and the central bank.

Longer-term treasury bonds were introduced through a primary auction in January 2005. Treasury bonds are auctioned every twenty-eight days. Bonds have provided an additional saving instrument and have helped deepen the capital market.[20]

Outstanding treasury bills were equivalent to just 2 per cent of GDP in June 1998. By June 2008 total outstanding domestic government securities had increased to 12 per cent of GDP. This increase, together with a much better functioning financial sector, has transformed the environment in which monetary policy operates. We next review fiscal policy in the 2000s, before returning to the implementation of monetary policy.

4.3 Implementing the budget

The 2000s saw a shift in fiscal strategy. In the face of increased aid inflows, it was decided in 2001/02 to lower the fiscal deficit before grants (see Chapter 13). This fiscal consolidation reduced the deficit from 11.6 per cent of GDP in 2001/02 to 6.8 per cent in 2005/06. In addition, the budget system has been strengthened by a series of reforms introduced during the 1990s (see Chapter 8). Making sure that fiscal consolidation sustained low inflation, and ensuring that public spending helped boost growth, both depended on whether the budget was actually implemented as planned.

A key change in fiscal management from the 1990s was the shift from monthly to quarterly cash releases. This loosened some constraints on spending by line ministries, with lumpiness in expenditure being absorbed by changes in net credit to government from the Bank of Uganda. The intention was to programme quarterly spending releases in coordination with the programming of monetary policy (see below). The frequency of 'Cashflow Committee' meetings decreased accordingly—there no longer being a decision point each month. Indeed, for several years the group only met when there was a

---

[20] Treasury bills securities have maturities of 91 days, 182 days, and 364 days in the primary market, with auctions now held fortnightly. Treasury bonds have two years, three years, five years, and ten years maturities.

change in the spending programme, or some other need for coordination between MoFPED and the Bank.

Table 3.5 shows the quarterly implementation of spending (excluding interest, net lending, and investment)—in terms of the extent to which quarterly releases matched the quarterly programming for fiscal policy—for the three fiscal years 2004/05 to 2006/07. These show only modest overruns on total spending, but persistent shifts in the composition of spending.

In 2004/05 Poverty Action Fund (PAF, see Chapter 13) spending was reasonably well protected. It was higher spending in the fourth quarter, under the heading 'other recurrent ministries', that caused the overrun on total spending. The *Background to the Budget* reported 'over-expenditures (supplementaries) of UGX21.5 billion on the recurrent budget' in 2004/05 (MoFPED 2005).

In 2005/06 spending under 'other recurrent ministries', together with un-programmed statutory expenditures, accounted for higher than budgeted total spending. Outlays on PAF wages and salaries were, in addition, consistently UGX10 billion higher than programmed in the second, third, and fourth quarters. There was a modest offset to these over-runs from below-budget spending on PAF domestic development in the first and third quarters of 2005/06. The *Background to the Budget* reported: 'there were some overruns on account of unforeseen outlays on public administration and security . . . The slight overrun in the non-wage category was largely accounted for by frontloading non-wage releases to State House and Office of the President' (MoFPED 2007).

In 2006/07 the outturn for total spending was only 1 per cent over the budget, but the composition of spending shifted significantly. PAF spending was below budget; defence wages and salaries (which includes allowances), and 'other recurrent ministries' and district spending were all significantly over-budget, with the net overrun taking place in the fourth quarter.

Taking a broader view, the aggregate budget and Cashflow outturn for the ten years 1997/98–2006/07 as shares of GDP[21] is shown in Table 3.6. In general, the record of strong implementation established in the 1990s has been maintained. In all but three years, domestic financing (as a share of GDP) was tighter than budgeted.

In 1998/99 there was a shortfall of donor support which was not wholly offset by expenditure cuts; although financing from the BoU was negative, it was smaller than the repayment provided for in the budget. In 1999/2000,

---

[21] This table is from data held by the MoFPED Macroeconomic Policy Department. It is compiled on a similar basis to Table 3.3, with donor financed project grants, expenditures, and loans excluded. However, in this table the lines for the cheque float and changes in arrears are shown as part of domestic financing—strictly a more correct presentation than their treatment as an adjustment to cash item in Table 3.3. Note that nominal GDP is given as originally projected in the budget, with the outturn reflecting the revision and re-basing of GDP by the Uganda Bureau of Statistics in 2008. As a result, there is some variation between the levels of GDP projected in the budget column, and the estimates of actual GDP shown in the outturn column for each fiscal year.

Table 3.5 Quarterly Cash Spending Limits and Outturn, 2004/05–2006/07[1]

| | 2004/05 | | | | | | | | 2004/05 Fiscal year | | | |
| | Q1 | | Q2 | | Q3 | | Q4 | | | | | |
	Programme	Outturn	Programme	Outturn	Programme	Outturn	Programme	Outturn	Programme	Outturn	Deviation: UGX	%
Total[2]	470.7	485.7	612.8	586.3	632.4	647.9	511.0	618.3	2,226.9	2,338.2	111.3	5%
Wages & Salaries	189.3	175.2	190.6	184.6	192.1	212.9	193.7	203.7	765.8	776.3	10.5	1%
PAF	79.9	70.5	80.6	77.9	81.3	92.3	82.1	85.3	323.9	326.1	2.1	1%
Defence	33.4	33.4	33.4	33.4	33.4	33.4	33.4	33.4	133.6	133.6	0.0	0%
Non PAF non-defence	76.0	71.3	76.7	73.3	77.4	87.2	78.2	84.9	308.3	316.7	8.4	3%
Transfers to URA	14.4	14.4	14.4	14.4	14.4	16.4	14.4	18.1	57.7	63.4	5.7	10%
Recurrent Expenditure	188.5	189.4	252.0	231.3	226.9	227.0	183.1	256.8	850.5	904.6	54.1	6%
PAF	22.2	36.5	66.6	54.5	64.7	48.5	31.4	38.3	184.8	177.9	-6.9	-4%
Defence	49.3	48.9	65.8	51.5	41.1	54.9	41.1	46.3	197.4	201.6	4.2	2%
Statutory	39.4	30.1	39.4	30.4	39.4	37.7	29.2	55.0	147.4	153.3	5.9	4%
Other recurrent ministries	66.0	62.3	68.8	83.4	70.2	74.2	69.8	104.1	274.7	324.0	49.2	18%
District recurrent	11.5	11.5	11.5	11.4	11.5	11.8	11.5	13.2	46.1	47.9	1.8	4%
Domestic Development	73.5	102.4	144.4	136.5	165.2	159.1	114.8	120.7	497.9	518.8	20.9	4%
PAF	37.5	60.8	102.6	98.8	114.4	104.3	58.3	77.3	312.9	341.3	28.4	9%
Defence	4.0	4.0	4.0	1.9	4.0	2.7	4.0	3.2	16.1	11.8	-4.2	-26%
Non PAF, non-defence	31.9	37.6	37.8	35.8	46.8	52.2	52.5	40.1	168.9	165.6	-3.3	-2%
Arrears	5.0	4.2	11.3	19.4	33.8	32.5	5.0	19.0	55.0	75.2	20.2	37%

2005/06

	Q1		Q2		Q3		Q4		2005/06 Fiscal year			
	Programme	Outturn	Programme	Outturn	Program	Outturn	Programme	Outturn	Programme	Outturn	Deviation: UGX	%
Total[2]	581.3	565.7	694.0	686.3	590.7	677.7	615.1	656.6	2,481.0	2,586.2	105.2	4%
Wages & Salaries	206.5	210.7	207.9	217.6	209.6	217.9	211.3	222.2	835.2	868.4	33.1	4%
PAF	83.1	86.1	83.8	93.9	84.6	94.1	85.4	95.5	336.9	369.5	32.7	10%
Defence	33.8	33.8	33.8	33.8	33.8	33.8	33.8	36.7	135.2	138.1	2.9	2%
Non PAF non-defence	89.6	90.9	90.3	90.0	91.2	90.0	92.1	90.0	363.2	360.8	-2.4	-1%
Transfers to URA	17.0	17.0	17.0	17.0	17.0	17.0	17.0	17.0	68.0	68.0	0.0	0%
Recurrent Expenditure	229.9	228.8	246.0	265.1	233.0	300.3	242.8	255.3	951.8	1,049.5	97.7	10%
PAF	53.5	50.0	56.5	56.4	55.0	52.8	55.0	53.3	219.9	212.4	-7.5	-3%
Defence	50.4	50.4	50.4	48.9	50.4	64.7	50.4	38.3	201.6	202.3	0.7	0%
Statutory	40.2	33.3	40.2	57.7	40.2	66.5	40.2	64.2	160.6	221.7	61.1	38%
Other recurrent ministries	75.1	86.3	88.1	88.3	76.7	88.4	86.5	88.0	326.3	350.9	24.6	8%
District recurrent	10.8	8.8	10.8	13.8	10.8	27.9	10.8	11.5	43.3	62.0	18.7	43%
Domestic Development	123.7	96.7	145.9	136.9	131.0	127.4	140.4	149.2	541.0	510.2	-30.8	-6%
PAF	75.8	64.1	84.4	82.9	80.1	71.4	80.1	79.0	320.2	297.4	-22.9	-7%
Defence	2.6	2.6	2.6	2.6	2.6	1.4	2.6	3.8	10.4	10.4	0.0	0%
Non PAF, non-defence	45.3	30.1	58.9	51.4	48.4	54.5	57.8	66.4	210.4	202.4	-8.0	-4%
Arrears	4.3	12.5	77.2	49.7	0.0	15.1	3.5	12.9	85.0	90.2	5.2	6%

(Continued)

Table 3.5 (Continued)

| | Q1 | | Q2 | | Q3 | | Q4 | | 2006/07 Fiscal year | | | |
	2006/07											
	Programme	Outturn	Programme	Outturn	Programme	Outturn	Programme	Outturn	Programme	Outturn	Deviation: UGX	%
Total²	666.1	640.7	821.6	823.3	758.3	743.0	816.0	880.9	3,062.0	3,087.9	25.8	1%
Wages & Salaries	227.6	234.8	242.8	249.0	249.3	249.1	255.7	254.1	975.4	987.0	11.7	1%
PAF	126.2	125.9	140.1	137.8	146.5	138.7	150.3	142.5	563.1	544.9	-18.2	-3%
Defence	34.5	41.0	34.5	41.0	34.1	41.0	35.0	41.0	138.1	164.1	26.0	19%
Non PAF non-defence	67.0	67.8	68.2	70.2	68.6	69.4	70.4	70.6	274.2	278.0	3.9	1%
Transfers to URA	17.0	17.0	17.0	17.0	17.0	17.0	17.0	17.0	68.0	68.0	0.0	0%
Recurrent Expenditure	237.9	238.7	288.5	290.6	271.3	280.7	266.9	310.5	1,064.5	1,120.5	56.0	5%
PAF	56.7	56.8	64.5	59.4	69.6	62.5	60.7	61.4	251.5	240.0	-11.4	-5%
Defence	53.5	53.6	50.2	49.9	42.3	55.4	54.7	45.0	200.6	203.9	3.2	2%
Statutory	35.5	35.5	34.2	41.9	31.6	40.5	38.1	38.7	139.3	156.5	17.3	12%
Other recurrent ministries	81.2	81.8	128.7	127.0	116.7	111.5	102.3	135.0	428.9	455.4	26.5	6%
District recurrent	11.0	11.0	11.1	12.5	11.2	10.8	11.0	30.4	44.2	64.7	20.5	46%
Domestic Development	168.6	134.0	206.4	195.6	183.5	158.5	246.7	267.2	805.3	755.2	-50.1	-6%
PAF	68.0	63.9	89.2	86.3	70.3	67.7	75.8	89.4	303.3	307.3	4.0	1%
Defence	2.9	2.9	2.9	1.9	2.9	6.1	2.9	3.9	11.6	14.8	3.2	28%
Non PAF, non-defence	97.8	67.2	114.3	107.3	110.3	84.7	168.0	173.8	490.4	433.1	-57.3	-12%
Arrears	15.0	16.2	66.9	71.2	37.2	37.7	29.8	32.1	148.9	157.2	8.3	6%

¹ This information reflects programmed releases (cash limits) and release outturns. It does not reflect the quarterly programme that determines the 'Policy Support Instrument' benchmarks. Actual expenditure outturns vary from releases depending on absorption patterns of the spending agencies.

² Excluding interest, net lending, and investment.

Source: Ministry of Finance, Planning and Economic Development.

Table 3.6 Actual Budget and Cashflow Outturn, 1997/98–2006/07[1]

	1997/98		1998/99		1999/00		2000/01		2001/02		2002/03		2003/04		2004/05		2005/06		2006/07	
	Budget	Outturn	Budget	Outturn	Budget	Outturn	Budget	Outturn	Budget	Outturn	Budget	Outturn	Budget	Outturn	Budget	Outturn	Budget	Outturn	Budget	Outturn
	(As a percentage of GDP, except where otherwise indicated)																			
Revenue & grants	14.2	12.8	14.3	13.2	16.00	13.7	16.1	15.2	15.7	16.2	16.5	15.2	17.2	17.7	16.3	17.1	16.8	15.4	16.4	16.5
Revenue	12.3	10.3	12.0	11.3	12.7	10.9	12.0	10.5	11.3	11.8	12.4	11.5	13.1	11.9	12.9	11.9	13.3	12.7	13.5	13.0
Grants	1.9	2.5	2.3	1.9	3.3	2.8	4.2	4.7	4.3	4.4	4.2	3.6	4.2	5.8	3.4	5.1	3.5	2.7	2.9	3.5
Expenditures & net lending	12.2	10.6	11.6	12.0	14.7	18.4	16.0	13.7	16.9	16.2	16.8	16.2	17.5	16.6	16.8	15.4	15.9	15.0	16.1	15.3
Recurrent	10.2	9.2	10.3	10.2	11.5	10.4	12.4	10.8	12.8	12.6	13.9	12.6	13.4	13.6	12.9	12.4	12.5	12.3	12.5	11.7
Domestic development & net lending	2.0	1.4	1.3	1.7	3.2	8.1	3.6	2.9	4.0	3.5	2.9	3.6	4.1	3.0	3.9	3.0	3.5	2.7	3.7	3.7
Overall balance	2.0	2.2	2.7	1.2	1.3	4.7	0.1	1.6	1.2	0.1	0.3	1.0	0.3	1.2	0.6	1.7	0.8	0.4	0.3	1.2
Financing	2.0	2.2	2.7	1.2	1.3	4.7	0.1	1.6	1.2	0.1	0.3	1.0	0.3	1.2	0.6	1.7	0.8	0.4	0.3	1.2
External	0.0	0.1	1.4	0.2	1.4	0.3	2.0	1.2	4.9	5.5	1.7	2.6	0.1	0.5	0.1	0.9	0.4	0.6	0.2	1.5
Domestic	2.0	1.9	4.1	1.9	2.7	5.1	2.1	1.6	3.7	2.8	1.4	1.5	0.1	0.5	0.4	1.7	1.3	0.1	0.5	2.7
Of which:																				
Bank of Uganda	0.8	1.3	2.6	0.3	1.3	5.1	2.0	0.4	2.6	1.7	4.6	1.7	0.3	1.2	0.5	2.9	0.9	0.7	0.0	3.5
Arrears cheque float	0.9	0.9	1.4	1.7	1.6	0.7	1.2	1.9	1.2	1.8	0.4	0.7	0.3	0.9	0.4	0.0	0.6	1.1	0.8	1.1
residual	0.0	0.2	0.0	0.5	0.0	0.1	0.0	1.2	0.0	2.8	0.0	0.1	0.0	0.2	0.0	0.9	0.0	0.1	0.0	0.0

(Continued)

Table 3.6 (Continued)

Items	1997/98 Budget	Outturn	1998/99 Budget	Outturn	1999/00 Budget	Outturn	2000/01 Budget	Outturn	2001/02 Budget	Outturn	2002/03 Budget	Outturn	2003/04 Budget	Outturn	2004/05 Budget	Outturn	2005/06 Budget	Outturn	2006/07 Budget	Outturn
Memorandum Items:																				
GDP (at current market prices UGX bn.)[2]	7,207	7,830	7,824	8,435	8,861	9,241	9,422	10,296	11,455	10,907	11,585	12,438	12,921	13,972	14,515	16,026	17,229	18,172	19,070	20,953
Domestic Financing (UGX bn.)	144	150	322	163	237	472	196	163	429	303	160	180	14	69	61	265	218	13	98	567
Of which: Bank of Uganda	56	103	205	24	114	470	192	42	302	190	535	207	39	168	75	471	147	136	0	743
Arrears & cheque float	65	67	106	146	143	68	113	195	132	193	50	91	45	127	55	7	101	202	149	240
Underlying inflation (period average, %)		1.0		2.8		5.0		5.3		3.5		2.4		2.9		4.6		7.0		7.4
Annual Inflation (period average, %)		5.1		0.2		5.8		4.5		2.0		5.7		5.0		8.0		6.6		7.4
Annual Inflation (end-period, %)		1.6		5.2		1.9		5.9		2.5		10.1		0.9		0.7		7.4		5.9

[1] data on a 'cash' basis, excluding donor-financed projects; fiscal years from July 1st to June 30th.

[2] GDP data for budgets are as used in original projections, where available; for outturns they are either the most recent re-based data spliced back to 1997/98, or the series in use in the 1990s for prior years.

Sources: Ministry of Finance, Planning and Economic Development; Bank of Uganda; Uganda Bureau of Statistics.

following a shortfall in revenue, and with limited scope for cutting spending (on a spectrum ranging from Universal Primary Education, re-capitalization of the Bank of Uganda, the compensation of depositors of banks closed in 1998/ 99, through to a new presidential jet), the net result was an increase in domestic financing (IMF 2000). In 2005/06 expected foreign financing did not material- ize following the arrest of the opposition candidate in the Presidential elections, and a smaller than programmed surplus was financed from a small increase in domestic claims on government (IMF 2006).

The performance of budget implementation in terms of the Uganda Shilling outturn against the original budget is less good—with shortfalls in domestic financing in 2000/01 and 2001/02. However, when viewed in terms of macro- economic outcomes, overall budget implementation up to 2006/07 was impres- sive. Average inflation over the eleven years to June 2008 was 5.1 per cent, with growth in GDP averaging 7.1 per cent (see Tables 3.1 and 3.4). However, two problem areas in fiscal management persisted into the 2000s: supplementaries and domestic arrears.

SUPPLEMENTARIES

The reforms to the budget process, particularly the MTEF and the PAF, sought to defend the allocation of resources, and the effectiveness of spending, against the predations of supplementaries. Nonetheless, supplementaries and realloca- tions during the course of the fiscal year have featured regularly in the accounts of fiscal performance in recent editions of *Background to the Budget*. For example, the 2004/05 edition notes that:

The overall management of the budget in 2003/04 was complicated by the emergence of supplementary expenditure pressures in the last quarter of the financial year ... Given the need to fund supplementary expenditures in the fourth quarter of the financial year, adjustments have been made. These adjustments have had a negative affect on the discretionary non-wage and development expenditures. (MoFPED 2004)

The report on the implementation of the budget[22] in 2007/08 includes a table illustrating the magnitude of supplementaries approved during the course of the year, which amounted to more than 5 per cent of originally approved spending.[23] The main source of over-run was additional spending on the Commonwealth Heads of Government Meeting in Kampala in 2007 and another presidential jet (IMF 2008).

[22] MoFPED has changed the presentation of the fiscal accounts to conform to the IMF 2001 Government Finance Statistics methodology, and now reports on the outturn for the budget both in financial terms and in terms of physical outputs (www.finance.go.ug).

[23] This exceeded the statutory 3 per cent of budgeted spending ceiling but was approved by a resolution of Parliament, given exceptional circumstances related to the Commonwealth Heads of Government Meeting.

ARREARS

The second persistent symptom of dysfunctional budget implementation is the accumulation of domestic arrears. These are a result of ministries contracting with suppliers, and then finding that they do not have the cash to pay—in part a consequence of a lack of budget discipline being tackled through tight control of cash releases. The accumulation of such arrears is, in effect, involuntary non-bank domestic financing. Since the problem first emerged in the 1990s—as discussed above—it has proved stubbornly persistent. In the 2000s it was compounded by a spate of court awards, or discretionary government decisions to make large compensation payments, which had not been included in the budget.

The Commitment Control System (see Chapter 15), which was introduced in 1999, was unable to prevent the accumulation of new arrears. It did not have comprehensive coverage, despite the extension to all non-wage spending in 2002. In particular, arrears on pensions were omitted from the system.

There was a succession of efforts to get to grips with the outstanding stock, and continued accumulation, of arrears. During 1999/2000 new non-wage recurrent arrears amounted to UGX45 billion; during 2001/02 new arrears were UGX32 billion. In June 2002 the stock of arrears (not fully verified by the Auditor-General) amounted to UGX181 billion (1.75 per cent of GDP). During 2001/02 newly identified past pension obligations amounted to UGX103 billion. At June 2004, the stock of verified domestic arrears, including on wages and pensions, amounted to 3.5 per cent of GDP, significantly higher than the unverified estimate from June 2002.

In 2007/08 attempts were made to use an integrated personnel and payroll system under the Integrated Financial Management System (see Chapter 15) to prevent further accumulation of arrears, and to verify the new pension and gratuity arrears from 2006/07. A budget of 1.3 per cent of GDP was allocated to clear old arrears. This was supported by a new debt strategy published in 2007, which sought to clear existing verified arrears, prevent the diversion of resources budgeted for arrears clearance, and stop new arrears accumulating.[24] As with supplementaries, the prospects for progress depend on high-level political backing.[25]

4.4 Managing monetary policy

In the 1990s monetary policy instruments did not work because there were only a few treasury bills in circulation, and the banking system was shallow,

---

[24] The new debt strategy was also set out in the 2008/09 *Background to the Budget*.

[25] The 'president and the prime minister emphasized to the mission that existing regulations prohibiting accounting officers from exceeding budget ceilings would be strictly enforced' (IMF 2005).

inefficient, and highly liquid. Increased issuance of treasury bills through the late 1990s sometimes just offered banks the opportunity to reduce excess reserves by increasing their holdings of treasury bills. This did not change broad money, or affect inflation, but simply switched unremunerated excess reserves into treasury bills on which interest was paid, for no particular monetary policy purpose. As a result, the share of treasury bills in banks' portfolios grew from 6 per cent in 1995 to 34.2 per cent in 2002. However, commercial banks' excess reserves were largely eliminated after 2003. The connection between base money under BoU control and broader monetary conditions—the 'money multiplier'[26]—appears to have been relatively stable since 2005, having earlier been prone to jumps (see Table 4.4). BoU has also been building capacity to guide the conduct of monetary policy. In particular, from the early 2000s the Bank has been able to report on its balance sheet with greater speed and accuracy; the lags shown in Table 3.2 for the compilation of the monetary survey have been significantly shortened.

With the foundation provided by fiscal consolidation, the reform of the financial system and the development of capital markets (discussed above), the scope for effective monetary policy has increased since the turn of the century.

In the 2000s there have been two main instruments for tightening monetary conditions and thereby sustaining low inflation—the sale of government securities and the sale of foreign exchange. The costs of these instruments were an increased bill for interest payments on the budget and higher (and sometimes more volatile) interest rates, or the risk of an appreciated exchange rate, respectively. The balance between these instruments fluctuated during the early 2000s. The choice of instrument was complicated by the pursuit of the twin objectives of inflation and exchange rate stability. The declared policy of BoU was that it did not take a view on the level of the exchange rate—its primary role was inflation control. In practice, however, the Bank has had at times to take measures intended to avoid an appreciation of the currency.[27]

In 2001/02 net issuance of bills amounted to 3 per cent of GDP, and net official interventions in the foreign exchange market reached nearly 4 per cent of GDP. With a further net issuance of 1.1 per cent of GDP in 2002/03, the outstanding stock of treasury bills reached a peak of 10 per cent of GDP.[28]

---

[26] This indicates the extent to which changes in base money—the monetary liabilities on the BoU balance sheet—over which the Bank more or less has control, directly and reliably drive broad money.

[27] This tension mainly revealed itself when the Bank had to absorb an increased resource transfer from abroad, for example in 2004/05.

[28] The stock of treasury bills fell to 6 per cent in June 2008 mainly owing to investors switching out of shorter-term treasury bills into longer-term treasury bonds. Taken together, the outstanding stock of treasury bills and treasury bonds was equivalent to 12 per cent of GDP in June 2008.

During 2003/04 large variations in government liquidity injections led to substantial interest rate volatility, though treasury bill sales fell significantly in the final quarter of the fiscal year with intensified sterilization through foreign exchange sales. In 2004/05 the emphasis switched back to treasury bill sales, with the Bank of Uganda cutting back on foreign exchange sales to avoid pressure on the exchange rate; the corollary was concern over the amount of domestic interest payments that would be required in the 2005/06 budget at a time when the government was a net creditor to the banking system as a whole. Accordingly, the bulk of the burden of monetary policy fell on exchange rate intervention during 2005/06. There was a corresponding drop in interest rates, which supported private sector credit growth.

The declared approach for 2006/07 was a 'mix of foreign exchange sales and open market operations to sterilise foreign exchange inflows' (IMF 2006). However, from late 2006 into 2007 foreign exchange inflows intensified. These were in part due to foreign demand for government securities. In response, BoU halted repo operations and cancelled treasury bill auctions. Short-term interest rates fell back, and the pressures for exchange rate appreciation eased. However, by the end of 2006/07, the domestic interest cost of monetary policy remained substantial at 1 per cent of GDP.

In 2007/08 the fiscal cost increased by some 0.25 per cent of GDP. In the face of persistent foreign inflows BoU had sustained currency intervention and some sales of treasury securities. Nonetheless, surging inflows over both these years, much of which appears to have been private capital, was also reflected in increased creation of private credit, which grew by 48 per cent in 2006/07 and 28 per cent in 2007/08. From the middle of 2008, increased inflation[29] presented the first major challenge to macroeconomic stability for many years.

Chapter 13 discusses the broad approach to macroeconomic management of aid inflows. There is also a broad theoretical and empirical literature tackling the appropriate monetary response to aid surges.[30] BoU and MoFPED have sought a pragmatic balance between the use of treasury bills and foreign exchange sales to keep domestic monetary conditions on track. Over the course of the 2000s the choice of instrument has fluctuated as the balance of costs and benefits has see-sawed.

During the 2000s the foundation for sustaining macroeconomic stabilization has remained the prudent implementation of the budget. There has been an increased deployment of more orthodox instruments of policy. The outcome, in terms of reasonably low inflation and robust economic growth over an extended period, has been among the best in Africa. The costs include the fiscal burden of outstanding domestic debt at a time when the government continues

---

[29] Headline inflation was 14.2 per cent, and underlying inflation 12.6 per cent, as at December 2008.

[30] See Adam et al. (2007); Buffie et al. (2008).

to build a position as a net creditor to the banking system in most years. There may also be an opportunity cost: the availability of government instruments yielding significant positive returns has eased the pressure on banks to be more active in searching out profitable opportunities for lending to the private sector. Although credit from commercial banks to the private sector has grown significantly, from 4 per cent of GDP on average between 1992/93 and 1996/97 to 12 per cent of GDP at June 2008, much of the increase is very recent; the figure was still only 8 per cent of GDP in 2006. Nonetheless, the sustained macroeconomic outturn provides justification for the fiscal adjustment during the 2000s and the deployment of more conventional instruments of monetary policy, which together have underpinned macroeconomic stability.

5. Conclusions

This chapter has set out the changes in Uganda's macroeconomic management since the early 1990s. There were three main phases in the transition from the sustained high inflation of the late 1980s to macroeconomic stability and growth.

First was the legalization of the *kibanda* foreign exchange market in 1990 and the sharp fiscal adjustment that succeeded in stopping inflation within three months in 1992. These two reforms were important as they brought an end to domestic instability and a failing foreign exchange control regime, putting Uganda's economy on to the path of monetary security and open trade at a market-determined exchange rate. Moreover, they made further liberalization possible. The policy changes were not the result of donor conditionality, but succeeded in large part because they were formulated, debated, and implemented by the government of Uganda itself.

The second phase was one of dogged pursuit of macroeconomic stability in the 1990s in the face of shocks. Internal shocks arose primarily from budget indiscipline in the form of supplementaries, but also from volatility in a thinly monetized economy. The main external shock was the coffee boom of the mid-1990s. That inflation remained reasonably low was in large part due to careful short-term fiscal implementation using the Cashflow. In effect, Uganda ran an inflation-targeting regime with short-term fiscal adjustment as the main instrument of stabilization policy.

The third phase, largely since 2000, has been more conventional. The basis for low inflation has remained careful implementation of a sound budget. Monetary policy now operates more independently from fiscal policy, and in a more orthodox fashion, in sustaining low inflation. Despite continuous efforts to improve the quality and focus of the budget, fiscal shocks persist—particularly demands for supplementary expenditures within fiscal years.

Uganda has seen a transformation in macroeconomic management since the early 1990s. Central to the reforms was the establishment and maintenance of fiscal discipline—in the face of economic shocks and the threats posed by incessant supplementaries. Since 1992 inflation has been tamed, the exchange rate has been broadly stable while remaining market-determined, and the financial sector has become much stronger. These developments laid the foundations for the sustained growth and significant poverty reduction since 1992.

4

Public Service Restructuring and Pay Reform

Mary Goretti Sendyona

1. Introduction

The Uganda Public Service of the 1950s and 1960s is remembered with nostalgia both for its efficiency and effectiveness, as well as its role in spearheading the transition from colonial rule to an independent state. However, the political turmoil of the 1970s and early 1980s led to almost the complete breakdown of its administrative structure. From being one of the best in Africa, the public service went into rapid decline: discipline broke down, hiring went out of control, and salaries fell drastically in real terms. When the National Resistance Movement government came to power in 1986, the rebuilding of the public service was seen as a pre-requisite for long-term national reconstruction.

This chapter focuses on two elements of public service reform which were of particular importance for the overall economic reform programme. First, it looks at the restructuring of the public service. This was critical not only for efficiency reasons but because, with limited scope for increasing the wage bill in the medium term, the only way to increase wages was to reduce the number of public servants. The chapter discusses how Uganda managed to achieve one of the most rapid and dramatic reductions in the number of public servants ever seen in Africa. It looks at the retrenchment and voluntary retirement schemes, and the recruitment freeze, as well as the controls on new posts, payroll reform, and divesture. Second, it examines the extent to which the financial resources released through restructuring and increases in the wage bill succeeded in improving incentives to work.

2. Restructuring and reorganization

In 1989 the Public Service Review and Reorganization Commission (PSRRC) was set up to advise government on how to rehabilitate and reorient the public service.

The Commission highlighted a number of weaknesses in the public service including: a lack of discipline; the erosion of rules and regulations; obsolete procedures; poor remuneration; limited managerial and technical skills; and poor attitude among public servants (Ministry of Public Service 1990).

The Commission's report provided the blueprint for the public service reform agenda over the next decade. Its key recommendations covered: restructuring and downsizing of ministries and agencies; retrenchment and voluntary redundancies of public servants; progressive salary enhancements and monetization of benefits; and improved personnel management systems. These recommendations guided the design of the Public Service Reform Programme (Ministry of Public Service 1994b).[1] The objective of the Programme was to create a public service with the right size and structure to meet service delivery needs, whilst minimizing the financial and administrative burden on government, and promoting the role of the private sector as a service provider. This involved redefining the roles and functions of government, liberalization of the economy, hiving off of non-core functions, privatization of public enterprises, and reducing the size of the public service to an affordable level.

One fundamental problem facing government is illustrated in Table 4.1. Salaries had collapsed to such an extent that by 1991 a graduate entry public servant received a monthly salary of just USD7, while even a permanent secretary only received USD23. Such salaries were insufficient for survival, let alone to motivate public servants to perform. However, with the government facing a fiscal crisis (see Chapter 3), there was no scope to increase the size of the wage bill. In the short term, therefore, there was no alternative to reducing the size of the public service if salaries were to be increased.

The restructuring programme effectively started in 1992 with the reduction of the number of ministries from thirty-eight to twenty-one through a presidential directive. A radical downsizing plan was prepared with the objective of reducing

Table 4.1 Monthly Salaries for Various Grades in 1991 and 2005

Salary Scale	UGX		USD	
	1991	2005	1991	2005
U1S	18,256	2,145,366	23	1,225
U1	14,400	1,252,116	18	742
U3	8,800	737,805	11	451
U4(Graduate)	5,600	344,102	7	196
U7	4,312	158,506	5	90
Support Staff	3,200	96,038	4	55

Source: Ministry of Public Service: Salary Structures for 1991 and 2005.

---

[1] Until 1997 it was called the Civil Service Reform Programme.

the total public service from some 320,000 to 145,000 'comprising of Traditional Civil Service 30,000; Teaching Service 90,000; and Police and Prisons 25,000' (Ministry of Public Service 1994b). This was to be achieved through retrenchment, the abolition of the Group Employee Scheme (see below), voluntary retirement, a recruitment freeze, and the elimination of 'ghost workers'. These measures were accompanied by military demobilization, which reduced the size of the army from 90,000 to 50,000.

2.1 Retrenchment

In 1992 6,339 established staff identified by the PSRRC as overdue leavers were retrenched from the public service. In 1993 a further 7,241 officers in the same categories were retrenched, followed by 6,613 overdue leavers from the teaching service in the same year (Ministry of Public Service 1994b).

The number of group employees[2] was reduced by 50 per cent in July 1990. By 1993 another 15,000 were removed. The abolition of the Group Employee Scheme resulted in the redundancy of a further 11,500 employees by December 1995 (Ministry of Public Service 1994b).

An important lesson was learnt from the retrenchment exercise in 1992—retrenchment needed to be handled strictly within public service regulations. Retrenched staff were not paid pension benefits on the basis that they had entered the service irregularly, or were non-performers; they should have already left the service (Ministry of Public Service 1994b). The letters of removal indicated that they were 'retrenched', a term that was not provided for under the regulations. The only circumstances under which an officer should not be paid terminal benefits were upon dismissal, resignation, or abandonment of duty. The affected officers sued the government and won since they had been retrenched and not dismissed, leaving the government to pay their pension benefits and the legal costs (High Court of Uganda 1998).

Openness and broad understanding of the selection criteria became important factors in minimizing bias, claims of illegal removal, and the successful implementation of the retrenchment programme (Ministry of Public Service 1998a). In this regard, the government ensured that the criterion for removal was clear and that the retrenchment process was transparent. Administrative guidelines were always provided to public servants by the Ministry of Public Service,

---

[2] Group employees were staff at the bottom of the salary scale recruited on temporary terms by line ministries to perform casual and unskilled work (e.g. road repair gangs, construction workers, grass cutters) or permanent and skilled work (e.g. drivers, junior copy typists, messengers, cleaners, cooks, mortuary attendants, and nursing assistants). In 1994 the scheme was abolished. Some functions were phased out and others contracted out to private service providers. Retained staff were appointed on permanent and pensionable terms with effect from July 1995.

clearly spelling out the procedure for removal, the selection process, and the terminal benefits to be paid. Sample letters were provided to Responsible Officers[3] to ensure consistency.

Providing for an appeal mechanism gives confidence to affected staff that the retrenchment exercise will be handled in a fair and transparent manner. The institution mandated to handle the appeals must have legal backing. Public officers in central government use the appeal mechanism provided for in the Standing Orders and can also appeal to the Inspector General of Government for redress. Article 166 1(e) of the Constitution provides that local government staff can appeal to the Public Service Commission for redress against decisions of District Service Commissions.

The revision of the Constitution in 1995 also had major implications for the organization, staffing, and responsibilities of the public service. In particular, Article 189 gave local governments residual responsibility for all functions and services not specifically reserved for central government (Ministry of Public Service 1995). A second major restructuring exercise was therefore undertaken in 1997 in order to align ministries' and departments' mandates with the provisions of the Constitution. As a result, by 1999 over 9,000 staff had either been retrenched on abolition of office or had retired voluntarily.

2.2 Voluntary retirement

A voluntary retirement scheme was introduced in 1994 as an equitable way of achieving rapid reductions in staff numbers to enable the government to move quickly towards pay reform. It provided a means of limiting the level of resentment and grievance of those who had to leave the service. Since it was optional, those who left were more likely to explore opportunities elsewhere and contribute towards private sector development. A voluntary scheme was also easier to implement, as the extensive process of review necessary for compulsory retirement was avoided (Ministry of Public Service 1994b, 1998a).

Under this scheme 4,500 staff retired voluntarily in 1994 and 5,511 in 1998 (excluding support staff). Voluntary retirees received an *ex gratia* payment of UGX1 million (about USD1,000) more than the severance package paid to retrenched staff. In 1997 a special voluntary retirement scheme for support staff was introduced (Ministry of Public Service 1997a). A total of 7,740 staff retired voluntarily and were paid a lump sum of UGX1 million.

It is commonly observed that those who can easily get jobs elsewhere are the first to apply for voluntary retirement. It was decided, therefore, that certain critical personnel, namely police and prisons staff, health professionals, qualified teachers, engineers, research staff, state attorneys, magistrates and judges,

---

[3] A Responsible Officer is the chief executive in a ministry, autonomous department, district, or municipality.

should not be allowed to apply (Ministry of Public Service 1994a). In this case, Responsible Officers were given the right to reject an application based on the needs of the public service.

Successful implementation of compulsory and voluntary retirement schemes clearly requires that a government has adequate funds to pay the severance packages. Donors funded much of the Ugandan programme. Table 4.2 shows the costs of the retrenchment and voluntary retirement programme between 1992 and 2005. The average cost of the various schemes over the period was about USD650 per employee.

2.3 Recruitment freeze, 1992–1998

In 1992 the government introduced a selective freeze on the creation and filling of posts until further notice. Between 1992 and 1998 the annual recruitment exercises for graduates and school leavers were suspended while the restructuring programme was undertaken. In other words, there was virtually no recruitment of new public servants for six years. Posts that fell vacant through attrition were not filled. Moreover, officers who retired voluntarily were not allowed to rejoin the public service for five years.

While its impact is difficult to measure, the recruitment freeze undoubtedly played a significant role in reducing public service numbers. Attrition levels were unusually high during the early 1990s because of the HIV and AIDS pandemic, which affected urban areas disproportionately. However, the freeze was not without problems, and the effective monitoring and enforcement of the policy across a service with different appointing authorities proved difficult.

Table 4.2 Retrenchment and Voluntary Retirement Costs of Severance Packages, 1992–2005

Year	Number of staff	UGX billion	USD thousand
1992	6,339	1.167	991
1993	7,241	1.333	1,113
1994	2,784	6.073	6,280
1995	958	2.410	2,487
1996	11,744	6.543	6,202
1997	7,740	3.763	3,523
1998	5,511	6.570	5,320
1999	3,199	4.045	2,780
2000	673	1.385	868
2001	117	0.107	62
2002	26	0.026	144
2003	12	0.017	9
2004	10	0.017	10
2005	349	2.065	1,179
TOTAL	**46,703**	**35,521**	**30,967**

Note: Some retrenched public servants were not paid severance packages. These included the over aged, illegal entrants, and group employees removed before 1994.

Source: Ministry of Public Service, Final Accounts 1992–2005.

The recruitment freeze was lifted in 1996 for primary school teachers and for institutions receiving wage subventions from government, such as public universities and local governments (Ministry of Public Service 1996a). It was finally lifted completely in 1998 following the completion of the restructuring programme (Ministry of Public Service 1998b).

Restructuring and reorganization requires strict control over the creation of new posts. Responsible Officers were encouraged, therefore, to identify posts that could be traded off in exchange for the creation of critical new posts. Care was taken not to trade off critical vacant posts.

2.4 *Eliminating 'ghost workers'*

In the early 1990s about 42,000 'ghost workers'—staff who had left the public service or did not exist but whose names were assigned a payroll number—were removed from the payroll. Efforts were particularly successful in the teaching service where, largely through the removal of ghost workers, the payroll was reduced from 120,000 in 1990 to 95,000 in 1993.

The Ministry of Public Service issued directives relating to payroll management which provided sanctions for public servants caught creating 'ghosts' (Langseth 1995). The computerization of the payroll for the traditional public service in 1989 and for teachers in 1991 was a landmark in public service reform. This enabled the government to have a clearer picture of employment numbers and to monitor the size of the public service on a monthly basis. It also provided a rational basis for controlling the public service establishment (Ministry of Public Service 1994b).

Addressing the issue of ghost workers was helped by the establishment of a Payroll Monitoring Unit, to verify entry and exit from the payroll. In 1994 control measures were introduced with regard to payroll management and wage bill management. These included the introduction of wage allocations based on approved structures and staff establishment ceilings for ministries, local governments, and the teaching service.

Over time payroll internal controls and wage bill management have been strengthened. The establishment of the Inter-Ministerial Taskforce on Payroll Management in 1998[4] and the Wage Bill Committee in 2003 helped to ensure that emerging issues relating to payroll and wage bill management were promptly addressed. This led to continuous improvements in management processes such as reducing delays in accessing the payroll and improving the reliability and timeliness of salary payments.

---

[4] The Taskforce comprised the ministries responsible for public service, finance, education, health, and local government.

2.5 Divesture of non-core functions

One of the aims of the restructuring exercise was to identify non-core functions to be divested. In some cases this resulted in creation of new agencies and authorities. Since 1992 internal revenue collection, customs and exercise, vehicle licensing, civil aviation, national social security, agricultural research, environmental management, forest management, roads maintenance, and information and broadcasting functions/services have all been divested and are now operated by autonomous public sector institutions.

In determining which functions to divest it is important to consider the prospects for financial sustainability of any new institution. The decision in 1998 to divest the Administrator General's Office, Meteorological Services, Uganda Computer Services, and the Virus Research Institute was subsequently reversed since they could not finance their own operations.

2.6 Impact on public service numbers

The combined effect of the above measures (mainly retrenchment, voluntary retirement, elimination of ghost workers, and the recruitment freeze) was a reduction in the size of the public service from 320,000 in 1990 to 156,803 by June 1995 (see Table 4.3). This is one of the largest and most rapid reductions ever seen in any public service. The largest categories of staff removed were group employees and teachers (see Table 4.4).

Although there were fears that such large scale downsizing might cause social unrest, the exercise was implemented surprisingly smoothly. This can be attributed to a number of factors. First, there was strong political commitment from the President to reduce the size of the public service. In a country emerging from military dictatorial government, public servants were accustomed to obeying government directives. Second, significant reductions were achieved by removing ghost workers from the government payroll. Third, generous severance packages, well in excess of retrenchees' annual salary, were offered (Langseth 1996). Fourth, public service labour unions and associations were very weak. Finally, the low pay of public servants played a role too; the loss of a job is easier to bear when the salary is well below a 'living wage' and only represents part of family income.

2.7 Expansion of the public service from 1998

Since the mid 1990s the government's political reform agenda has strongly influenced the size of the public service. The restructuring programme had largely run its course by 1995, with most surplus posts eliminated. In addition, by this time, macroeconomic stability had been established and increased fiscal resources were becoming available to implement government programmes (see

Table 4.3 Public Service Numbers and Wage Bill, 1990–2005

Year	Number of public servants	Wage bill USD million	Wage bill as % of GDP	Wage bill as % of recurrent expenditure
1990	320,000	59.8	2.6	14
1991	269,000	60.0	2.6	15
1992	229,000	53.5	2.3	17
1993	214,943	70.5	2.2	21
1994	177,225	140.5	3.1	27
1995	156,803	172.8	3.1	29
1996	158,969	215.5	3.7	39
1997	157,189	238.8	3.8	40
1998	173,657	276.2	4.4	40
1999	177,520	268.8	4.6	41
2000	177,525	296.4	5.1	42
2001	196,129	318.0	5.3	43
2002	211,420	337.1	5.6	43
2003	219,110	337.0	5.4	44
2004	227,172	438.2	5.5	45
2005	228,463	487.7	5.3	48

Source: Ministry of Public Service, Payroll Monitoring Unit.

Chapter 3). Moreover, the 1993 decentralization policy (see Chapter 14) and, even more importantly, the launch of the Poverty Eradication Action Plan in 1997 with its commitment to increasing services to the poor (see Chapter 7), implied a substantial increase in public service numbers. New government programmes, such as free Universal Primary Education (1997) and Primary Health Care (1999),[5] required a significant expansion in the number of skilled workers. Public service numbers started increasing again in 1998 and reached 228,463 by June 2005, a 45 per cent increase over the 1995 figure (see Table 4.3). Teachers alone accounted for 51,000 of the 71,000 increase between 1995 and 2005 (see Table 4.4).

3. Pay reform

One of the key objectives of public service reform was to have a properly motivated public service. The political turmoil of the 1970s and early 1980s led to a collapse in government revenue and, in turn, in the real value of public service wages. Allowances, such as transport, were often of much greater value

---

[5] The 1999 National Health Policy and the Health Sector Strategic Plan 2000/01–2004/05 emphasized the 'minimum health care package' and the establishment of health centres at village, parish, sub-county, and county levels throughout the country to provide services to the rural population and promote primary health care.

Table 4.4 Number of Public Servants by Grade in Selected Years

Salary Scale	1990	1995	2005
U1	781	1,130	756
U2	2,225	1,541	1,436
U3	3,223	2,077	1,788
U4	9,172	8,463	13,961
U5	23,759	18,765	25,353
U6	13,177	10,127	6,643
U7	95,608	43,550	125,879
U8	62,055	42,650	52,647
Group employees	110,000	28,500	—
Total	**320,000**	**156,803**	**228,463**
of which: Teachers	162,984	90,521	141,981
of which: Health workers	18,029	13,998	17,265

Source: Ministry of Public Service, Payroll figures for June 1990, 1995, and 2005.

than the salary.[6] It was simply not possible for public servants to support their families on their official salaries alone. Often they were forced to supplement their salaries through allowances, through ('moonlighting') activities such as rural farming and petty trading, as well as less desirable practices such as office pilferage, embezzlement of public funds, and outright corruption (Ministry of Public Service 1990).

Clearly, salaries had to be increased substantially if progress was to be made in rebuilding public services. The PSRRC recommended achieving a 'minimum living wage' for public servants by 1996. This meant both increasing the size of the wage bill and spreading it less thinly by cutting the size of the public service. As noted above, the size of the public service was cut dramatically between 1990 and 1995. However, in the short term, fiscal pressure limited the government's ability to redistribute savings from retrenchments to the remaining staff. Instead of increasing the wage bill, government was forced to cut it (in real and in US Dollar terms) in the short term as part of the measures to tackle the 1991/92 fiscal crisis. It fell from USD60 million in 1990/91 to USD53.5 million in 1991/92, or from 2.6 per cent of GDP to an exceptionally low 2.3 per cent of GDP. However, once the crisis had been overcome the wage bill rebounded, climbing steadily from 1993/94 until 2001/02 when it peaked at 5.6 per cent of GDP (see Table 4.3).

While the average public service wage increased from USD174 per annum to USD1,102 between 1990 and 1995 (see Table 4.3), salaries were still extremely low compared to the private sector and parastatals, and the salary compression ratio was only 6.8:1.[7] The government recognized the need to provide remuneration to public servants that was competitive with the private sector to

---

[6] A total of seventy-six allowances were being paid by 1989. Some were paid on a monthly basis while others were duty-facilitating allowances such as *per diems*.

[7] The compression ratio is the ratio between the highest paid public servant and the lowest.

facilitate the recruitment, motivation, and retention of professionals and managerial staff. In 1995 a new Public Service Remuneration Policy and Pay Structure was announced. It set out four key principles:

1. The total cost of the public sector wage bill must be affordable within the context of a rational and non-inflationary public expenditure policy.
2. All public servants should receive at least a 'living wage', i.e. a wage sufficient to maintain an adequate standard of living for himself and his immediate family, at the level of his appointment.
3. The remuneration package should be as transparent and simple as possible, and should ideally consist of a single consolidated taxable salary without additional allowances or non-cash benefits. This package should also be sufficiently attractive to motivate and retain public servants to perform to the highest standard of which they are capable and by which they should be judged.
4. The public service salary structure should be harmonized, rationalized, and equitable throughout Uganda for all groups of staff. Selective salary awards should be discouraged (Ministry of Public Service 1995).

As a result of the new policy, in 1996 all allowances of a salary nature, such as housing and transport, were consolidated with the basic salary into a single taxable package (Ministry of Public Service 1996b). The remaining allowances were rationalized or abolished. Government pool houses were divested,[8] except for institutional houses (Ministry of Public Service 1994c). Public servants who were still housed had to pay for the accommodation at rates equivalent to the housing allowance.

This represented a more transparent and fair pay system for public servants at the same grade. However, when the decision was taken to consolidate allowances into salary the financial implications for salary related benefits—especially pensions—were not taken into account. For instance, in 1994 the government made a decision to increase pensions in line with annual pay increases (Pensions (Amendment) Statute 1994). This increased the government's annual pension bill by UGX103 billion (USD97 million) per annum.[9] It raised concerns about the sustainability of the public service pension scheme[10] as no comprehensive actuarial valuation had been undertaken (Ministry of Public Service 1997b).

---

[8] Public servants who were sitting tenants were given first priority to purchase the houses on mortgage terms over a period of ten to fifteen years.

[9] The policy decision to revise the pensions was implemented in 1999 and arrears were paid to the beneficiaries. The specific increase to each pensioner depended on the length of service and the current salary attached to an equivalent post.

[10] The public service pension scheme is a defined benefit scheme and unfunded. Government meets its obligations to current pensioners from current revenue. The benefits are based on salary at the date of retirement.

From 1998 budget constraints and the growth in public service numbers started to erode the early gains in wages. Despite low inflation, increases in the wage bill were not sufficient to maintain, let alone improve, the real value of public service wages. With rapid economic growth and rising wages in the private sector, serious problems were experienced in retaining public servants with critical skills. The fiscal situation did not allow for substantial salary enhancement across the board. A decision was taken, therefore, to accelerate the salaries of those categories that were in high demand or short supply, and were deemed critical for the social transformation of the country. The problem was that selective pay awards resulted in endless demands for pay increases from other groups who felt they deserved the same treatment. Appendix 4.1 illustrates some of the selective awards implemented since 1989.

With increasing resources being allocated to the social sectors, government was concerned at the inability of local governments in remote areas to recruit and retain certain categories of front line service delivery personnel because of inadequate incentives. A number of measures were introduced to address the issue including: improved access to further education, flexibility in recruitment by lowering job specifications, and undertaking targeted local recruitment. For example, due to increased demand for primary school teachers as a result of universal primary education, 'ordinary' and 'advanced' level school leavers were hired as untrained primary school teachers for a period of three years. The introduction of non-formal education resulted in the recruitment of untrained personnel to teach primary school pupils in pastoralist areas. Tailored training programmes aimed at professionalizing staff were developed and implemented by the Ministry of Education and Sports.

A pay reform strategy was adopted in 2002. The key features were:

1. Implementation of the recommendations of the job evaluation exercise conducted in 2000. A key objective was to eliminate the glaring distortions and inequalities in the salary structure among jobs that had been evaluated at the same level. This resulted in the abolition of the multiple salary structure and the adoption of a single spine salary structure from July 2003. As a result, the number of salary grades was reduced from fifteen to ten (Ministry of Public Service 2003).

2. Implementation of agreed salary targets over a ten-year period based on the recommendations of the job evaluation exercise.

3. Achieving market benchmarked salary targets for critical roles and skills for middle and senior level managers and professionals, where serious problems in recruitment and retention of staff were being experienced.

4. Implementation of cost efficiency measures.

5. Development of a comprehensive pay policy[11] for public service institutions to provide a rational basis for determining pay across the public service.

6. Restoring and preserving the purchasing power of salaries for all public servants.

7. Establishing a sustainable retirement benefits scheme (Ministry of Public Service 2002).

Average wages increased rapidly between 1993 and 1997, as the wage bill increased from 2.2 per cent of GDP to 3.8 per cent while the number of public servants continued to decline. While the wage bill continued growing as a share of GDP until 2002, wages increased more slowly from 1998 as additional public servants were recruited to meet the commitments to increased service delivery in the Poverty Eradication Action Plan. The wage bill peaked at 5.6 per cent of GDP in 2002 and has subsequently been in the range 5.3 per cent–5.5 per cent (see Table 2.3). While this represents a substantial increase on the levels of the early 1990s, it is still well below the average for sub-Saharan Africa of 6.5 per cent of GDP (Kiragu and Mukandala 2005: 281).

The rapid increase in the wage bill around the turn of the century was facilitated by increased flows of budget support, debt relief, and aid earmarked for Poverty Action Fund activities from 1999/2000 (see Chapter 13). It was increasingly recognized that expanding social service delivery meant increased recurrent—and particularly wage—expenditure. The wage bill share of recurrent expenditure has increased steadily from 14 per cent in 1990 to 48 per cent in 2005 (see Table 4.3).

Table 4.1 shows that, as a result of the reduction in public service numbers and—more importantly—the increase in the wage bill, public service salaries increased substantially between 1991 and 2005. The monthly salary of a graduate (U4) increased from USD7 to USD196 and that of a permanent secretary (U1S) from USD23 to USD1,225 over the period. These rates are still below the pay reform salary targets of 2002 and government still has difficulty retaining key personnel such as medical workers and legal professionals. Nevertheless, it is now at least possible for a public servant to survive on his or her salary.

Little progress has been made in harmonizing pay levels across the public service. Two problems can be identified. First, a number of autonomous and semi-autonomous institutions/agencies have been established since the early 1990s, which are authorized by law to determine their own terms and conditions. Second, to ensure the projects they were funding were implemented successfully many donors established Project Implementation Units (PIUs) in

---

[11] Previous pay policies were fragmented. There was no comprehensive policy to guide pay decisions for all government institutions.

which Ugandan members of staff were paid well above public service rates. This inevitably resulted in many public servants moving to PIUs, further weakening government capacity. The damage caused by PIUs to government systems (throughout Africa) was acknowledged in the Paris Declaration on Aid Effectiveness (OECD 2005), in which donors committed to phasing out the practice. As a result of this and the switch by many donors from project to budget support (see Chapter 13), the number of PIUs has been reduced.

4. Conclusions

Significant progress has been made in rebuilding the Ugandan public service following its virtual collapse during the 1970s and 1980s. The number of public servants was halved between 1990 and 1995 through a number of measures such as the elimination of ghost employees, retrenchment, voluntary retirement, abolition of group employees, and a recruitment freeze. The number of ministries was reduced and many non-core government functions were divested. The reduction in numbers, the monetization of benefits, and increases in the wage bill as the economy revived, together contributed to significant real salary increases.

However, despite rationalization of the salary structure, these were not sufficient to properly motivate public servants or to retain those with skills demanded in the private sector. Increasingly, *ad hoc* pay awards were made to selected groups. A new wave of recruitment started in 1998 as government began implementing its commitments to improved service delivery, particularly free universal primary education, in the Poverty Eradication Action Plan.

Most progress in public service reform was made during the first half of the 1990s when the President was closely involved in driving the process. The dramatic reduction in the size of the public service and the restructuring of ministries would not have been possible without strong political leadership. Despite the approval of a new pay reform strategy in 2002, government failed to commit substantial resources for salary enhancement on the grounds that more pressing political objectives assumed precedence over the pay of public sector employees, notably free universal primary education and increases in defence expenditure on account of the ongoing war in northern Uganda (Robinson 2006: 17).

With the wage bill stagnating at about 5.5 per cent of GDP since 2002, government pay reform targets are unlikely to be achieved in the foreseeable future.

APPENDIX 4.1

Selective Pay Awards

Year	Pay Decision
1989	• Professional allowance introduced for specific groups, e.g. lecturers, medical workers, auditors, finance officers, system analysts/programmers, judicial officers, research scientists, economists, engineers, and technicians
1990	• Categories of employees to be paid professional special allowance expanded
1991	• Consolidated monthly allowance introduced for staff not receiving professional allowance
	• Consolidated allowance for Permanent Secretaries introduced
1992	• Professional/top up allowance for teachers introduced
1993	• Auditors and legal/judicial officers, medical officers and dental surgeons were awarded additional 40% salary increase over and above other public officers
1994	• Auditors and medical workers awarded an additional 40% over and above other public officers
	• Legal professionals awarded enhanced salaries
	• Mulago Hospital consultants and other medical staff teaching at Makerere University awarded salaries equivalent to their counterparts in the Makerere Medical School
1995	• Special teachers allowance for primary school teachers introduced
2001	• Following a strike of medical workers, all health workers entitled to lunch allowance and exempted from housing deductions
2004	• Following a strike of academic staff in public universities, they were awarded a pay increase
	• Hardship allowance paid to primary school teachers in selected hard to reach districts

Source: Circular Standing Instructions on Salary Structures issued by the Ministry of Public Service.

5

Tax Reform

Gerry Cawley and Justin Zake

1. Introduction

The prolonged political unrest and civil strife which ended in 1986 caused a sharp reduction in government revenue. During the first five years of the NRM government, Uganda's tax revenue/GDP ratio averaged 5.8 per cent, one of the lowest levels in sub-Saharan Africa (see Table 5.1). Tax policy had become volatile, unpredictable, and constituted a serious hindrance to trade, investment, and enterprise. Moreover, tax administration capacity had deteriorated greatly, smuggling and evasion were rampant, and decisions about tax issues were heavily influenced by rent-seeking behaviour. Information about tax laws, rules, and regulations was not generally available or easily accessible even to policy makers and administration officials. This encouraged corruption, created serious inequities in tax outcomes, and undermined revenue collection.

While Uganda received substantial external aid after 1986 (see Chapter 13) the government could not rely on it indefinitely. Tax reform began in earnest in 1991 when responsibility for tax administration was transferred from the Ministry of Finance (MoF) to the newly established Uganda Revenue Authority (URA). To help achieve fiscal sustainability and reduce dependence on aid the government announced, in 1992, its objective to raise the revenue/GDP ratio by one percentage point every year.

This chapter examines Uganda's tax policy and tax administration reforms, and their impact on revenue collection and taxpayer compliance. Section 2 outlines the government's tax policy reforms, including efforts to improve the export competitiveness of local industry, broaden the tax base, and increase revenue collection. It discusses reductions to Uganda's trade taxes, the introduction of Value Added Tax, and new income tax legislation. Section 3 focuses upon reforms to develop a modern and professional revenue administration, and a culture of tax compliance. It discusses the formation of the URA and the Large Taxpayer Department, as well as efforts to automate and modernize tax

Table 5.1 Average Tax Revenue in Selected Sub-Saharan African Countries (as % GDP), 1985–1996

	1985–1990	1991–1996	1985–1996
Zimbabwe	32.4	30.9	31.6
South Africa	24.4	25.0	24.7
Kenya	19.9	22.7	21.3
Malawi	18.6	17.0	17.8
Zambia	18.1	16.2	17.0
Mozambique	16.2	17.4	16.8
Tanzania	14.3	12.0	13.2
Nigeria	13.7	12.5	13.1
Ghana	11.6	14.2	12.9
Ethiopia	12.2	8.5	10.4
Rwanda	9.9	7.6	8.8
Uganda	5.8	7.8	6.8
Sub-Saharan Africa un-weighted averages	17.3	16.4	16.9
Oil-producing countries	20.0	18.2	19.1
Non-oil producing countries	16.9	16.2	16.6

Source: Ghura (1998).

processing, increase taxpayer education, and strengthen enforcement. Section 4 evaluates the collective impact of these reforms on revenue collection before concluding with some lessons from Uganda's experience.

2. Tax policy reform

Tax policy formulation has always been the responsibility of MoF. When URA was established there was a large transfer of MoF staff dealing with the tax function to the new agency, leaving little capacity within the Ministry on tax policy issues. Not surprisingly, during its first two years of operation URA became heavily involved in tax policy formulation. However, this diminished significantly as a programme to strengthen the Ministry of Finance, Planning and Economic Development (MoFPED)[1] Tax Policy Department got underway in 1994 (involving new appointments, technical assistance, training, better accommodation, and computerization). Subsequent URA interventions were restricted to the provision of information and discussion of proposed amendments to tax law; and a clear separation between tax policy and administration was gradually achieved. It was not uncommon for the two institutions to disagree over tax policy propositions; this is normal and healthy in a dynamic

---

[1] MoF merged with the Ministry of Planning and Economic Development in 1992. Since 1998 the combined ministry has been called the Ministry of Finance, Planning and Economic Development (see Chapter 2). For convenience the acronym MoFPED is used for the merged ministry throughout this chapter.

environment. Ultimate responsibility for tax policy remained with MoFPED, which had to take account of political and socioeconomic considerations.

2.1 Taxes on international trade

The initial focus of tax policy in the late 1980s and early 1990s was on reducing the heavy dependence on trade taxes that had developed since the 1970s. While heavy dependence on international trade taxes is not uncommon in low-income countries, Uganda was unusual in its reliance on revenue from export taxes. During the 1980s export duty, mainly from coffee exports, contributed as much as 50 per cent of total government revenue. This became a major deterrent to export production and an impediment to economic growth. The phasing out of export taxes in the early 1990s signalled a deliberate change to the tax system designed to reduce anti-export bias and encourage increased international trade.[2]

A gradual scaling down of import tariffs complemented the removal of export duties. In the early 1990s import tariffs ranged as high as 350 per cent, making them the largest single contributor to total revenue. By the end of the decade the highest import duty rate had been reduced to 20 per cent and the duty rate regime had been greatly simplified. In addition, import bans and other non-tariff barriers were scaled down and various discriminatory taxes on imports were reduced.

The tax treatment of imported raw materials for industry remained a contentious policy issue in Uganda. This helps explain the volatile tariff pattern for these imports in the late 1980s and throughout the 1990s. Duty on imported raw materials was suspended in 1987, reintroduced at a rate of 10 per cent in 1990, abolished again in 1992, only to be reinstituted the following year. In 1994 a remission of duty was allowed on raw materials not available locally before, in 1995, a duty rate of 5 per cent was applied to imported raw materials. Apart from what was provided in the tariff code, exemptions from duty on imported raw materials were frequently granted on an *ad hoc* basis.

---

[2] A notable exception to this phasing out of export taxes was the Coffee Stabilization Tax (CST) introduced in 1994 following a sharp rise in international coffee prices. The CST was passed in response to the impact of high international coffee prices on Uganda's export competitiveness. Between 1993 and 1994 the US dollar price of Ugandan coffee rose by 125 per cent and remained high for about two years. Given the dominance of coffee in total exports (77 per cent), the sharp rise in prices led to a 20 per cent appreciation in the nominal exchange rate of the Ugandan shilling against the US dollar, implying a sharp deterioration in the competitiveness of non-coffee exports. When introduced the CST was progressive: a rate of 20 per cent applied to export values above UGX1,100 (USD1.20) per kilogram and a 40 per cent rate above UGX2,200 (USD2.40). In 1995 the CST was revised to a single rate of 25 per cent for export values exceeding UGX1,500 (USD1.55) per kilogram. As the international coffee price boom subsided, the CST was abolished in 1996. Over the three years 1994/95 to 1996/97, the CST contribution to total government revenue was a modest UGX56 billion (USD58 million).

Despite liberalization of the trade regime through reductions in tariff and non-tariff barriers, the development of exports was still inhibited by relatively high effective protection for local industries.[3] The combined effect of low rates of duty on imported materials with much higher rates on finished products was high rates of effective protection. Although the average nominal tariff was well below 20 per cent, the World Bank (1995) calculated that rates of effective protection for local industries averaged almost 100 per cent against imports not covered by preferential tariff regimes. The average rate of effective protection against imports from the Common Market for Eastern and Southern Africa (COMESA) was much lower, at about 65 per cent.[4] The COMESA preferential tariff regime is particularly important in Uganda because a high proportion (usually more than 25 per cent) of total imports come from Kenya, its nearest COMESA neighbour and largest trading partner.

Ugandan exporters, on the other hand, faced negative rates of effective protection because the tariffs increased the cost of their imported inputs. This was often aggravated by non-tax factors such as the poor road and rail connections between Kampala and Mombasa, expensive airfreight services, and long delays getting goods cleared at Mombasa Port and at Uganda's borders. The cost of corruption (much of it tax-related) was also significant. These extra costs were often higher than the tax costs and substantially increased effective rates of protection and the anti-export bias.

To reduce the disincentive for exporters resulting from the tariff system a 'duty drawback' operated for most of the 1990s. Under the drawback scheme, direct taxes on exports were refunded based on the product type, as well as for the raw materials and intermediate goods used in their production. The system was revised in 1999 to allow a refund of both direct and indirect taxes, including high fuel duty that was an important additional cost for many exporters. Coefficients were calculated for different export products and, once quantities exported were verified, the calculation of the drawback due should have been a relatively simple task. However, the system required regular updating of the drawback coefficients for different export products to take account of the frequent changes in taxes payable on inputs used in export production. Moreover, with revenue collection being URA's highest priority and continuing problems with allocating resources to pay refunds, the amounts received by exporters were never significant. The implication of high effective protection rates for local industries without an effective duty drawback system for exports was to favour investment in low value-added import-substitution projects and to compound the anti-export bias.

---

[3] Effective protection refers to protection in terms of local value added. It is a more meaningful measure than nominal protection (IMF 1995).
[4] COMESA is a twenty-four-member group with a trade liberalization agenda.

As a member, Uganda was party to COMESA's programme to gradually move towards zero tariffs on trade with other member countries. While this was being implemented on a gradual basis during the 1990s, the government was frequently forced to apply additional tariffs on imports from Kenya in response to pressure from local producers. Given the dominance of Kenya in imports from COMESA, the result was often to cancel out the effect of the COMESA tariff preference scheme. Competition from Kenyan imports has always been a major concern for Ugandan firms. Ugandan producers consider their Kenyan rivals to have a competitive advantage in areas such as utility and labour costs, infrastructure, and port access. These concerns have driven much of the agenda on the treatment of imported raw materials and intermediate goods.

Efforts to liberalize trade were revitalized with the signing of a Treaty for an East African Community (EAC) in 1999 and a commitment to move to a common market between the three signatories. However, given the dominance of Kenya in regional trade, it was recognized that there would have to be a slow transition to zero tariffs on imports from Kenya into the other two countries. Regional integration efforts have been further complicated by the different, and sometimes contradictory, tariff strategies pursued by the regional groupings of COMESA, EAC, and the Southern African Development Community. Tanzania's decision in 2000 to withdraw from COMESA, while remaining a member of the Southern African Development Community (which has its own integration plans) compounded the problem of developing a coherent EAC tariff system.

2.2 Tax exemptions

The use of tax exemptions was a continuing concern during the 1990s, not only because of the direct revenue loss but also for the inevitable equity problems associated with them. The ability of some individuals and groups to exercise undue influence, and the opportunities for abuse provided by exemptions, resulted in significant revenue losses. The revenue losses associated with exemptions for non-governmental organizations (NGOs) and for activities presented as supporting welfare and humanitarian work were often particularly high. A series of measures were taken during the 1990s to stem losses from exemptions.

To achieve more transparency in the exemption process, the use of discretionary powers allowed to the Minister was sharply curtailed. Provisions for specific exemptions were set out in relevant tax laws and regulations. For example, the 1996 Value Added Tax and 1997 Income Tax Acts virtually eliminated the discretionary powers allowed in the previous laws. This greatly assisted tax administration, obviating the need to formulate administrative criteria and create mechanisms to administer exemptions.

Changes were also made to limit the damage caused by blanket exemptions in agreements with donor agencies and NGOs. The list of goods eligible for relief was limited to essential inputs for implementing projects, while measures were taken to reduce the preference for imported over local goods.

Tax inclusive tendering for public sector procurement was introduced in 1996. This meant there were fewer opportunities for suppliers to 'piggy back' on an exemption given for inputs needed to fulfil public sector contracts. Government departments and public enterprises were required to budget for and pay taxes on all goods and services purchased.

The granting of exemptions under the Investment Code, 1991 (administered by the Uganda Investment Authority) from various taxes on inputs required by investors to implement their projects was gradually restricted and then terminated completely in 1995. After 1995 the import duty exemption on capital and other inputs needed to implement projects was provided for in the tariff code. This was achieved essentially by fixing a zero rate of import duty for important capital items like plant and machinery. As a result, goods such as building materials and passenger vehicles no longer enjoyed exemptions. When Value Added Tax (VAT) was introduced in 1996, investors were facilitated by a deferment facility for the VAT payable on imported plant and machinery. Finally, the obligation to report regularly to Parliament about tax exemptions was given more attention as the decade advanced.

2.3 Introduction of Value Added Tax

By the 1990s it was widely recognized that VAT was superior to other forms of indirect taxation in terms of both economic and administrative efficiency.[5] To widen the tax base and make the tax system more equitable for businesses and consumers, a VAT was introduced in Uganda in 1996. It replaced Sales Tax and the Commercial Transactions Levy (CTL). A standard rate of 17 per cent was chosen to keep the new tax revenue neutral in the short term—i.e. to achieve much the same yield from VAT as was previously obtained from Sales Tax and CTL—and avoid any increased tax burden which might jeopardize the launch of the new tax.

With MoFPED keeping a relatively low profile in the implementation of the project, there were doubts initially about political commitment to the VAT project. Responsibility for managing the process and sensitizing the public and parliamentarians fell disproportionately on URA. Poor communication between MoFPED and URA contributed to initial administrative hiccups and created uncertainty in the trading community about the government's precise

---

[5] A VAT is a broad based tax, levied at multiple stages of production. The essential feature is that tax paid on inputs is allowed as a credit against tax on outputs. By collecting the tax at successive stages in the production process the revenue flow is made more secure. By allowing credits for tax paid on inputs, the VAT does not distort production decisions, unlike Sales Tax and CTL (Ebrill et al. 2001).

VAT strategy. For example, it is widely recognized that when introducing a VAT government should refrain from other changes that may disrupt the process. Contrary to URA advice, the 1996/97 Budget introduced some additional tax measures, in particular, a higher rate of duty on imported second hand clothing and increased fuel taxes. This provoked a strong reaction from the 30,000 small traders affected.

To compound matters, the VAT threshold was set (with hindsight) too low. As a result, the population of about 16,000 VAT registered enterprises included traders who were unable to cope with the accounting rigours of the new tax system—a reflection of Uganda's cash economy. In September 1996 the small traders launched a 'VAT strike', which threatened to derail the reforms.

To avert a crisis, the President made radio and television broadcasts stating clearly that there would be no turning back on VAT. He personally conducted sensitization sessions for representatives of the trading community to allay fears about the tax, emphasizing the advantages of the new tax on business (especially keeping books and records), and the economy at large. A key factor that helped to end the strike was support for VAT by larger traders and manufacturers. They saw the new tax system as reducing their cost of doing business and saw advantage in the transitional arrangements that allowed crediting of sales tax incurred within six months of the start of VAT. The receipt of sales tax credits by importers of second-hand clothing also helped calm the situation. In addition, to ease the burden of administering an excessively large VAT register, the VAT threshold was increased from UGX20 million (USD19,000) to UGX50 million (USD47,000). The strike was eventually called off in October 1996. In retrospect, it is clear that the strike was largely instigated by non-compliant taxpayers who were not prepared for the additional scrutiny required by the self-accounting VAT mechanism.

To ensure a smooth transition from sales tax to VAT and to get prompt feedback from the public, press briefings and field visits were made every week for two months by the URA Commissioner General and senior management. In recognition of their information dissemination role and the need to get the print and electronic media on the side of tax administration, special VAT education sessions were held for staff of media organizations. As expected, tax compliance was poor in the early stages of the new system, partly because URA had to 'go easy' with enforcement procedures so as not to endanger the entire VAT project. Also, URA's audit capacity did not develop quickly enough to allow adequate follow-up of those who were least compliant. Nevertheless, despite these 'teething troubles' the new tax eventually became well established.

Additional difficulties arose when, during the first year of implementation, MoFPED decided to administratively withhold the VAT portion of payments to its suppliers, remitting it directly to URA instead. The decision resulted in non-timely remittance of deductions to URA by the government and a build up of arrears. The government experienced difficulties in cross-matching deductions with taxpayers' monthly VAT returns. Moreover, further delays arose whilst staff carried out 100 per cent audits to ascertain the accuracy of returns on which withholdings had been made. Multiple checking points had to be introduced within URA to minimize loss of revenue arising from fraudulent trader refund claims. The VAT-withholding practice disabled the automatic crediting process by the taxable person, distorted the VAT system and undermined taxpayer confidence in VAT. It was not until 2005 that the government discontinued this system.

The payment of VAT refunds has been a continuing problem, constraining the cash flow of enterprises and compounding the anti-export bias elsewhere in the tax system. An inefficient refunds system undermines the credibility of the VAT system as a whole. In a number of instances, even when the refund claims had been audited and approved, the monthly appropriation was inadequate and lead to rationing.[6] Insufficient funding led to many complaints of delayed refunds and created fertile ground for corruption, as a number of taxpayers attempted to jump the queue through inducements to tax officials.

Once VAT had taken root, it was anticipated that the VAT yield would increase over the medium term towards the regional norm of 5 per cent of GDP. However, the highest yield so far is 4 per cent of GDP in 2005/06. It then fell back to 3.7 per cent in 2006/07 (see Table 5.2). This relatively slow progress is largely attributable to the gradual extension of the exempt and zero-rated lists and the fact that administration capacity and compliance did not improve as much as expected. The main items in the zero-rated list were exported goods and services, international transport services, medical goods, milk, and maize meal. The main items in the VAT-exempt list were education and health services, financial services, unprocessed food stuffs, and excisable petroleum fuel products.

2.4 Petroleum fuel duty

Apart from a spike in 1996/97 (caused by an increase in duty rates at the same time VAT was introduced), petroleum product duties have consistently contributed between 1.9 per cent and 2.5 per cent of GDP to government revenue since the early 1990s (see Table 5.2). The convenience of this tax, in terms of the relative ease and low cost of collection, make it an attractive source of revenue for government. However, the fact that fuel taxes have generally been higher in Uganda than in Kenya has often led to sizeable pump price differentials between the two countries. Combined with weak border administration, this has led to high levels of fuel smuggling and hence revenue losses. Kenyan pump prices effectively limit the scope for increased petroleum taxes in Uganda.

---

[6] URA was allowed to retain one-twelfth of the fiscal year refunds estimate irrespective of the value of refund claims.

Table 5.2 URA Collections (as % GDP), 1991/92–2006/07

	1991/92	1992/93	1993/94	1994/95	1995/96	1996/97	1997/98	1998/99	1999/00	2000/01	2001/02	2002/03	2003/04	2004/05	2005/06	2006/07
Total revenue	6.8	7.6	9.2	10.0	10.7	11.3	10.7	11.6	11.2	10.6	11.2	11.4	11.8	12.1	12.5	12.7
Income taxes	0.9	1.2	1.4	1.5	1.4	1.6	1.7	2.1	2.0	2.2	2.6	2.8	3.1	3.5	3.6	3.7
Individual	0.1	0.3	0.3	0.4	0.4	0.6	0.6	0.8	0.9	1.0	1.3	1.4	1.4	1.5	1.7	1.8
Corporate	0.8	0.8	0.6	0.5	0.4	0.4	0.4	0.5	0.5	0.5	0.6	0.7	0.9	1.0	1.0	0.9
Other [a]	0.0	0.0	0.4	0.6	0.6	0.6	0.6	0.7	0.6	0.6	0.7	0.8	0.8	1.0	0.9	1.0
Import duties (non-oil)	0.8	1.0	1.4	1.4	1.5	1.1	1.1	1.2	1.2	1.4	1.1	1.1	1.0	1.0	1.3	1.3
Petroleum product taxes	2.1	2.2	2.2	2.3	2.5	3.0	2.5	2.4	2.2	1.9	2.0	1.9	1.9	1.9	2.1	2.2
Non-petroleum excise duties	0.6	0.5	1.0	1.0	1.1	1.6	1.5	1.6	1.5	1.2	1.3	1.2	1.3	1.2	1.0	1.1
Non-oil imports	0.0	0.0	0.1	0.1	0.1	0.3	0.2	0.3	0.3	0.2	0.2	0.3	0.4	0.3	0.1	0.3
Local goods	0.6	0.5	1.0	0.9	1.0	1.3	1.3	1.3	1.2	1.0	1.1	0.9	0.9	0.8	0.9	0.9
VAT/sales tax/CTL (net) [b]	1.8	2.3	2.7	3.0	3.4	3.3	3.3	3.7	3.7	3.4	3.7	3.8	3.9	3.9	4.0	3.7
Imports	0.8	1.0	1.3	1.4	1.6	2.1	2.0	2.3	2.2	2.0	2.1	2.1	2.4	2.3	2.4	2.5
Local goods/services	1.1	1.3	1.5	1.6	1.8	1.4	1.5	1.7	1.8	1.7	2.0	2.0	1.7	1.9	1.9	2.0
Refunds	0.0	0.0	0.0	0.0	0.0	-0.1	-0.2	-0.3	-0.3	-0.3	-0.4	-0.3	-0.3	-0.3	-0.4	-0.8
Export/stabilization taxes	0.1	0.0	0.0	0.3	0.2	0.0	0.0	0.0	0.0	0.0	0.0	0.0	0.0	0.0	0.0	0.0
Non-tax revenue	0.6	0.4	0.5	0.6	0.6	0.6	0.6	0.6	0.6	0.4	0.5	0.6	0.7	0.6	0.5	0.5

[a] Includes presumptive, rental, bank interest, and withholding taxes.
[b] In 1996/97 VAT replaced sales tax and commercial transactions levy (CTL).

Sources: Various Uganda Revenue Authority reports; GDP from IMF (2006) up to 1999/2000, and Uganda Bureau of Statistics from 2000/01 onwards.

In preparing for the introduction of VAT in 1996, a decision had to be made about the treatment of dutiable fuel products: whether the standard 17 per cent VAT rate should apply or whether they should be included in the VAT-exempt list. Because of their important contribution to total revenue and to avoid creating opportunities for claiming VAT credits on fuel not used as business inputs, it was decided to include dutiable fuels in the list of VAT-exempt goods and services.

2.5 Reform of the income tax system

Once VAT had become established, attention turned to modernization of the income tax system. The income tax law dated from 1974 and had been extensively amended. While tax rates on business and personal income had been reduced significantly since 1986, it was necessary to review important aspects such as the definition of taxable income, the deductions allowable in calculating taxable income, and the treatment of pensions along with other forms of long term savings. There was also a need to provide for the treatment of income from mining operations. It was important to enhance the contribution of income tax to total revenues. By the mid 1990s income taxes contributed only 15 per cent of total revenue, or 1.5 per cent of GDP (see Table 5.2), exceptionally low figures even for low-income countries.

By the late 1980s the income tax base had been greatly narrowed by a wide range of statutory and discretionary exemptions. Important exempt categories included the salaries of public servants and security personnel (including the army, police, and prison service), income derived from donor-funded operations, and the income of most parastatal organizations. In addition, the law provided for a wide range of non-taxable allowances and allowed employers to construct remuneration packages with large non-taxable components.

In 1994 the exemptions for public servants and most parastatals were eliminated. Corporate and personal tax rates were reduced and the personal tax exemption threshold was raised; the corporate tax rate and the top personal tax rate were both reduced progressively from 60 per cent to 30 per cent between 1988/89 and 1993/94. In 1995 the personal income tax exemption threshold was raised from UGX840,000 to UGX1,200,000 (USD840 to USD1,200)—equivalent to 5.5 times per capita income, much higher than the prevailing figure for comparable countries—simultaneously with the termination of non-taxable lunch and transport allowances of UGX30,000 (USD30) per month. This undermined somewhat the objective of a rapid improvement in the contribution of personal tax to total revenue.

With an outdated income tax law and very limited availability of the text of the law, it was decided in 1996 to prepare an entirely new income tax law. Following a detailed study, a new Income Tax Bill was presented and promulgated in 1997 to replace the Income Tax Decree 1974. The new Act included the following important reforms:

* The granting of income tax holidays provided to investors under the Investment Code was terminated and replaced with a generous scheme of allowances for investment expenditure.
* A new scheme for taxing income from mining operations was established.
* Gross income was redefined to substitute a worldwide concept of income for the more limited Ugandan definition.
* Virtually all remaining non-taxable allowances were abolished and most benefits-in-kind were made fully taxable.
* The scope of, and discretion to grant, exemptions was sharply curtailed (however, the exemption for security services personnel was retained).
* The allowable deductions used in calculating taxable income were more precisely defined to limit eligibility to expenses incurred in producing income, and to allow generous deductions for expenditure on training and research.
* Up to date provision was made for taxing pensions and other forms of long-term savings, taking account of the obstacle created by the constitutional requirement to exempt pension income from tax.
* Provision was made for self-assessment.
* Capital gains realized on disposal of business assets became taxable.

The special scheme for taxing house rental income of individuals, which had been introduced in 1993, was retained. This scheme applied an effective tax rate of 16 per cent on all house rental income above the personal income tax exemption threshold. This low rate applied to gross income made administration easier and made due allowance for costs, such as repairs, maintenance, and interest.

The Act also restored a presumptive tax system of 'tax deposits' for small enterprises, with an option to file and be assessed by URA—albeit with a simplified format. Prior to 1995 tax deposits ranged from UGX5,000 to 5 million (USD5.20 to USD5,200), with over 100 different categories of business enterprise. The tax deposits were payable annually in advance and were a means of obtaining at least some income tax from small-scale enterprises. The tax deposits system was terminated in the 1995 Budget. Instead the 70,000 or so small businesses were now required to file income tax returns and to be assessed by URA. Given URA's capacity constraints, the inevitable result was a collapse in income tax from small businesses. The new system applied a small fixed percentage of total turnover as the tax payable—2 per cent for trading enterprises and 3 per cent for those engaged in service activities. It only applied to enterprises with a turnover of less than UGX50 million (USD47,000) per annum and could not be used by individuals engaged in specified activities, such as professional services or construction. However, because of tax administration constraints, the new scheme failed to deliver commensurate revenue.

Table 5.2 suggests that the above reforms were largely successful, with collections of income taxes increasing from 0.9 per cent of GDP in 1991/92 to 3.7 per cent in 2006/07. Personal income tax, collected under the Pay As You Earn system, and corporate tax have provided the bulk of the increased income tax yield since 1995; the contribution from the self-employed and small business sector has been negligible. Revenue trends are discussed in Section 4.

The 1974 Income Tax Decree provided for a 4 per cent Withholding Tax on a wide range of transactions as an advance payment of income tax due. This tax applied to most payments by public sector organizations for goods and services supplied and to most import transactions. The law provided that the tax withheld from a taxpayer could be offset against the taxpayer's final liability for tax. The 1997 Act retained this provision but with some refinement, notably that the 4 per cent tax would not be withheld in cases where URA certified that a taxpayer's affairs were in order. In practice, there have been serious problems obtaining URA certification. Similarly, it has proved difficult for taxpayers to get credit for tax amounts paid or withheld. The result is that withholding tax is effectively a final tax.

2.6 Tax appeals tribunal

Prior to 1997, there was no institutionalized arrangement for taxpayers to appeal against URA decisions on tax issues. Although various provisions had been made in law for a tax appeals process, these were never made operational. The result was that formal appeals were rarely made and disputes taken up by taxpayers were rarely pursued. Making an appeal to senior officials of URA and/ or MoFPED offered little prospect of a successful outcome. The 1995 Constitution included a provision that Parliament would establish tax tribunals for the settling of tax disputes.

As a result, the Tax Appeals Tribunal Act was passed in 1997; followed by the establishment of the tribunal and the appointment of staff to commence the tax appeals service. The Act sets out the procedures to be followed by taxpayers in pursuing appeals. It includes provision for a taxpayer to appeal to the High Court, but only when there is need for a decision on legal interpretation.

3. Tax administration reform

3.1 Formation of the Uganda Revenue Authority

Tax reform began in earnest with the formation of the Uganda Revenue Authority (URA) in September 1991. Much the most significant tax administration reform measure, it consolidated the operations and management of domestic tax and customs administrations previously carried out by separate departments of MoF.

The move to establish URA was spearheaded by the Minister of Finance following discussions on revenue administration reform with his Ghanaian counterpart during a Commonwealth Finance Ministers meeting in 1990. As part of the implementation preparations, a World Bank mission studied the efficiency of the revenue collecting departments in MoF and recommended a review of the existing arrangements. A delegation from the Ministry then visited Ghana to familiarize themselves with the revenue administration developments in that country. This was followed by a study to firm up the revenue authority concept (Coopers and Lybrand 1991), and a decision to implement the recommendations with assistance of a team from Ghana.

The key objectives in setting up URA were to improve revenue collection and address the human resource constraints through improved remuneration, recruitment, staff development and training, and ethical conduct. It was expected that a semi-autonomous institution would be more responsive to the day-to-day challenges of domestic revenue mobilization than one operating under the constraints of the public service. URA was financed by a specific appropriation under the MoF vote, rather than (as in some revenue authorities) by retaining a percentage of collections.

The mandate of URA was to assess and collect specified tax revenue,[7] administer and enforce taxpayer compliance, and account for the revenue collected (Government of Uganda 1991a). Although not responsible for tax policy, it was expected to provide input into the government's policy formulation process on revenue-related matters. The statute provided for a Board of Directors composed of private sector members and *ex officio* representatives from the ministries of finance and trade, and the Bank of Uganda.[8] The Board reported to the Minister of Finance and was charged with providing operational policy guidance to URA. The URA Commissioner General reported directly to the Board, but for day-to-day operations was answerable to the Minister. This reporting relationship was problematic, as the Commissioner General did not necessarily have to inform the Board prior to engaging with the Ministry. Below the Commissioner General were five commissioners and their deputies who supervised operations of customs and excise, domestic taxes and fees (income tax, sales Tax/VAT, and fees and licences), internal audit, tax investigations, and support services (including finance, human resources, administration, research and planning, and information technology).

Managing mergers can be a daunting task, especially when it involves the revenue lifeline of a country. There is the need to maintain revenue collection while at the same time absorbing staff, managing their expectations, and introducing them to a new corporate culture. Additional challenges include

---

[7] Specified taxes included collection of all national taxes on gains and profits (income taxes), indirect taxes (sales, international trade, and excise taxes), and drivers permits and motor vehicle licensing fees.

[8] The Bank of Uganda was removed from the Board in the mid 1990s.

115

integrating and harmonizing different work cultures and systems, and adequately financing the new agency. In April 1991, five months before the establishment of URA, the Minister of Finance constituted a full-time implementation committee reporting to his office that included both local and expatriate staff.[9] The committee's key tasks included a review of various revenue administration improvement reports, preparing an implementation timetable, supervising the drafting of the URA legal framework and its submission to Parliament, and making recommendations to the Minister on legal, administrative, and human resource requirements. The committee also proposed remuneration scales for URA staff. Establishment of the committee was critical to the successful launch of URA.

The key human resource challenge was how to maintain revenue collection while at the same time bringing quality to revenue administration. All staff employed by the former customs and excise, income tax, and inland revenue departments were initially seconded to the authority pending screening. The screening process lasted about six months. Unsuccessful seconded staff returned to their substantive employer, the Ministry of Public Service, for redeployment. Not surprisingly, revenue declined during the first month of operations (September 1991). However, following measures to reassure staff about their employment tenure, collections rose from October 1991. Skills gaps, especially in finance, legal, human resource, and information technology areas, were covered by direct recruitment from the labour market.

To ensure a smooth and swift URA take-off, experienced expatriate line managers were recruited, with donor funding, as Commissioner General, commissioners for customs, income tax, and finance and administration, and at deputy commissioner level for sales tax, tax audit, and investigations. They were expected to mentor local personnel to be able to take over their positions in due course. Towards the end of their contracts the expatriates assumed the role of advisors to substantive local managers; the transition worked well. URA staff initially received competitive remuneration in comparison to both the private sector and the public service, providing some incentive for better performance and attracting skilled personnel from the private sector. However, this was eroded in the mid-to-late 1990s and there was a reverse flow of staff to the private sector—especially in taxation management related disciplines. It is an open question whether the loss of competitive remuneration advantage is correlated to the perceived high levels of corruption that have dogged URA.

---

[9] The government of Ghana released some senior revenue administration staff to assist in establishing URA. They were financed by UNDP.

3.2 *Formation of the Large Taxpayer Department*

Following the introduction of VAT a long term strategy for strengthening domestic tax administration was needed. A 1997 IMF review recommended, *inter alia*, integrating the VAT and Internal Revenue Departments, beginning with the establishment of a large taxpayer unit in Kampala. The strategy was to offer good corporate services to the few large and better-organized players in the economy—and in the process secure at least 70 per cent of domestic tax revenue. Government would at least be assured of this portion of revenue. Further, it would allow URA to devise better taxpayer assistance and compliance strategies for medium and small taxpayers. It was anticipated that the new processes, procedures, and systems developed in managing the large taxpayer segment would be rolled out to medium and small taxpayer groups. Subsequently, a unified domestic tax department would be established under one accountability centre, so as to avoid differential application of the law (primarily VAT, income tax, and excise duty).

In pursuit of this objective, a Large Taxpayer Department (LTD) was formed in November 1998 as a 'one stop' management centre for all tax matters of the largest taxpayers. The LTD started with a list of about 250 taxpayers that was a mix of private sector entities and government. It was charged with securing tax collections; improving services to large taxpayers; introducing modern collection, audit procedures, and systems; and providing a pilot site to develop a function-based organization. The implementation of the LTD paid dividends; in its first full year of operation (1999/00) it collected 74 per cent of domestic tax revenue.[10] One benefit of establishing the LTD was that it highlighted the extent to which management of medium and small taxpayers was underdeveloped and the effort required to improve compliance for these segments.

The creation of the LTD brought the number of URA departments managing domestic taxes to three: LTD, VAT, and Inland Revenue. The latter two managed VAT and income tax respectively for the medium and small taxpayers but contributed to a top-heavy URA structure, and complicated the task of harmonizing domestic tax administration approaches. For example, the three departments administered the same VAT and income tax laws for different segments of the taxpayer population. As a consequence, there were instances of varying legal interpretations for each of the segments. The domestic tax departments ended up competing with one another instead of working towards the common goal of modernizing operations. What was required was a single centre of operational accountability for domestic taxes, something that was not achieved until 2005.

Some of the large taxpayers resented the deeper scrutiny of their affairs by LTD and the increasing capacity of URA to question the treatment of

---

[10] URA internal reports.

transactions, particularly for income tax. Some accounting firms representing large taxpayers alleged that URA was harassing them. This explains why LTD was disbanded in 2001. It was re-established in 2005 under a unified domestic tax department. With the benefit of hindsight, while the integration strategy and the drive to use LTD as a reform and modernization model was sound, the concept was not well explained to and therefore not wholly owned by URA's management and staff. It would have been better to map out a clear, time-bound 'road-map' to integrate domestic tax administration under a single accountability centre.

3.3 *Automation of tax administration*

Automation of tax administration processes is an important element in facilitating service delivery, and frees resources that can be redirected to value-adding activities such as taxpayer services, taxpayer self-assessment, audit, and enforcement. Furthermore, by reducing contact between tax administration officials and taxpayers, particularly in customs administration, automation can reduce the scope for corruption. There was negligible automation prior to the formation of URA in 1991. URA's automation objective was to work towards a one-taxpayer ledger with an overall single view of the tax position, whilst increasing its ability to manage taxpayer compliance. There was a need for a unique taxpayer identification number (TIN) common for all tax liabilities payable by the same person/ entity; this was designed and implemented in 1993.

TIN implementation had a number of problems in the early stages. First, there was no ownership of the system by the managers of the domestic tax units and the TIN was not taken seriously. The taxpayer register was managed by the information technology division, because capacity to manage the TIN in the income tax department (where it truly belonged) was low. Second, duplicate TINs and mutating taxpayers were rife and no meaningful clean-up of the taxpayer register could be undertaken because the system was not being managed by the proper responsibility centre. Third, except in customs administration, there was continued use of other identification numbers such as the income tax file number and (after VAT introduction) the VAT number. The TIN coexisted with the other registration numbers and was also widely used by entities such as the electricity and water utilities as proof of identity by their customers. However, the expected linkages to local authority management information systems that were potentially a good validation source of business registrations did not materialize. These and infrastructural deficiencies limited the exploitation of the TIN as a primary identifier of business transactions.

The initial phases of automation in URA gave priority to customs administration because of the 'retail' nature of operations and pressure from the public for improved services, comparatively greater risks to revenue, and the need to augment audit trails. The only automated customs administration process prior to the establishment of URA was the compilation of trade statistics for the Statistics Department (see Chapter 11). In 1994 this system was augmented by an (in-house developed) transactions processing module developed over the first URA local area network in the main customs processing centre. The system was replaced in 1996 with UNCTAD's Automated System for Customs Data (ASYCUDA).[11] These developments greatly facilitated the clearance of goods, improved revenue, and strengthened the compilation of trade statistics. Deployment of these systems was initially confined to the key stations contributing up to 85 per cent of customs revenue. These included Kampala Long Room, Kampala Railway Goods shed, Entebbe Cargo, Entebbe passenger terminal, Jinja, Busia, Malaba, Tororo, Mbarara, and Mutukula.

Progress in automating domestic tax processes was much slower due to the lack of recognized and tested integrated tax administration systems available in developing countries. The costs of such systems were of the order of USD3–5 million, whereas ASYCUDA only cost about USD600,000. As a result, several in-house transactions processing solutions were developed for income tax accounting and for motor vehicle and driver licensing. These filled the void, but the lack of comprehensive automation solutions denied URA opportunities to improve compliance management and focus on value addition. A 1999 Swiss government financed external evaluation found that the level of automation in URA and the national communication infrastructure were inadequate and made recommendations to address these issues (Lortie 1999).

The introduction of VAT in 1996 included the implementation of the Crown Agents' VAT Information Processing System, the first major domestic tax management application in the country. The application was later supplemented with an in-house solution to address the millennium changeover issues and additional requirements for electronic data interchange, VAT offsets, penalties, report printing, and implementation of direct banking arrangements for the large taxpayers in LTD. Implementation of the VAT system underlined the importance of using IT tools in tax administration, especially to keep track of compliance in the face of a growing taxpayer population.

3.4 Tax evasion and corruption

Table 5.2 shows that, following a steady increase from 6.8 per cent of GDP in 1991/92 to 11.3 per cent in 1996/97, revenue collection stagnated in the late

---

[11] Customs first installed ASYCUDA version 2.6 in 1996, though this was upgraded to version 2.7 in 1999. A complaint about the early versions of ASYCUDA was the difficulty of extracting trade statistics without making numerous conversions first into a database and then spreadsheets. In 2002 the more robust ASYCUDA++ version was implemented with several modules, including declaration, accounts, statistics, manifest, transit broker (agent), warehousing, and examination selectivity.

1990s. This has been attributed in part to poor tax administration, and the inability to curb tax evasion and corruption:

firms estimated the informal economy (part of the economy evading taxes, duties, or laws and regulations) to be as high as 43 per cent. In 1998 this perception remained, with tax evasion considered the leading constraint from unfair competition. [Moreover] among the firms that were audited, at least every third firm had to pay additional taxes, while every fourth firm incurred additional costs, such as bribes... All firms whose tax assessment differed by 100 per cent or more 'always'... had to pay bribes to URA officials. (Chen et al. 2001: 292–4)

URA's response on tax evasion was multi-pronged. First, taxpayer education and information was intensified in order to increase awareness. Second, enforcement action, including field spot-checks on businesses, was carried out. The law allowed URA to temporarily close premises of recalcitrant traders, although this instrument was used only in extreme cases. However, the trading community regarded this as harassment and in the late 1990s petitions were made to the government, particularly by the small importers. These succeeded in getting the measure suspended, which was a serious setback to revenue administration and to URA's credibility. Despite the requirement for increased revenue, fair enforcement of non-compliant taxpayers was being restricted.[12] Not surprisingly, compliant taxpayers complained about the lack of enforcement and called for widening of the tax net. URA had to change strategy and carried out limited but targeted enforcement. In what appears to be a contradiction, concern about ineffective URA taxpayer compliance enforcement gave rise to the formation by government of parallel enforcement structures such as the Special Revenue Police Service.

URA's internal anti-corruption response was to use disciplinary mechanisms to dismiss proven culprits in cases that had been brought to its attention either by taxpayers, through informers, or from internal investigations. Evidence of malpractice was critical in this process as the principles of equity and natural justice were important. Prosecution of offenders was rarely pursued as resolution of cases through the court system tended to take too long.

3.5 Improved transparency and taxpayer education

The introduction of VAT and the Income Tax Act created a much more transparent tax environment. As well as improving transparency, the wider availability of legal texts helped with developing capacity in tax policy formulation and tax administration and assisted those working as tax advisers and

---

[12] A 2007 IMF revenue administration mission observed that URA prosecution of tax evaders was still not receiving full support from some sections of government.

practitioners. Comprehensive and up-to-date texts of important tax laws were also useful for businesses and for those involved in tax education activities.

Taxpayer education was a key element in addressing Uganda's very poor taxpaying culture. It is best practice for revenue agencies to provide taxpayers with detailed information on the tax system and how to comply with the obligations, including making returns, payment modalities, and sanctions relating to non-compliance. From the formation of URA, taxpayer education took a number of forms: leaflets; publishing details of contact points for taxpayers requiring assistance; issuance of practice notes that advise the taxpayer of the Authority's interpretation of the law; conducting regular taxpayer workshops; visiting schools; interacting closely with the media to disseminate tax-related information; and publishing a bulletin (*Revenews*) that was distributed to key external stakeholders, including legislators.

The process of taxpayer education was greatly facilitated when the private sector became more organized in representative groups that URA collaborated with. These groups included the Uganda Manufacturers Association (UMA), which was formed to promote the interests of all local manufacturers irrespective of size. Believing that in practice UMA represented the larger and more influential enterprises, some manufacturers formed the Uganda Small Scale Industries Association. Other private sector institutions included: the Uganda National Chamber of Commerce and Industry; the Uganda Importers and Exporters Association, a group that had been particularly vocal about high taxes; the Kikuubo Traders Association, which looked after the interests of small-scale traders and importers in Kampala; the Uganda National Farmers Association; the Uganda National Coffee Association; and the Uganda Clearing and Forwarding Agents Association. Interaction with taxpayers often yielded solutions to outstanding problems. For example, many medium and small taxpayers preferred paying income tax in instalments to alleviate liquidity problems; this was incorporated into the tax system. A request to pay taxes through more than just the single bank URA was using was also accepted (Zake 1995).

3.6 The fight against smuggling

When URA was formed customs preventive staff took on the fight against smuggled goods but were no match for the sophistication, and in some instances the armed nature, of the smugglers. In response, an Anti-Smuggling Unit (ASU), a core armed unit of about twenty officers headed by an army colonel, was formed in 1992 to assist URA in managing this threat. The Unit reported directly to the URA Commissioner General. Along with other measures, such as the escorting of goods by convoy, automation, and payment of taxes through the banks, the presence of the ASU had a deterrent effect on smuggling. Anecdotal evidence and data suggest that ASU operations had some positive revenue impact. For example, there was an increase in (non-oil) import duty from 0.8 per cent to 1.5 per cent of GDP between 1991/92 and 1995/96 (see Table 5.2). However, misbehaviour by some ASU operatives, and the 'militarisation of revenue' (Therkildsen 2003), led to an outcry by sections of the public and cases being filed against URA. The Unit's credibility waned and the government disbanded it in early 1996. The absence of an effective enforcement arm in customs administration was deeply felt and inevitably led to a resurgence of smuggling. Import duty dropped back to 1.1 per cent of GDP in 1996/97.

In 1998, dissatisfied with the low customs collections and poor compliance enforcement, the government formed a Special Revenue Police Service (SRPS) that collaborated with, but did not report directly to, URA. As well as countering smuggling, SRPS was charged with investigating URA staff suspected of aiding and abetting smuggling and tax evasion. While all these measures were implemented in good faith, parallel systems, multiple reporting centres, and external management of part of the enforcement function created their own problems. Taxpayers were often unsure where to appeal for redress (URA or SRPS); and when SRPS was involved in a case, the URA usually directed taxpayers to the Attorney General for remedy. There was frequently operational tension between URA enforcement officers and SRPS;[13] the public was aware of this state of affairs and some taxpayers took the opportunity to settle scores.

4. Impact of the reforms

Looking at the trends in revenue collection between 1991/92 and 2006/07, three phases can be discerned. Total revenue increased steadily from 6.8 per cent of GDP in 1991/92 to 11.3 per cent in 1996/97 (see Table 5.2). This can be attributed largely to more effective collection following the establishment of URA, a task made easier by reductions in the highest tax rates and a simplification of the tax regime. Total collections then stagnated up to 2000/01 as continued increases in collections from income taxes were offset by the fall in petroleum taxes from 3.0 per cent of GDP in 1996/97 to 1.9 per cent in 2000/01. Smuggling of petroleum products was a key factor in the decline, coupled with weak capacity of URA to decisively deal with the problem and exacerbated by a scaling down of anti-smuggling operations in 1996. Other factors contributing to the decline included the continued implementation of solely specific duty rates—rather than a combination of *ad valorem* and specific—that were not frequently adjusted to reflect market conditions and therefore did not provide the needed revenue buoyancy. In 2001/02 the upward trend in total collections

---

[13] The SRPS was disbanded in 2007 and the enforcement function fully reverted to URA.

resumed, increasing from 10.6 per cent of GDP in 2000/01 to 12.7 per cent in 2006/07.

4.1 *Effects of tax reform on revenue collection*

The breakdown of total revenue shows that almost all the improvement has been in two areas, VAT and income taxes. Sales Tax and CTL increased from just 1.8 per cent of GDP in 1991/92, to 3.4 per cent in 1995/96. The introduction of VAT in 1996/97 was intended to be revenue neutral until the new tax had taken root. VAT collections during the first two years, at 3.3 per cent of GDP, were about the same as the combined sales tax and CTL collections in 1995/96. They started to increase in 1998/99 (3.7 per cent of GDP) and had reached 4.0 per cent of GDP by 2005/06, before declining to 3.7 per cent in 2006/07. Entry into the Uganda market of a number of international telecommunications and supermarket operators—large payers with more transactions—and some administrative improvements had a noticeable impact on VAT collections. Despite the increased collections, Uganda's average VAT efficiency ratio[14] of 0.23 for the period 1998/99 to 2005/06 was still well below the average of 0.27 for sub-Saharan Africa (Ebrill et al. 2002).

The improvement in import and excise duties in the early 1990s was not sustained. Import duties (non-oil) increased from 0.8 per cent to 1.5 per cent of GDP between 1991/92 and 1995/96 despite the reduction in rates over the period. However, as noted above, collections declined subsequently as a result of the lowering of tariffs in line with regional trade agreement commitments, and problems with smuggling and corruption. A similar pattern is observed with excise duties.

Income taxes increased steadily from the exceptionally low level of 0.9 per cent to 3.7 per cent of GDP between 1991/92 and 2006/07, with a notable acceleration after 2000/01. However, the pattern was very different for the three categories of income tax: individual, corporate, and other taxes. Most of the increase came from individual income tax, which increased steadily from 0.1 per cent to 1.8 per cent of GDP between 1991/92 and 2006/07. This was underlined by improvements in tax administration and compliance. The steady growth of the Ugandan economy, particularly in the service and manufacturing sectors, also increased the taxable base (the number and value of formal sector incomes). This was helped by the substantial increase in the number of public servants and the government wage bill from 1998 (see Chapter 4). Collections were further boosted by the abolition of many tax-free allowances in 1994 and the tighter treatment from 1997 of end-of-contract gratuities and benefits.

---

[14] The VAT efficiency ratio is the ratio of VAT revenue to GDP divided by the standard VAT rate, which was 17 per cent in Uganda during that period.

Housing, the use of company cars, and interest free loans all became taxable at values nearer to market rates.

By contrast, the yield from corporate taxes halved between 1991/92 and 1997/98 (from 0.8 per cent to 0.4 per cent of GDP), before slowly increasing to 1.1 per cent of GDP by 2006/07. The initial slump was largely attributable to the generous tax holiday regime for new investments provided under the Investment Code of 1991, which undermined the revenues that would otherwise have resulted from the strong growth of the formal economy. The subsequent replacement of tax holidays with depreciation and investment allowances under the 1997 Income Tax Act meant that strong company profits growth was reflected in increased corporate tax revenue. However, the effect was somewhat delayed because tax holidays granted before the 1997 Act were allowed to run their full course. Growth in the service sector, particularly banking and telecommunications, contributed to the accelerated improvement from 2001/02. Other income taxes (mainly withholding tax, presumptive tax, tax on bank interest, and rental tax) have assumed steadily increasing importance over the period, reaching 0.9 per cent of GDP in 2006/07.

4.2 Impact on trade

One of the objectives of the tax policy reform was trade promotion. While this is not the place for a detailed assessment of the trade regime, a recent World Trade Organization review (WTO 2001) notes substantial increases over the period 1991 to 2004 (see Table 5.3). Total merchandise exports and imports increased from USD175.4 million to USD647.2 million and from USD545.0 million to USD1,321.4 million, increases of 269 per cent and 142 per cent respectively. These were accompanied by increases in the GDP shares of industry from 11.6 per cent to 19.5 per cent and manufacturing from 5.4 per cent to 8.4 per cent.

4.3 What could have been done better?

Although the formation of URA sought to create a modern institution to implement tax policy reforms, revenue administration modernization was not an explicitly stated strategic objective. The main focus was on meeting revenue targets and not enough was done to embed non-revenue performance objectives and indicators, dedicated headquarters functions, self-assessment, taxpayer segmentation, and large taxpayer operations. The opportunity for in-depth modernization was missed and with it the development of a more tax compliant society.

An important objective for any tax administration is to have a robust and flexible delivery structure. This framework should ensure that the expected workload is ascertained, measured, and distributed to the various functions. The delivery structure should also be lean and compact. Over time, URA

Table 5.3 Uganda, Selected Trade Data, 1991–2004

	1991	1992	1993	1994	1995	1996	1997	1998	1999	2000	2001	2002	2003	2004
Total merchandise exports (FOB USD million)	175.4	172.1	157.1	253.9	595.3	590.3	670.9	458.4	549.1	459.9	462.9	479.0	507.9	647.2
Total merchandise imports (CIF USD million)	545.0	450.6	530.5	671.7	1,085.5	1,218.3	1,246.3	966.1	1,039.4	954.3	953.3	1,003.9	1,130.6	1,321.4
Industry (% GDP)	11.6	12.5	12.3	12.8	13.1	14.7	15.9	16.4	18.0	18.5	18.6	19.8	19.6	19.5
Manufacturing (% GDP)	5.4	5.8	5.6	6.0	6.2	7.1	7.8	8.3	9.0	8.9	8.8	9.1	8.6	8.4

Source: World Bank, African Indicators (2006) database.

developed into a top-heavy structure without an identifiable headquarters function separate from field delivery. In essence most staff, from the chief executive to the lowest operative, were involved in field delivery work. With hindsight, design of the delivery structure was flawed. However, this has been largely corrected since 2005.

Operationally, modern revenue administration aims at efficient and client-centred services. Performance should be assessed using both revenue and non-revenue performance indicators. The latter were not explicitly used in the areas of taxpayer services, taxpayer registration, returns and filing processing, audit and investigation, intelligence and risk management, compliance enforcement, and dispute resolution.[15] A major drawback to operations was the absence of taxpayer segmentation that led to applying the same strategies to large, medium, and small taxpayers. While the formation of LTD in 1998 was intended to be a first step in this direction, the concept was not extended to medium and small taxpayers.

As noted above, investment in an integrated and responsive system is an important ingredient in modern tax administration. Although the concept of a single taxpayer ledger was conceived in 1993, no holistic strategy was developed nor resources allocated to meaningfully achieve it. A 1999 external evaluation found that the national communication infrastructure was inadequate and made recommendations to address these issues (Lortie 1999). It is perhaps just as well that full automation was not achieved in such a fragmented administrative environment, as the old systems would have been scrapped anyway and the investment lost.

The aim of any revenue organization should be to develop a cadre of reliable professional staff with a high level of integrity operating with a client-centred approach. This requires establishing operating standards, staff monitoring and evaluation mechanisms, and a transparent and enforceable code of ethics that is owned—and preferably policed—by the institution's staff. Mechanisms for the timely dispensation of justice, including prosecution of cases where appropriate, are also needed. To support this process, it is important to implement systems that eliminate non-value-adding processes and unwarranted bureaucracy, promote self-assessment, and employ risk management principles in managing compliance of the different taxpayer segments. Moreover, they should minimize contact between revenue agency staff and taxpayers, and avoid external interference in the management of the agency.

From the outset URA had a code of conduct, an assets declaration requirement, and an administrative disciplinary and appeals system—with the staff committee of the board in the role of the 'high court' and the board as the

---

[15] This should include enforcement of registration, filing returns, timely payment of tax, and management of delinquent accounts.

'supreme court'.[16] There was also an internal audit mechanism and an internal affairs unit to detect malpractice. However, some ingredients were missing. The verification of staff asset declarations was non-systematic, offenders were not prosecuted where warranted, and a robust support system to minimize offences was absent. Some staff and taxpayers took advantage of the fragmented nature of operations, and committed offences in the knowledge that it would take a long time for the offence to be detected, if ever.

With the benefit of hindsight, it is clear that preparations for the introduction of VAT should have been more thorough. The lack of initial political commitment undermined URA effectiveness during the critical early stages of its implementation. Key aspects which should have been done better include fixing a higher registration threshold and developing a stronger administration infrastructure—in particular, auditing/investigation capacity and an adequate IT system. The continuing problems with VAT refunds mean that producers of zero-rated goods and services are denied the intended benefits—undermining Uganda's international competitiveness.

5. Conclusions

Uganda has made substantial progress in tax policy and in building the revenue function since the early 1990s. An extremely distorted tax structure, which strongly discouraged production for export, has been replaced by a stable, liberal regime, which is broadly in line with international best practice. This was an important factor in the substantial increase in trade since the mid 1990s. Reduced reliance on taxing international trade has been accompanied by increased taxation of consumption and incomes and profits. Despite teething troubles, a robust revenue raising institution—URA—has been established from scratch.

Concerned at the collapse of revenue during the 1970s and 1980s and the resulting dependence upon donor funds, in 1992 the government announced the objective of increasing revenue by 1 per cent of GDP every year. Table 5.2 shows that total revenue increased from 6.8 per cent of GDP in 1991/92 to 12.7 per cent in 2006/07. While this is below half of the improvement in revenue performance implied by the 1 per cent of GDP annual (political) target, it nevertheless represents substantive progress since the early 1990s. Uganda is no longer the outlier it appears in Table 5.1. When account is taken of the rapid growth in GDP over the period (see Chapter 3) the real value of collections has increased dramatically.

---

[16] URA was the only government agency requiring staff to declare their assets in the early 1990s.

Despite this undoubted progress, Uganda's revenue/GDP ratio of 12.7 per cent in 2006/07 still lagged well behind the sub-Saharan average of 18 per cent, and was lower than many other countries with similar economic circumstances. This situation is largely attributable to four factors. First, the poor tax compliance culture, which became strongly rooted during the prolonged period of civil disorder and weak government between 1971 and 1986, has proved very difficult to overcome. Second, the low level of political commitment to tax compliance has made it difficult to deal with corruption and has not permitted URA to enforce taxes effectively. It has also contributed to a relaxed attitude towards the granting of exemptions. Third, Uganda's informal sector remains significant, with a large proportion of the population engaged in subsistence or small-scale agriculture. The use of cash in business transactions remains prevalent. It is difficult and usually revenue-ineffective to collect tax from small operators and from those who conduct business mostly on a cash basis. Last, the full potential of tax administration has not yet been realized—the full range of taxpayer services have still not been offered, compliance management is still weak, and dispute resolution mechanisms are not yet sufficiently robust.

On the tax policy side, a key lesson from Uganda's experience is the importance of clarity, consistency, and visible political commitment in tax policy decisions. Reforms to the tax laws and regulations and the reduction of discretionary powers with regard to tax exemptions have resulted in a more transparent regime and contributed to improved revenue performance. Strong political commitment is a critical element in undertaking serious tax reforms. This was noticeably absent during the early stages of VAT preparation and made implementation of VAT much more difficult.

The creation of a semi-autonomous revenue administration cannot deliver a rapid improvement in tax administration on its own. It must be accompanied by other measures, such as giving the new organization the freedom to act, making it fully accountable for meeting agreed targets, providing it with adequate resources, delivering the full suite of taxpayer services, and paying more attention to the largest taxpayers and high-risk areas. In establishing a revenue authority it is important to be clear from the outset about issues such as the roles and responsibilities of the governing board vis-à-vis management and the authority's role with respect to tax policy. Even with a sound programme of action to improve tax administration, revenue gains may be slow to materialize and difficult to quantify in the absence of these factors. To significantly increase Uganda's revenue/GDP ratio there is no alternative but to make revenue administration more effective. Having made significant strides during the 1990s in creating a lower tax regime, raising tax rates is now a more difficult option.

6

Planning and Development Budget Reform, 1990–1995

Alan Whitworth[1]

1. Introduction

Since the late 1990s Uganda's public expenditure management system has been one of the most highly regarded in Africa. Yet just ten years earlier public expenditure management had been, like most government systems in Uganda at the time, in a state of collapse. This and the following two chapters attempt to show how this transformation was brought about. This chapter discusses the initial reforms of the planning system and shows how they provided the springboard for reform of the budget system and public expenditure management generally, beginning with the Development Budget. It is structured as follows. Section 2 looks at the initial measures adopted between 1986 and 1990 to revive the planning system. Section 3 discusses the weaknesses of the system identified by a 1991 internal review, particularly the separation of the plan from the budget, and the failure to address the dependence on foreign aid and to manage counterpart funding. Section 4 discusses the reforms to the planning and development budget system following the review, such as the integration of the plan and development budget, efforts to bring all aid within the system, and measures to strengthen the finance ministry's capacity to discharge its 'challenge function'. Section 5 assesses the impact of the reforms on the credibility of the budget, on counterpart funding, and on the quantity of aid and its alignment with government priorities. Finally, Section 6 presents the main conclusions.

[1] The author gratefully acknowledges helpful comments from Martin Brownbridge, Tim Lamont, Mary Muduuli, Ritva Reinikka, and Samuel Wanyaka.

2. Planning in the early National Resistance Movement years

Until the merger of the two ministries in March 1992, responsibility for planning and for preparing the Development Budget lay with the small Ministry of Planning and Economic Development (MoPED) while responsibility for preparing the Recurrent Budget and for implementation of the entire budget lay with the Ministry of Finance (MoF).

Economic planning had been an interest since President Museveni's student days and he attached particular importance to rebuilding the planning system. However, it was not clear what 'planning' meant in practical terms. With revenue insufficient even to finance basic recurrent expenditure and civil service salaries, there were negligible funds available for public investment. Despite the President's interest in input–output analysis and promotion of inter-sectoral and inter-industry linkages, little could be done in such areas because of the almost total lack of reliable data. The MoPED Statistics Department virtually ceased operations in the late 1970s and many old records were lost or destroyed. Clearly a precondition for serious planning was the rehabilitation of the department. Beginning in 1988 the World Bank funded extensive rehabilitation of the Statistics Department and by the early 1990s regular statistical series were again being published (see Chapter 11).

With the scope for macroeconomic planning (as opposed to management) limited by political instability and statistical constraints, MoPED planning activity in the early NRM years was largely confined to project planning. In March 1987 the NRM government's first Rehabilitation and Development Plan (RDP) was published, covering the four years to 1990/91. The term 'rehabilitation' was included to emphasize that, following fifteen years of turmoil, the rehabilitation of existing infrastructure took priority over new investment. The first RDP was essentially an update of the Recovery Programmes produced during the Obote II period (1981–85), rather than a totally new plan.

The 1987 RDP was published in two volumes. Volume I covered macroeconomic policies and projections and sector policies, while Volume II listed details of development projects government was hoping to undertake, classified by sector. Since government had negligible funds of its own to invest, Volume II was essentially a 'shopping list' designed to attract donor funding. The total 'planned' capital expenditure over the period was—at USD1.29 billion—highly optimistic. A revised Volume II (project list) was published in June 1988, covering the period 1988/89–91/92. Total Plan Period expenditure was now estimated at USD1.67 billion. Volume I was only revised in late 1989, in time for a Consultative Group meeting with donors.

These plans had limited practical significance. The government had yet to draw up coherent sector policies reflecting current conditions, so the projects listed did not reflect policy priorities. Moreover, in the aftermath of the civil war, most of the priorities for rehabilitation (such as main roads, electricity generation, and urban water supplies) were starkly obvious. Donors did not need government plans to point this out, and had already started funding projects in these areas.

In late 1990 Volume II of the RDP was 'rolled over' for the third time since 1987. It covered the period 1990/91–93/94. A number of changes were made. All donor-funded projects included in the 1990/91 Development Budget[2] were automatically included (with identical expenditure estimates) in the RDP, along with selected projects funded by government. In addition, ministries were invited to submit new project proposals for which aid could be sought. These were reviewed by the MoPED committee set up to oversee the exercise and classified either as 'Priority', 'Reserve', or 'Rejected' projects.

The 1990/91–93/94 RDP was a rushed job. It combined weak estimates from the 1990/91 Development Budget with extremely rough 'guesstimates' for those ongoing projects for later years. It also included projections for new projects, many of which had little or no prospect of securing funding. Moreover, it subsequently transpired that many fully donor-funded projects had been left out altogether. Little attempt was made to ensure compatibility with macroeconomic projections of available resources over the plan period, mainly because the MoPED Macroeconomic Planning Department was in no position to make meaningful projections. As a result, total plan period expenditure of USD1.75 billion was again highly optimistic.

Nevertheless, the 1990/91–93/94 RDP represented an advance on previous editions. It was the first Plan to be overseen by a committee—a precursor to the Development Committee (see below). It was also the first Plan to be directly linked to the Development Budget, even if only retrospectively, and had a common list of projects and identical expenditure and funding estimates for 1990/91. While the process of prioritizing projects (largely on the basis of funding availability, economic returns, and consistency with sector policy) was also quick and crude, it nevertheless represented a move towards a more assertive role for MoPED in project planning. Perhaps the most significant aspect of the third RDP was the initiative to collect and store detailed financial information on all RDP projects on a computer database. This developed into a key instrument of budget and aid management (see Box 6.1).

3. 1991 review of the planning system

Following publication of Volume II of the 1990/91–93/94 RDP, MoPED undertook an internal review of the planning system in 1991. By now Uganda had

---

[2] The Development Budget is meant to cover capital expenditure and projects, as distinct from the Recurrent Budget.

enjoyed five years of relative political and economic stability. As the dust settled, Uganda's new circumstances stood out more clearly. The most dominant feature of the landscape was the country's heavy dependence on aid. With the collapse of domestic revenue, it was clear that if the economy was going to be rebuilt this would have to be largely financed from abroad. The heavy debt burden (see Chapter 12) meant that commercial loans were out of the question, and that Uganda's rehabilitation was dependent upon the availability of concessional aid.

Fortunately, the international community was keen to support the new government. Idi Amin, the civil war, and the HIV and AIDS pandemic had all attracted international attention and sympathy for Uganda. The country's social indicators were awful. Thus, once the new government had demonstrated that it could secure peace and stability, and that the National Resistance Army was much more disciplined than its predecessors, aid began to flow. Official gross aid flows reached 13.8 per cent of GDP in 1992/93 (USD443 million, see Table 13.2) from 2.7 per cent of GDP in 1986/87. As a consequence 'aid covers more than 80% of all public investment and a substantial share of other public outlays, such as recurrent expenditures and debt service' (World Bank 1995: 18).

The implications of such donor dependence for public investment planning were profound. The traditional approach to planning was premised upon governments having a significant degree of control over the resources whose use was being allocated. However, when virtually all investment funds were provided by donors this clearly did not apply. While the government could exercise negative control by refusing offers of aid, it could not force donors to support particular projects. Donors had their own policies and priorities and, if they differed from those of the government, there was little the latter could do about it. It was no longer sufficient, if it ever had been, for a national development plan to simply list government expenditure priorities without considering where the resources were coming from. Planning and aid management were now inextricably linked.

With this backdrop, the review identified three fundamental weaknesses in the 'planning system' as embodied in the RDPs. First, despite the publication of the RDPs, the set of projects which were being financed and undertaken was largely determined by the donors themselves, albeit in consultation with line ministries, with little reference to MoF or MoPED. This reflected the lack of capacity in both ministries as well as the fragmentation of responsibility for aid coordination. MoF handled all lending donor agencies (because of government repayment guarantee requirements) while MoPED was responsible for most bilateral and grant aid. Given properly motivated staff and good inter-ministerial working relations this division of responsibility might have worked. Unfortunately, neither condition applied.

The general problem of low public service salaries combined with the mutual suspicion between MoF and MoPED made central government aid coordination and project planning virtually impossible in the early years of the NRM government. Yet this was a time when donors were keen to 'do something' in Uganda and to re-establish aid operations. In the absence of coordination from the centre donors took to dealing directly with line ministries. The latter welcomed this arrangement because, with negligible non-salary funding from government, they saw it as a much more effective way of attracting resources into their ministries than conventional planning/budgeting procedures.

The practice developed, therefore, of donors designing projects jointly with line ministry staff. Frequently, the first that MoF or MoPED heard of a new project was when the donor, following its own appraisal, made an offer to finance it. MoF or MoPED had to sign the loan or grant agreement respectively, but were effectively presented with a *fait accompli*. This was, of course, the antithesis of government 'planning' which seeks to ensure that resources are distributed according to (central) government priorities. It carried the danger that those ministries with relatively eloquent ministers and officials would attract a disproportionate share of donor resources. Many ministers and top officials saw canvassing donors for project aid as part of their job description.

MoF and MoPED's ability to address this situation was complicated by lack of information on donor activities. Following publication of the 1990/91–93/94 RDP it became apparent that many donor-funded projects had been omitted. Since the RDP was based on the 1990/91 Development Budget and 100 per cent donor-funded projects were deliberately excluded from the Budget at the time, few such projects had been picked up. Ministries' RDP and Development Budget submissions tended to focus on projects requiring 'counterpart funding' from government (see below). While detailed information on all donor-funded projects should have been available in the MoF and MoPED Aid Coordination Departments—because between them they had to sign all financing agreements with donors—poor communications within and between the two ministries meant that such information frequently failed to reach the MoPED department responsible for preparing the RDP and Development Budget.

The second key weakness highlighted in the review was the separation of the Plan and Budget. One of the main reasons for the failure of many African plans was that the ministry that produced the plan did not actually control the necessary resources to implement it. If the finance ministry (or donor) did not provide the necessary funds in the budget—and release them—the plans could not be realized. In Uganda the problem was slightly different. MoPED was responsible for producing the Development Budget, in consultation with MoF, which covered capital expenditure. However, although the same MoPED desk officers were responsible for both RDP and Development Budget preparation, these were undertaken as largely separate exercises. Until the 1990/91–93/94 RDP rollover, the lists of projects appearing in the two documents were quite different. Where they overlapped there was little correspondence between their annual expenditure estimates for common projects. In other words, project expenditures (particularly the government contribution) were not being planned in any real sense: annual Budget estimates were prepared one year at a time with little or no reference to the Plan.

The third weakness was the absence of any real coordination within MoPED in the preparation of either the Plan or the Development Budget. Individual sections prepared the plan sector chapters or ministry budget expenditure estimates for which they were responsible with little management oversight, guidance, or checks for consistency with available resources. This was compounded by the lack of communication between the two Aid Coordination Departments in MoF and MoPED. The failure of the system was vividly illustrated in the 1990/91 Budget. Line ministries were given no financial limits within which to prepare their Development Budget submissions, while the MoPED desk officers chairing Budget meetings had virtually no guidelines within which to work. Not surprisingly, when the 'agreed estimates' for government funding of the Development Budget were aggregated at virtually the last minute of Budget preparation, they exceeded the resources expected to be available by a large margin. The 'agreed estimates' were then slashed dramatically over the weekend before the Budget Speech by one officer from MoF and one from the MoPED Macro Department.

There was no consultation with MoPED sector desk officers in this exercise. In other words, substantial arbitrary cuts were made by (macro) officers to projects of which they had little knowledge. Inevitably, many of the cuts were in the wrong places. Where this resulted in, say, failure to honour clear counterpart funding commitments to donor funded projects this had to be rectified by 'supplementary' appropriations during the course of the year. Partly as a result, actual expenditure in the Development Budget in 1990/91 exceeded the Approved (by Parliament) Estimates by 35 per cent (see Table 6.1).

The 1990/91 Budget fiasco highlighted the significance of planning and budgeting for local counterpart funds in aid dependent countries. The rules of the major multilateral lending agencies, such as the World Bank and African Development Bank, which accounted for 36 per cent of donor disbursements to Ugandan projects in 1992/93, meant they could not lend more than 90 per cent of a project's financing requirements. The balance had to be funded by the recipient government (or parastatal), in part to demonstrate local 'ownership' of the project. A few bilateral donors (notably Germany) also insisted on a government financial contribution, while some could not finance certain categories of local expenditure (such as land compensation, office accommodation, local salaries). In such cases, the government had to provide counterpart funding in the Development Budget.

Though typically constituting only 10–20 per cent of total project financing, counterpart funding was frequently cited as the main bottleneck to project implementation in the early 1990s. If it was insufficient, donor funds were held up. Also it typically covered activities, such as vehicle operations and maintenance as well as salaries and allowances of local staff, which were critical to project implementation. Despite efforts to rectify the situation, the arbitrary last minute cuts made to the 1990/91 Development Budget caused considerable disruption to many donor-funded projects.

In early 1992 MoPED undertook a stock-take of the extent of Uganda's counterpart funding obligations. It soon became clear that the government was vastly over-committed. The stock of outstanding commitments to the World Bank alone, the country's largest donor, in 1992 exceeded USD100 million—a figure which took the bank by surprise when announced.[3] While this was to be discharged over about four years, it compared with a total government Development Budget contribution (for all projects funded by all donors) in 1991/92 of USD22.5 million (see Table 6.1).

This situation had arisen because in the early NRM years everyone had been desperate to secure aid to finance rehabilitation of the devastated economy. When a donor offered to fund 80 or 90 per cent of a project the response from MoF and MoPED was invariably 'yes please'. No one bothered to check whether government would in fact be in a position to contribute its 10 or 20 per cent share of project costs. This was simply taken for granted. That this situation should have developed in prevailing Ugandan conditions was not surprising. What was surprising is that the responsible donors failed to monitor the rapidly rising stock of counterpart funding obligations they were imposing on Uganda. Clearly an important part of the planning function had to be the management of Uganda's counterpart funding obligations.

4. Reform of the planning system

Following completion of the review, a number of reforms were initiated in MoPED from 1991 with the aim of increasing both the volume of aid attracted to Uganda and government's influence over its allocation. The reforms were based on three basic principles. Firstly, donor resources should be allocated on the basis of government, not donor, policies and priorities. Secondly, all resources, including aid, should therefore be allocated through the planning and budgeting systems; and thirdly, the Plan should be integrated with the Budget.

While it was inevitable that project decisions were donor-driven in the early NRM years, this was no longer considered acceptable now that the country had

---

[3] Following the announcement World Bank management commissioned a stock take of counterpart fund commitments throughout Africa.

stabilized and the government had begun to develop its own policies and priorities.[4] Allocation of resources by donors was objectionable not only on grounds of sovereignty, but also of allocative efficiency. A fundamental principle of both planning and budgeting is that resources are allocated most efficiently in support of government objectives when all available resources are considered together, allocated in one process, and according to a single set of criteria. By contrast, in Uganda in 1991 roughly half of the resources available for public expenditure were being allocated by government through the budget process, while decisions regarding the other half were being made individually by donors.[5] This was bound to result in an inefficient allocation of scarce resources.

Clearly, if the government was to start influencing the distribution of donor funds, all projects had to be brought within the planning system. The principle was established therefore that all resources, whether local or from donors, should be captured in the planning and budgeting system. This, in turn, meant that all project aid of any size should henceforth be included in both the Plan and the Development Budget.

It was recognized at the outset of the reform process that there were a number of key constraints on the application of these principles and that full application would take several years. Even where they were considered low priority by government, it rarely made sense to terminate on-going donor-funded projects prematurely. In practice, government priorities could only be applied to decisions on new projects. Importantly, if donors were to pay serious attention to government priorities in allocating their resources, MoF and MoPED needed to establish credibility as technically competent custodians of policy priorities. They had to learn to say 'no thank you' to donor proposals where necessary. Building technical capacity meant developing both individual skills and appropriate institutional arrangements to review project proposals.

4.1 Integration of the Plan and Development Budget

The other important principle adopted following the review was that for the RDP to be implementable it had to be integrated with the Development Budget. One of the first major reforms, therefore, was the decision to transform the RDP into a 'rolling' plan integrated with the Budget. Instead of producing the RDP (occasionally) and the Development Budget (annually)

---

[4] MoPED published two papers, Way Forward I (macro) and II (sectoral), in 1990 and 1991 respectively setting out the Ministry's new policy thinking. Much of this was incorporated in Volume I of the RDP, 1991/92–94/95 published in September 1992.

[5] Almost all Budget resources were pre-committed to 'non-discretionary' items such as debt service, salaries, and counterpart funds. The only significant 'discretionary' resources available to support government priorities were donor resources, therefore.

as two separate exercises, it was decided to henceforth 'roll over' Volume II (the project list)[6] every year as part of the annual Budget process. The Development Budget estimates for the relevant year would be the first year of the Plan. In this way it was also possible to address the issue of consistency of the RDP with macro estimates of available resources, at least for the Budget year—year 1 of the RDP.

Until 1991/92 the Development Budget had two sections:

- Section 1 comprised wholly government-financed projects. This covered a 'ragbag' of activities ranging from genuine development projects (such as Mityana–Fort Portal road) to various small activities that did not fit into the Recurrent Budget (such as vehicles, office repairs, and photocopiers); and
- Section 2 comprised projects jointly financed by donors and government. This was the counterpart funding budget.

Prior to 1992/93 wholly donor financed projects were omitted altogether from the Budget and received little attention from MoF and MoPED. Yet MoPED could hardly plan future public expenditure if it was unaware of many projects that were already underway. While it was of little concern to some donors whether or not their projects were included in the Plan and Budget it was important for MoPED, which had wider concerns than counterpart funding. Many projects gave rise to additional recurrent costs and manpower requirements, which became government's responsibility when the donor withdrew; these needed to be planned for.

From 1991 the coverage of the RDP was extended to all public sector development projects, regardless of how they were financed, and to all donor project aid. This meant that the RDP comprised all jointly financed projects (Section 2 of the Development Budget), government funded projects (part of Section 1), and 100 per cent donor-funded projects (which had been excluded from the Development Budget).

In order to integrate the Plan and Budget, therefore, with effect from 1992/93 the Development Budget was reorganized into:

- Part A, comprising all RDP projects; and
- Part B, comprising the remaining non-RDP, non-recurrent activities that did not represent 'genuine' projects.

Part A expenditures were identical to those for year 1 of the new Plan. Part B was produced as a separate part of the Budget process.

The first rolling Plan to be produced as part of the Budget process was published in 1992. It covered the period 1991/92 (for historical comparison

---

[6] Since policies change little from year to year, Volume I did not need 'rolling over'. A revised Volume I was published in December 2003.

purposes only) to 1994/95. In reality, it was a three-year plan commencing in 1992/93. The 1992/93 estimates were produced during the Budget process. Both the list of projects and the expenditure and funding estimates in the RDP for that year were identical to those published in Part A of the Development Budget. Part B Estimates were produced separately and were added to the Part A Estimates to arrive at the consolidated 1992/93 Development Budget (see Table 6.1). RDP projections for the same projects for 1993/94 and 1994/95 and for new project proposals, as well as project write-ups, were prepared after the Budget. The RDP was published in September.

To emphasize the rolling nature of the RDP, the year 2 projections were used as the initial indicative limits for preparing the following year's RDP/Budget submissions. For example, if the 1992/93 RDP indicated government funding of UGX x million for a particular project in 1993/94 this was a warning to the relevant project/ministry that it should not expect more than this amount in the following year's rollover. Such limits were not cast in stone, but significant deviations needed to be carefully justified.[7] As officers became more familiar with the new system, project expenditure estimates were updated three years at a time rather than (as in 1992) one year for the Budget followed by two more years for the Plan.

Each project included in the RDP normally had a two page entry. This consisted of: a project synopsis, a one page write-up indicating the project's background, objectives, description, financing, plan of action, etc. and a financial form (see Appendix 6.2 for an example) giving annual expenditure estimates for each of the three years along with anticipated sources of funding. Donor funding was clearly distinguished from government funding. Where no, or insufficient, funding had been lined up for a project a 'funding gap' was shown to indicate that donor funding was being sought.

As noted above, Part A of the Development Budget was taken—without change—from year 1 of the RDP. This meant that the Budget Estimates document included not only government funding, but also estimated donor disbursements. Since disbursements were mainly managed by the donors themselves—outside the Consolidated Fund—these estimates were not part of the Budget on which Parliament voted. The Appropriation Act only covered government funding, which was printed in bold to distinguish it from donor funding. However, the latter was included in the document (as a 'memorandum item') for transparency reasons. Given that most government funding was counterpart funding, Parliament could not assess whether the government estimates were reasonable without details of expected donor disbursements.

Being also Budget Estimates, the aggregate 1992/93 expenditure figures in the RDP, 1991/92–94/95 were by definition equal to macroeconomic estimates of

---

[7] No limits were applied to donor funding at this stage.

government resources available for projects in that year. However, aggregate RDP expenditure did not represent the government's forecast for aggregate public sector investment over the Plan Period as a whole. The RDP Volume II comprised individual three-year expenditure estimates for some 300 projects. Since many projects had 'funding gaps' in 1993/94 and 1994/95 (years 2 and 3 of the Plan Period)—not all of which would be filled—year 2 and 3 aggregate expenditures for the listed projects were invariably too high. On the other hand, some totally new projects being considered by donors were not listed at all. It was not possible initially to match exactly aggregate RDP project expenditure estimates with macroeconomic projections of resource availability for the outer years of the Plan Period. However, as the quality and comprehensiveness of successive Plans improved and with the development of the Medium Term Expenditure Framework (MTEF, see Chapter 8), macroeconomic consistency also improved.

The RDP was renamed the Public Investment Plan (PIP) in 1994, recognizing that Uganda's rehabilitation phase was ending. Meanwhile the importance of Part B of the Development Budget steadily diminished. The establishment of a system of rolling plans completely integrated with the annual budget was completed when the Part A/Part B division was abolished with effect from the 1995/96 Budget. Since much Part B expenditure was seen as being ad hoc and of lower quality than Part A, it was decided that it should henceforth be subjected to the same screening process as Part A. Major categories of Part B expenditure were packaged together into 'projects' for inclusion in the Plan so that, for example, the Plan now contained defence equipment and government equipment purchase (vehicles, computers, etc.) projects. An important benefit of the integrated system was the rationalization of desk officers' work loads, since they were now only required to produce a single document each year. This released time for project monitoring and broader policy issues.

The PIP was a credible three-year rolling plan only at the level of individual projects. As illustrated in Appendix 6.2, for each project three-year estimates were presented for: expenditure, broken down by budget classification; donor funding; and government funding. For year 1 only, total expenditure and 'secured funds' were equal. Development Budget estimates for year 1 were taken directly from the PIP; aggregate government funding for all PIP projects was equal to the limit specified in the Budget Framework Paper (see Chapter 8). Many projects had 'funding gaps' in years 2 and 3, indicating that donor funding was not yet confirmed. The main significance of year 2 figures was that they represented initial indicative limits for the following year's budget and PIP rollover process. Year 3 figures were purely indicative.

The 'planning system', therefore, had little in common with Soviet planning or the planning literature of the 1960s and 1970s. Not only was recurrent expenditure ignored, but aggregate PIP expenditure estimates did not even represent an accurate three year estimate of aggregate development expenditure. In practice, the PIP was used less for 'planning' than as a tool for preparing the Development Budget. It was essentially a means of keeping track of donor disbursement plans and managing government counterpart funding obligations within approved macro limits. Meaningful planning had to await the development of the MTEF (which incorporated both recurrent and development expenditure), the formulation of the Poverty Eradication Action Plan, and sector wide approaches (see Chapters 8, 7, and 9 respectively).

4.2 Political support

If the reforms to the planning system were to be taken seriously by donors and ministries it was vital to demonstrate that they had strong political support. In 1991 the Presidential Economic Council, the political committee that had to approve the RDP, decreed that henceforth Volume II of the RDP constituted the government's 'Priority Project List'. 'These are the Government's highest priority development projects and are the only ones for which funding is being sought during the plan period' (Ministry of Planning and Economic Development 1990/91–93/94, Volume II: i). The policy was established that all new project proposals should be submitted by line ministries to MoPED for consideration for inclusion in the RDP before being put to donors for funding.

The new policy was not easy to enforce. Many donors continued to approach line ministries directly, fearing the additional layer of bureaucracy.[8] MoPED's only real stick with which to force ministries and donors into the RDP system was its control over counterpart funding in the Budget: since the Development Budget was now integrated with the RDP, non-RDP projects could not receive counterpart funding. However, this did not necessarily mean that MoPED got to review new project proposals before they had gone too far: once a project financing agreement was signed MoPED had little alternative but to incorporate it in the RDP. Moreover, this only affected projects requiring counterpart funds. Many projects were fully funded by (mainly bilateral) donors and could easily proceed outside the planning and budgeting systems—until they ended, when government had to take over their recurrent costs.

To underline the political priority attached to bringing aid within the planning system, a Presidential directive was issued in August 1992. Noting that the Ministry of Finance and Economic Planning (MoFEP), as it now was, 'is the only

---

[8] Following the 2005 Paris Declaration on Aid Effectiveness, most donors now accept the principle that donors should align their support behind government plans and priorities. However, things were very different in Uganda in the early 1990s. Given the lack of capacity in central government, most donors understandably felt they were better placed to decide how to allocate their funds. Line ministry endorsement of their proposals was taken as sufficient 'ownership'.

Ministry authorised by law to commit Government financially abroad' the President directed, *inter alia*, that 'All dealings with donors are to be coordinated by the [MoFEP] Aid Management Department', and that 'Donor funding should only be sought for projects included in the RDP' (Museveni 1992).

4.3 Comprehensiveness of the Plan

If the revised RDP was to become an effective means of establishing government control over the allocation of donor resources, it was vital that it cover all aid to the public sector. From 1991 a major effort was made to 'capture' ongoing projects missing from the RDP database. The initial emphasis was on ensuring comprehensiveness of the RDP, with little attention paid to projects' consistency with government priorities. Government needed to establish the scale of available resources and how they were being used before it could expect to influence their allocation.

Since from 1992/93 government counterpart funds could only be budgeted for donor-funded projects if those projects were first included in the RDP, this provided a strong incentive to both line ministries and donors requiring counterpart funds to ensure that their projects were properly submitted for the RDP. Most multilateral projects were covered from 1992/93, therefore. A concerted effort was then made to capture remaining missing bilateral projects for 1993/94. Donors were approached directly, presented with the disbursement projections contained on the RDP database and requested to report any gaps or errors. Historical disbursement data back to 1991/92 were also collected as part of an exercise by the Aid Data Unit to establish a solid time series of aid data (see Box 6.1). Partly to encourage donor cooperation in this exercise, the results were published in a 'league table' of aid disbursements in the RDP from 1993/94. This had the desired effect of uncovering more missing projects as donors sought to improve their position in the table.

By the time the renamed PIP was published in August 1994 it was a reasonably comprehensive inventory of project aid to Uganda (MoFEP 2004). Only small projects, below USD1 million, such as technical assistance were less than fully covered.

4.4 Development Committee

The review of the planning system highlighted a number of weaknesses in MoPED institutional arrangements. In particular, it observed that the absence of any single body to oversee preparation of the Plan and Development Budget was a major omission. The Development Committee was therefore established early in 1991 to take on this role. All MoPED Departments were represented on the Committee. Its main functions were:

Box 6.1 AID DATABASE

One of the main outputs of the reforms was the development of a detailed project expenditure and donor disbursement database. In 1990 MoF and MoPED were unaware of the existence of many donor-funded projects, let alone their expenditures. In late 1990 a database was established to collect detailed financial information for all projects to be included in the RDP, 1990/91–92/93. By 1994 virtually all the significant projects had been captured. For each project, estimates were entered every year for: (i) expenditure; (ii) donor funding; and (iii) government funding, in the format at Appendix 6.2.

Actual disbursement data was collected from donors and entered alongside the forecasts for that year (a useful measure of the accuracy of donor forecasts). During 1994/95 the separate RDP/PIP and aid data databases were integrated into a single 'Development Management System' covering all aid data—project and non-project—and documentation. Budget Directorate desk officers entered expenditure forecasts and government funding for their projects on the database while the Aid Liaison Department entered donor disbursement figures. The Development Budget and PIP documents were printed directly from the database from 1994/95 through 2008/09. The regular updating and extension of the database since 1990/91 generated a consistent time series of project expenditure and aid disbursement data, which has been invaluable for budgeting and aid management (as well as national accounts and balance of payments analysis). The data is published and analysed in annual Development Cooperation Reports.

- To vet all new project proposals prior to their inclusion in the Plan;
- To oversee preparation of both Plan and Development Budget expenditure and funding estimates, ensuring consistency of aggregate expenditure with anticipated resources and of sectoral allocations with policy priorities;
- To manage the government's counterpart funding commitments; and
- To advise on general (sectoral) policy issues.

From 1991 the preparation of all RDPs/PIPs and Development Budgets was overseen by the Development Committee. New project proposals were assessed on such criteria as economic viability, consistency with government policy, counterpart funding, recurrent cost implications, and availability of donor funds. Terms of reference for studies were also to be reviewed by the Committee before being forwarded to donors.

One of the 'traditional' roles of planning ministries, which the Committee was now responsible for, was to determine the desired sectoral distribution of public investment. However, the statistical base was so poor and government influence over donor resources so weak that there was little point trying to come up with precise target shares. Instead, following a World Bank-led Public Expenditure Review, a number of 'Priority Programme Areas' (essentially 'pro-poor' sub-sectors) were identified which clearly required increased public sector funding: primary health care, primary education, main road maintenance, rural feeder roads, rural water supplies, and agricultural research and extension

(World Bank 1991). In 1991 the government committed itself (publicly and through conditions for the first World Bank Structural Adjustment Credit) to real increases every year in government appropriations to these sectors and to protect these appropriations from expenditure cuts when revenue fell short of estimates. Donors were also encouraged to focus on these priority sectors.

These sector priorities were applied to both development and recurrent expenditure. The development during the early 1990s of this concept of giving priority to sub-sectors identified as 'pro-poor' led to two institutional innovations, which have received considerable international attention and been widely copied. First, a 'Financial Tracking Study' of primary school teacher salaries commissioned (in house) by the Development Committee in 1992 inspired a new sub-discipline of expenditure research (Public Expenditure Tracking Surveys, see Box 6.2), which has been heavily promoted by the World Bank.

Box 6.2 PUBLIC EXPENDITURE TRACKING SURVEYS

One of the conditions attached to a World Bank Structural Adjustment Credit in 1991 was that the government would increase budgetary appropriations in real terms to certain priority sectors each year and protect these sectors from within-year budget cuts. The Development Committee was responsible for implementing the policy and developed systems to ensure that monthly budget releases to the priority sectors were protected.

One of the priority sectors was primary education. Although the Committee had both increased appropriations and ensured regular budget releases, reports were received that schoolteachers in rural areas had not noticed any improvement and were still not receiving their salaries. To try and establish where the extra funds being released for primary education were actually going, in 1992 the Committee established a team of Budget Directorate officers to track the progress of funds from MoFEP to the teachers via Ministry of Education headquarters, regional/district offices, and head teachers. The survey concluded that only 25 per cent of funds for primary teacher salaries were actually reaching the teachers. Most of the funds were getting diverted at Ministry of Education headquarters and District Education Offices.

Armed with this information, Budget Directorate instituted a number of measures to try and ensure budgeted funds reached the intended beneficiaries, such as publishing details of how much was released each month in newspapers. This was highly successful. A follow up survey showed that the proportion of funds reaching teachers had increased substantially.

The success of the survey attracted the attention of the World Bank. In 1996 the Bank and the Decentralization Secretariat undertook a 'Public Expenditure Tracking Survey' (PETS) of primary school non-wage capitation grants. This took the same idea of tracking funds through government systems, but used much more systematic survey methods. It found that just 13 per cent of capitation grants reached schools between 1991 and 1995. Following a programme of publishing grant details in newspapers and on school notice boards, the proportion of grants reaching schools increased to 82 per cent by 2001 (Reinikka and Svensson 2006). The success of this and subsequent Ugandan PETS led to a new sub-discipline of expenditure research, which the Bank has rolled out in numerous countries.

Second, the Poverty Action Fund developed as part of HIPC negotiations in 1997 drew on the experience with priority sub-sectors (see Chapter 13).

4.5 Merger of finance and planning ministries

In March 1992 MoF and MoPED were merged to form the Ministry of Finance and Economic Planning (MoFEP, see Chapter 2). The former Minister and Permanent Secretary of MoPED took over the leadership of the new ministry, with a political mandate to bring government expenditure and inflation under control. This was arguably the single most important event in Uganda's economic reforms. The merger facilitated the establishment of fiscal discipline and macroeconomic stability, providing a springboard for subsequent reforms (see Chapter 3). The merger had equally profound implications for planning and expenditure management. Not only did it facilitate the completion of the integration of the Plan and Budget but, critically, responsibility for all aspects of the Plan and Budget was now under one roof.

The merger allowed a number of immediate efficiency gains. Despite the severe shortage of skilled manpower throughout government, many functions in the two ministries overlapped. Of particular relevance here are the aid management and budgeting functions. Both ministries had aid coordination departments, one handling loans (MoF) and one grants (MoPED). Similarly, MoF handled the Recurrent Budget while MoPED was responsible for the Development Budget. Merging these respective departments allowed a much more effective use of scarce manpower, improved internal communications and greatly strengthened the capacity of central government relative to sector ministries.

An immediate benefit of the merger was that Development Committee membership was extended to all parts of the combined ministry with responsibilities for economic management. Initially, the Committee had focused upon MoPED's responsibilities—the RDP, the Development Budget, and projects. MoF's responsibility for loan-funded projects represented a weak link here. The merger not only removed this anomaly, but also opened up the prospect of looking at the Development and Recurrent Budgets together. For the first time, therefore, there was now a single body within central government looking at the details of all public expenditure. While the new Budget Directorate provided most of the members and staffed the secretariat, representatives from the Macroeconomic Policy and Aid Management Departments were responsible for ensuring the Committee worked within a realistic 'resource envelope' and was aware of donor constraints.

A key longer term benefit of the merger was the opportunity it provided to develop sectoral technical expertise within the new Budget Directorate, enabling it to play an increasingly important leadership role in driving policy reform across government. Prior to the merger, the small MoPED Sector Planning Department had lead responsibility within central government for sector policy development and implementation. Desk officers, mostly economists, were expected to engage in policy discussions with their respective ministries and appraise project proposals. They were also responsible for relevant sections of 'Background to the Budget',[9] the RDP, and the Development Budget. However, in practice the system was ineffective. Apart from the general problem of under-staffing and low pay, as noted above, most decisions on projects were being made by donors—not government. Moreover, recurrent expenditure was handled by MoF finance officers, who had a narrower policy remit than MoPED economists.

If government was going to develop sufficient credibility with donors to be able to influence the shape of future aid programmes it was important not only to bring aid within the plan and budget, but also to strengthen the technical capacity of the Budget Directorate.

The merger of the MoF Budget Department and the MoPED Sector Planning Department to form the MoFEP Budget Directorate was very significant. For the first time, all aspects of public expenditure management (i.e. policy, planning, budgeting, and implementation; capital and recurrent) were now the responsibility of a single division. Long-standing problems of communicating across divisional and ministerial boundaries largely disappeared. The Directorate's operations were overseen by the Development Committee, which was chaired by the Budget Director. Bringing together MoF finance officers and MoPED economists both increased the range of skills available and meant the Division had a large enough establishment to have an effective division of labour.

The Budget Directorate was organized along sectoral lines. Initially, sections were established for the following sector groupings: Agriculture, Social Services, Transport, Energy/Environment, Industry, and Public Administration. For each ministry in its portfolio the section was responsible for central government input into policy development on the one hand and the financial resources (whether from government or donor) to implement policy priorities on the other. On the resource side, the same section or officer was responsible for all phases of the project cycle (appraisal, planning, budgeting, releases, as well as monitoring and evaluation) within the merged ministry, as well as for recurrent funding.

Over time this arrangement proved increasingly effective. By assigning competent officers complete responsibility for their ministries—and keeping them in post for several years—the Budget Directorate was able to develop a sufficient degree of technical competence and experience to engage meaningfully with ministries and donors on both policy and budgetary issues (now termed the 'challenge function'). The combination of desk officers' sector expertise and the Development Committee's overview of all sectors meant that for the first time there was an institutional mechanism enabling central government to engage

---

[9] Background to the Budget is the key text presented to Parliament explaining the background to the detailed estimates of revenue and expenditure.

effectively in sector policy and to attempt to allocate resources across government on the basis of policy priorities. It was becoming harder for donors and line ministries to 'stitch up' project proposals on their own. While the detailed institutional arrangements continued to develop over time,[10] a technically strong Budget Directorate responsible for all aspects of planning and budgeting—a 'one stop shop'—was critical to the success of subsequent public expenditure reforms.[11]

5. Impact of the reforms

5.1 Releasing budgeted funds

One of the first measures of the merged ministry was to transfer responsibility for releasing Development Budget funds (mainly counterpart funds) to the (former MoPED) desk officers responsible for producing the Budget estimates in the first place. Prior to the merger MoF had handled releases. This arrangement had compounded the problems with counterpart funding because, when Development Budget funds could not be released in full—and revenue shortfalls were a recurring problem—cuts were often arbitrary and very damaging. Now the officers most familiar with the projects could administer cuts, helping to minimize the inevitable damage.

Managing Development Budget releases assumed particular significance in the aftermath of the merger. Chapter 3 notes that the merger was precipitated by the realization that the 1991/92 fiscal deficit target would be missed by a wide margin (because of over-ambitious revenue estimates and delayed release of donor import support funds). Immediately following the merger, severe expenditure cuts were imposed during the fourth quarter of the fiscal year (April–June 1992) in a desperate attempt to meet the target. Since the Recurrent Budget comprised largely salaries and debt service, which could not be touched in the short term, the adjustment burden fell disproportionately on the Development Budget. Table 6.1 shows that actual expenditure in 1991/92 was only USD30.8 million, compared to the approved estimate of USD52.1 million. Inevitably, this caused considerable short-term disruption to projects dependent on counterpart funding. Nevertheless, the merger meant that the cuts were managed better than they had been on previous occasions.

---

[10] Chapter 9 shows how some Development Committee and Budget Directorate functions were delegated to sector working groups.

[11] The Budget Office in the South African National Treasury has played a similar central role in that country's reforms. More common is the arrangement in Malawi, where sector policy is the responsibility of a separate planning ministry while finance ministry budget desk officers are relatively junior. With both ministries under-staffed and with poor inter-ministry cooperation, central government is simply unable to engage on sector policy or to allocate resources across government on the basis of inter-sectoral priorities.

Table 6.1 Development Budget Approved Estimates and Actual Expenditure (USD million), 1990/91–1995/96

	1990/91		1991/92		1992/93		1993/94		1994/95		1995/96
	Budget	Actual	Budget	Actual	Budget	Actual	Budget	Actual	Budget	Released	Budget
Original Categorization (pre-1992/93)											
Government funded development ($1)	28.3	38.2	29.6	17.3	18.1	11.3	16.5	22.9	25.2	34.6	16.4
Government/Donor funded ($2)	11.3	15.5	22.5	13.5	19.8	15.5	32.6	28.5	49.4	49.0	52.0
New Categorisation (1992/93 onwards)											
Project allocations (Part A)	20.1	28.7	26.3	19.6	26.8	19.8	37.8	33.4	58.5	58.9	68.4
Other development (Part B)	19.5	25.0	25.8	11.2	11.1	7.0	11.3	18.0	16.1	25.0	0.0
Total	39.6	53.7	52.1	30.8	37.9	26.8	49.1	51.4	74.6	83.9	68.4
Part B Share, %	49.2	46.5	49.5	36.5	29.4	26.1	23.1	34.9	21.5	29.8	0.0
Section 1 Share, %	71.5	71.1	56.8	56.3	47.7	42.0	33.7	44.6	33.8	41.2	24.0

Notes:
a. Part A comprises RDP/PIP projects; Part B comprises non-RDP, non-recurrent activities.
b. Section 1 comprises wholly government financed projects; Section 2 comprises joint government/donor financed projects.
c. For 1990/91 and 1991/92 Section 1 and Section 2 estimates have been reclassified by the author to correspond to the Part A/Part B classification adopted from 1992/93.
d. From 1992/93 Part A and Part B estimates have been reclassified by the author to correspond to the Section 1/Section 2 classification used until 1991/92.
e. UGX have been converted to USD using the average annual Bureau Middle Rate recorded by the Bank of Uganda.
f. For 1994/95 only data on funds released is available.

Source: Ministry of Finance and Economic Planning: Estimates of Revenue and Expenditure, 1990/91–1995/96; Treasury Office of Accounts.

Building on this experience, a Development Budget Releases Committee (a sub-committee of the Development Committee) was formed in October 1992 and charged with responsibility for 'rationing' Development Budget funds. The Cash Flow Committee (see Chapter 3), which managed government's cash flow, advised the Releases Committee of the funds available each month. If this was less than one twelfth of the annual budgeted amount the Releases Committee recommended where the axe should fall. A computerized system of monthly releases was developed which greatly improved the management and predictability of counterpart fund releases.

5.2 Improved development budgeting

What impact did the above reforms have on the management and effectiveness of the Development Budget? This is best seen in Table 6.1, which is discussed in detail in Appendix 6.1. Initially, both the size of the Development Budget and the proportion of Approved Estimates that was actually spent fluctuated widely as MoFEP struggled to establish fiscal discipline from 1992. Stabilization of the fiscal situation from 1993/94 facilitated both a substantial increase in the Development Budget (from USD39.6 million in 1990/91 to USD68.4 million in 1995/ 96) and a closer relationship between Approved Estimates and outturns.

As significant as the size of the Development Budget were the changes in its composition. Table 6.1 shows a steady decline in the share of the non-project domestic Development Budget (Part B) between 1990/91 and 1995/96, when it was dropped. Since this comprised *ad hoc*, (usually) one year expenditures which just did not fit in the Recurrent Budget, it was generally of lower quality than the genuine projects (Part A) taken from the PIP which had passed through a screening/appraisal process.

The increase in project allocations from USD20.1 million (50.8 per cent of the total) in 1990/91 to USD68.4 million (100 per cent) in 1995/96 indicates a substantial increase in both the size of the Development Budget and the proportion representing planned expenditure. *Ceteris paribus*, this should indicate an improvement in the quality of expenditure. It also had major implications for counterpart funding.

5.3 Counterpart funding

Following the merger of MoF and MoPED in 1992, MoFEP began getting to grips with the counterpart funding issue. First, it was re-emphasized that no new project agreements should be signed without the project first being included in the Plan. All new project proposals had to be reviewed by the Development Committee, which was responsible for ensuring that future counterpart funding obligations were minimized and were acceptable.

Second, the Minister of Finance and Economic Planning wrote to the donors acknowledging that the government had taken on substantially more counterpart funding obligations than it could possibly honour in the short term and seeking their assistance in managing the situation. Where their rules permitted, donors were requested to 'front load' their funding: if possible financing 100 per cent of project costs in the early years, with government contributing correspondingly more in later years. The plea to donors had some effect. From 1992 new World Bank projects attempted to minimize counterpart funding requirements, particularly in the early years. Increased allowance was made for government contributions in kind. For example, a Bank transport project counted road maintenance appropriations in the Recurrent Budget towards the counterpart funding obligations.

Third, as discussed in Appendix 6.1, the budgeted government contribution to projects in the Development Budget (Part A) steadily increased and, within this, the proportion appropriated for counterpart funding (relative to 100 per cent government funded projects) also increased. In addition, an attempt was made to utilize funds from outside the Consolidated Fund to meet counterpart funding obligations. For example, in 1993/94 USD4.2 million of US Government PL 480 commodity aid local currency funds were appropriated for counterpart funding, effectively increasing project (Part A) funding in the Development Budget by 11 per cent. MoFEP also started using some of the proceeds of the parastatal divestiture programme (see Chapter 16) for the Development Budget.

Government's counterpart funding increased substantially between 1990/91 and 1994/95. The Approved Estimates for 'Section 2' in 1994/95 were over four times (in Dollar terms) those of 1990/91 or over three times actual 1990/91 expenditure. *Prima facie*, this should indicate improved 'productivity' of Development Budget funding; counterpart expenditures had substantial multiplier effects (typically five–ten times) because they triggered much larger donor disbursements.

Counterpart funding increased both in real terms and as a proportion of the Development Budget. However, this would only represent an easing of the constraint on project implementation if counterpart funding had increased relative to donor disbursements. Reliable project aid disbursement data is only available from 1991/92. Analysis by the author in 1995 found that actual (Section 2) government expenditure, as a proportion of donor disbursements to the same projects, was 6.1 per cent (of USD222.4 million) in 1991/92, 6.2 per cent (of USD251.6 million) in 1992/93, and 9.8 per cent (of USD291 million) in 1993/94. Only budgeted estimates were available from 1994/95. Budgeted Section 2 expenditure was 11.8 per cent and 11.0 per cent of budgeted donor disbursements in 1994/95 and 1995/96 respectively.

It appears therefore that, even though disbursements of project aid for 1995/96 were more than double 1991/92 disbursements (see Table 13.2), the ratio of counterpart funds to donor funding also increased over the period. Moreover, this may understate the improvement in the situation because some donors reduced their counterpart funding requirements, and the above figures ignore the contribution to counterpart funding from PL 480 and other local currency sources.

5.4 Impact of reforms on aid

The reforms discussed here had two main objectives: to increase the volume of aid to Uganda and to improve the effectiveness of aid through increased Government influence over its allocation. Looking first at aid volume, in the early 1990s inadequate counterpart funding was perceived to be the major bottleneck to project implementation by many donors, particularly the multilateral lending agencies. Tackling the counterpart funding issue was critical, therefore, to facilitating increased project aid. Table 13.2 shows that project aid disbursements steadily increased from USD136 million in 1991/92 to a peak of USD400 million in 1996/97. The improved management of counterpart funding, which was brought under control by 1995, was undoubtedly a key factor here. Along with non-project aid, the increase was of sufficient magnitude to pose problems for macroeconomic and exchange rate management (see Chapter 13). While counterpart funding was not the only factor,[12] the reforms clearly contributed to increasing project aid volumes.[13]

What about increasing government influence over aid allocations? Although by 1994 the Plan covered most donor activity, this did not necessarily indicate that donors were paying more attention to government priorities than before. Public sector investment was still very much 'donor driven'. Not only was over 80 per cent of the Development Budget still funded by donors, most of the government contribution was 'counter-parting' donor funds. Donors had picked up very few projects that had been declared a priority by government in the early 1990s. MoFEP was still reacting to donor proposals (albeit more critically than in the past) rather than initiating proposals itself together with line ministries. There were still cases where MoFEP only found out about new project proposals at the last minute. Some donors still considered requests direct from ministers.

Nevertheless, government influence over the shape of donor projects was starting to increase. Most donors were now anxious to see their projects included in the Plan (as an indication of government support) and required an official request from MoFEP for project aid. This greatly increased MoFEP's leverage

---

[12] Political stability and improved macroeconomic management were particularly important.
[13] In 2004 the World Bank dropped its requirement for counterpart funds, as part of a general review of its expenditure eligibility policies (World Bank 2004).

over project design, especially if counterpart funds were involved. Donors could no longer take it for granted that MoFEP would answer 'yes please' to any offer of aid.[14] New project proposals were routinely examined by the Development Committee for their counterpart fund and/or recurrent cost implications, as well as for economic viability and consistency with sector policy. Chapters 7, 8, 9, and 13 show how the above reforms were taken forward in the second half of the 1990s and how government was able to increase its influence over the allocation of donor resources.

6. Conclusions and lessons

This chapter has shown how the foundations of Uganda's planning and development budget systems were laid down in the early 1990s. From the chaos of the late 1980s, when aid started to arrive on a large scale but with no central direction, a degree of order was established. The principle was established that aid should be allocated on the basis of Uganda government priorities and a start was made on building the institutional arrangements and professional skills to enable central government to apply policy priorities to the allocation of all resources, domestic and foreign. The authority and credibility of the budget was re-established, helping government, *inter alia*, to manage and meet its counterpart funding obligations. All of this increased donor confidence in government's capacity to utilize aid effectively and contributed to a tripling of project aid inflows between 1991/92 and 1996/97.

A number of key lessons can be drawn from the above experience. One lesson that has been widely learnt is that for a plan to be useful it must be integrated with the budget. Since policies can only be implemented if funds are allocated for them through the budget, plans that are not integrated with the budget are likely to be academic exercises. This explains why the five-year plans which used to be so common in Africa are increasingly being replaced by MTEFs. Comparing Ugandan economic management before and after 1992 also strongly suggests that fiscal discipline and sound expenditure management are easier when they are the responsibility of a single combined ministry of finance and planning rather than of separate ministries.

A fundamental budgeting principle is that all public resources should be considered together and allocated through the budget on the basis of a single set of criteria. For aid dependent countries like Uganda this means that aid needs to be incorporated in the planning and budgeting processes. Whether or not aid passes through government systems (and is voted on by Parliament), a

---

[14] The rejection in 1995 of offers by the Spanish and French governments to finance the purchase of railway wagons and construction of a control tower at Gulu airport respectively represent the first significant rejections of aid.

government needs to have a complete picture of its resource envelope in order to allocate its own resources efficiently. Uganda was one of the first countries to establish an aid database completely integrated with the plan and development budget. This was invaluable in increasing government influence over aid allocations.

Ensuring that scarce public funds are allocated in accordance with political priorities both across and within sectors is the responsibility of central government. By the 1980s the capacity of MoF and MoPED to discharge what is now termed the challenge function had collapsed. As a result, the budget process had lost credibility and donors and line ministries were effectively making decisions on allocations to public investment. Building technical capacity in MoFEP was critical to Uganda's progress in public expenditure management. This had two dimensions—institutional and technical. In addition to the planning and budgeting systems and documents described above, critical to the strengthening of institutional capacity was the establishment of an oversight committee (the Development Committee, comprising senior officials from all relevant divisions), which genuinely 'challenged' sector budget submissions for consistency with policy and managed the resource envelope.

Effective discharge of the challenge function requires a degree of technical expertise on individual sectors within central government. This is something few African governments have been able to develop. Even within consolidated finance and planning ministries, responsibility for sector policy/planning is frequently separated from the (more junior) budget desk officer function. Few governments have sufficient manpower resources or can retain staff in post long enough to allow this division of labour to work. With particularly acute manpower problems in the early 1990s, Uganda addressed this issue by consolidating responsibility for all aspects of sector policy and expenditure within the Budget Directorate. By keeping officers in post for relatively long periods, MoFEP was able to develop sufficient technical competence to engage meaningfully with both sector ministries and donors on policy and budgetary issues.

CHANGES IN THE DEVELOPMENT BUDGET, 1990/91–1995/96

Table 6.1 shows both the 'Approved (by Parliament) Estimates' and the expenditure outturn for the Development Budget for the six years 1990/91–95/96. Only direct government funding, but no donor funding, is included. This is broken down in two ways: (i) between Parts A (RDP/PIP projects) and B (non-RDP, non-recurrent); and (ii) between Sections 1 (fully government funded projects) and 2 (joint donor/government funded projects). Since the Part A/Part B division was only introduced in 1992/93, the figures have been adjusted to produce consistent time series for both breakdowns.

A striking feature of Table 6.1 is the fluctuation in the total size of the Development Budget. The Approved Estimates increased from USD39.6 million in 1990/91 to USD52.1 million in 1991/92, before falling to USD37.9 million in 1992/93. They subsequently increased rapidly to USD49.1 million and USD74.6 million in 1993/94 and 1994/95 respectively. It is also striking that in 1990/91 actual expenditure exceeded the Approved Estimates by 35 per cent. This reflected both the inevitable corrections following the *ad hoc* cuts made in the 1990/91 Development Budget and the general lack of budgetary discipline at the time.

While the Approved Estimates increased in 1991/92, actual expenditure at USD30.8 million was only 57 per cent of the 1990/91 outturn, or 59 per cent of the 1991/92 Estimates. As noted above, the Development Budget bore the brunt of expenditure cuts in the merged Ministry's frantic attempt to limit the 1991/92 fiscal deficit. The reduction in the 1992/93 Approved Estimates reflected a move towards more realistic budgeting, while still representing a 23 per cent increase over 1991/92 actual expenditure. The imposition of strict fiscal discipline during 1992/93 succeeded in bringing inflation down to single figures and establishing macroeconomic stability. This facilitated both a significant increase in the size of the Development Budget from 1993/94 and a closer relationship between Approved Estimates and outturns.

As significant as the size of the Development Budget were the changes in its composition. The share of Part B in the total approved Development Budget fell steadily from USD19.5 million in 1990/91 to USD16.1 million in 1994/95 in nominal terms, or from 49.2 per cent to 21.5 per cent. The corresponding increase in Part A from USD20.1 million (50.8 per cent) to USD58.5 million (78.5 per cent) indicates a substantial increase in the proportion of the Development Budget representing planned expenditure. The essential difference between Parts A and B was that the former covered genuine projects which had passed through some screening/appraisal process and for which there were multi-year expenditure forecasts, while Part B was a set of *ad hoc*, (usually) one year expenditures which just did not fit in the Recurrent Budget.

Ceteris paribus, one would expect a relative increase in Part A expenditure to indicate an improvement in the quality of expenditure for two reasons. First, Plan/Part A expenditures were more closely scrutinized. Second, they comprised mainly counterpart funding and therefore had substantial multiplier effects because they triggered much larger donor disbursements. The distinction between Parts A and B was dropped from 1995/96.

Trends in counterpart funding are measured by the Section 2 row of Table 6.1. This shows that counterpart funding increased substantially between 1990/91 and 1994/95. The Approved Estimates for Section 2 in 1994/95 were over four times (in US Dollar terms) those of 1990/91, or over three times actual 1990/91 expenditure. Not only did the size of the Development Budget as a whole increase from USD39.6 million in 1990/91 to USD74.6 million in 1994/95, but also Section 2 increased at the expense of Section 1. The Section 1 share dropped from 71.5 per cent to 33.8 per cent over the period.

The drop in the shares of Part B and Section 1 is less pronounced if we look at actual expenditures, instead of Approved Estimates. The share of Part B in actual expenditure dropped from 46.5 per cent in 1990/91 to 34.9 per cent in 1993/94, while Section 1 went from 71.1 per cent to 44.6 per cent over the same period. Actual Part B expenditure in 1993/94 was USD18.0 million, well above the USD11.3 million approved figure. Substantial 'Supplementary' (unbudgeted) expenditures were authorized during the course of the financial year, a problem that persists to this day.

APPENDIX 6.2

Example of Format for Project Financial Estimates in RDP/PIP and Development Budget

Budget Head: 108—Finance and Economic Planning

Project Code: HI10(A)—108/PCAR/91

Project Name: South West Integrated Health and Water

	1993/94 Budget		1994/95 Budget			1995/96 Planned			1996/97 Planned			Plan Total		
	Donor	Local	Donor	Local	Total	Donor	Local	Total	Donor	Local	Total	Donor	Local	Total
	USD (m)	UGX (bn)	USD (m)	UGX (bn)	UGX (bn)	USD (m)	UGX (bn)	UGX (bn)	USD (m)	UGX (bn)	UGX (bn)	USD (m)	UGX (bn)	UGX (bn)
Expenditure														
100—Fixed Assets														
Construction and Building	2.381					1.310		1.310				1.310		1.310
Machinery and Equipment														
Roads														
Transport Vehicles														
Trucks	0.220					0.712		0.712				0.712		0.712
Cars/Pickups														
Other Vehicles	0.020		0.173		0.173							0.173		0.173
Other Fixed Assets		0.051	1.585		1.585							1.585		1.585
200—Payments to Personnel														
Long Term Experts	0.883		0.586		0.586	0.905		0.905				1.491		1.491
Consultants			0.075		0.075	0.163		0.163				0.238		0.238
Local Salaries and Wages	0.125	0.031	0.246	0.028	0.274	0.056	0.028	0.084				0.302	0.056	0.358
Incentives and Allowances	0.417	0.287	0.390	0.261	0.651	0.430	0.280	0.710				0.820	0.541	1.361
300—Non-Wage Goods and Services														
Training	0.359		0.301		0.301	0.874		0.874				1.175		1.175

(Continued)

(Continued)

		1993/94 Budget		1994/95 Budget			1995/96 Planned			1996/97 Planned			Plan Total		
		Donor	Local	Donor	Local	Total	Donor	Local	Total	Donor	Local	Total	Donor	Local	Total
		USD (m)	UGX (bn)	USD (m)	UGX (bn)	UGX (bn)	USD (m)	UGX (bn)	UGX (bn)	USD (m)	UGX (bn)	UGX (bn)	USD (m)	UGX (bn)	UGX (bn)
Vehicle O and M		0.316	0.072	0.527	0.069	0.596	0.648	0.113	0.761				1.175	0.182	1.357
Consumables		0.051		0.195	0.046	0.241	0.500		0.500				0.695	0.046	0.741
Utilities			0.005	0.034	0.022	0.056							0.034	0.022	0.056
Property Costs				0.069	0.025	0.094							0.069	0.025	0.094
Other Goods and Services		0.394	0.017	0.110	0.019	0.130	0.131	0.025	0.156				0.241	0.044	0.285
TOTAL EXPENDITURE		5.166	0.462	4.291	0.471	4.762	5.729	0.446	6.175				10.020	0.917	10.937
Funds Secured															
UNICEF	Plan	5.166		4.291		4.291	5.729		5.729				10.020		10.020
	Actual	4.855													
GoU	Plan		0.462		0.471	0.471								0.471	0.471
	Actual		0.462												
TOTAL SECURED FUNDS	Plan	5.166	0.462	4.291	0.471	4.762	5.729		5.729				10.020	0.471	10.491
	Actual	4.855	0.462												
FUNDING GAP								0.446	0.446					0.446	0.446

Source: Ministry of Finance and Economic Planning, Public Investment Plan 1994/95–1997/98.

7

The Poverty Eradication Action Plan

Kenneth Mugambe[1]

1. Introduction

By the mid 1990s the return of peace and the reforms that are the subject of this volume had brought Uganda nearly a decade of continuous rapid economic growth. Despite evident economic progress, it appeared that the benefits of the reforms were bypassing the poor. There were increasing calls for the government to pay greater attention to poverty eradication. Despite the improvements to the planning process described in Chapter 6, there were concerns that public expenditure was poorly allocated.

The calls to address poverty provided the impetus for a second wave of planning and budgetary reforms led by the Ministry of Finance, Planning and Economic Development (MoFPED). At the apex was the development of the Poverty Eradication Action Plan (PEAP), which is the subject of this chapter. The PEAP built on the improvements in the planning system and evolved alongside parallel, but complementary, reforms such as the Medium Term Expenditure Framework (MTEF), sector wide approaches (SWAps), and fiscal decentralization (see Chapters 8, 9, and 14 respectively).

This chapter charts the evolution of the PEAP. It starts with the political demands to address poverty, the process that led to the development of the first PEAP in 1997, and initial efforts to ensure its implementation. It then examines subsequent iterations of the PEAP, including how the process became increasingly consultative; how it served as the first Poverty Reduction Strategy Paper; how it became a guide for sector planning and budgeting; and how it set out the principles for the relationship between the government and donors. The chapter concludes by examining the role the PEAP has played in spearheading reforms and the challenges that emerged, including the arrangements for preparing the successor National Development Plan.

---

[1] Helpful comments from Tim Lamont are gratefully acknowledged.

2. The 1997 Poverty Eradication Action Plan

The economic reform programme had visibly begun to pay off by the mid 1990s, with a decade of unprecedented economic growth. Yet it was widely perceived that the strong performance of the economy had failed to improve the economic situation of the poor. The 1994 Constituent Assembly elections and the 1996 Presidential and Parliamentary elections provided a platform for these frustrations to be vented (Ssewakiryanga 2005). In the course of the election campaigns it became evident from interaction with the electorate that there was need for the government to do more to tackle poverty. The government's initial response tended to be *ad hoc*. For example, in 1995 it set aside substantial sums for the *Entandikwa* programme—a micro-credit scheme meant to help the poor access cheap credit. Though well intentioned, the programme was poorly administered. The disbursement of loans was politicized and subsequently recovery of loans became difficult because they were widely perceived as political handouts (Goodwin-Groen et al. 2004).

In parallel, pressure was also emerging from the international community to address poverty more comprehensively. At the Consultative Group meeting between government and donors in Paris in 1995, donors raised concerns about poverty in Uganda. The United Nations and some bilateral donors openly criticized the World Bank's 'trickle down' development strategy for Uganda based on structural adjustment reforms, and called for bolder, novel approaches to tackling poverty.

A national conference on poverty eradication was organized by the then Ministry of Planning in late 1995 to discuss the findings of the World Bank Country Economic Memorandum 'The Challenge of Growth and Poverty Reduction'. The conference was addressed by President Museveni and was attended by senior government officials, parliamentarians, donors, the private sector, non-government organizations (NGOs), academics, and the general public. It discussed several issues related to poverty and noted that strong macroeconomic policies were necessary but not sufficient to eradicate poverty. A National Task Force on Poverty Eradication was formed to develop an action plan to address poverty. This marked the beginning of a long collaboration between government and its development partners, particularly donors and civil society, in tackling poverty reduction.

The Task Force carried out wide consultations with stakeholders, principally government officials, Members of Parliament, local government officials, employers' and workers' organizations, donors, NGOs, social researchers, academics, and civil society organizations (CSOs). The Task Force formed seven thematic groups, with representation from government, civil society, and donors, to analyse themes such as economic growth, social services, agriculture, and cross-cutting issues. Seminars, meetings, and retreats were organized to discuss sector issues. In these meetings, government was often hard-pressed to defend its policies. The consultative process enjoyed extensive outreach in terms of regional and district coverage. A team of local and international experts, who both organized the process and drafted the documentation, supported the Task Force. The initial involvement of stakeholders from civil society and the private sector was somewhat limited because the number of such organizations was much smaller than it is today and they often lacked the expertise and interest necessary for meaningful participation.

The Task Force's first outputs were a background paper and an inventory of policies and initiatives on poverty reduction. These were translated into a strategy that was published in the annual government publication 'Background to the Budget' in June 1996. The consultants supporting the Task Force then began drafting the first PEAP. Groups were set up to prepare sector action plans, setting out strategies for government, donors, NGOs, and communities, and recommending changes to public expenditure. These appeared as PEAP annexes in the form of detailed matrices showing objectives, constraints, priority actions, monitoring indicators, and timing/responsibilities for all the critical sectors in the PEAP.

The first draft PEAP was produced in early 1997. It was discussed at regional and national workshops, and received feedback from the Consultative Group meeting with donors. While participation was relatively broad, verification of PEAP priorities by the poor was shallow, with only two consultations. The draft was subject to a lot of criticism, and was subsequently revised extensively. Cabinet finally approved the PEAP later that year.

In terms of content, the PEAP represented a significant step forward from previous initiatives. It provided a comprehensive strategy covering all the major areas of public and private activity. It had three 'pillars': increasing the incomes of the poor, increasing the quality of life of the poor, and strengthening good governance (see Box 7.1). These were underpinned by a foundation of continued macroeconomic stability. Within these broad pillars, five areas of service delivery were given priority: free universal primary education (UPE, a central part of President Museveni's 1996 election manifesto), primary health care, rural feeder roads, provision of safe water and sanitation, and the modernization of agriculture.

The launch of the PEAP as the national planning framework in 1997 marked a new chapter in economic policy and sector priorities. It built on the reforms to the planning framework and macroeconomic management of the early 1990s. The PEAP replaced Volume 1 of the Public Investment Plan (PIP), which had previously just summarized macroeconomic and sector policies. To implement the strategies for eradicating poverty set out in the PEAP, resources had to be allocated or reallocated from non-priority areas to priority areas. As a result, Volume 2—the project list—of the PIP (see Chapter 6) had to be revisited to bring it into harmony with the poverty focus of the PEAP; thereafter the PIP was labelled Volume 2 of the PEAP. Projects in the PIP were reviewed and categorized

---

Box 7.1 THE MAIN FEATURES OF THE 1997 PEAP

Increasing the incomes of the poor through the provision of roads (so that farm produce can reach markets), improved land laws (to guarantee security of tenure), support for the modernization of agriculture (to improve total factor productivity on the farm), improved rural market infrastructure; strengthening rural credit and financial services; telecommunications and rural electrification (to facilitate development of rural agro-processing and other non-farm employment in rural areas). The key objective here was to provide the necessary infrastructure and an enabling environment, as well as to facilitate private and community efforts in promoting the income generation activities of the poor.

Improving the quality of life for the poor through increased provision of primary health care, water and sanitation, and primary education, as well as preserving the environment. These essential services primarily met the basic needs of the poor. They also helped build human capital, thus enhancing the income earning potential of the poor.

Strengthening good governance through improved security, decentralization, transparency, accountability, and popular participation. Improved security is a fundamental precondition for all forms of progress. Institutional arrangements are of vital importance, such as a clear delineation of the role of the state vis-à-vis the private sector and civil society, the role of central agencies vis-à-vis district administrations, and the efficiency and integrity with which the public sector carries out its functions.

These pillars stood on a foundation of continued macroeconomic stability. A sound macro economic environment was required to build confidence, to lengthen the planning horizons of economic agents, to motivate people to save and invest, and thereby to promote economic growth.

Source: Ministry of Finance, Planning and Economic Development (1997)

---

on the basis of their expected impact on poverty reduction. The first category comprised on-going projects, which had a direct impact on poverty. These were to enjoy preference in terms of budgetary resources. Some projects outside the PIP list that were deemed more poverty focused were added to the relevant sector investment programmes. The second category comprised projects of national priority, even if they did not directly target poverty. These included projects to do with the enabling environment, sustainable development, good governance and accountability. The third category comprised projects approved by the MoFPED Development Committee but which had no funding.

   This exercise was an attempt to provide a priority ranking of public investment activities. Inevitably, some projects were downgraded. This was no easy task as projects often had strong backing from line ministries, politicians, or donors. The fact that the exercise was seen through to fruition underlines the government's commitment to PEAP implementation. However, the PIP continued to be dominated by donor projects, and the influence of the review was arguably limited to prioritizing which projects should have the first call on budgetary resources for counterpart funding.

Ultimately, the PEAP needed additional resources to be implemented—not just for public investment, but also for wages and operational costs of primary education, primary health care, agricultural extension, etc. Fortunately, the increasing domestic and international focus on poverty eradication, the advent of debt relief, and the shift towards programme aid meant that increased government and donor resources were becoming available to finance the PEAP. The introduction of the MTEF in 1997/98 as an integral part of the planning and budgeting system provided an opportunity to realign resources towards PEAP priorities. Major shifts in resource allocations followed Uganda's qualification for HIPC (see Chapter 12) and the formation of the Poverty Action Fund (PAF, see Chapter 13). The government committed itself to channelling debt relief and additional budget support as additional resources to the five priority areas in the PEAP. Within three years of the launching of the PEAP, resource allocations to those basic services had nearly tripled in real terms, rising from 17 per cent to 37 per cent of the rapidly increasing government budget (Williamson and Canagarajah 2003).

The 1997 PEAP also focused the attention of policy making and strategy formulation at the sector level on poverty eradication. Sectors were widely involved in the PEAP formulation process and the development of sector action plans helped generate ownership of the PEAP. The importance attached by MoFPED to the PEAP priorities in the budget process via the PAF added credibility to the poverty eradication agenda. A requirement for a sector to benefit from the PAF (whose programmes were all receiving rapidly increasing resources) was that they were prioritized in the PEAP and that they provided services directly to the poor. The profile of the PEAP steadily increased; it was clearly the apex of Uganda's national planning framework.

3. First revision of the PEAP

The three-year period following the adoption of the first PEAP was one of rapid reform in a number of areas. To ensure its continued relevance, in 1999 an exercise was initiated to revise the PEAP. This was an opportunity to review and learn from the challenges of implementation of the first PEAP. It also enabled the inclusion of new and existing policies, which were subsequently deemed priorities for poverty reduction.

The revision process involved much deeper consultation than during the first PEAP:

- Sector Working Groups (see Chapter 9), which were now well established as part of the budget process, were charged with preparing position papers for the PEAP. By the time of the revision, many sectors had developed sector strategies and SWAp processes were maturing—notably in roads, health, education, water, and agriculture. It was important that the revised PEAP drew from and built upon the policies and strategies that had been developed at the sector level.

- Regional PEAP workshops were held for local governments to canvas opinion. By the time of the PEAP revision local governments had seen their resources expanded and districts were now implementing UPE, maintaining rural roads, delivering basic health care, and recruiting agricultural extension workers.

- Involvement of CSOs and the private sector increased noticeably. Many CSOs had developed advocacy skills and broadened their focus beyond policy dialogue to service delivery. Twelve workshops covering forty-two districts (75 per cent of all districts) were conducted by CSOs (Isooba 2005).

The revision process was again supported by local and international expertise. Importantly, there was a high degree of continuity in both the Ugandan and international personnel from the previous PEAP, which helped deepen the process.

One of the most influential exercises feeding into the PEAP revision was consultation with the poor themselves through the Uganda Participatory Poverty Assessment process (PPA, see Chapter 10), which commenced in 1998. The PPA process vitally brought the views of the poor into the policy planning process (Isooba 2005). It affirmed that most priorities of the 1997 PEAP were still valid, while giving important new insights into the priorities of the poor. A key finding was the importance of security as a prerequisite for poverty eradication. The PPAs also observed that water and sanitation was a far higher priority to the poor than was reflected in budget allocations. These findings had a major influence on the content of the revised PEAP and future budget allocations.

This leads to another feature of the revision process—the use of information on poverty in the revision of the PEAP. The 1999 Poverty Status Report was particularly influential. The Report drew from three main types and sources of data. The first source was the Uganda Bureau of Statistics surveys, particularly the Demographic and Health and Household Surveys, which allowed the monitoring of national progress against many poverty indicators. The second was the management information systems in sector ministries developed in the context of Sector Wide Approaches (see Chapter 9). The third source was the PPAs. The Poverty Status Report provided a sound body of evidence for the revision of the PEAP. Crucially, MoFPED leadership was willing to use the analysis and information in the Poverty Status Report in their decision making.

A key feature of the 2000 PEAP was the introduction of security as a major component, following its identification as a major issue by the poor during the PPA process. There was also a greater emphasis on economic growth. Overall, the 2000 PEAP included a broader spectrum of government programmes and services, building on the sector strategies that had been developed since the 1997 PEAP. For example, it embraced strategies from the Plan for Modernization of Agriculture (Ministry of Finance, Planning and Economic Development 2000a), which ranged from land reform to agricultural advisory services.

The strategies in the 2000 PEAP were better supported by analysis and evidence than the original PEAP. A review of the causes of poverty drew from the 1999 Poverty Status Report. There was also an increased focus on results, with the specification of sector output targets. In addition, the 2000 PEAP laid out the framework for monitoring poverty, which would later be elaborated in the 2002 Poverty Monitoring and Evaluation Strategy (PMES, see Chapter 10). This included both the priority indicators to be monitored and the institutional arrangements and instruments.

A preliminary cost of implementing the PEAP was also presented, drawing from costing exercises that had taken place at the sector level. The projected costs were compared against the likely availability of resources. The exercise

---

Box 7.2 THE MAIN ELEMENTS OF THE 2000 PEAP

Goal 1: Rapid and sustainable economic growth and structural transformation

- Poverty cannot decline unless the economy as a whole grows; and
- Economic growth requires structural transformation in the context of economic openness: agriculture must modernize and competitive modern manufacturing and services must develop.

Goal 2: Good governance and security

- Security, accountability, transparency of public actions, respect for human rights, and zero tolerance for corruption are both dimensions of, and conditions for, poverty eradication.

Goal 3: Increased ability of the poor to raise their incomes

- Maximizing economic growth requires the participation of the poor, who in turn require access to services and information to develop skills and increase the returns to their assets;
- Poor people get their incomes mainly from self-employment or wage employment. So another way of describing this goal is as the promotion of employment; and
- This goal includes provision for the livelihoods of those who are disadvantaged, including orphans, internally displaced people, etc.

Goal 4: Enhanced quality of life of the poor

- Health, education, and housing are basic requirements of a full life in the modern world;
- Achieving these goals requires tackling the cross-cutting issues of AIDS and large family size; and
- Achieving these goals requires improved service delivery and public information.

Source: Ministry of Finance, Planning and Economic Development (2000)

showed that there was a significant, but bridgeable, gap between projected costs and available resources. An increase of 60 per cent in budget allocations over and above 2000/01 levels would be required.

Another important and influential element of the 2000 PEAP was a set of 'partnership principles' (see Box 7.3)—commitments that government and donors would make regarding the implementation of the PEAP. These built on principles identified at a conference 'Making Partnership Work on the Ground' held in Stockholm in 1999, attended by the governments of Uganda, Tanzania, and Vietnam, the Nordic donors, and the World Bank.

Box 7.3 THE 2000 PEAP PARTNERSHIP PRINCIPLES

Shared commitments: **Donor support will only be sought/provided for programmes that are in the Poverty Eradication Action Plan.**

In addition government will:	*In addition donors will:*
1. Continue with increased focus on poverty eradication (at minimum PAF funded programmes as a share of total budget will remain constant);	1. Jointly undertake all analytical work, appraisals and reviews;
2. Continue with increased tax revenue effort;	2. Jointly set output/outcome indicators;
3. Assume full leadership in donor co-ordination process (at central, sectoral, and district levels);	3. Develop uniform disbursement rules;
	4. Develop uniform and stronger accountability rules;
4. Decline any offers of stand-alone donor projects;	5. Ensure all support is fully integrated into sector wide programmes and is fully consistent with each sector programme's priorities;
5. Strengthen monitoring and accountability (including value for money evaluations);	6. Continue to increase the level of untied sector budget support;
6. Continue to improve transparency and combat corruption;	7. Increase the level of delegation to country offices;
7. Continue to strengthen district capacity;	8. Abolish topping up of individual project staff salaries;
8. Develop comprehensive, costed, and prioritized sector wide programmes eventually covering the whole budget;	9. End individual, parallel country programmes, and stand-alone projects; and
9. Further develop participation and coordination of all stakeholders (including MPs); and	10. Progressively reduce tying of procurement.
10. Strengthen capacity to coordinate across government (so that it speaks with one voice).	

Source: Ministry of Finance, Planning and Economic Development (2000)

The Stockholm conference was held in the context of broader reforms to the architecture of international aid, over which the PEAP had significant influence. For example, the World Bank had launched its Comprehensive Development Framework (CDF) in the same year, which would guide relations between the Bank, other donors, and recipient countries. The CDF laid particular emphasis on poverty reduction as a goal of international aid and espoused the principles of countries developing a long-term vision, country 'ownership', country led partnerships, and a results focus. The PEAP was seen as a vehicle for implementation of CDF principles when the Framework was adopted by the World Bank in 1999, because it embodied one of the key CDF principles—country ownership (Tumusiime-Mutebile 1999). The 2000 revision process, which started in 1999, was therefore a central test case for the new CDF paradigm.

In addition, under the Enhanced HIPC Initiative (see Chapter 12) the World Bank and IMF made the preparation of a Poverty Reduction Strategy Paper (PRSP) a requirement for accessing debt relief. The original PEAP was again influential in developing the PRSP concept. In early 2000 discussions took place between MoFPED and the World Bank and IMF on whether the 2000 PEAP met the requirements for a PRSP; for some reason, the World Bank and IMF were unwilling to accept the PEAP. It was agreed to prepare a 60-page summary of the (nearly 300-page) PEAP. This summary became the first full PRSP approved by the World Bank and IMF. In the lead up to qualification for the Enhanced HIPC Initiative the government committed to channelling the savings from the initiative to PEAP priorities via the PAF. It was announced that a major share of the savings from debt relief would be allocated to water and sanitation, as the sector was identified as a key priority of the poor during UPPAP.

At around the same time the World Bank was discussing how to provide programme aid to Uganda in a post structural adjustment setting. With the revised PEAP, Uganda was seen within the World Bank as the best setting in which to develop a new lending instrument to support the new CDF paradigm. The instrument proposed by the World Bank in the lead up to the 2001/02 Budget was initially called a Public Expenditure Reform Credit. However, given the parallel HIPC PRSP agenda and that implementation of the PEAP was at the heart of the discussions on this new instrument, the term Poverty Reduction Support Credit (PRSC) was adopted. The pillars of the PEAP provided the structure of the 'PRSC matrix', which was used for monitoring the implementation of 'prior actions', which the government proposed and committed to undertake as conditions for PRSC funding. So in 2000 Uganda became the first country to develop a PRSP and to benefit from a PRSC, both of which are now standard instruments across the developing world.

The Partnership Principles were elaborated upon in a separate document, PEAP Volume 3 entitled 'Building partnerships to implement the PEAP', in 2001. These stated that general budget support was government's preferred instrument for supporting the implementation of the PEAP, followed by PAF budget support, sector budget support, and then project support. The principles also built on the early experience of SWAps (see Chapter 9). In 2003 MoFPED refined the Partnership Principles further. Many of the principles were subsequently embodied in the 2005 Paris Declaration on Aid Effectiveness, in particular those relating to ownership, alignment, and harmonization (OECD 2005).

Between 2000 and 2003 the key PEAP implementation mechanisms of the MTEF, PAF, and SWAps matured. A 2002 review of the PAF advocated a move towards more comprehensive mechanisms for allocating funding and monitoring the budget, in line with the broader focus of the 2000 PEAP (Ndungu and Williamson 2002). By 2003 the rate of increase in budget allocations had slowed significantly. As a result, there was no longer room to mobilize significant additional resources to implement new PEAP priorities. This resulted in some disillusionment in sectors that had only recently developed sector strategies, such as justice, law and order.

4. Second revision of the PEAP

A second revision of the PEAP was undertaken in 2003. Again the process involved consultation with a wide range of stakeholders from the public sector, local government, civil society, and the private sector (Canagarajah and van Diesen 2006). With wide consultation came the need to define the process and keep it focused. So MoFPED (2003) issued a PEAP Revision Guide that set out clear parameters for the consultative process. It was important to continue with wide stakeholder participation beyond the consultative stage and into the prioritization and drafting processes, so as to avoid disillusionment and the inference that the consultation was for its own sake (Canagarajah and van Diesen 2006).

By the 2003 revision the level of organization in civil society and the private sector was much improved. Their consultations and input were modelled on the same framework as that of the sector working groups. There were at least fourteen civil society sector groups covering themes such as water, HIV and AIDS, natural resources, accountability, and the enabling framework for the private sector. Each group prepared a report covering the issues they felt should be incorporated in the PEAP. The NGO Forum and the Private Sector Foundation provided coordination. The technical assistance from the previous PEAPs was engaged again for the revision process.

The second PEAP revision benefited from the availability of richer information on poverty, from sources such as the Demographic and Health and Household Surveys, the Poverty Status Reports, and PPA. These instruments were also becoming institutionalized. However, the information they contained was not always positive. A major challenge for the second revision was that, while poverty had fallen dramatically during the 1990s, household surveys indicated that the proportion of people below the poverty line increased from 34 per cent to 38 per cent between 2000 and 2003 (see Chapter 10). This was compounded by a marked increase in inequality, with the Gini coefficient rising from 0.35 in 1997 to 0.43 in 2003. The revision process had to look into the causes of this deterioration and ensure that policy strategies were more evidence based.

The PEAP 2004 put greater emphasis on the economic functions of government, as well as security and governance issues, in order to tackle the challenges of increasing poverty and inequality. The number of PEAP pillars was expanded from four to five. The PEAP 2004 adopted a more deliberate focus on linking public expenditure to PEAP priorities. A specific chapter was created for this purpose. While the previous PEAPs prioritized social spending, the PEAP 2004 proposed more of a balance between social spending and spending on productive sectors. Despite this, arguably the third iteration of the PEAP had the least impact on budget allocations, largely because there was limited room in the budget to shift resources towards more economically productive sectors, because the budget was increasing less rapidly.

Box 7.4 THE MAIN ELEMENTS OF THE 2004 PEAP

The PEAP is premised on the understanding that while economic growth is necessary for poverty reduction and eventual eradication, there are many other factors that need to be addressed. The 2004 PEAP is anchored on five thematic pillars:

Economic Management: Continued prudent economic management is critical for sustainable growth. Inflation control and private sector development are vital levers. Subsequently, keeping the budget deficit and government borrowing under control while: improving the investment climate; commercializing agriculture; enhancing access to finance by rural communities; and developing small and medium enterprises are priority actions under this pillar. Emphasis is also placed on the quality of public expenditure. Other priorities include deepening of the financial sector and increasing the savings rate.

Enhancing Production, Competitiveness, and Incomes: The focus here is on improving rural incomes through increasing agricultural production and productivity and through the activities of micro and small enterprises. Agricultural extension services, livestock disease control, and rural access to financial services are priority action areas. To address competitiveness, the expansion of the capacities of local firms to innovate and adapt modern technologies is emphasized, along with scientific research. Infrastructural improvements in transport and energy are also emphasized.

Security, Conflict Resolution, and Disaster Management: Security is essential for the poor to share in the benefits of economic growth. Measures to address insecurity, conflict, and natural disaster related concerns include improving the capacity of security forces to deal with insurgency and exploring peaceful means to conflict resolution through CSOs, faith-based organizations, traditional leaders, and diplomatic efforts.

Good governance: Three facets of good governance are emphasized—democratization, justice, law and order, and public sector management.

Human development: The focus here is on primary and secondary education, health care, and water and sanitation.

The 2004 PEAP also incorporated a greater focus on results. A comprehensive policy and results matrix was prepared to enhance the PEAP's results focus and to facilitate monitoring and evaluation. Monitoring of PEAP implementation plus coordination of general budget support through the PRSC dialogue was moved to the Office of the Prime Minister (OPM). The rationale for this was that, as the Prime Minister was the leader of government business, he should also be responsible for the coordination and monitoring of the implementation of government policies.

Meanwhile, OPM had been developing a comprehensive National Integrated Monitoring and Evaluation Strategy (NIMES). It was agreed that NIMES, which built on the PMES, should be the vehicle for monitoring PEAP implementation. A key initiative under NIMES was the Annual PEAP Implementation Review (APIR). The purpose was to assess regularly whether PEAP implementation was on track and take corrective action if necessary. It was also intended to build linkages and synergy between implementers across sectors (OPM 2006). An underlying motivation was a requirement by donors that government produce Annual Performance Reports on PRSP implementation. The first APIR was held in 2006. Although led by OPM, consultants conducted the bulk of the work. There was little ownership of the findings amongst sector institutions, the key implementers of the PEAP. Moreover, the final report was only produced in October 2007, a year after the review. Therefore, it was neither well oriented towards national decision making, nor accountability of PEAP implementers. Nevertheless, a number of lessons emerged from the process, and future APIRs are expected to be far lighter-touch—drawing from budget and sector performance reports.

5. From the PEAP to the National Development Plan

There have been two further and significant developments since the third version of the PEAP was published in 2004. First, the PEAP is to be succeeded by the National Development Plan (NDP). The change of name reflects the change of political emphasis from poverty eradication to wealth creation during the 2006 election campaign. This change of emphasis is understandable given that the poverty eradication banner was over a decade old. It was an important step in ensuring that the political relevance and ownership of the national policy and planning framework was maintained.

Second, institutional responsibility for preparation of the NDP was assigned to the newly formed National Planning Authority (NPA) in 2007. During the constitutional review process in the early 1990s, parliamentarians had argued that there was a need to have a separate body responsible for long term planning, even in the context of the newly merged MoFPED. The NPA was duly provided for under Article 125 of the Constitution, and pressure continued for its formation, even after the first PEAP was prepared by MoFPED. However, little progress was made towards its establishment during the 1990s. This was partly due to the reluctance of the MoFPED leadership to split the planning and budgeting functions once more, especially given how critical the 1992 merger of the finance and planning ministries had been to the success of economic reform in general and the PEAP in particular. However, following pressure from Parliament, the National Planning Authority Act was passed in 2002, and the Authority became operational at the time the 2004 PEAP was being finalized. Since the Authority's primary function under the Act is to produce comprehensive and integrated development plans for the long and medium term, it was logical that it be made responsible for the preparation of the NDP.

The need for collaboration between NPA, OPM, and MoFPED in the preparation of the NDP is widely recognized. However, responsibilities are now much more fragmented than before. Ensuring coherence between the plan, budget allocations, and monitoring of policy implementation will almost certainly become much more challenging.

6. Lessons, challenges, and future prospects

The PEAP has impacted on economic management and on government generally in a number of ways, including:

- Raising the profile of poverty in policy making at the sector level and beyond;
- Facilitating the mobilization of additional resources for poverty reduction;
- A reorientation and huge expansion of budget allocations towards poverty reduction priorities;
- Improving accountability for the achievement of public sector (policy) outcomes; and
- Broadening ownership of the development agenda through consultation.

The process of design, implementation, and review of the PEAP has valuable lessons for planning in Uganda and for the role of PRSPs in other countries. The fact that the PEAP was an indigenous, domestically formulated, and driven process from the outset was critical to its success as a poverty reduction strategy. The 'bottom-up' and consultative manner through which successive iterations of the PEAP were prepared and reviewed helped ensure that proposed solutions were practical and addressed the peculiarities of the Ugandan situation. This helped keep the PEAP effective and relevant to the goal of poverty reduction. Where, on the other hand, a PRSP is adopted primarily in order to gain access to debt relief or an IMF or World Bank programme it is unlikely to have nearly as much domestic impact.

The use of a sequential, incremental, and decentralized approach to policy formulation helped build ownership and momentum, and contribute towards the success of the programme. The PEAP built on the planning and budgeting reforms of the early 1990s. The MTEF and the processes for sector planning and expenditure prioritization were developed alongside the first PEAP. Sector working groups were charged with development of sector strategies and the sector elements of the PEAP. Successive iterations of the PEAP built on existing sector strategies, policies, and processes and guided the development of future ones. The PEAP required that policy and expenditure priorities were to be informed by a broad sectoral outlook, with inputs from a range of sector stakeholders. The problems with the centralized approach to the 2006 APIR underline the importance of delegation of policy processes to the sector level and the promotion of accountability at that level.

A key success factor was that the PEAP directly influenced the allocation of public resources through the budget towards basic service delivery, via the PAF. As noted earlier, there was a substantial increase in the share of the budget allocated to PAF programmes between 1997 and 2001. This share was maintained subsequently and total allocations to PAF programmes more than quadrupled in real terms between 1997 and 2005 (see Table 9.1). The majority of these allocations were made to local governments, as they were responsible for the delivery of basic services. This accelerated and shaped the decentralization process (see Chapter 14).

These increases, in turn, changed the behaviour of government institutions. The rapid increases to budget allocations for PAF programmes meant that government institutions sat up and took notice of the PEAP, as well as the budget process. This added credibility to subsequent PEAP processes. The coincidence of interests of the political leadership, MoFPED, and donors over the PEAP agenda in 1997 was a crucial factor underpinning the credibility of the Plan. However, the impact on budget allocations diminished with each iteration of the PEAP. As a result, less attention has been paid to the instrument by government institutions.

The PEAP was not a static document, but a flexible framework. Both the national budget and SWAp processes provided opportunities to periodically revisit policies and budget allocations during PEAP implementation, and to constantly improve upon them. These built-in revision mechanisms not only ensured that PEAP implementation and sector priorities remained on course, but also helped take new issues into account and keep the Plan relevant.

The principle of ensuring the widest possible participation contributed greatly to the success of the PEAP. The number and expertise of civil society and private sector actors in the PEAP process has increased considerably since formulation of the first PEAP and their input is highly valued. The decentralization policy and the PPA process helped strengthen consultation with and feedback to the grassroots. Widespread participation helped ensure that the PEAP process benefited from a diversity of viewpoints from different stakeholders and addressed the real concerns of the poor. This prevented it from becoming an academic exercise.

The anchoring of the process in sound technical analysis also contributed to its credibility and effectiveness. Considerable effort was put into building appropriate technical databases and undertaking analysis on which the strategy processes are anchored. Since 1995 poverty analysis and monitoring has been top of the agenda. The establishment of the Uganda Bureau of Statistics as an autonomous institution with a network down to the lowest levels, the institutionalization of annual Household Surveys, Service Delivery Surveys, poverty assessments, and the PMES all played a crucial role (see Chapter 10). In analysing Household Survey data since 1992, Uganda has used international expertise both to ensure credibility of the analysis and to build local capacity.

Another important lesson is that the use of monitoring and evaluation data in decision-making is more important than the formal products of monitoring processes. The real product of monitoring is not reports or facts *per se*, but a higher quality of decision making. Critically, monitoring systems need to provide a continuous flow of actionable information about the interrelationship between operational activities—especially those of government—and the reality of poverty on the ground. This in turn should help guide changes in strategy and the design of new interventions (Hauge 2001).

Challenges have emerged with successive iterations of the PEAP. In particular, in the process of becoming a comprehensive strategy for eradicating poverty the PEAP has become less clearly prioritized (Canagarajah and van Diesen 2006). At 300 pages the 2004 PEAP was undeniably a detailed and well-researched plan. However, articulating the shift in emphasis from social sectors towards the productive sectors posed challenges, given the many competing demands. Furthermore, whilst the PEAP provided a flexible framework, the level of explicit political support for the PEAP as an instrument waned over time. The need to keep plans fresh from a political perspective is important. The move towards the NDP responds to this.

Finally, the changes to the institutional framework for preparing the NDP are likely to pose new challenges as well as opportunities. The fact that the original PEAP was overseen by a unified ministry responsible for finance and planning, made it easier for PEAP priorities to be reflected in the budget. The link between the National Development Plan and the MTEF and budget will no longer be automatic. The challenge for the future will be how to build on the successes of the three PEAPs given changing institutional and political circumstances and dynamics.

8

Budget Reform and the Medium Term Expenditure Framework

Martin Brownbridge, Giulio Federico, and Florence Kuteesa

1. Introduction

The budget reforms introduced in the early 1990s were designed to enhance the credibility of the budget process and establish fiscal discipline (see Chapter 6). By the mid 1990s, with macroeconomic stability restored (see Chapter 3) and the political imperative to redirect public expenditure towards poverty eradication (see Chapter 7), the Ministry of Finance, Planning and Economic Development (MoFPED) embarked on a second wave of budget reforms. These were designed to ensure that resource allocations were consistent with political priorities, while continuing to underpin the role of fiscal policy in supporting macroeconomic stability. The reforms were wide ranging, but at their core was the gradual implementation of the Medium Term Expenditure Framework (MTEF), which was to become instrumental in implementing the Poverty Eradication Action Plan. Uganda was one of the first low-income countries to introduce an MTEF, and has made more progress in developing the concept than most other countries.

This chapter documents, and draws lessons from, the main budgetary reforms adopted in Uganda since the mid 1990s including, most notably, the implementation of the MTEF. Section 2 sets out the rationale behind, and key features of, an MTEF. Section 3 describes the consultative budget process that has come to underpin the MTEF. Section 4 discusses other budget reforms, which were introduced in parallel with the MTEF. Section 5 examines how the MTEF is formulated during the budget process, including how the projections of the budget resource envelope are made. Sections 6 and 7 provide an empirical assessment of the extent to which the MTEF facilitated a shift in sectoral allocations and contributed to enhanced credibility and predictability of the budget respectively. Section 8 examines the main challenges to budget reform, while Section 9 offers some conclusions, both for Uganda and other developing countries.

2. Evolution of the Medium Term Expenditure Framework

A Medium Term Expenditure Framework is a tool for budget planning, designed to provide a framework and incentives for budget planners to formulate medium term budget plans within a hard budget constraint[1] on the basis of prioritizing expenditures to best meet strategic policy objectives. It provides a framework for linking policy formulation with budget allocations and hence is often referred to as a tool for policy based budgeting. The key features of the MTEF which allow budget allocations to be made on the basis of strategic budget policies are threefold: first, the division of the budget into sectors; second, the medium term perspective (which allows budget priorities to be aligned with the objectives set out in medium term strategy documents); and, third, the integration of all expenditures into a single unified budget.

Uganda's MTEF was introduced gradually, starting with the preparation of an annual Budget Framework Paper in 1992/93,[2] to help consolidate the measures taken to deal with the 1992 macroeconomic and fiscal crisis (see Appendix 8.1). The intention was to strengthen fiscal discipline at the stage of budget preparation, by ensuring that budgets were planned within a medium term fiscal framework, which was consistent with macroeconomic stability. Macroeconomic stability required that government maintained strict control over its domestic borrowing requirement. Driven by this imperative, the emphasis of the MTEF was on fiscal aggregates rather than the details of expenditure. The framework comprised aggregate expenditure projections for the largest components of locally funded recurrent and development expenditure, such as wages, non-wage recurrent, defence, 'priority programme areas', and development projects, covering a three-year period.

With the establishment of macroeconomic stability and sustained economic growth, the focus of public policy shifted towards poverty reduction—encapsulated in the 1997 Poverty Eradication Action Plan (PEAP, see Chapter 7). The MTEF was the logical instrument for translating the PEAP priorities into expenditure allocations within a coherent multi-year macroeconomic and fiscal framework. During the second half of the 1990s the budget resource envelope expanded by about 5 per cent of GDP, mainly as a result of debt relief and increased budget support (see Table 13.1). Ensuring that expanded budget

---

[1] Hard budget constraints refer to situations where spending agencies (and the government as a whole) face binding limits on their expenditures. Hence they imply that over-expenditures in one area need to be matched by budget cuts in another area.

[2] The evolution of Uganda's MTEF is discussed in Bevan and Palomba (2000).

resources were effectively directed towards the strategic priorities set out in the PEAP became an increasingly important goal of fiscal policy; the MTEF took on an increasingly important role, therefore and its formulation became an integral part of the annual budget process.

In 1997/98 the MTEF was incorporated in the budget documentation. The publication of the MTEF table in the Budget Speech and the 'Background to the Budget' document reinforced the link between the planning and budgeting systems and provided an opportunity to realign resources towards PEAP priorities. The table allowed all stakeholders in the budget process to see how the government planned to allocate resources among the major sectors and programmes over the coming three years. Budget allocations were now more clearly linked to the expenditure priorities outlined in the PEAP.

2.1 Key features of the MTEF

Uganda's MTEF is prepared on a rolling three year basis. It consists of an aggregate fiscal framework which determines the overall budget resource envelope, combined with a presentation of the budget by sectors, defined according to major functional classifications (health, education, etc.). Expenditures within sectors are further classified by programmes and/or budget agencies, as well as by the major economic classifications (wage, non wage recurrent, and development). The MTEF comprises all expenditure by central government, including transfers to local governments but excluding arrears payments. The medium term aggregate budget resource envelope is divided into sector expenditure ceilings, which are intended to act as hard budget constraints for planning expenditures at the sectoral level.

The MTEF captures total expenditures disaggregated by two sources of funding: Government of Uganda (GoU) and donor funded projects. The GoU budget includes all expenditures funded from domestic revenues, domestic borrowing, and donor budget support, while donor funded projects are financed through project aid. Appendix 8.2 provides an illustration of the MTEF from the 2006/07 budget.

2.2 Rationale for the introduction of the MTEF

There were four key motivations behind the introduction of the MTEF. First, by providing a hard budget constraint, the MTEF aimed to provide incentives for budget planners to improve the allocative efficiency of scarce budget funds, while maintaining the achievements of macroeconomic stability.

Second, the categorization of the budget into sectors and programmes, and the introduction of a three year horizon for budget planning, facilitated policy-based resource allocation. As most strategic policies are formulated at the sector level, the sectoral organization of the MTEF made it easier to translate policies into budget allocations. The medium term planning horizon encouraged a shift from input or line item based annual budgeting, where it is usually only possible to make incremental changes, to a more strategic planning perspective where more significant and rational resource reallocations can be achieved over the medium term. Accordingly, spending agencies were encouraged to develop quality medium term strategic plans and realistic expenditure projections within sectors of the MTEF, in the form of Sector Budget Framework Papers. This in turn would result in better prioritization of budget resources and their alignment with strategic policy objectives.

Third, by providing a comprehensive picture of expenditure allocations across sectors within the three-year macro-fiscal framework, the MTEF promoted transparency in the budget resource allocation process. Budget allocations, including donor project aid, could be tracked against central government programmes or specific basic services delivered by local government within a particular sector. Over time, better appreciation of the hard budget constraint encouraged a decision making process that emphasized efficiency in the use of additional resources to the sector as well as mobilization of potential savings to address critical priorities.

3. The consultative budget process

The introduction of the MTEF required a lengthening of the budget process, to provide more time for strategic budget policies to be formulated and adopted before the more routine stages of the annual budget process.[3] This also enabled more meaningful participation by Parliament, sector spending agencies, and other stakeholders. Consequently, in 1998 the start of the budget preparation process was brought forward to October, eight months before the presentation of the draft budget estimates to Parliament in June.

To raise political and public support for budget policy, the budget process was made increasingly participatory. Since 1998 a national consultative budget workshop, open to the public, has been held at the start of the budget process in October to disseminate the macroeconomic and fiscal framework, present the initial sector ceilings, and initiate the consultative budget process. A Budget Framework Paper (BFP) is presented to Cabinet and Parliament by 1 April. The BFP, which is prepared by MoFPED with inputs from the sectors, sets out the fiscal framework, the expenditure priorities, and the plans of the individual sectors. The BFP enhances the understanding of budget policy by legislators and

---

[3] The annual budget process previously involved issuing the budget call circular four or five months before the end of the fiscal year, requesting submissions of estimates by ministries, departments, and agencies. Negotiations at the technical and political level were conducted three months before the Budget Statement was tabled in Parliament.

thereby contributes to their making a more effective contribution to the budget process in Parliament.

Sector Working Groups (SWGs, see Chapter 9) were formed with representation from sector spending agencies, donors, and civil society. They were charged with the preparation of Sector Budget Framework Papers, and became central to the consultative process. MoFPED decentralized some decision making over budget allocations to SWGs. This approach, from which Sector Wide Approaches (SWAps) evolved, provided a vehicle for dialogue and collaboration within sectors. SWAps provided a platform for bringing together sector ministries and stakeholders to participate in determining sector priorities and discussing intra-sectoral resource allocations under the umbrella of the MTEF. In the context of SWAps, most SWGs instituted annual or biannual sector reviews, open to stakeholders, at which performance against targets was evaluated, and sector expenditure priorities and proposed resource allocations were presented and discussed.

The budget process was divided into three major stages, as illustrated in Appendix 8.3.

1. Stage one, from October to December, started with the development and dissemination of the macroeconomic and fiscal framework plus the indicative MTEF and the convening of SWGs. SWGs then held consultations, reviewing past performance and developing medium term spending plans. This culminated in the preparation of sector budget framework papers.

2. Stage two involved budget hearings, which reviewed sector BFPs, with a view to aligning expenditure priorities with the resource allocations under the MTEF. Sector BFPs were then consolidated into the national BFP, which was submitted to Cabinet for consideration in March. Later the Budget Act 2001 required submission of the BFP to Parliament by 1 April.

3. The final stage involved the revision of the MTEF and issuance of the budget call circular in May for the preparation of draft annual budget estimates.

4. Other budget reforms

The MTEF and consultative budget process were conceived for budget planning purposes rather than budget implementation. Alongside these reforms to budget formulation and reporting, complementary reforms have focused on strengthening budget implementation, such as the commitment control system to curb expenditure arrears, and procurement reforms (World Bank 2004).

While the MTEF provided the overall framework for the budget process, it was not the only instrument employed. Other budget reforms implemented alongside the MTEF included the Poverty Action Fund, increased focus on results, adoption of the SWAp (see Chapter 9), local government planning and budgeting, and public expenditure reviews.

4.1 Poverty Action Fund (PAF)

The PAF is a virtual fund which is an integral part of the GoU budget. It comprises a set of designated expenditures, which are directly linked to poverty reducing priority programmes in the PEAP.[4] It was set up in 1997/98 as an institutional mechanism to show that HIPC debt relief would be used to fund poverty reducing expenditures. In addition to HIPC debt relief, bilateral donors also provided grants for the PAF, for the reasons discussed in Chapter 13. PAF expenditures have a somewhat privileged position within the budget in two key respects. First, up to 2002/03 there was a direct link between the external resources provided for the PAF and PAF expenditures. Second, during budget implementation, releases to PAF programmes were protected from cuts.

PAF expenditures were also subject to more intensive monitoring than other components of the budget, with 5 per cent of budgeted PAF expenditures allocated specifically for this purpose. To strengthen incentives for more efficient budget planning with a stronger focus on budget outcomes, the PAF required fully elaborated plans together with the introduction of a results-oriented work planning and reporting process for local governments effective from 1999. Disbursement of budget funds was made conditional on these requirements being fulfilled.

The PAF encouraged some donors to switch from project aid to budget support by demonstrating that poverty reducing expenditures were being prioritized in the budget (see Chapter 13). As a result, PAF resources expanded; its share of the GoU discretionary budget rose from 17 per cent to 37 per cent between 1997/98 and 2001/02 (Williamson and Canagarajah 2003), and reached almost 39 per cent in 2004/05 (MoFPED 2006).[5] The growth of PAF expenditures eventually began to impinge on the government's flexibility to allocate budget resources in an optimal manner. As a consequence, the direct link between donor resources for the PAF and PAF expenditures was replaced from 2002/03 onwards with a commitment by government to maintain a minimum share of PAF spending within the discretionary budget. This and related issues are discussed in more detail in Chapter 13.

---

[4] These include: primary education, primary health care, rural roads, agricultural extension, and safe water and sanitation.

[5] The PAF target for monitoring purposes is defined as follows: total PAF expenditure as a percentage of discretionary GoU expenditure. GoU discretionary expenditure is defined as total GoU expenditure minus interest and arrears payments. The PAF share of the budget is about three percentage points lower if the total GoU budget is used as the denominator (MoFPED 2001b).

4.2 *Output oriented budgeting*

The introduction of output oriented budgeting for the 1998/99 budget cycle brought into the budget planning process a focus on results rather than simply the provision of inputs. Output oriented budgeting supported the efforts by the Ministry of Public Service to introduce results oriented management across the public service. All sectors were required to ensure that their plans and budgets were output and outcome oriented. Outputs became the driving force for planning and budgeting, with emphasis placed on costing of interventions. The cost of achieving targeted sector outputs or expenditure priorities guided sector budget formulation, specifically decisions on resource allocations within sector expenditure ceilings.

However, reporting on the overall performance of the budget and linking this to its impact on poverty reduction was weak, which impeded the task of monitoring the impact of the MTEF. MoFPED therefore introduced a number of measures to strengthen reporting and accountability for the use of public funds. Monitoring and reporting of outputs and outcomes has begun to take centre stage in the budgeting process. There was a gradual shift from the mechanistic collection of data to the establishment of management information systems that could facilitate the monitoring and tracking of expenditures and progress towards planned results and outputs. The requirements of the PAF for stronger planning and reporting reinforced the shift in the focus of budget planning towards the achievement of results.

4.3 *Fiscal transfers to local governments (see Chapter 14)*

Uganda introduced decentralization in the mid 1990s, giving local governments the responsibility for delivering basic public services such as education, health, and rural roads. The share of the GoU budget implemented through local governments increased from 14 per cent in 1994/95 to 34 per cent in 2004/05. Decentralization was motivated by both political goals and a desire to improve efficiency and accountability in the delivery of public services. The key local government administrative units are municipalities and districts. However, while a large degree of administrative decentralization has been achieved, decentralization of responsibility for allocating expenditures has been much more circumscribed. There is an unavoidable tension between the need to ensure that the allocation of resources spent at the local government level accords with national priorities, especially poverty reduction programmes,[6] and the desire to allow local governments discretion to allocate resources according to locally determined priorities.

---

[6] More than two thirds of the PAF is spent at the local government level administered under sector specific planning, budgeting, and accounting guidelines formulated by central government.

Local governments receive budget resources mainly from two sources: trans-fers from central government and locally raised revenues.[7] The latter are relatively small and represent only about 10 per cent of local government budget resources, because all major taxes in Uganda are collected by central government. Hence budgetary transfers from central government constitute the bulk of resources available to fund spending by local governments.

Transfers are comprised of unconditional grants, which can be allocated by local governments according to their own priorities, and conditional grants which must be spent in areas specified by central government, such as primary education, primary health care, district water, and rural roads maintenance. Unconditional grants are included under the public administration sector for presentational purposes. Their allocation to each local government is determined by a formula. Conditional grants are included under the ceiling for the relevant sector and responsibility for their allocation rests with central government, through MoFPED and the relevant sector ministry. Conditional grants are the main tool used to ensure that local government expenditures accord with the national budget priorities of the MTEF. Of the UGX825 billion of expenditures on local government programmes in the 2004/05 MTEF (i.e. expenditures funded from transfers from central government), 81 per cent comprised expenditures funded from conditional grants. This left only 19 per cent for transfers, over which local governments had some degree of discretion in allocating expenditures; these transfers comprised unconditional grants, equalization grants and transfers under the Local Government Development Project. Given the limited control which local governments have in determining expenditure allocations, Uganda's local government system has been described as one of 'deconcentration rather than decentralisation' (Ahmad et al. 2006: 13).

To help local governments manage these increases in funding a medium term consultative budget process was introduced, mirroring the process at the centre. In 1998 MoFPED introduced Local Government Budget Framework Papers (LGBFPs) to foster integrated and medium term planning and budgeting within a decentralized framework. Local governments had already been made responsible for preparing three-year district development plans in the Local Government Act (1997). The LGBFPs set out three-year rolling expenditure plans guided by the indicative resource ceilings for each grant under the MTEF. The paper was an outcome of a consultative process conducted at two levels:

- Local governments were invited to the National Budget Conference, while MoFPED also led teams from central government to facilitate regional LGBFP

---

[7] Expenditures made by local governments from locally raised revenues are not included in the MTEF.

179

workshops. Both helped to build constructive dialogue between the centre and local governments on budget issues.

• At the district level the process involved review of the performance of individual sectors and specification of the outputs to be achieved over the medium term, as well as allocating resources from the various sources, including local government revenues.

The LGBFP then guided the preparation of the district's annual plan and budget. MoFPED also included issues raised by local governments in the national Budget Framework Paper.

Planning and budgeting at the district and lower levels was impeded by weak capacity in local governments. The linkage between the budget, budget framework papers, and district development plans remained very weak. Many budget submissions were prepared solely to meet administrative requirements rather than as a decision making tool for linking proposed expenditures to council priorities (World Bank 2004: 20–2). The credibility of the LGBFP was undermined by unreliable indicative grant allocations, which were often changed by sector ministries late in the budget process.

4.4 Public Expenditure Reviews

During the early 1990s a series of Public Expenditure Reviews were conducted by the World Bank which highlighted weaknesses in the efficiency of public expenditure, both between and within sectors. Most of the work was undertaken by Bank staff and consultants during short, intensive missions with relatively little involvement from government. In the late 1990s it was decided to mainstream the Reviews into the budget preparation. This was motivated by the recognition that increases in the level of public spending by themselves were not sufficient to guarantee greater access to public services if spending was inefficient. Studies were undertaken on selected strategic issues and cross-cutting issues with budget implications. They focused on areas such as value for money, procurement, operational efficiency, payroll management, deployment of human resources, and unit costs. Since the mid 1990s annual Public Expenditure Review meetings have been held, which have become an important forum for government to present its budget policies to donors and other stakeholders (see Chapter 13).

4.5 Legal implications of budget reforms

The public finance sections of the Constitution provided the necessary legal framework for the MTEF, including key clauses that give only the executive the authority to submit an expenditure appropriation to Parliament and require all government expenditures to be appropriated by Parliament. The former is essential because if Parliament could appropriate expenditures that had not been submitted to it by the executive, there would be a danger that aggregate expenditure would exceed the budget resource envelope. The latter is essential to ensure consistency between budgeted and actual expenditures. While the budget reforms did not require amendments to the Constitution or the overall legal framework, some revisions to budget related legislation and the regulatory framework did occur, in particular to buttress the consultative process and results orientation.

The 2001 Budget Act, *inter alia*, clarified the role of the legislature in the budget process and specified a schedule of budget consultations. It was introduced at the initiative of Parliament, originating as a private member's bill. Parliament was concerned that it had limited input into the budget process, which was dominated by the executive. The Act requires the executive to lay before Parliament indicative medium term estimates of revenue and expenditure two months before tabling the budget estimates in Parliament. To provide all the information demanded by the Act, the BFP was upgraded to a public document. The BFP proposals and preliminary budget estimates are presented to Cabinet by the beginning of March for consideration and approval before onward submission to Parliament by 1 April. Parliament, led by the Budget Committee, reviews the three-year macroeconomic plan and programmes for economic and social development and then submits comments to the President to take into account during the finalization of the budget estimates. The Act also established a parliamentary budget office to provide technical and advisory support to MPs in the early stages of the budget process.

The 2003 Public Finance and Accountability Act, which replaced the Public Finance Act 1964, harmonized the new budget practices, strengthened procedures for the accounting and reporting of public expenditures, and imposed a requirement for Parliamentary approval of supplementary expenditures before they can be incurred (see Chapter 15).[8] Two features were particularly important for budgeting. First, the Act explicitly required donor project funding to be part of the appropriation by Parliament, elaborating on the requirements of the Constitution. Second, it embedded results orientation into the budget process with requirements for statements of outputs alongside appropriations.

4.6 *Evaluating new policy proposals*

The PEAP had wide ranging implications for public and budget policy in such areas as the review of sector policies and investment programmes, the enactment of new laws, and the restructuring or creation of public bodies. Such

---

[8] Previously, much supplementary expenditure had been approved retrospectively by Parliament.

initiatives often imposed substantial expenditure demands, which had to be incorporated in the MTEF.

Policy proposals were frequently approved without considering the budgetary implications, undermining the predictability and integrity of the budget. In 2000, therefore, guidelines were issued on the incorporation of policy formulation into the MTEF and budget process. Henceforth, Cabinet approval of new policy proposals was subject to confirmation of their affordability over the medium term by the Finance Minister. Ministries were required to submit policy proposals or draft bills well in advance to MoFPED and the Ministry of Public Service to examine, *inter alia*, whether the resource implications could be accommodated within the applicable sector ceiling and the overall MTEF. The adoption of these procedures helped to focus policy formulation on issues of funding and affordability. The policy formulation process increasingly recognized the role of the MTEF as a budget planning tool with a hard budget constraint. This further strengthened the link between policy, planning, and budget formulation and also underscored the principle that policies, plans, and new legislation must be developed within a binding fiscal constraint.

5. Resource allocation and the Medium Term Expenditure Framework

The determination of expenditure ceilings in the MTEF follows a clear ordering implemented at three separate levels of aggregation. First, the aggregate expenditure ceiling is determined from the fiscal framework and is driven by macroeconomic objectives and projections. Although the aggregate expenditure ceiling is revised during the budget process, to take account of updated macroeconomic and fiscal projections, it is never revised simply to accommodate spending pressures which would not otherwise be able to be included within the budget. Hence at the aggregate level the macroeconomic objectives of fiscal policy are paramount and are not compromised to meet demands for higher expenditures. The second level entails the allocation of the aggregate expenditure ceiling to the various sectors and programmes in the MTEF. The third level allows the division of each sector ceiling into allocations for central government spending institutions and local government grants within each sector.

5.1 *The fiscal framework and the budget resource envelope*

Aggregate fiscal policy is formulated by the MoFPED Macroeconomic Policy Department. Projections of the budget resource envelope are generated using a financial programming methodology (termed a macro frame). The macro frame includes fiscal policy targets (such as a target for the overall fiscal deficit before grants) and three-year projections for each of the components of the budget resource envelope. The macro frame ensures that the fiscal projections and targets are consistent with a set of macroeconomic projections (GDP, inflation, the exchange rate, and the balance of payments), which are drawn up in collaboration with the Bank of Uganda. The major components of the budget resource envelope are: i) recurrent revenues; ii) budget support loans and grants; iii) external debt repayments; and iv) net domestic financing.

The fiscal framework is included in the BFP presented to Cabinet and Parliament in March. Although Cabinet could, in principle, revise the fiscal framework prepared by MoFPED to allow for higher expenditure in the MTEF, it has never done so. In effect, the determination of the fiscal framework is treated as an essentially technical exercise.

5.2 Inter-sectoral allocations and sector ceilings

Having determined the medium term budget resource envelope, MoFPED then allocates aggregate expenditure among the sectors and key programmes. The indicative allocations are then discussed with stakeholders and revised during the consultative budget process. Allocating budget resources among competing expenditure demands is an inherently more political exercise than the determination of the fiscal framework. In principle, allocations are guided by budget priorities and by whether or not sectors have prepared coherent and realistic expenditure plans that can deliver the policy objectives.

In practice, MoFPED prepares an initial allocation of sector ceilings at the start of the budget process based on a few key criteria such as the need to accommodate unavoidable expenditures and targets for specific priority expenditures, such as those covered by the PAF, many of which have been agreed with donors. During the budget process, unallocated funds are then distributed depending on where the needs are most pressing. This allows some scope for MoFPED to allocate a share of each year's increase in budgetary resources to strategic priority areas, and avoid a return to incrementalism.

However, aligning the sector ceilings with strategic national priorities is not straightforward for several reasons. First, although strategic budget priorities are set out in the PEAP, this provides no firm guidance on the quantitative allocations that each sector should receive. Moreover, the PEAP is not the only source of budget priorities, as there are strong political pressures to accommodate programmes or projects which are not prioritized in the PEAP; for example, the creation of new districts. Second, there is no transparent institutional mechanism within the process for determining the medium term inter-sectoral allocations in a way that can automatically command political consensus. Instead, allocations are determined in a somewhat *ad hoc* manner. Third, the room for inter-sectoral reallocations is highly circumscribed because a large share of the budget is effectively non discretionary (e.g. most of the wage bill, and all statutory expenditures).

5.3 *Intra-sectoral allocations*

Each of the sectors receives a three year sector ceiling at the start of the budget process. The SWG, which is usually chaired by the main line ministry in the sector, then convenes to discuss the policy priorities for the sector and prepares sector expenditure plans for discussion at sector review conferences.

In principle sectors have some scope for allocating the ceiling to their own expenditure priorities, such as those set out in sector expenditure plans. However, there are constraints on the extent to which intra-sectoral reallocations can be made. The wage bill, which comprises 30 per cent of total GoU expenditure, is effectively determined separately in the budget process, mostly without any direct reference to strategic priorities, by the Ministry of Public Service (MoPS).[9] Hence there is limited scope for sectors to shift expenditures between the wage and non-wage components of the budget. In addition, sectors have to accommodate all statutory expenditures and cannot reallocate funds away from PAF expenditure, as this would jeopardize the targets for minimum PAF expenditures agreed with donors. In addition, sectors have little control over donor project allocations, while allocations are sometimes needed for the counterpart funding of donor projects. Thus, in practice, discretion is limited. The lack of accurate data on key expenditure items also impedes the realism of expenditure plans.

While the MTEF and SWAps have undoubtedly contributed to improved budget planning at the sector level, the quality, and degree of realism, of sector expenditure plans varies considerably between and within sectors. From a budgetary perspective, SWAps have been relatively successful in sectors that are dominated by a single line ministry (such as education and health) because this reduces the scope for conflict between different spending agencies within the sector over budget resources. They have been less successful in sectors with multiple line ministries, such as public administration, justice, law and order, and the economic functions and social services sectors. This is because the more powerful ministries in these sectors can ignore the sector as a forum for discussing budget resource allocation and negotiate allocations directly with MoFPED. Moreover, in a sector with multiple line ministries and multiple objectives, it is very difficult to achieve any sort of consensus at the sector level over the optimal allocation of scarce budget resources. Consequently, sector ceilings in these sectors were rather meaningless as budget planning tools.

---

[9] MoPS must allocate the wage bill within an aggregate wage ceiling determined by MoFPED.

6. Did the MTEF facilitate a shift in sectoral allocations of the budget?

The MTEF is a strategic medium-term planning tool which should help budget planners to shift budget resources over time to the strategic spending priorities of government. Given that budget priorities were often identified in terms of priority sectors, a strategic shift in budget allocations should be reflected in changing sector shares of the budget over time. Figure 8.1 illustrates the substantial increase in public expenditure since the mid 1990s. The trends refer to total expenditure, 'discretionary' GoU expenditure (i.e. excluding donor projects and interest payments), and directly poverty-reducing expenditure (as reflected in the PAF). Real MTEF expenditure more than doubled[10] over the period 1994/95 to 2004/05. Discretionary expenditure increased even more rapidly, partly reflecting the shift of aid from project to budget support over the period, as well as debt relief.

The rapid growth of expenditure facilitated strategic shifts in the budget because it is much easier to increase the budgets of priority sectors when the overall budget envelope is expanding, as this does not require cuts in non-priority sectors. Figure 8.2 illustrates the trend in the sectoral composition of MTEF expenditures, which changed significantly towards the priority poverty

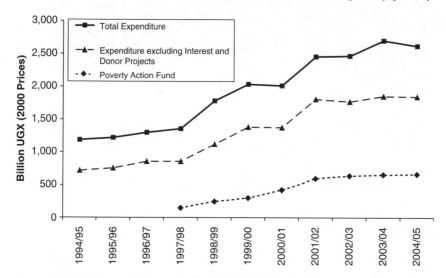

Figure 8.1 Public Expenditure under the MTEF, 1994/95–2004/05, constant prices

Source: Ministry of Finance, Planning and Economic Development, Budget Speeches and Budget Performance Reports.

[10] This is derived by deflating current expenditures by the price deflator for public consumption and development expenditure by the price deflator for investment.

reducing sectors identified in the PEAP. In 1994/95 the three largest sectors in the MTEF were public administration, defence, and education.[11] By 2004/05 education was much the largest sector with a 23 per cent share. The health sector increased its share from 7 per cent to 9 per cent over the period, while the shares of the new water and accountability sectors also increased. In contrast, the overall share of public administration fell from 25 per cent in 1997/98 to 21 per cent (including the accountability sector). The education sector's share rose from just under 20 per cent of the GoU budget in 1994/95 to 26 per cent in 1997/98, following the introduction of free Universal Primary Education in 1997. It reached 27 per cent the following year before falling back to 23 per cent as other priority sectors expanded more quickly.

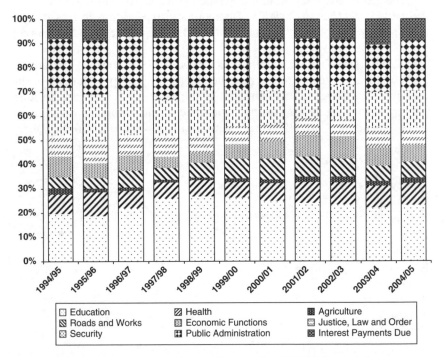

Figure 8.2 Sectoral Composition of the MTEF, 1994/95–2004/05 (Annual Outturns, Budget Releases)

Note: the Water sector is shown under Economic Functions. Accountability is shown under Public Administration.

Sources: Bevan and Palomba (2000) for 1994/95 to 1998/99; Ministry of Finance, Planning and Economic Development (Budget Performance Reports) for all other years.

[11] The Public Administration sector covers all functions related to execution of the general administration and operation of the public service provided by central line ministries, including State House, Office of the President, Office of the Prime Minister, MoPS, Ministry of Local Government, and associated public agencies.

The MTEF also demonstrates a marked shift in intra-sectoral allocations towards priority areas, most notably in the education, agriculture, and health sectors. For instance, in health the share of primary health care expenditure increased from less than one third in 1997/98 to two thirds in 2002/03 (Foster and Mijumbi 2002). In education, 60 per cent of total sector discretionary resources were earmarked for Universal Primary Education throughout the period.

7. Did the MTEF improve the predictability of the budget?

One of the main objectives of the MTEF is to provide predictable resource flows to spending agencies, to enable them to properly plan and manage their expenditures. In particular, it is important to ensure that spending agencies actually receive the resources required to implement their appropriated budgets. If spending agencies suffer cuts in their appropriated budgets during budget implementation, or are able to obtain additional resources over and above their appropriated budgets, the sector expenditure ceiling loses its credibility as an *ex ante* budget planning tool and the incentives for sectors and ministries, departments, and agencies (MDAs) to plan their budgets within their expenditure ceilings are weakened.

The predictability of budget resource flows to sectors requires, first, accurate projections of the budget resource envelope and, second, that sectoral allocations are guided by realistic expenditure projections for the priorities. This section examines how closely budget outturns, at both aggregate and sectoral levels, compared with projected resources and appropriated budgets.

7.1 Budget resource envelope: projections compared to outturns

Table 8.1 shows the projections and outturns for each of the components of the budget resource envelope for the six fiscal years from 1999/2000–2004/05. The largest component is recurrent revenue (mostly tax revenue). Apart from 1999/2000 and 2000/01, when a strong external terms-of-trade shock (falling world coffee prices and rising oil prices) caused revenues to fall short of the budgeted amounts by 9 per cent and 4 per cent respectively, the recurrent revenue outturns were quite close to the projections. Moreover, revenue projections improved over time, with the shortfalls becoming smaller. To provide a buffer against revenue shortfalls and other fiscal shocks (such as supplementary expenditures), MoFPED included a macroeconomic contingency in its fiscal framework, which was approximately 2 per cent of total budgeted expenditures.[12] Table 8.1 shows that the contingency was sufficient

---

[12] The contingency is not appropriated in the budget.

Table 8.1 Projections and Outturns of the Budget Resource Envelope and its Components, 1999/2000–2004/05, in billion UGX

	1999/2000			2000/01			2001/02		
	programme	outturn	deviation	programme	outturn	deviation	programme	outturn	deviation
Recurrent Revenue	1,109	1,010	−99	1,126	1,083	−43	1,290	1,254	−36
Budget Support	496	314	−182	686	573	−113	1,165	736	−429
External Amortization	−101	−87	14	−98	−102	−4	−102	−102	0
Net Domestic Financing	−189	59	248	−191	−129	62	−450	−35	415
Macro Contingency	26			40			32		
Resource Envelope	1,289			1,483			1,871		
GOU Expenditure	1,289	1,248	−41	1,483	1,448	−35	1,871	1,864	−7

	2002/03			2003/04			2004/05		
	programme	outturn	deviation	programme	outturn	deviation	programme	outturn	deviation
Recurrent Revenue	1,429	1,434	5	1,691	1,669	−22	1,867	1,915	48
Budget Support	818	832	14	696	871	175	689	829	140
External Amortization	−133	−104	29	−138	−129	9	−163	−159	4
Net Domestic Financing	−59	−53	6	99	−125	−224	117	57	−60
Macro Contingency	50			37			63		
Resource Envelope	2,005			2,311			2,447		
GOU Expenditure	2,005	2,034	29	2,311	2,384	73	2,446	2,540	94

The data pertains to the GoU budget (excluding externally financed projects). External amortization includes arrears repayments and exceptional financing. Budget support includes grants and loans.

Source: Ministry of Finance, Planning and Economic Development.

or almost sufficient to cover revenue shortfalls every year except for 1999/2000. It was not, however, large enough to also cover demands for supplementary expenditure.

There was much greater variance between projections and actual disbursements of budget support grants and loans, primarily because budget support disbursements were often subject to delays. Large shortfalls in budget support were incurred in the first three fiscal years of Table 8.1. Given the importance of budget support as a share of the resource envelope, this would have caused severe disruption to the budget if no alternative resources were available to bridge the shortfalls. To avoid disrupting budget implementation, the government used domestic borrowing to substitute for the shortfall in budget support, with an equivalent reduction, below programmed levels, in the Bank of Uganda's (BoU) accumulation of foreign exchange reserves to ensure that the net impact on money supply growth was neutral. In effect, the government borrowed from the foreign exchange reserves to fund the shortfall in budget support; this was only possible because BoU had built up its foreign exchange reserves in the 1990s. By the beginning of 1999/2000, BoU's foreign exchange reserves had reached almost USD750 million and exceeded five months' of imports. However, using foreign exchange reserves to fund shortfalls in budget support is only possible on a temporary basis—otherwise the reserves will eventually be depleted. Consequently, from 2002/03 MoFPED began making more conservative projections of budget support by applying a discount factor to each component, to allow for the possibility that it might not be disbursed during the fiscal year. This helped eliminate the shortfalls between budgeted amounts of budget support and actual disbursements in the final three years of Table 8.1.

As noted above, the motivation for accurate projections of the budget resource envelope and for mechanisms to provide buffers against shortfalls is to ensure that, at least at the aggregate level, sufficient resources are available to fund budgeted expenditures. Table 8.1 shows the budget and outturns for aggregate GoU expenditure and net lending. In general, actual expenditures were quite close to the budgeted levels at the aggregate level,[13] with the largest shortfall amounting to only 3 per cent (in 1999/2000), when the resource envelope was affected by the terms of trade shock noted above. Hence the methods used to generate resource envelope projections and to provide buffers against shortfalls in budget resources can be judged to have been relatively successful.

---

[13] Larger cuts were made to individual spending programmes because of the need to accommodate supplementary expenditures.

7.2 *Sector expenditure ceilings: budgets versus outturns*

Appendix 8.4 shows the GoU expenditure ceilings for each sector of the budget in terms of appropriated expenditures and outturns in the eight fiscal years 1997/98–2004/05. The expenditure comprises non-wage recurrent expenditure and domestic development expenditure and excludes wages.[14] Wages are excluded because this component of the budget was not subject to cuts during budget implementation.[15]

Significant deviations between appropriated budgets and outturns occurred at the sector level. They were more severe in the discretionary parts of the budget, such as the development budget and non-wage recurrent expenditure. Non-discretionary budget expenditures, such as statutory expenditure, poverty reducing expenditure and utilities were for the most part protected from cuts during budget execution. Some sectors persistently spent above their original budget appropriations, notably security and public administration, by an average of 10 per cent in both cases. The justice, law and order, and accountability sectors also persistently overspent, although being two of the smaller sectors, the deviation in absolute terms was much less significant.

Such overspending in those sectors where it was most prevalent reflected not just a lack of budget discipline but a more fundamental problem. Although the GoU budget expanded substantially in real terms from the mid 1990s, many sections of the budget were chronically under-funded, with insufficient funds budgeted to meet normal recurrent costs, or for counterpart funding of donor funded projects. Examples of under-funding include: road maintenance, medicines, subscriptions to international organizations, the State House recurrent budget, pensions, and diplomatic missions abroad. The under-funding reflected weaknesses in budget planning. Government took on too many new activities, including new development projects and new semi-autonomous bodies (of which there are over eighty).[16] These new activities drew funds away from existing budget activities. Commitments to fund activities were incurred without proper consideration of affordability; this was particularly the case with regard to compensation payments, which were often motivated by political considerations. Budget support donors pressed government to increase expenditures on new activities, such as the Local Government Development Programme and activities within the justice, law and order sector. There were too many donor-funded

---

[14] The outturn data are based on releases of funds to the accounts of the MDAs. Actual spending was slightly lower in some cases where MDAs were unable to spend all their available resources.

[15] In fact the wage bill sometimes underperformed because of unfilled vacancies, which freed up budget resources that could be used to fund overspending in other areas.

[16] Donors have contributed to the proliferation of quasi autonomous government agencies, often by pressing strongly for their creation as a perceived solution to a problem in a particular sector and by funding some of the capital and start up costs. An example of this is the Road Agency.

projects which imposed a burden on the GoU budget for counterpart funds, taxes, and recurrent costs. The cost implications for the budget were not properly taken into account when these projects were initiated. Finally, funds were diverted from core areas of spending to fund political directives.

The MDAs that overspent their budgets received supplementary budget appropriations. Supplementary appropriations became a persistent characteristic of budget implementation (see Chapter 3); in 2003/04 supplementaries amounted to UGX127 billion, which was more than 5 per cent of the MTEF. As the magnitude of supplementaries usually far outstripped the macroeconomic contingency, funding them required cuts in other items of the budget. Around 75–80 per cent of the budget, including wages, statutory expenditures, PAF expenditures, unconditional grants to districts, and expenditures of politically powerful MDAs, was effectively protected from cuts during budget implementation. Consequently, the burden of cuts fell disproportionately on a small part of the budget, comprising the non wage, non PAF, and non statutory expenditures of the less influential MDAs; these items often suffered large cuts relative to their budget appropriations to accommodate supplementary expenditures. As can be seen from Appendix 8.4, the roads and works sector and the economic functions and social services sector (in both of which PAF expenditure is a relatively small share of total spending) suffered the largest cuts in appropriated budgets, with outturns falling below appropriations by an average of 8 and 9 per cent respectively.

The expectation among politically powerful MDAs that they will be able to access supplementary resources, together with the likelihood that less influential MDAs will suffer cuts in their non protected expenditures undermines the incentives facing both sets of MDAs to prepare realistic budget plans in line with their MTEF expenditure ceilings. As such, it reduces the value of the MTEF as a budget planning tool which can force MDAs to prioritize their expenditures within a hard budget constraint. Cuts to MDA budgets below appropriated levels have also contributed to the persistent accumulation of expenditure arrears, despite the introduction of the commitment control system (see Chapter 15). The need to repay arrears reduces the scope for reallocating budget resources towards priority expenditures.

A further weakness of the MTEF is that the outer years of the framework were often an unreliable guide to future expenditure ceilings, and not given much focus during the budget process. The outer years were occasionally adjusted for major policy decisions, such as stepping up recruitment of teachers over time with the introduction of UPE, and some sectors made output projections for three years. However, the major focus was invariably on the first year of the MTEF. Importantly, the first year of the MTEF was always entirely consistent with the annual budget appropriations since it was also the annual budget. Despite the pressures mentioned above, the predictability of the annual budget has improved significantly since the MTEF was introduced.

8. Challenges in budget reform

Despite the progress made since the early 1990s, serious weaknesses in the budget process continue to impede a more efficient allocation of public resources. Rectifying these weaknesses represent the major challenges for future budget reforms, and are briefly discussed below.

8.1 *Budget indiscipline*

A serious weakness in budget implementation is the lack of budget discipline in politically powerful MDAs, such as those in the public administration and security sectors. These MDAs persistently overspend their budget appropriations, thereby requiring supplementary appropriations which can only be funded at the expense of cuts in the budgets of less politically powerful MDAs which do not enjoy the protection accorded by PAF status. The frequent supplementary approvals and resultant cuts in non-priority expenditures undermine the value of the MTEF as a budget planning and decision making instrument.

8.2 *Determining sector ceilings*

Another significant constraint is the inadequate institutional procedures and mechanisms for determining medium term inter-sectoral allocations in a manner which builds political consensus and commitment. The budget ceilings for some sectors, such as public administration, are determined in a somewhat *ad hoc* manner and are subject to political pressures during the budget process, which undermines the link between budget allocations and strategic policies. Sectors which include a number of line ministries and agencies do not function effectively as institutions for determining strategic intra-sectoral allocations, which undermines the usefulness of the ceiling as an instrument for strategic decision making and expenditure prioritization. This is attributable to a number of factors, including the lack of accepted sector specific strategic plans, unrealistic budgeting, weak capacity for planning and budgeting within line ministries, and, in some cases, the inability of line ministries to impose disci pline on each spending agency within their sector.

8.3 *Managing donor support*

Despite the shift towards budget support in the late 1990s, managing the various modalities of donor inflows to the MTEF remained problematic and still, to some extent, constrained the strategic allocation of budget resources. Even donors that shifted to budget support wanted to retain some degree of control over their aid, by emphasizing 'additionality' of their support (meaning that they expected to see their aid lead to increased expenditure in specific sectors relative to some benchmark level), or notionally earmarking their support to a specific sector or form of expenditure, such as the PAF (see Chapter 13).

In addition, few donors provided credible estimates of external project flows over the three year period of the MTEF. Although *ex ante* estimates of donor project expenditures are captured in the MTEF, donor disbursement estimates for projects were not initially integrated into sector ceilings in the MTEF, and accurate *ex post* expenditure data was never available. This reflected the difficulties of capturing realistic aid projections needed to plan public expenditure and enforce fiscal discipline if all sectors and sources of funding (domestic and donor) were covered within the framework. These issues partially undermined some of the objectives of the MTEF, such as the provision of credible and predictable expenditure ceilings to each sector, the adoption of integrated ceilings (including both recurrent and development expenditure, whether funded by the government or directly by donors), and the strategic reallocation of resources across sectors.

8.4 Absorption constraints

While predictability in the level of fiscal transfers to support the delivery of basic services improved, the rapid growth in the level of spending during the late 1990s outstripped the implementation capacity of the public sector. Capacity issues were more acute within local governments, resulting in delayed implementation of programmes and return of significant un-spent funds to the treasury at the end of the fiscal year. Deficiencies in budget planning and implementation led to poor scrutiny of costs of inputs and outputs, unrealistic budgeting, delayed procurement, and cost overruns. In addition, the numerous grants, each with far-reaching planning and accountability obligations, to some extent undermined efficiency in the execution of the budget.[17]

8.5 Mainstreaming of cross-cutting issues

The Poverty Status Report 2000 revealed that the marginalization of cross-cutting and equality issues, including gender equality, in the planning and budgeting processes was undermining the effectiveness of the budget and the achievement of desired poverty eradication outcomes (MoFPED 2001a). Failure

---

[17] Transfers to each priority sector were administered under three sub-grants: wages, recurrent, and development. Each category had a set of planning and accountability guidelines. With over ten national priority programmes, each with three specific transfers, a total of twenty-six grants were being transferred to each local government in 2004.

to address the specific needs of the different categories of vulnerable groups during policy formulation had adversely impacted access to, and effectiveness of, service delivery. Weak inter-sectoral coordination led to inadequate public action, wastage of resources, or duplication of expenditure. For instance, infant, child, and maternal mortality all remained high despite increasing budgetary allocations to social sectors. The deterioration in some of the social and human indicators of development called for a reorientation of budgeting to deal with specific needs of vulnerable groups.[18] In response, government revised the criteria for the allocation of resources from conditional grants to incorporate gender and poverty issues, and to enhance the relevance of the criteria and the effectiveness of the conditionalities of the various grants. This was later complemented with the formulation of guidelines to promote mainstreaming gender and equity issues in the budget process.[19]

9. Conclusions

Uganda's decade of experience with implementing the MTEF has provided valuable lessons. It is clear that the MTEF can bring about important benefits in formulating budget policies and expenditure priorities. However, some critical aspects of the MTEF have proved difficult to implement and it is not a panacea for the many deep-rooted structural problems in budgeting. Tackling these problems is essential if the MTEF is to be a more effective tool of budget resource allocation.

The MTEF can be judged as relatively successful in three important respects. First, it has reinforced sound fiscal policy formulation at the aggregate level by ensuring that medium term budgets are planned within a resource envelope and fiscal framework fully consistent with the government's policy objectives and macroeconomic projections. It thus built on, and helped to entrench, the macro-fiscal reforms of the early 1990s (see Chapter 3). Critical to this was political acceptance of the need for sound fiscal policy, realism of the resource envelope projections, and the imperative of respecting the constraints of the budget resource envelope. Second, was the shift in inter-sectoral budget allocations in line with the strategic priorities in the PEAP and predictability of funding necessary for their implementation over the medium term. This shift was reinforced by the PAF, which provided a strong stimulus to increase funding

---

[18] The Report also pointed out that the positive trend in income distribution had been reversed and inequality had been increasing since 1997 (see Chapter 10).

[19] The guidelines were intended to help SWGs take into account gender and equity concerns in sector reviews and in the formulation of BFPs. They underscored the importance of addressing equity issues and ensuring that all vulnerable groups access and benefit from government programmes. They were not intended to impose additional tasks on SWGs, but to strengthen analysis aimed at improved delivery of public services.

for priority sectors and poverty reducing programmes. Third, was the formation and operation of SWGs and the associated improvement in budget planning at the sector level. Particularly in the health and education sectors, SWGs have strengthened sector planning and brought about a better expenditure allocation.

As a budget planning tool, a number of challenges have limited the efficacy of the MTEF. Unrealistic budgeting in politically powerful MDAs, which are then able to access funds for supplementary expenditures, undermines the credibility of the MTEF. Budgeting for the wage bill is still largely carried out as a separate exercise from the rest of the budget, albeit within a clearly defined wage bill ceiling which is compatible with the overall budget resource envelope. Sectors do not yet have the capacity to allocate their own sector ceilings between wage and non-wage items, which undermines optimal sector planning. Donor projects, and their funding, are effectively outside the MTEF planning and thus are not fully integrated into MTEF sector ceilings.

A distinguishing feature of Uganda's budget reforms was the role of the political leadership. Political buy-in and commitment, particularly from the President, was central to the reforms' success. As discussed in Chapter 2, the merger of the finance and planning ministries in 1992 was critical in establishing fiscal discipline and in building links between policy and budgeting. Over time, the merged ministry became one of the technically strongest institutions in government.

The value of both the knowledge of the leadership and their commitment was essential in the design and sustained implementation of the reforms. A critical mass of reform minded politicians and technocrats were instrumental in initiating the reforms and spreading commitment to budget reform across government. Balancing capacity enhancement with behavioural change was crucial in linking policy formulation and budgeting. The reforms aimed at not only promoting compliance with reform principles and objectives, but also at encouraging changes in attitudes towards the budget and consequently practices regarding allocation of public funds. The emphasis on transparent decision making and effective communication of budget decisions, spearheaded by MoFPED, was instrumental in enhancing understanding of the reforms and securing the collaboration of all agencies involved in the budget reform agenda.

APPENDIX 8.1

Evolution of the MTEF in Uganda

Dimensions	Design Features	Key Features	1992/93–1996/07	1997/08–2001/2	2002/03–2005/06
General	Scope	Sectors included	None	All sectors. Quality and realistic expenditures limited to education and health	All sectors. Most sectors committed to prioritization and production of realistic expenditures
	Format	Type of expenditure	Recurrent and Capital	Wage, non-wage recurrent, and capital/development	Wage, non-wage recurrent, and capital/development
		Budget classification	Functional (through mapping) and organizational	Functional, organizational, and programme	Functional, economic, organizational, geographical, and programme
	Levels	Central and local	Central	Central	Central and districts
Technical	Macro/Fiscal Framework	Basis	Financial programming approach	Financial programming approach, funding commitments, strategies, and obligations	Financial programming approach, funding commitments, strategies, and obligations
		Content	Aggregate, and selected line ministries ceilings	Aggregate, line ministries ceilings, and programmes	Aggregate, sectoral, line ministries, and districts (grants for sector programmes)
	Sector Expend. Framework	Sector Policy Framework	RDP. With unrealistic sector strategic plans	PEAP with gradual formulation of realistic sector policies and strategies led by education, health and followed by water and justice, law and order	Defence plus social development formulate strategies and investment programme. Public service and administration action completed by 2005/06 process

	Type of costing		
Organizational			
Status in budget process	Focus on RDP/PIP. More incremental budgeting for recurrent budget	Adoption of investment programmes, activities; criteria for grants and units costs where applicable	Programmes and activities
Fit in budget process	Adopted as tool for resource allocation at aggregate level	Adopted for allocation of resources at aggregate, sectors, grants, and programmers	Focus on rationalization of donor funds
		Key feature in Budget Framework paper sent to Cabinet and Parliament before tabling budget	Key feature in the LGBFP submitted to district council for approval before onward submission to centre
Approval Centre	MoF	Cabinet	Cabinet
Management structure	Departments of Budget and Economic Affairs, MoF	Directorates of Budget and Economic Affairs, MoFPED	Directorates of Budget and Economic Affairs, MoFPED
Sector	Selected line ministries	SWGs and technical committees at local governments	SWGs, and donor specific working groups

Source: Adapted from Houerou and Taliercio (2002).

APPENDIX 8.2

Example of MTEF Table (in billion UGX, nominal) attached to Budget Speech, 2005/06

SECTOR/VOTE		Wage	Non-Wage Recurrent	Domestic Dev	Donor Project	Total excl. Donor Project	Total incl. Donor Project
SECURITY							
158	ISO	14.40	9.48	1.04	—	24.92	24.92
004	Defence excl. LDUs	135.17	201.59	10.42	1.89	347.18	349.07
159	ESO	—	—	—	—	—	—
	SUB-TOTAL SECURITY	**149.57**	**211.07**	**11.45**	**1.89**	**372.10**	**373.98**
ROADS AND WORKS							
016	Works and Transport	3.95	3.10	53.47	217.24	60.52	277.76
016	Trunk Road Maintenance	—	23.13	50.73	0.40	73.86	74.27
501–850	District Road Maintenance	—	18.01	—	—	18.01	18.01
501–850	Urban Road Maintenance	—	4.10	—	—	4.10	4.10
	SUB-TOTAL ROADS	**3.95**	**48.34**	**104.20**	**217.65**	**156.50**	**374.15**
AGRICULTURE							
010	Agriculture, Animal Industry and Fisheries	2.38	6.79	24.31	51.71	33.47	85.18
142	National Agricultural Research Organisation (NARO)	—	2.80	9.20	13.27	12.00	25.27
501–850	District Agricultural Extension	3.08	2.92	—	—	5.99	5.99
501–850	National Agricultural Advisory Services (Districts)	—	—	24.75	2.71	24.75	27.45
152	NAADS Secretariat	—	2.52	2.44	—	4.95	4.95
	SUB-TOTAL AGRICULTURE	**5.46**	**15.02**	**60.69**	**67.68**	**81.16**	**148.85**

EDUCATION

Code	Item						
140	Uganda Management Institute	—	0.40	—	39.47	0.40	0.40
013	Education and Sports (incl. Prim Educ)	7.31	39.62	19.26	17.56	66.18	105.65
136	Makerere University	—	33.44	0.13	—	33.57	51.13
137	Mbarara University	4.03	2.40	0.41	—	6.84	6.84
139	Kyambogo University	6.07	4.93	0.28	—	11.27	11.27
132	Education Service Commission	0.46	1.78	0.05		2.29	2.29
138	Makerere University Business School	—	4.19	—		4.19	4.19
149	Gulu University	—	3.15	1.20		4.35	4.35
501–850	District Primary Educ incl. SFG	254.00	33.49	51.10	—	338.59	338.59
013	District Secondary Education	76.32	6.51	—	—	82.82	82.82
501–850	District Tertiary Institutions	15.71	8.25	—		23.96	23.96
501–850	District Health Training Schools	2.46	1.77	—	—	4.23	4.23
	SUB-TOTAL EDUCATION	366.35	139.92	72.42	57.03	578.69	635.72

HEALTH

Code	Item						
014	Health	4.30	25.65	13.51	213.98	43.46	257.44
162	Butabika Hospital	1.57	1.59	6.92	43.28	10.07	53.35
161	Mulago Hospital Complex	12.58	11.79	1.39	—	25.75	25.75
134	Health Service Commission	0.42	1.23	0.03	—	1.69	1.69
107	Uganda Aids Commission	0.69	0.63	1.51	10.21	2.83	13.05
501–850	District NGO Hospitals/ Primary Health Care	—	17.73	—	—	17.73	17.73
501–850	District Primary Health Care	73.01	22.91	6.09	—	102.01	102.01

(Continued)

(Continued)

SECTOR/VOTE		Wage	Non-Wage Recurrent	Domestic Dev	Donor Project	Total excl. Donor Project	Total incl. Donor Project
501–850	District Hospitals	—	10.61	—	—	10.61	10.61
163–173	District Referral Hospitals	17.03	7.26	—	—	24.29	24.29
151	Uganda Blood Transfusion Service (UBTS)	0.30	1.53	—	0.91	1.83	2.74
	SUB-TOTAL HEALTH	109.90	100.93	29.45	268.38	240.28	508.66
WATER AND ENVIRONMENT							
019	Water	1.59	0.78	16.29	60.27	18.66	78.93
501–850	District Water Conditional Grant	—	1.50	29.66	—	31.17	31.17
150	National Environment Management Authority	—	0.03	0.40	6.74	0.43	7.17
	SUB-TOTAL WATER	1.59	2.28	45.96	60.27	49.83	110.09
JUSTICE/LAW AND ORDER							
144	Uganda Police (incl. LDUs)	38.82	33.42	3.42	—	75.66	75.66
145	Uganda Prisons	10.04	10.40	1.09	—	21.53	21.53
009	Internal Affairs	2.21	21.57	0.27	3.45	24.05	27.50
133	DPP	2.53	1.18	0.29	—	4.00	4.00
007	Justice Court Awards (Statutory)	—	2.03	—	—	2.03	2.03
007	Justice, Attorney General excl. Compensation	1.23	2.50	19.59	—	23.32	23.32
007	Justice, Attorney General - Compensation	—	1.23	—	—	1.23	1.23
101	Judiciary (Statutory)	7.23	7.58	2.64	4.11	17.44	21.55
148	Judicial Service Commission	0.50	0.92	0.03	—	1.46	1.46
105	Law Reform Commission (Statutory)	0.38	1.54	0.10	—	2.02	2.02
109	Law Development Centre	—	1.17	—	—	1.17	1.17
	SUB-TOTAL JUSTIC/LAW AND ORDER	63.02	83.58	27.43	7.55	174.03	181.59

ACCOUNTABILITY							
001	Ethics and Integrity	0.11	0.36	0.66	0.46	1.14	1.61
008	MFPED (excl. URA)	2.34	18.13	25.57	85.44	46.04	131.47
131	Audit	1.98	4.05	0.16	1.91	6.19	8.10
103	Inspector General of Government (IGG) (Statutory)	1.68	5.87	0.91	3.01	8.46	11.48
501–850	District Grant for Monitoring and Accountability	—	11.11	—	—	11.11	11.11
143	Uganda Bureau of Statistics	—	8.89	—	—	8.89	8.89
153	PPDA	—	1.00	0.70	—	1.70	1.70
	SUB-TOTAL ACCOUNTABILITY	**6.10**	**49.42**	**28.00**	**90.82**	**83.52**	**174.35**
ECONOMIC FUNCTIONS AND SOCIAL SERVICES							
017	Energy and Minerals	1.59	2.00	64.04	65.83	67.64	133.47
015	Tourism, Trade and Industry	1.48	11.68	5.15	12.96	18.31	31.27
012	Lands, Housing and Urban Development	1.43	2.26	4.65	12.01	8.34	20.36
018	Gender, Labour and Social Development	1.61	4.67	4.18	7.32	10.45	17.78
003	Office of the Prime Minister (Development)	—	—	5.66	88.56	5.66	94.22
011	Local Government Dev (excl. Roads)	—	—	1.35	28.94	1.35	30.29
501–850	District Functional Adult Literacy Grant	—	1.60	—	—	1.60	1.60
501–850	District Equalisation Grant	—	3.49	—	—	3.49	3.49
501–850	Local Government Development Programme (LGDP)	—	—	64.30	—	64.30	64.30
501–850	Non-Sectoral Conditional Grant	0.72	5.45	—	—	6.18	6.18

(Continued)

(Continued)

SECTOR/VOTE		Wage	Non-Wage Recurrent	Domestic Dev	Donor Project	Total excl. Donor Project	Total incl. Donor Project
501–850	District Women, Youth and Disability Councils Grants	—	1.36	—		1.36	1.36
501–850	District Natural Resource Conditional Grant	0.80	0.25			1.05	1.05
	SUB-TOTAL ECONOMIC FUNCTIONS AND SS	**7.64**	**32.77**	**149.32**	**215.64**	**189.73**	**405.38**
PUBLIC SECTOR MANAGEMENT							
003	Office of the Prime Minister (excl. Dev)	0.85	2.77	—	—	3.62	3.62
108	National Planning Authority (Statutory)	0.93	0.76	0.43		2.12	2.12
005	Public Service	1.61	1.82	0.71	7.99	4.15	12.14
146	Public Service Commission	0.66	1.36	0.26	—	2.28	2.28
011	Local Government (excl. Dev)	0.68	3.60	—	—	4.27	4.27
005	Public Service Pension/Comp (Statutory)	—	75.24	—		75.24	75.24
147	Local Govt Finance Comm	0.47	0.77	0.11	—	1.35	1.35
501–850	Unconditional Grant (Urban Authorities)	12.16	5.89	—		18.04	18.04
501–850	Unconditional Grant (District)	73.35	31.15	—		104.49	104.49
	SUB-TOTAL PUBLIC SECTOR MANAGEMENT	**90.70**	**123.34**	**1.51**	**7.99**	**215.55**	**223.54**
PUBLIC ADMINISTRATION							
006	Foreign Affairs	1.01	17.28	0.80	—	19.09	19.09
201–223	Missions Abroad	7.77	15.67	0.71	—	24.15	24.15
141	URA	—	68.03	—	7.69	68.03	75.72

Code		Col1	Col2	Col3	Col4	Col5	Col6
002	State House	2.14	31.15	14.67	—	47.96	47.96
001	Office of the President (excl. E&I)	4.67	4.27	0.45	—	9.39	9.39
100	Specified Officers - Salaries (Statutory)	0.37	—	—	—	0.37	0.37
104	Parliamentary Commission (Statutory)	7.40	33.39	3.96	1.09	44.75	45.83
106	Uganda Human Rights Comm (Statutory)	1.34	1.29	0.04	7.28	2.67	9.95
102	Electoral Commission (Statutory)	5.09	39.06	0.33	—	44.49	44.49
	SUB-TOTAL PUBLIC ADMINISTRATION	32.17	212.59	21.19	16.05	265.95	282.01
INTEREST PAYMENTS DUE							
	Domestic Interest	—	231.79	—	—	231.79	231.79
	External Interest	—	58.84	—	—	58.84	58.84
	SUB-TOTAL INTEREST PAYMENTS	—	290.63	—	—	290.63	290.63
	Total Centre	376.05	670.32	366.21	989.30	1,412.57	2,401.87
	Total Local Government Programmes	435.28	181.60	175.90	2.71	792.78	795.49
	Line Ministries + Loc. Gov't Programmes	811.33	851.92	542.10	992.01	2,205.36	3,197.36
	Statutory Interest Payments	—	290.63	—	—	290.63	290.63
	Statutory excluding Interest Payments	25.11	167.38	9.93	25.70	202.42	228.12
	GRAND TOTAL	836.45	1,309.93	552.03	1,017.71	2,697.83	3,716.12

Source: MoFPED (2006).

APPENDIX 8.3 The Consultative Budget Process

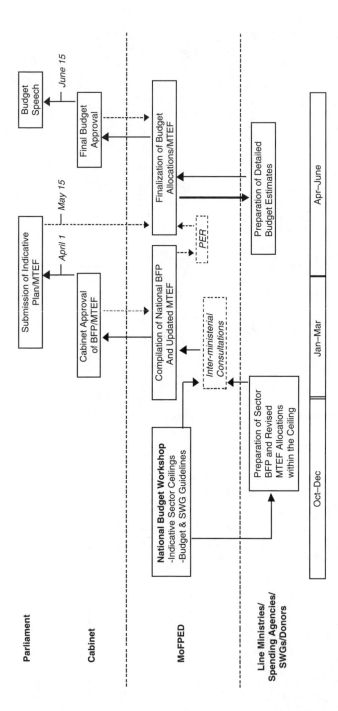

Source: Ministry of Finance, Planning and Economic Development.

Stage 1 Development and approval of the macroeconomic and fiscal policy plus indicative MTEF (October–December): The major activity is the dissemination of the indicative MTEF to provide a basis for sector consultations. The process is spearheaded by the SWG and involves the following: review of budget performance; progress on policies and programmes; identification of achievements and challenges; assessment of budgetary implications of new policies and programmes and their affordability; alignment of sector expenditures with indicative ceilings; submission of policy proposals to deal with challenges. These are all articulated in sector BFPs.

Stage 2 Consultations and Approval of National Budget Framework Paper (January–March): This involves budget hearings aimed at aligning expenditure priorities with the resource allocations under the MTEF and consolidation of sector BFPs into the national BFP, which is submitted to Cabinet for consideration before submission to Parliament by 1 April.

Stage 3 Finalization of the MTEF and preparation of Budget estimates (April–June): Consideration and approval of the macroeconomic policy and

APPENDIX 8.4

Approved Budget and Outturns (Non-wage recurrent and domestic development only) by Sector, 1997/98–2004/05

UGX billion

	1997/1998			1998/1999			1999/2000		
	Approved Budget	Outturn	Deviation	Approved Budget	Outturn	Outturn as % of Budget	Approved Budget	Outturn	Outturn as % of Budget
Security	83.8	86.9	104%	95.5	128.1	134%	86.0	83.2	97%
Roads & Works	48.0	39.0	81%	74.3	61.8	83%	103.9	99.3	96%
Agriculture	10.0	7.7	77%	11.1	8.4	75%	14.0	15.4	110%
Education	75.4	73.2	97%	90.6	118.7	131%	177.8	172.6	97%
Health	44.9	40.1	89%	46.0	43.8	95%	49.1	53.4	109%
Water	5.1	3.7	73%	12.8	12.4	97%	18.0	18.0	100%
Justice, Law & Order	42.0	45.2	108%	44.8	42.6	95%	52.9	56.3	106%
Accountability	2.7	2.8	107%	4.0	4.9	121%	5.6	8.6	154%
Econ Functions & Social Services	31.0	30.5	98%	27.2	25.2	93%	76.7	54.3	71%
Public Administration	149.9	165.1	110%	150.6	167.9	112%	192.7	200.9	104%
Interest Payments Due	76.2	62.4	82%	82.4	72.1	88%	89.6	94.7	106%
TOTAL	569.1	556.7	98%	639.1	685.9	107%	866.3	856.6	99%

(Continued)

(Continued)

UGX billion	2000/2001			2001/2002			2002/03		
	Approved Budget	Outturn	Outturn as % of Budget	Approved Budget	Outturn	Outturn as % of Budget	Approved Budget	Outturn	Outturn as % of Budget
Security	87.4	86.1	99%	101.2	109.6	108%	121.4	158.8	131%
Roads & Works	136.2	126.2	93%	168.0	154.9	92%	147.7	152.4	103%
Agriculture	19.6	19.3	99%	45.2	38.7	86%	41.6	44.1	106%
Education	204.9	192.5	94%	237.3	218.0	92%	235.0	218.2	93%
Health	77.5	75.5	97%	108.7	105.5	97%	127.7	130.3	102%
Water	36.0	36.0	100%	53.6	48.6	91%	48.2	54.6	113%
Justice, Law & Order	54.7	58.8	108%	71.4	73.5	103%	83.1	90.4	109%
Accountability	15.1	14.3	95%	19.9	19.0	96%	23.4	23.4	100%
Econ Functions & Social Services	90.0	72.1	80%	135.3	118.9	88%	144.1	146.9	102%
Public Administration	207.5	244.9	118%	266.0	305.3	115%	291.7	299.4	103%
Interest Payments Due	107.1	127.6	119%	155.1	153.4	99%	144.6	180.8	125%
Contingency	6.9			11.5			2.0		
TOTAL	1,043.0	1,053.4	101%	1,373.1	1,345.5	98%	1,410.6	1,499.3	106%

UGX billion

	2003/2004			2004/2005		
	Approved Budget	Outturn	Outturn as % of Budget	Approved Budget	Outturn	Outturn as % of Budget
Security	183.9	192.1	104%	224.2	223.5	100%
Roads & Works	166.2	143.2	86%	152.8	157.2	103%
Agriculture	43.4	40.4	93%	42.6	47.7	112%
Education	231.0	207.7	90%	214.4	214.3	100%
Health	149.3	139.7	94%	130.2	128.1	98%
Water	60.3	52.2	87%	58.9	55.0	93%
Justice, Law & Order	101.6	137.7	135%	104.4	111.8	107%
Accountability	74.6	75.3	101%	64.4	65.2	101%
Econ Functions & Social Services	123.1	118.1	96%	112.2	110.1	98%
Public Administration	275.7	295.0	107%	316.4	350.7	111%
Interest Payments Due	227.8	248.2	109%	258.9	220.6	85%
Contingency	1.1					
TOTAL	1,638.1	1,649.5	101%	1,679.5	1,684.1	100%

Source: Ministry of Finance, Planning and Economic Development.

9

Sector Wide Approach and Sector Working Groups

Ishmael Magona[1]

1. Introduction

From the time it came to power, the National Resistance Movement government grappled with the challenge of how to rebuild public infrastructure and services—from roads, to water, sanitation, education, and health. This agenda was pursued in a complex environment of structural adjustment, decentralization, and civil service reform. Public enterprises were being privatized (see Chapter 16); a policy of fiscal and administrative decentralization of service delivery was being developed (see Chapter 14); and central ministries and agencies were being rationalized and the civil service reduced (see Chapter 4). These policies and processes impacted in many different ways upon both institutions and service delivery at the sectoral level.

As early as 1987 sector ministries embarked on a process of reform, developing ambitious new policies and strategies to rebuild service delivery. However, the policies that emerged required levels of funding that were far greater than the resources available at the time. Government recurrent budgets were very small, with the bulk of public investment and a large share of service delivery being funded by donors. Despite these sector level reforms, and reforms to the planning process (see Chapter 6), donor funded projects were fragmented and poorly aligned to the government's emerging policies. Public investments and services were consequently being delivered inefficiently and inconsistently across the country.

While Uganda's Sector Wide Approach (SWAp) evolved in parallel with sector ministry led policy reforms, it benefited from new sector-based planning and budgeting processes introduced by the Ministry of Finance, Planning and

[1] Helpful comments from Robert Yates are gratefully acknowledged.

Economic Development (MoFPED) in the context of the Poverty Eradication Action Plan (PEAP, see Chapter 7) and Medium Term Expenditure Framework (MTEF, see Chapter 8). A key feature of both processes was the delegation of responsibility for planning and the allocation of resources to sector institutions. In this context, innovative and consultative approaches to dialogue, resource allocation, performance monitoring and review, aid delivery, and conditionality emerged. In the sectors that developed SWAps, there has been a significant rehabilitation of public sector infrastructure and expansion in basic services.

This chapter discusses how SWAps evolved, their achievements and limitations. Their evolution is described along three dimensions: sector policy reform, strategic planning, and coordination; Sector Working Groups (SWGs), the budget process, and changes in aid delivery; and sector coordination, reporting, and review processes. The chapter concludes by trying to assess the contribution of, and the dilemmas facing, sectors a decade after the emergence of SWAps.

2. Sector policy reform, strategic planning, and coordination

The reform process which sector ministries embarked on from the late 1980s involved evaluation of the state of service delivery and the development of laws, policies, and implementation strategies. However, these policies tended to be unprioritized and were usually unaffordable. In most sectors investment was largely aid funded while in some, such as Health and Education, this applied to recurrent expenditure too. Many early donor interventions aimed at alleviating the costs of structural adjustment, focusing on the rehabilitation and provision of services to Uganda's most vulnerable groups and districts. Nonetheless, this and subsequent aid was often fragmented and poorly aligned to the Government's emerging policy priorities. Consequently, sectors found it difficult to put new policies into operation.

Universal Primary Education (UPE) provides an illustration of the problems faced by ministries (see Box 9.1). UPE was one of the central policies of the 1992 Education White Paper and the 1993 Primary Education Reform Programme. Little was achieved early on. It was only when President Museveni made UPE a central element of his 1996 election manifesto that the impetus was provided to implement the agreed policy. The Roads sector was another key priority during the 1996 election. Health was put under the political spotlight when the President announced, ten days before the 2001 elections, that all fees would be abolished at government health units. This subsequently put pressure on the Health sector to deliver results.

The Roads and Education sectors were the first to develop sector plans, partly in reaction to the problems they faced in delivering the President's political priorities, just as the PEAP was developed by MoFPED to address poverty nationally. Roads was the first sector to develop a comprehensive costed plan,

---

Box 9.1 EARLY REFORMS IN THE EDUCATION SECTOR

Uganda's education reforms began in 1987, with the formation of the Education Policy Review Commission to evaluate the education system and chart a way forward. The Commission's report was published in 1989. A White Paper on Education was approved by Cabinet in 1992. One of the key goals was the achievement of Universal Primary Education (UPE) by 2000. The Primary Education Reform Programme was launched in 1993. It comprised a comprehensive list of ideas and programmes for improving education, but was not prioritized and did not include a budget for implementation. This meant that little progress was made in implementing the programme.

The impetus for implementation was provided by the political commitment to free UPE in President Museveni's 1996 election manifesto. Implementation began in January 1997 and saw nationwide enrolment increase from 2.6 million children to 5.2 million in 1998 with most increases at the first and second grades. In 1997 the Ministry of Education and Sports (MoES) and related line ministries, in collaboration with donors, civil society, and local governments, formulated the Education Sector Investment Plan, 1998–2003. This marked the beginning of the SWAp in the Education sector.

The initial structure set up to drive the education reform was the Education Sector Consultative Committee comprising Government, donors, and civil society. This Committee was assisted by working groups in areas such as financial management, monitoring and evaluation, and sector policy management.

Source: Ward et al. (2006)

---

the ten year Road Sector Development Plan (RSDP), in 1996. The Education Sector Investment Plan quickly followed the decisive launch of UPE in 1997. Plans for both the Health and Water and Sanitation sectors, which had been developing new policy frameworks, soon followed.

In addition, it was recognized that if the new plans were to be delivered, greater coordination of actors was needed at the sector level—from policy, planning, financing, and budgeting through to implementation, monitoring, and evaluation. As part of the process of preparing policies and plans, new coordination mechanisms were developed. For example, the RSDP Steering Committee, the Education Sector Coordination Committee, and the Inter-Ministerial Committee for Rural Water were formed to monitor progress in the implementation of their respective sector policies and plans. As well as bringing representatives of government institutions together in collaborative fora, donors and civil society were also involved. MoFPED was represented through its sector desk officers, enabling it to play an active role in policy and plan development at the sector level without driving the process.

However, the sector policies and investment plans still needed resources if they were to be put into operation. The plans meant that the government was getting a better picture of the cost of delivering the new policies. These costs needed to be reflected in budget allocations. However, it was clear that most plans remained unaffordable, at least in the short term. Budgetary resources were limited, while most donor resources were still committed to projects that were not well aligned to the new policies.

3. MTEF and Sector Working Groups

The planning reforms of the early 1990s were critical in establishing a degree of central control over broad allocations of donor and government funding between sectors, as well as screening and budgeting project proposals (see Chapter 6). Initially, sectors were dependent upon desk officers in MoFPED to relay their respective expenditure priorities to the Development Committee. Nor was there much opportunity for stakeholders at the sector level to engage in dialogue with the Committee, and the process of (donor-funded) investment budgeting remained fragmented. However, by the mid-1990s MoFPED was sufficiently confident in the basic budgeting framework to start 'decentralizing' some of its functions to sectors and to draw sector expertise (wherever it resided) into the budgeting process. MoFPED acknowledged that responsibility for determining sector expenditure priorities must rest largely within the sector, with MoFPED retaining the 'challenge function'.

Two initiatives were central to this development: the MTEF and SWGs. The three-year MTEF introduced in 1997 represented a more comprehensive, strategic, and integrated approach to budgeting. A key feature was that the MTEF was presented by sector, made up of those ministries, departments, and agencies as well as the relevant local governments (or elements of them) involved in a certain function of government. The MTEF for a sector combined all the relevant central budget allocations along with grants to local governments. This presentation had two advantages. First, it made inter-sectoral allocations clearer, and thereby facilitated the alignment of overall sector allocations with national policy priorities, such as those elaborated in the PEAP. Second, it also made intra-sectoral resource allocations clearer. The recurrent and development budget components of the government budget and donor project aid for all institutions in a sector were set out together. By grouping together the budgets of all institutions in a sector, the allocation of resources towards policies and the delivery of services were made clearer. This basic innovation in the presentation of the MTEF has been a cornerstone of the budget process for over a decade. Appendix 8.2 illustrates the format.

The new presentation of budget allocations in the MTEF could not by itself ensure that expenditure choices were efficient and well linked to policy objectives. MoFPED felt that, rather than leaving individual institutions to allocate resources in isolation from one another, bringing them together at the sector level would increase coherence and reduce duplication. Therefore, as part of the consultative budget process, SWGs were formed. These comprised representatives from spending institutions within the sector as well as other stakeholders, such as civil society and donors—similar to the consultative sector fora which had already emerged in some sectors. The sectors' lead line ministry chaired these SWGs, while the sector desk officer from the MoFPED Budget Directorate served as secretary.

SWGs were charged with the preparation of Sector Budget Framework Papers, the medium-term budget strategy documents. These documents set out objectives, priorities, and resource allocations for the following three years, fitting within preliminary MTEF budget ceilings. Moreover, SWGs were tasked with setting out sector policies and plans, reviewing past performance in their implementation, and projecting future resource allocations in the light of existing and emerging policy priorities—as well as future spending pressures. From 1998 they were also asked to identify sector outcomes and outputs under the banner of 'output oriented budgeting'. This involved the identification of output performance targets for the sector, consistent with the policies and plans, and ensuring resource allocations reflected the costs of achieving those targets. While falling short of formal performance budgeting, for which there was limited capacity, it ensured that efforts were made to identify the intended results of sector expenditures at an aggregate level, and to link them to the achievement of policy objectives. This helped sectors focus on more tangible results of service delivery (e.g. number of outpatients) rather than outcomes (e.g. child mortality), which were difficult to measure. Outcomes were also difficult to attribute to specific sector interventions.

The SWGs proved very useful fora for consultation and discussion of sector performance and expenditure priorities in the context of the budget process. An external review of their functioning highlighted their importance as a basis for linking the sectoral nature of planning with the institutional nature of budgeting within the annual budget process (Folscher 2002). However, not all sectors formed coherent groups. Institutions in sectors such as Roads, Water and Sanitation, Health, and Education worked relatively well together through their respective SWGs. However, this was not the case for the Public Administration, Economic Functions, and Social Services, which were composed of a broader variety of institutions. The capacity of groups also varied. Consequently, the usefulness and performance of SWGs varied across sectors.

4. Supporting changes in sector financing and donor coordination

Another influence on the evolution of sector budgeting and coordination mechanisms was the change in the way donors financed sectors. This was prompted by Uganda's qualification for debt relief in 1998 (see Chapter 12), together with donor interest in budget support.

As a result of debt relief, the government had significantly more resources available to channel towards priorities in the PEAP, via the Poverty Action Fund (PAF, see Chapter 13). Many donors saw the PAF as an opportunity to provide budget support to either specific sector programmes, such as primary health care and classroom construction, or to the PAF overall. The majority of these resources were channelled as grants to local governments, providing resources for the new decentralized structures to fulfil their functional mandate (see Chapter 14). A move to un-earmarked general budget support followed in 2000, linked to the implementation of the second iteration of the PEAP. The World Bank and the UK Department for International Development led this shift.

Uganda's qualification for debt relief and donors' shift to budget support meant that between 1997 and 2000 there was a considerable increase in resources channelled via the mainstream budget, as opposed to fragmented projects. There was substantial fiscal space, therefore, for MoFPED to allocate resources towards new policy priorities laid out in the PEAP, and for SWGs to allocate resources towards the implementation of their new policies and associated strategic plans. Table 9.1 shows that between 1997/98 and 2004/05 allocations to PEAP priorities in the Education, Health, Water and Sanitation, and Roads sectors more than quadrupled in real terms, increasing from 43 per cent to 63 per cent of overall sector budgets.

The PAF was useful at the sector level in ensuring prioritization towards basic service delivery and greater allocative efficiency. For example, the Ministry of Health's planning department was constantly under pressure to increase funding allocations to tertiary hospitals and central ministry programmes. MoFPED's rules with respect to the PAF ensured that the main funding increases were at the level of primary health care.

With the shift towards budget support, and their engagement in sector consultative committees and SWGs, the nature of donor interaction with the government was changing. Despite this, conventional project aid remained significant and needed to be aligned with new sector policies and strategies. Transactions costs of bilateral relations between different donors at the sector level were seen as high. Hence, donor coordination became increasingly important, both for coordinating aid interventions and for improving the consistency of policy dialogue with sector institutions. As the sector coordination committees developed, donors started forming themselves into groups to match that structure. The first of these was the Education Funding Agencies Group (see Box 9.2).

Table 9.1 Domestic Budget Allocations to Sector PEAP Priorities, 1997/98–2006/07 (excludes donor projects)

	(Pre-PAF) 1997/98	1998/99	1999/00	2000/01	2001/02	2002/03	2003/04	2004/05	2005/06	2006/07
UGX Billion (2000 prices)										
Universal Primary Education	167	236	277	318	379	386	389	390	396	433
Primary Healthcare	6	29	25	72	146	174	176	183	204	192
Safe Water and Sanitation	5	17	23	44	62	66	61	60	48	58
Agricultural Extension, Advisory Services and Strategic Exports	1	0	6	5	32	35	33	38	53	58
Rural Roads	12	28	32	39	48	47	52	43	41	38
Other Poverty Action Fund	6	12	30	74	115	129	148	154	163	261
Total Poverty Action Fund	**196**	**323**	**393**	**552**	**782**	**836**	**859**	**866**	**904**	**1040**
% of Sector Budgets										
Universal Primary Education	57%	62%	65%	68%	65%	65%	65%	64%	68%	68%
Primary Healthcare	8%	31%	24%	52%	70%	76%	74%	78%	85%	85%
Safe Water and Sanitation	97%	97%	95%	97%	99%	99%	100%	100%	100%	100%
Agricultural Extension, Advisory Services and Strategic Exports	6%	2%	25%	18%	59%	58%	62%	66%	65%	69%
Rural Roads	21%	32%	24%	24%	24%	25%	31%	25%	26%	23%
% of GDP										
Universal Primary Education	1.5%	2.0%	2.3%	2.5%	2.7%	2.6%	2.4%	2.3%	2.2%	2.2%
Primary Healthcare	0.1%	0.2%	0.2%	0.6%	1.0%	1.2%	1.1%	1.1%	1.1%	1.0%
Safe Water and Sanitation	0.0%	0.1%	0.2%	0.3%	0.4%	0.4%	0.4%	0.3%	0.3%	0.3%
Agricultural Extension, Advisory Services and Strategic Exports	0.0%	0.0%	0.0%	0.0%	0.2%	0.2%	0.2%	0.2%	0.3%	0.3%
Rural Roads	0.1%	0.2%	0.3%	0.3%	0.3%	0.3%	0.3%	0.2%	0.2%	0.2%
Other Poverty Action Fund	0.1%	0.1%	0.2%	0.6%	0.8%	0.9%	0.9%	0.9%	0.9%	1.3%
Total Poverty Action Fund	**1.8%**	**2.8%**	**3.3%**	**4.3%**	**5.6%**	**5.6%**	**5.3%**	**5.1%**	**5.0%**	**5.3%**

Sources: MoFPED 1998–2007a–d; Uganda Bureau of Statistics.

Box 9.2 EDUCATION FUNDING AGENCIES GROUP

An important feature of the education sector development process was the Education Funding Agencies Group (EFAG). This was created in 1999 by the education sector donors to provide an effective forum for the partnership between government—chiefly MoES—and the donors, and to reduce transaction costs to government. A Memorandum of Understanding sets out the roles and responsibilities of both parties.

The chair of EFAG rotates on an annual basis. The group meets monthly to discuss education issues and to agree common positions to take with government on matters of policy, financing, and strategy. EFAG communicates with government solely through channels agreed with MoES. These consist of verbal and written communications between the EFAG coordinator and the Permanent Secretary, MoES. Technical advice is communicated to MoES in the form of an EFAG Technical Note, whilst agreed EFAG positions on matters of policy or critical issues in the sector are conveyed under the EFAG letterhead.

Source: Adapted from Ward et al. (2006)

---

5. Sector reporting and review processes

As the policy and budgetary framework strengthened, the focus of the dialogue amongst the various coordination bodies turned towards monitoring—and improving—the implementation of those policies and plans. The sector coordination and decision making structures were increasingly formalized, and took on formal monitoring roles. Although these evolved in different ways, there were a number of common features:

- a government decision making body, usually headed by the responsible minister;
- a consultative/technical body which may serve as the decision making body, made up of stakeholders from the different institutions involved in the sector. In some sectors this is also the SWG;
- a series of technical working groups dealing with specific issues of sector performance to inform the decision making process; and
- a separate donor coordination group.

For example, in the Education sector the government decision making body was the MoES' top management meeting, chaired by the Minister. The consultative body was the Education Sector Consultative Committee, chaired by the Permanent Secretary, MoES. Technical working groups were formed covering issues such as sector policy and management, finance and budgeting (the SWG), as well as monitoring and evaluation. EFAG was the donor coordination group.

In this context, Joint Sector Reviews became synonymous with SWAps in Uganda as consultative fora for reviewing past performance and agreeing future undertakings to improve sector performance. Joint Sector Reviews were first introduced in the Education sector in April 1999. Health followed in October of the same year. Joint Sector Review processes became the home for the initiation, dissemination, and follow up for a series of sector diagnostic studies. These looked at various aspects of resource use and service delivery, particularly within local governments. They included the flow of funds to service providers through Public Expenditure Tracking Surveys (PETS); the cost effectiveness of delivery through value-for-money studies; and overall efficiency and effectiveness of sector expenditures through sector Public Expenditure Reviews.

Within the Health and Education sectors two reviews were initially held each year. The first was convened in April to focus on sector performance and whether donors would disburse budget support in the following financial year. These decisions were arrived at following an assessment of the government's implementation against undertakings agreed at previous reviews. Successful achievement of sector undertakings at sector reviews also became conditions for the disbursement of general budget support from its introduction in 2000. The second review, in October, was to discuss the following year's budget priorities and education targets. These intense, high profile events were extremely valuable in shifting attention of stakeholders from the review of individual donor projects towards the implementation of policies and strategic plans overall.

The Education, Health, and Water and Sanitation sectors undertook the most sector diagnostic studies. Studies were also completed in Roads, Agriculture, and the social development sectors. Primarily, they enabled central government to assess local government performance in the achievement of national objectives. A unit cost study was conducted for Roads and several value-for-money studies for Water and Sanitation, identifying several inefficiencies. However, since PETS and value-for-money studies were usually carried out on a sample basis they were a complement to, rather than a replacement for, other routine systems of monitoring and assessing local government performance. Furthermore, a number of stakeholders expressed concern that there was no effective follow up of recommendations from such studies.

6. The maturing of SWAps

By the early 2000s the foundations for the formalization of SWAps had been laid through development of sector policies, the introduction of a sector-based MTEF and SWGs, and the establishment of sector coordination and review mechanisms. The typical SWAp had three main elements (see Figure 9.1):

- a strategic plan to put into operation the sector policy and legal framework;
- the sector Budget Framework Paper, the medium-term budget strategy for the implementation of the strategic plan; and

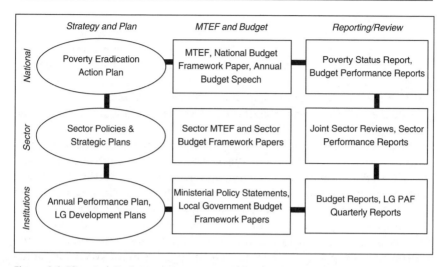

Figure 9.1 Planning, Budgeting, Reporting, and Review Processes in the Early 2000s

Source: Adapted from Williamson (2003).

- consultative sector reporting and review processes to review implementation of the budget and strategic plan.

Underlying these elements was the sector dialogue and coordination between government institutions in the sector, civil society, and donors. It was further underpinned by donors' move towards budget support, which helped shift attention away from projects and towards sector policy and the budget.

The number of formal SWAps has increased; by 2007/08 eight[2] out of eleven sectors had some kind of SWAp established or under development, covering over two thirds of the budget. This increasing scope meant that SWAps, and their constituent components of sector planning, budgeting, and review filled an important gap between the high-level policy priorities of the PEAP and the institutions charged with delivering policies and services. As ownership of the PEAP increased, through participation by SWGs, so the second iteration of sector plans was more explicitly aligned towards PEAP objectives. A key underlying incentive was that for a sector to qualify for funding under the PAF (which was the most rapidly rising part of the budget) it was required to demonstrate that its programmes were directly poverty reducing. It was clearly in a sector's interest both to develop sector plans, and to orient them towards the delivery of PEAP objectives.

---

[2] These were Roads, Agriculture, Education, Health, Water and Sanitation, Justice, Law and Order, Accountability, and Public Sector Management. Security, Public Administration, and Economic Functions and Social Services were the only sectors without any kind of SWAp under development.

In 2002 MoFPED started to raise concerns over the size of the budget deficit, and the effects that high levels of donor inflows were having on the private sector (see Chapter 13). In addition, the composition of expenditure had become increasingly skewed towards the social sectors. The government decided, therefore, that it could no longer guarantee the 'additionality' of donor aid—whether budget support or project aid—to sector allocations, either within or outside the PAF. This meant that those sectors that had not already developed SWAps faced weaker incentives to do so.

The review processes around SWAps, although valuable, created transaction costs of their own. Biannual sector review processes in Health and Education proved overly burdensome, involving a lot of time and effort on the part of both government and donors—including field trips and drafting reports. In 2003 stakeholders from the Education and Health sectors decided to reduce this to a single review combined with an annual sector performance report every October. Successful annual sector reviews remained a trigger for both sector and general budget support. This became standard practice in the Water and Sanitation, Decentralization, and Justice, Law and Order sectors. Some sectors also convened a smaller meeting to discuss the draft sector Budget Framework Paper. In addition, annual sector performance reports have become increasingly common tools for focusing the dialogue on performance in the context of sector review processes.

In 2003 donor–government relationships were formalized in the form of the jointly agreed Partnership Principles (see Box 9.3). Donors formally committed themselves to: work through lead donors, in the context of donor coordination groups; use government reporting processes; accept integrated budget ceilings; and use sector review processes.

As SWAps matured, not all sectors were keen on working within the framework of the PEAP, Sector Working Groups, and the MTEF. For example, in the late 1990s the Agriculture sector developed a plan outside the context of the sector working groups, which was inconsistent with the 1997 PEAP. The Ministry of Agriculture wanted government funding, but MoFPED was very uneasy. In response, MoFPED initiated the preparation of the Plan for Modernization of Agriculture, which took a cross-sectoral consultative approach to developing agriculture (Ministry of Finance, Planning and Economic Development 2000b). Whilst this ensured a more coherent policy and plan, ownership from the Ministry of Agriculture was understandably weaker than in other SWAps. For a long time there was no clear sector investment plan for the agriculture sector.

The Health sector faced a number of challenges during the early 2000s. A combination of changes in political and technical leadership and the arrival of global health initiatives (such as the Global Fund for HIV and AIDS, tuberculosis and malaria, and the United States President's Emergency Plan for AIDS Relief) meant that resources were less clearly directed towards implementation of the

---

Box 9.3 EXTRACTS FROM THE PARTNERSHIP PRINCIPLES RELATING TO SECTORS

Working More Effectively at the Sector Level

All donor partners, whatever the modality of their assistance, should also be represented (possibly as a silent partner) in a single SWG that focuses on policy, strategy, prioritizing expenditures, monitoring and evaluation, and service delivery.

Development partners participating in the SWG should endeavour to communicate with government through a 'lead donor' and with a common voice.

Government reporting mechanisms should be strengthened so that they can be adopted by development partners. As this is accomplished, development partners should seek to utilize the government reporting systems and not demand separate reporting mechanisms for their own funds. All stakeholders should adopt a common set of outcome indicators for monitoring progress at the sector level.

Joint financing committees should only address administrative issues related to the basket. All resources provided by development partners must be reflected in the government budget. Joint financing reviews, although necessary for accountability, should become a smaller component of a larger review.

Sector expenditure ceilings must be determined by the government through the budget process, independently of any sector financing and in particular, independently of any 'additional' sector funding made available or promised by development partners... Development partners should not attempt to influence Line Ministries to undertake expenditures which have not been identified as priorities by the SWG, using their own sector support or project aid as a lever.

Joint Sector Reviews/Missions

Joint missions are preferable to bilateral consultations... A sector review should provide the single opportunity for all development partners to comprehensively review policy, strategy, performance, and capacity needs.

Joint reviews must be open to all stakeholders. This should be reflected in the Terms of Reference for the joint review.

The outcomes of sector reviews should feed into the overall PRSC review.

Source: MoFPED (2003)

Health Sector Strategic Plan. Much donor project aid was provided off budget, outside the purview of the SWAp. Data from a survey of aid conducted in 2006 (Overseas Development Institute 2007) showed that 25 major donors were supporting 108 different projects in the Health sector, with over half of project aid not appearing in the sector's budget. Whilst 90 per cent of mainstream government budgetary funding was being channelled to service delivery, this only represented 44 per cent of sector funding. The financing of parallel service providers has meant that scarce human resources are also being attracted away from mainstream government employment. The sector was also distracted by major corruption scandals, which discouraged donors from moving towards sector budget support, even though the scandals related to project aid and were facilitated in part by donors refusing to channel their aid through the budget.

7. Achievements and limitations of SWAps

There has been a rapid expansion in service delivery since the mid 1990s. This expansion was largely a consequence of major policy decisions. For example, enrolment in Primary Education doubled following the introduction of UPE in 1997. Outpatient attendance at health centres increased substantially following the abolition of user fees in 2001 (see Figure 9.2), and immunization rates have also increased markedly. Safe water coverage has climbed steadily since the early 1990s, despite the rapidly expanding population (see Figure 9.3). SWAps, along with budget reforms and PEAP, emerged as instruments to help plan for and manage the rebuilding and expansion of services.

Although the level of services has increased there have been major and legitimate concerns over the *quality* of service delivery. Few pupils attending primary schools leave with basic literacy or numeracy skills, and completion

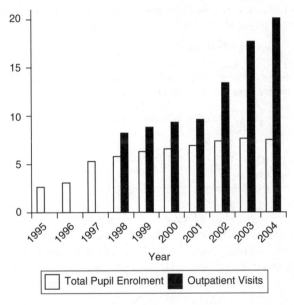

Figure 9.2 Primary Health Care and Education Services (Millions of Pupils/Visits)

Source: Lister et al. (2006).

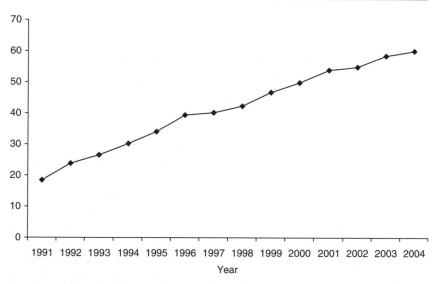

Figure 9.3 Rural Safe Water Coverage (% of Rural Population Served)

Source: Lister et al. (2006).

rates are very low (see Table 9.2). No resident of Kampala is happy with the state of the roads in the capital city. Although there have been improvements, even in the context of the policy of free basic healthcare significant problems remain with the availability of staff and medicine at health facilities.

Given the unprecedented increases in the levels of service delivery, but the less positive story on the quality of those services, what has been the role of sector reforms and SWAps? To what extent have SWAps facilitated this expansion? Have they been able to deal with issues such as quality?

Over time a stronger, more coherent set of policies and plans has been developed at the sector level. The delegation by MoFPED of much of the

Table 9.2 Quality of Service Delivery in Health and Education Sectors

Health	1999/00	2004/05	Education	2000	2004
Proportion of approved posts that are filled by trained health personnel	33%	68%	Literacy P3	18%	38%
			Literacy P6	13%	30%
			Numeracy P3	29%	41%
Percentage of facilities without any stock-outs of chloroquine, ORS, cotrimoxazole and measles vaccine	29%	35%	Numeracy P6	42%	43%
Percentage of children < 1 yr receiving DPT 3	41%	89%			

Sources: Lister et al. (2006); Ministry of Health (2007).

Box 9.4 ROLE OF MoFPED SECTOR DESK OFFICERS

Following the 1992 merger of the Ministries of Finance and Planning, Finance Officers and Economists from the two respective institutions were integrated into a single budget directorate, and their functions were also integrated. The new sector 'desk officers' became the key focal points for all sector planning and budgeting issues. Their functions include:

- representing MoFPED in sector meetings relating to policy development, planning, budgeting, and budget implementation, including SWGs and Joint Sector Reviews;

- reviewing Sector Budget Framework Papers, Recurrent and Development Budget Estimates, and preparing sector components of the National Budget Framework Paper;

- appraising sector projects and presenting them to the Development Committee;

- reviewing sector policies, plans, and performance reports;

- coordinating budget releases and the processing of reallocations and supplementary expenditures for sector institutions;

- monitoring, analysis, and evaluation of recurrent and development budget expenditures; and

- giving technical advice to ministries on budget and expenditure issues.

---

responsibility for planning and budgeting to the sectors, and the consultative manner in which policies were developed, has meant there has been strong ownership of those policies and plans by the people responsible for implementing them. The involvement of sector desk officers from the unified Budget Directorate gave MoFPED confidence in the process since it was represented in all sector fora (see Box 9.4).

The combination of clearer policies and stronger ownership contributed towards increasingly coherent and common approaches to their implementation. Government institutions are notorious for not communicating with each other. The coordination structures which regularly brought different sector institutions together directly addressed this and helped increase synergy amongst those institutions. In many sectors technical working groups deepened the dialogue. Sector reviews also increased the focus on policy implementation and, combined with improved working relationships between stakeholders, enhanced mutual accountability.

Furthermore, a key feature of the Ugandan approach has been the use of government systems. The move by some donors from project to sector budget support via the PAF in the late 1990s contrasts with countries where 'basket funds' have been more prevalent.[3] This has enabled the government to channel additional resources through its own systems, including local government,

---

[3] For example, Tanzania and Mozambique.

for service delivery. This, in turn, has helped to focus national policy dialogue and attention on strengthening those systems. Having to build and use their own capacity to deliver services has strengthened local government capacity for delivery significantly.

The move towards sector budget support has also allowed the government to allocate more resources to recurrent aspects of service delivery. This has included expanding the number of teachers and health workers, provision of instructional materials and medicines, and better road maintenance. Moreover, it has helped ensure that public investments are maintained and that there is a more sustainable balance between the recurrent and development budgets. However, they have not been a panacea for solving problems at the sector level. Not all sectors are suitable for conventional SWAps such as those in Education and Health. Consequently, while some sectors have made substantial progress, others have not and collaborative working relationships have yet to take off.

An important element of the budget process is that it is constrained by available resources—the 'macro ceiling'; this has ensured fiscal discipline and macroeconomic stability. A common complaint by sectors is that they do not understand the macro ceiling, and they certainly have not wanted to be bound by it. Sectors have either been unwilling, or have found it difficult to prepare realistic plans, despite being aware of the discipline of the budget. This in part reflects political reality. It is very difficult for the Minister of, say, Education to propose a plan that does not include significant investment in universities; or the Minister of Health one that does not include significant development of hospitals. Consequently, sector investment plans have often borne little relationship to the likely available resources at the sector level as set out in the MTEF. This has made it difficult to link MTEF and budget allocations to the implementation of sector investment plans, as the latter are usually significantly under-funded.

In the late 1990s and early 2000s there were clear incentives to develop a SWAp. The early sectors—Health, Education, Roads, Water and Sanitation, and Agriculture—created the impression that developing a SWAp led to significant additional resources. However, this no longer applied after MoFPED withdrew the commitment of additionality of sector budget support in 2002. Without the incentive of extra funding, there was less incentive for sectors to develop new policies and for more collaborative ways of working. Moreover, it has continued to be possible to obtain project funding directly from donors, even outside the context of SWAps and the official MTEF ceiling, as many sectors have done. As noted above, channelling aid outside the budgetary process had significant negative consequences in Health.

It is clear that sectors need strong technical leadership within government when establishing and implementing a SWAp, as well as political backing. The Education, Health, and Water and Sanitation sectors all benefited from such leadership early on. This enabled lead ministries in the sector to coordinate government and domestic stakeholders, and to show clear direction to donors. However, strong leadership has not been present in all sectors. The political leadership does not always engage in sector reviews, the permanent secretary may not chair the SWG regularly, and the leadership may not demonstrate ownership and accountability for the implementation of sector policies.

Whilst the establishment of donor coordination mechanisms represents a positive step, donor engagement in SWAps has not always been constructive. Some donors have tried to push their own agendas rather than letting the government take the lead, diverting dialogue away from issues important for overall sector performance. Donors are not always consistent, partly due to the high turnover of donor staff participating in the dialogue. Furthermore, they often 'connive' with sectors, sometimes taking strong positions against MoFPED in the budget process. They sometimes back sector requests for additional resources rather than push for the more effective use of existing resources at the same time that their colleagues in the donor economist group are endorsing overall MTEF allocations.

SWAps are also subject to influence from factors outside the sector. For example, public sector reform cuts across all sectors. Public service pay reform has not been effectively implemented (see Chapter 4) and has not had the desired impact on public service motivation. The creation of new districts has also had a negative impact on institutions at the local level. Many sector specific policy initiatives, such as free primary education and health care, have come from the political leadership rather than the consultative processes around SWAps. High-level political decisions have often been the biggest catalysts of change. Yet it is such high level political decisions made outside the context of SWAps that, rightly or wrongly, have given the expansion of access to free basic services greater priority than the quality of those services. For example, the 2006 decision to introduce free Universal Secondary Education has meant that there are fewer resources available for improving the quality of primary education, which remains poor. Nevertheless, SWAps have provided a framework to respond to these policy decisions more rationally—through stepping up funding for medicine for health centres, operational funding for schools, and the recruitment of health workers and teachers, for example. The Health sector was more successful at maintaining standards of quality in delivery than the Education sector.

The best policy or budgetary choices may not always have been made at the sector level, either within or outside the framework of SWAps. Yet SWAps and the associated review mechanisms have definitely provided opportunities for learning from mistakes and resolving issues which emerge during policy implementation. For example, the Health sector gradually came to realize its mistake in allowing increases in off-budget funding in the first half of the 2000s, and to appreciate the importance of using the inclusive coordination mechanisms of the SWAps for managing aid and domestic resources. In 2007 teacher absenteeism was revealed, through the review mechanism, as an increasing problem—

highlighting the importance of improving schools inspection. Overcoming one set of challenges leads to identification of further challenges. This is to be expected as reform is an ongoing process, and SWAps provide a useful framework for this.

8. Conclusions

Uganda has come a long way in policy making, planning, implementation, monitoring, and evaluation at the sector level and has learned many lessons in the process. Importantly, the approach (not a blueprint) has been allowed to evolve, and this evolution has fostered a process of learning. The use of government systems wherever possible, and minimizing parallel mechanisms, has helped focus attention on strengthening policy implementation. Two key principles embedded within the SWAp have proved important: collaboration and comprehensiveness. Together they have helped ensure that these approaches are strongly owned and are genuinely sector wide.

Mistakes have been made in the context of SWAps. Undoubtedly, better decisions could have been made, and some sectors would have benefited from stronger leadership. Yet the inclusive and collaborative processes around SWAps have endured and have helped keep a focus on overall sector performance.

The expansion of service delivery between 1997 and 2007 has been a substantial achievement. The decision to give higher priority to free universal access to basic services over the quality of services, which remains poor, has ultimately been a political one made outside the context of SWAps. Given this political context, SWAps have nevertheless had a significant positive effect on the way in which policy decisions and services have been delivered in Uganda.

10

Poverty Monitoring

Margaret Kakande

1. Introduction

Uganda experienced rapid economic growth from 1986 onwards. However, by the mid 1990s there were concerns as to whether the growth was reflected in rising living standards, particularly of the poor. The 1997 Human Development Report, for example, noted 'The perennial concern is that the benefits of strong growth have yet to translate into measurable improvements in the standard of living for the majority of people' (United Nations Development Programme 1997: 2). This chapter describes the measures taken by the government to measure and monitor poverty trends and discusses the substantial drop in income poverty between 1992 and 2006. It consists of six sections:

- Mainstreaming of poverty issues in budgets and programmes;
- Poverty Monitoring and Evaluation Strategy;
- Technical issues in measuring poverty;
- Poverty trends;
- Reforms and developments behind the poverty trends; and
- Findings and conclusions.

2. Mainstreaming of poverty issues in budgets and programmes

The budget is the most important policy instrument of government, reflecting its commitment to specific goals and priorities. It determines whether or not, and the extent to which, different groups of people benefit from the services provided by the state through public intervention. It sets spending and revenue patterns for all sectors of government, results in the implementation of broad economic choices and priorities and affects income distribution and social change within the country. Implementation of the Poverty Eradication Action Plan (PEAP, see Chapter 7), therefore, entailed mainstreaming of poverty concerns into budgets and programmes to ensure that poverty reduction was a reality and not merely rhetoric. This section discusses how the Ministry of Finance, Planning and Economic Development (MoFPED) set about mainstreaming poverty concerns in the Public Investment Plan (from which the Development Budget is taken, see Chapter 6) and in the budget as a whole.

2.1 *Revising the Public Investment Plan*

To ensure that the strategies identified in the PEAP were effectively implemented, a review of the Public Investment Plan (PIP) was undertaken in 1998 by MoFPED in order to identify projects which were poverty focused. The PIP was reviewed to ensure that only projects with a poverty focus were retained, while others were to be phased out.

The PIP review categorized projects into three sections, I and II for ongoing projects and III for new ones. The projects in section I formed the core programme for implementing the PEAP and they were to have first call on resources in the budget. Section II listed projects that focused on other priority areas, not directly targeting poverty. While the focus was on interventions that had a direct impact on poverty eradication, it was recognized that some ongoing projects contributed to an enabling environment for poverty eradication. Such projects targeted, for example, sustainable development, good governance and accountability, macroeconomic stability, and accelerated economic growth. These projects were to be implemented to completion. For future such projects to be included in the PIP they had to have clearly specified linkages to poverty reduction.

Section III listed poverty focused projects which had been approved by the Development Committee (see Chapter 6) for inclusion in the PIP, but which had not secured funding. It also included proposals at various levels of development, which formed the 'project bank'; these were continuously upgraded as the project preparation process advanced.

2.2 *Mainstreaming poverty in the budget*

In the 1999/2000 Budget Call Circular MoFPED mandated all sectors and ministries to integrate poverty issues in their Budget Framework Papers (BFPs, see Chapter 8). To enhance compliance, in 2000 the Ministry established a Poverty Eradication Working Group (PEWG) with members from:

- Ministry of Finance, Planning and Economic Development;
- Ministry of Gender, Labour and Social Development;

- Uganda Bureau of Statistics;
- Donors (represented by DFID and the World Bank);
- Makerere Institute of Social Research; and
- Civil Society (represented by Uganda Debt Network and Forum for Women in Development).

The key tasks of the Group were to:

- Make recommendations on the overall allocation of resources and allocations within sectors;
- Make recommendations on other budget policies that have an impact on the poor;
- Recommend which sectors should be covered by the Poverty Action Fund; and
- Guide the Sector Working Groups (SWGs, see Chapter 9) in applying the PEAP crosscutting principles to the BFPs. This entailed assessing the sector BFPs and making recommendations on how to enhance their alignment with PEAP policy and expenditure priorities.

The PEWG designed guidelines for the SWGs. These emphasized three PEAP crosscutting principles:

1. Addressing the needs of the poor within sectors;
2. Addressing geographical inequalities; and
3. Designing measures to empower the poor.

1. ADDRESSING THE NEEDS OF THE POOR WITHIN SECTORS

Sectors were asked to reflect on their service provision to the poor and vulnerable groups;[1] and to differentiate between poor groups as much as possible, in the light of data availability constraints. Apart from reviewing mechanisms for enhancing access and use of services by the poor, SWGs were encouraged to make budgetary provisions for programmes that would reduce the constraints that limited service access by the poor.

2. ADDRESSING GEOGRAPHICAL INEQUALITIES

This entailed analysing sector service delivery in different regions with a view to addressing inequalities. It was recommended that local transfers take three particular factors into account: population size, geographical area in terms of land size, and the poverty situation of the district.

---

[1] The vulnerable groups included orphans, street children, assetless widows, people with disabilities, chronically sick, ethnic minorities, internally displaced persons, and refugees.

3. DESIGNING MEASURES TO EMPOWER THE POOR

Sectors were asked to identify direct measures relevant to empowering people in their sector, as well as the obstacles that worked to disempower people.[2] Measures to address empowerment should be included within sector BFPs.

The biggest challenge in mainstreaming poverty into budgets was the availability of adequately disaggregated data for analysis. In addition, the limited number of PEWG members hampered effective interaction with sector working groups during BFP formulation. SWGs sometimes received comments too late for meaningful action.

In addition to the above poverty mainstreaming, special protection was given to priority expenditures under the Poverty Action Fund (PAF, see Chapter 13). PAF arrangements required line ministries to demonstrate that their expenditure plans had a clear poverty rationale. PAF rules and the role of PEWG helped ensure that the poverty focus was carefully assessed.

3. Poverty Monitoring and Evaluation Strategy

Implementation of the PEAP required a system that would ensure comprehensive monitoring from inputs, processes, outputs, through to outcomes. To spearhead the process, MoFPED established the Poverty Monitoring and Analysis Unit (PMAU) in 1999. The Unit was charged with the task of collating information and producing Poverty Status Reports to give a comprehensive review of progress in implementing the PEAP.

To institutionalize poverty monitoring, a Poverty Monitoring and Evaluation Strategy (PMES) was developed in 2002. The monitoring system had to be integrated with the policy process. This entailed having an institutional framework that facilitated interaction between the population, 'information workers', and policy makers. The PMES spelt out the roles of the various institutions involved: central and local government, Uganda Bureau of Statistics, research institutions, donors, non-governmental organizations, and the general public (Ministry of Finance, Planning and Economic Development 2002a).

MoFPED had overall responsibility for coordination—shared between the Departments of Economic Development, Planning, and Research (supported by PMAU), Macro, and Budget Policy and Evaluation. A poverty-monitoring network was set up to ensure collaboration between the key players within the above institutional framework.

The Uganda Bureau of Statistics (UBoS, see Chapter 11) is the key institution for collecting statistical data. It develops the National Statistical Plan and coordinates

---

[2] Empowerment was defined as a process of enhancing people's capacity to participate in their own development.

data collection activities of other institutions. It is also the clearing-house for all statistical data so as to ensure consistency of information, irrespective of source.

The PMES compiled comprehensive information covering the multi-dimensional aspects of poverty. Poverty monitoring entailed assessing budget performance viewed from various angles: inputs (budget efficiency); process (budget reach/adequacy); and outputs/outcomes (budget effectiveness). From the outset, monitoring of inputs focused on financial resources using administrative reports from sectors and local governments, supplemented by Public Expenditure Tracking Surveys (PETS, see Chapter 6). PETS findings in education and health that less than 40 per cent of funds were reaching their intended targets led to the formulation of measures to enhance transparency such as publishing disbursements to local governments in newspapers.

The monitoring of budget effectiveness entailed reviewing outputs and outcomes. Sector management information systems provided information on quantity of outputs, but little of the information on quality needed to assess value for money. A few civil society organizations collected information on the value for money of public expenditure on an *ad hoc* basis, but this was not comprehensive enough. The statistical series on household consumption produced by UBoS was a particularly rich information source for reviewing outcomes.

Additional information has been generated through the following specialized surveys and assessments:

- National Service Delivery Surveys, conducted every three years by UBoS since 2001, review beneficiary satisfaction with public provision of education, health, agricultural extension, roads, and justice, law and order services;

- National Integrity Surveys, conducted every two years by the Inspector General of Government, assess levels of corruption within public institutions; and

- The Uganda Participatory Poverty Assessment (PPA) process commissioned by MoFPED in 1997 enhanced qualitative and participatory poverty research that was already widely used by civil society organizations.

The PMAU commissioned a number of discussion papers and policy briefs to analyse and build upon the above research findings. Examples of studies that directly influenced policy include:

- A study of the criteria used to allocate funds from central to local governments (Ministry of Finance, Planning and Economic Development 2002b). Initially, population size and geographical area were the only criteria used. The study found that this was fostering geographical inequalities and recommended the inclusion of poverty criteria. A poverty criterion was added with a weight of 50 per cent;

- A study of persistent poverty and inequality in northern Uganda (Ministry of Finance, Planning and Economic Development 2002c) led to the

---

Box 10.1 PARTICIPATORY POVERTY ASSESSMENT

The Uganda Participatory Poverty Assessment (PPA) process originated in a context where poverty was becoming a key government priority. A significant level of consultation had been undertaken in developing the PEAP, across government and with donors, academia, and NGOs. However, the poor themselves had not been consulted.

PPA research of 1998/99 was conducted in nine out of (then) forty-five districts. The selection of these districts was based on purposive sampling to cover the diverse socio-economic conditions and various facets of poverty across the country.

Government led a multi-stakeholder partnership consisting of donors, research institutions, and NGOs. Oxfam lead the implementation because of their expertise in participatory methodologies. However, the PPA office was located in MoFPED.

The distinctive feature of PPA was its extensive use of the perspectives of the poverty experts —the poor themselves. The research explored definitions of poverty by the poor; trends in poverty; social issues; experiences with service delivery; implementation of policy; and governance and security issues (Norton et al. 2001). The findings revealed a highly complex picture of poverty—reaffirming the multidimensional nature of the problem. Poverty trends were said to have deteriorated, with the poor experiencing low access to public services. The study identified constraints in the processes of policy implementation in terms of poor information flow. In addition, local governments were faced with limited flexibility in use of funds from central government, which constrained their ability to address peculiar needs that were not national in nature. The importance attached by the poor to security, good governance, and water and sanitation were highly influential in revising priorities in the 2000 PEAP (see Chapter 7).

Two Participatory Poverty Assessments were conducted. The 1998/99 study was aimed at exploring poverty from the perspective of the poor themselves, while the 2002 study conducted in twelve districts deepened the understanding of poverty.

---

government decision to design and implement a development plan specifically targeting the region; and

- A review of the persistent poor performance in quality of life indicators (1995–2000), in terms of both infant mortality and maternal mortality (Ministry of Finance, Planning and Economic Development 2002d). MoFPED established a multi-disciplinary Task Force on Infant and Maternal Mortality to formulate a national strategy to address the issues (Ministry of Finance, Planning and Economic Development 2004b).

MoFPED's willingness to use research findings to propose adjustments in budget allocations and to encourage ministries and districts to review their policies was a significant factor in realizing the potential of the PMES.

To enhance coordination, the PMES was subsumed into the National Integrated Monitoring and Evaluation Framework (NIMES) in 2005. NIMES is

231

coordinated by the Office of the Prime Minister and is charged with the production of annual PEAP implementation review reports. Within this framework, PMAU is part of the Policy Research group charged with production of Poverty Status Reports,[3] as well as conducting and disseminating policy related research. Other institutions continue with their monitoring and evaluation (M&E) functions and are coordinated by relevant working groups. There are seven working groups: Local Government M&E; Policy Research; Evaluation Coordination; National Statistical Data; Sector Management Information Systems and Spatial Data Infrastructure; Civil Society M&E; and the Financial Information System.

3.1 Monitoring indicators

To assess performance in implementing the PEAP, a number of indicators were selected by the poverty monitoring network[4] in agreement with the sectors. The indicators covered the whole range of poverty monitoring from inputs through processes to outputs, outcomes, and impacts. The priority indicators corresponded to the outcome targets that had been agreed for the sectors, and to the key policy areas that had been identified as the necessary steps (intermediate outcomes or outputs) to achieve those results. PMES focused in particular on output and outcome indicators. This was a new focus as government was progressively moving towards accountability for results—no longer just inputs. This was aimed at ascertaining the contribution that sectors were making to the overall poverty eradication objective.

These indicators were linked to the budgeting process as they were used to assess sectoral performance when considering budget submissions.

The main challenge facing the PMES was the limited availability of timely and reliable data. While information on outputs was usually generated by the sectors, information on outcomes—the results actually attained—was much harder to find.

4. Technical issues in measuring poverty

Since poverty is multi-dimensional, its measurement raises issues of scope of coverage. The various facets of poverty include household incomes, access to social services, lack of 'voice', and social capital. The quantitative poverty measure that is most prevalent in Uganda is based on household consumption expenditure as a proxy for income. This has been complemented by quantitative

---

[3] Poverty Status Reports are produced every two years.
[4] The network consisted of MoFPED, selected sector ministries, UBoS, selected development partners, two research institutions, and an NGO.

assessments of access to social services as well as 'perceptions' of the people on voice and social capital.

4.1 Quantitative techniques

The quantitative approach entails choosing a welfare measure, a poverty line, and a poverty index for aggregation. The use of the household as the unit of analysis in itself has limitations as the individual aspects of poverty are ignored.

The use of private consumption as the measure for welfare has various technical concerns that have to be addressed. Two types of adjustments are made to derive consistent estimates of consumption for comparability: for sampling, and for prices. The aspects of sampling that can cause problems for comparison over time are geographical coverage, seasonality, and the panel aspect of the data.[5]

In the 1990s Uganda suffered insecurity in both the north and west and this affected survey coverage. The largest exclusions were in 1997 when large parts of four districts (Kitgum, Gulu, Kasese, and Bundibugyo) were not covered by the household surveys. For comparability these districts were always left out until 2002, when they were included. These districts are relatively poor and their omission may have understated poverty levels.

Another possible source of incomparability in sampling is that of duration. The time spent on data collection during the surveys varied from seven to thirteen months. This is problematic because food consumption is reported for a short recall period and is subject to seasonal variations. If the survey is conducted only during the lean season, poverty will be overestimated.

Where new items were introduced over time, strict comparisons were impossible. The best option would be omission from the consumption basket. However, this is inappropriate where new items have come on to the market which take large shares of the household budget for both the poor and the rich—for example, airtime.[6]

To estimate consumption in constant prices, three adjustments were made. First, home consumption of food was revalued to market prices. This was because the respondents had been requested to value their food consumption in farm-gate prices. The problem has been the capture of items in all the forms in which they are produced, sold, or received. Many items are non-standardized; for example, a small basket in one part of the country may not be the same as in other parts. Another problem is the issue of desegregation of food items into their different forms. For example, people consume maize either as

---

[5] A panel is when some enumeration areas are continually visited and, within those areas, some households are also repeatedly visited during every survey exercise.

[6] The introduction of mobile phones has revolutionized the telecommunications sector. Airtime has become a major expenditure item for many households since 2003.

grain or flour and these have different nutritional values because of the processing. The differences were difficult to capture in the consumption surveys.

The second adjustment was for inflation, where the national consumer price index was used as a deflator to convert expenditures into base values. Although the index appears relatively stable, it is limited to only eight major towns. In addition, it does not take into consideration the particular month that a particular household was interviewed. This has implications for seasonal producers, who experience highly variable prices depending on the season.

The third adjustment was for the regional variation in prices. Food prices are markedly higher in some areas, especially urban areas, than others. Regional food price indices were constructed and median unit values used to make the results insensitive to extremes. Non-food prices were assumed to be the same across the country.

4.2 Defining an absolute poverty line for Uganda

An absolute poverty line was constructed reflecting the monetary cost of meeting certain basic needs and was fixed in real terms. The line was derived by Appleton (1998) from food related needs and only indirectly estimated for non-food requirements. The food related needs were reduced to energy requirements, although this was a simplification, as proteins, vitamins, and other nutrients are also required from food.

The first step was to define how many calories are 'sufficient'. The energy requirements set by the World Health Organization were adopted. These vary by age, sex, and intensity of work, pregnancy, and lactation. The requirements of men aged 18–30 years engaged in moderate work were adopted, giving 3,000 calories a day as the sufficient level of calories. The rest of the population's energy requirements were allowed for in reference to the male population based on an equivalence scale.[7] The poverty line was based on the food basket of 1993 and the adult equivalents corresponded to an average requirement of 2,283 calories per capita. In adding the non-food requirements, consumption variations due to factors such as age or the household economies of scale reaped by larger households were not considered.

The second step was establishing the poverty line. Two lines were derived:

- The food poverty line that defined core poverty; and
- The absolute poverty line that combined food and non-food requirements.

In constructing the food poverty line, it had to be based upon the actual consumption patterns of the poor. The mean quantities of twenty-eight major food items consumed by the poorest 50 per cent of the population constituted

[7] The equivalence scales were used in reference to age but not sex.

the reference food basket. In deriving the calories generated by the reference food basket, calorific values of East African foods as reported by West (1987) were used.

The variety of staples across the different regions would have been an argument for regional poverty lines. This is because different staples have varying nutritional values, and different costs in different parts of the country depending on availability. However, a single food poverty line was adopted for the whole country.

As noted above, to derive the national absolute poverty line non-food requirements have to be considered. However, there was no attempt to itemize non-food requirements as this would have involved making controversial judgments about the necessity of a myriad of small or infrequently consumed goods and services. The solution was to derive non-food requirements indirectly by reviewing the non-food spending of the poor. The basic non-food expenditure was taken to be the expenditure of those whose expenditure is just equal to the food poverty line. The argument was that, since at this level of welfare the poor have sacrificed some of their need for calories, the non-food expenditures they have chosen to prioritize should be regarded as meeting essential needs.

The national absolute poverty line was the food poverty line plus the expenditure on non-food requirements of the core poor. This amounted to USD34 per capita per month (in 1993/94 prices) and was hence comparable to the USD1 a day poverty line used for international poverty comparisons by the World Bank.

4.3 Challenges of using consumption as a welfare measure

The approach used to track poverty reduction efforts has been robust, irrespective of the poverty line used. It benefited initially from technical support from the Universities of Oxford and Bath, in the UK. Capacity has now been built in-country and the Economic Policy Research Centre analyses survey data for poverty trends without external assistance. However, the variable used for assessing welfare, private consumption, still has major interpretation issues.

The use of private consumption as a household welfare measure implicitly assumes that the higher the consumption the higher the welfare. However, this has increasingly been questioned. It has been observed that some private consumption actually reduces household welfare. An example is the consumption of alcohol, mainly by male members of the household, which not only reduces consumption of other members but may also lead to domestic violence. Communities raised this phenomenon during the participatory poverty assessments, noting that many households were falling into poverty because of increased alcohol consumption.

Another example is increased expenditure on health, especially by families with members suffering from HIV and AIDS. Increasing private consumption, irrespective of the income bracket, increasingly reflects higher expenditure on health—partly in response to HIV and AIDS. The PPAs found that such families had reduced welfare as expenditure on other items was crowded out.

Before associating increased private consumption with poverty reduction it is important to understand the sources of increased consumption. For poverty reduction to be sustainable the sources of increased consumption must be sustainable. There are doubts as to the sustainability of at least two key sources of increased consumption. First, transfers from relatives abroad are an important source of income for many Ugandans. The proportion of the population with transfers as the main source of income increased from 4.4 per cent in 2003 to 4.9 per cent in 2006 (Uganda Bureau of Statistics 2006a). Transfers from nationals abroad amounted to USD731.3 million in 2006. Second, consumption may be financed from the sale of assets, particularly land and livestock. Many households were found to be depleting assets to meet education and health expenses.

4.4 Qualitative techniques

The main issue with qualitative information generated through the PPAs was that of representativeness. As already noted, the 1998/99 PPA was conducted in nine of the then forty-five districts. The aim was to select the most disadvantaged district in each of the seven agro-ecological zones, as assessed by ten selection criteria[8] indicative of the multi-dimensional nature of poverty. In total thirty-six communities were visited.

National trends in the various poverty dimensions were drawn from case studies. However, Appleton (2001) questioned the use of one community (from Moyo district) to project the overall national poverty trend. Despite these concerns about national representation, the clear articulation and detailed documentation of the methodology earned the study findings widespread acceptance.

5. Poverty trends

5.1 Income poverty trends

Household survey data (Appleton 2001; Appleton and Ssewanyana 2003; Uganda Bureau of Statistics 2006a) show that Uganda's good macroeconomic performance since the late 1980s was translated into broad-based growth of consumption. When measured in terms of consumption (a proxy for income), poverty decreased considerably between 1992 and 2000 (Appleton 2001;

---

[8] These were the Human Development Index, natural calamities, civil strife, social and physical isolation, population density, land fragmentation, environmental degradation, poor soils and yields, participation-social networks, and access to roads and water.

Deininger and Okidi 2003; Kappel et al. 2005). However, poverty rose slightly between 2000 and 2003, despite continued growth, before resuming its downward trend. The increased poverty between 2000 and 2003 was attributable to slower growth in agriculture,[9] the major employer, and declining farm prices. When growth in the sector declined after 2000 (Kappel et al. 2005), rural poverty was pervasive and crop farmers fared badly.

Figure 10.1 highlights three distinct periods in the relationship between growth and poverty reduction. From 1992–2000, and again from 2003–06, growth was broad based with substantial consumption increases for the whole population, which in turn led to poverty reduction. Since consumption growth was higher in urban areas and for the richer segments of the population, total inequality and inequality between urban and rural areas increased. Nevertheless, the two periods can be termed pro-poor because the growth effect outweighed the distributional effect. By contrast, between 2000–03 there was much lower growth in mean consumption with most segments of the population experiencing a decline in consumption (Kappel et al. 2005). Only the rich experienced growth, which increased inequality with the distributional effect dominating the growth effect. The end result was an increase in poverty levels over the period.

As illustrated in Figure 10.1, national poverty assessed by the poverty line declined from 56 per cent in 1992 to 34 per cent in 2000. It then increased to 39 per cent in 2003 before declining to 31 per cent in 2006. This absolute measurement calculates the proportion of the population that does not have enough income to consume an appropriate amount of food and other essentials to survive (monetized as USD1 per day). This is one of the largest and fastest reductions in income poverty recorded anywhere in modern times.

The indicator has fallen by an average of almost 2 per cent a year and if it continues to fall at this rate Uganda can expect to achieve the Millennium Development Goal of halving extreme poverty by the time of the next national measurement in 2008/09.[10]

Overall, the findings indicate a significant improvement in living standards but marked spatial unevenness in the improvement. While the decline in poverty occurred in both rural and urban areas (see Figure 10.1), it is clear that poverty is still mainly a rural phenomenon.

All regions saw reductions in income poverty. However, as shown in Table 10.1, the north lagged well behind other regions throughout the period, reflecting the continuing insecurity in the region. In terms of economic activity, farmers

---

[9] The real GDP growth rate for monetary agriculture fell from 4.5 per cent in 2000 to 3.9 per cent in 2003. However, the rate for non-monetary agriculture fell from 4.6 per cent to 0.1 per cent over the same period (Uganda Bureau of Statistics 2004).

[10] UBoS proposes to conduct a National Household Survey in 2008/09. If poverty continues to fall at the average of 1.77 per cent per year then the poverty headcount rate will be 25.8 per cent at the time of that survey.

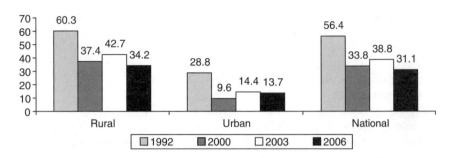

Figure 10.1 Trends in Income Poverty

Sources: Appleton (2001); Appleton and Ssewanyana (2003); Kappel et al. (2005); Uganda Bureau of Statistics (2006a).

continued to be poorer than the rest of the population. Among the farmers, women, who constitute 75 per cent of the labour force, are mainly engaged in crop farming.[11] Women therefore constitute the majority of the poor. Household heads employed in public services experienced the least poverty.

The biggest concern has been increasing income inequality. Uganda uses the Gini index[12] as the measure of inequality. The index increased from 0.364 in 1992 (Appleton 2001) to 0.408 in 2006 (Uganda Bureau of Statistics 2006a). However, this was an improvement from 0.43 in 2003 (Okidi et al. 2005), driven by improvements in urban equality as populations shifted into the urban based service and manufacturing sectors.

5.2 Qualitative findings on poverty trends

The qualitative findings from the PPAs traced changes in specific aspects of well-being and ill-being rather than in 'poverty' as a whole. The overall impression was that peoples' well-being was declining and the poor were getting poorer.[13] The overall trends discerned in particular dimensions of poverty included:

- The natural resource base was deteriorating, leading to increasingly frequent food insecurity. This was being exacerbated by rapid population growth;

---

[11] 60 per cent of women farmers are engaged in crop agriculture.

[12] The indicator is measured from 0–1 where 0 means that every person has an identical income and 1 means that a single person commands all the income from the entire country. The closer to 1 the measure is, the higher the degree of inequality.

[13] This finding contrasted with the quantitative income poverty measure, which showed a consistent decline.

Table 10.1 Poverty Trends by Region and Sector of Household Head

	% of the population below poverty line		
	1992	2003	2006
Region			
Central	45.6	22.3	16.4
Eastern	58.8	46.0	35.9
Northern	73.5	63.0	60.7
Western	52.7	32.9	20.5
Uganda	**56.4**	**38.8**	**31.1**
Sector			
Crop agriculture	63.0	48.9	36.8
Non-crop agriculture	55.0	32.5	28.1
Construction and mining	37.0	33.0	27.1
Manufacturing	44.0	31.0	21.8
Trade	26.0	20.5	14.9
Transport and communication	–	19.8	16.7
Public services	37.0	13.7	8.5
Other services	–	26.4	17.9
Inactive	59.0	43.1	37.2

Sources: Appleton (1999); Appleton and Ssewanyana (2003); Uganda Bureau of Statistics (2006a).

- Disposable household incomes were increasingly outstripped by needs. The main concern was user fees for public services that were limiting access by the poor;

- Increased ill-health in the wake of the HIV and AIDS pandemic, which had both direct and indirect costs to households. Directly, households had to spend more on health, while losing labour of productive family members. Indirectly, many households were reluctant to invest in the education of their children;

- Limited service coverage in the light of population pressure. Even with Universal Primary Education, where access was improved, there were major concerns about quality; and

- The civil strife that had displaced millions of people in western and northern Uganda, depriving them of meaningful livelihoods.

5.3 *Progress towards the Millennium Development Goals*

The United Nations' Millennium Development Goals (MDGs) focus attention on several important non-financial dimensions of poverty. This section assesses Uganda's progress in meeting the MDGs, drawing heavily on the detailed assessment in UNDP (2007).

MDG 1: ERADICATING EXTREME POVERTY AND HUNGER

The proportion of people who suffer from hunger was assessed based on the nutritional status of children. The proportion of underweight[14] children fell from 23.3 per cent in 1989 to 15.7 per cent in 2006. However, stunting[15] was persistent while wasting was on the rise.

MDG 2: ACHIEVING UNIVERSAL PRIMARY EDUCATION

Overall, the net primary school enrolment was 84 per cent (2006). However, the target of full completion of primary education is unlikely to be met. By 2006 38 per cent of pupils were completing the seven years of schooling (Uganda Bureau of Statistics 2006a); dropout rates were higher for girls than boys.

Literacy rates have risen steadily by about 1 per cent a year since 1990, although the rate has stagnated since 2002 (Uganda Bureau of Statistics 2006a). The rate rose from 56 per cent in 1990 to 69 per cent in 2006. This is explained by improved literacy in the north and strong progress in women's literacy, particularly in the central region.

MDG 3: PROMOTE GENDER EQUALITY AND EMPOWER WOMEN

Gender equality has almost been achieved in primary school enrolment. Secondary education enrolment has come a long way towards gender equality from a ratio of only 0.6 in 1998 to 0.83 in 2006. Tertiary education has not seen the same progress, although the absolute number of women gaining a university education has risen dramatically.

In terms of empowerment, female employment in non-agricultural wage labour is significantly below that of men. The average woman's wage is between 40 and 50 per cent that of the average man (Ministry of Finance, Planning and Economic Development 2007b).

MDG 4: REDUCE CHILD MORTALITY

Progress in reducing infant and under five mortality has been poor. The infant mortality and under five mortality rates have only reduced marginally, from 89 and 152 in 2000 to 75 and 137 in 2006 respectively (see Figure 10.2). At this rate it is unlikely that Uganda will attain the MDG infant mortality and under five target rates of 31 and 56 respectively.

---

[14] Underweight children have a low weight relative to their age.
[15] Stunted children have a low height relative to their age.

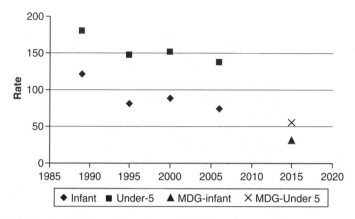

Figure 10.2 Trends in Infant and Under-5 Child Mortality Rates, 1989–2006

Sources: Uganda Bureau of Statistics and Macro International Inc (1996); Uganda Bureau of Statistics and ORC Macro (2001); Uganda Bureau of Statistics (2007).

MDG 5: IMPROVE MATERNAL HEALTH

The key MDG target for maternal health is to reduce the maternal mortality rate[16] by two thirds. The rate fell from 527 in 1995 to 435 in 2006 (Uganda Bureau of Statistics 2006a).

MDG 6: COMBAT HIV AND AIDS, MALARIA, AND OTHER DISEASES

The target of halting and reversing the prevalence rate of HIV and AIDS was achieved in Uganda even before the MDGs were set. By 2000 the effects were dramatic: the prevalence rate had fallen from 20 to 30 per cent in 1990 to 6.4 per cent in 2005. Committed and sustained political leadership, early intervention, a strong focus on prevention, and a multi-sectoral approach led to the reduction in prevalence rates that turned Uganda into a commonly cited example of best practice for tackling the disease (Okware et al. 2001).

Malaria is still the leading cause of morbidity and mortality in Uganda, with a prevalence of 40 per cent in 2006. Accurate data regarding prevalence and spread of the disease is constrained by difficulties in reporting disease incidence.

---

[16] Maternal mortality rate is the number of women deaths per 100,000 live births.

MDG 7: ENSURE ENVIRONMENTAL SUSTAINABILITY

Total forest coverage has reduced from 20.4 per cent in 1995 to 17.9 per cent in 2005. Fully stocked tropical high forest has reduced by approximately two thirds over the period, although a portion of the land area remains as depleted forest.

The main cause of the rapid depletion of forested land is demand for fuel. Approximately 60 per cent of wood consumption is for household fuel and another 20 per cent for charcoal. Over 90 per cent of total energy in Uganda is drawn from biomass. The volume of wood being felled for charcoal is growing at 7 per cent a year, double the population growth rate, while overall wood consumption is growing at 4.7 per cent per year.

The average distance travelled by the women and children usually responsible for collecting wood has increased dramatically from 0.06km in 1992 to 0.9km in 2002 (UNDP 2007).

In terms of safe water sources, Uganda is on track to meet the MDG target of improved access to water by 2015. The national level of access to safe water is 68 per cent (Uganda Bureau of Statistics and Macro International Inc. 2007). Steady progress in the provision of water despite rising population levels is a significant achievement. However, there is a wide range of access between districts; 10 per cent of districts have already achieved the MDG target of 77 per cent coverage whilst 9 per cent have coverage levels below 34 per cent, which is less than half the MDG target.

5.4 Explanation of differences in poverty trends

The PPA qualitative findings on poverty trends contrasted markedly with the quantitative income poverty trends. This, initially, created anxiety within government and some donors, who commissioned a study to explore the causes of the divergence (Bird and Booth 2000). The study concluded that the divergence was largely explained by differences in the definition of poverty, as well as by conceptual and methodological differences.

Income poverty defined poverty in terms of consumption. In contrast, during the PPAs people did not mention shortfalls in consumption at all when analysing poverty trends. Communities structured their qualitative responses around key events that culminated in crises or turning points in their lives.

The time frames varied markedly, with the quantitative surveys using time frames of one year. In the PPAs, on the other hand, people used timelines based on their own benchmarks, some as far back as the 1970s.

The quantitative poverty trends were derived from a nationally representative sample of both poor and rich persons. However, the PPA research was purposely focused on the poor, who may have been over-represented. Within the poor population poverty could actually have been getting worse, although this may have been concealed at the aggregate national level.

6. Reforms and developments behind the poverty trends

Income poverty reduction in Uganda has been attributed mainly to growth, as opposed to distributional effects. In the 1992–7 period, for example, when the total poverty headcount declined by 10.7 per cent, almost the whole decline (10.3 per cent) was attributed to growth and the rest to redistribution (Appleton 1999). Between 1997 and 2000 high growth contributed to large reductions in poverty, which more than offset the effects of rising inequality in both rural and urban areas.

Uganda has experienced continuous high economic growth rates since 1986. The growth record can be divided into two periods—post-war recovery and economic reforms. GDP grew by an annual 6.1 per cent between 1986 and 1990, mainly as a result of increases in productivity following the reactivation of productive capacity. After this recovery, the reforms that are the subject of this book helped sustain high GDP growth and poverty reduction (Kappel et al. 2005).

The reduction in poverty was a result of increased consumption expenditure by households. In the 1990s a critical factor in consumption growth was the increased prices that agricultural producers received for their crops. Of particular importance here was the liberalization of prices and exchange rates. The dismantling of the produce marketing boards and liberalizing of export crop prices meant increased competition and higher prices for farmers. The liberalization of agricultural marketing meant that farmers were able to benefit from increased world coffee prices (see Box 1.1). The unit export price for Ugandan coffee tripled from USD0.82 per kg in 1992/93 to a peak of USD2.55 per kg in 1994/95. The increase in export prices and the liberalization of the coffee sector (leading to higher prices for coffee farmers) allowed farm households to benefit directly from the increase in world prices (Appleton 2001). Not surprisingly, the most dramatic poverty reduction was among cash crop farmers in general and coffee farmers in particular. Deininger and Okidi (2003) show that coffee districts contributed more to overall poverty reduction than non-coffee districts between 1992 and 2000, but they also contributed slightly more to the poverty increase between 2000 and 2003 when world prices dropped.

As noted above, another source of consumption expenditure has been the increase in transfers from abroad, particularly remittances from citizens encouraged by the liberalized foreign exchange regime.

In addition to economic reforms, Deininger and Okidi (2003) show the importance of the supply of curative and preventive health services for poverty reduction. Higher levels of poverty in 2000 characterized households suffering from health problems in 1992. This is consistent with the PPA findings that identified ill health as the number one problem facing the poor. Health sector reforms were instrumental in poverty reduction. The removal of user fees in March 2001 was critical in enhancing the access of the poor to health services. Kappel et al. (2005) show that the poorest 20 per cent of the population received above average per capita transfers, implying that they benefited more from public health spending than the non-poor.

Deininger and Okidi (2003) also note the importance of asset endowments, in terms of both human and physical capital. Households' initial endowments clearly enhanced subsequent growth. Public investment in education, especially Universal Primary Education, was therefore targeting a critical area. However, households that were poorly endowed often used the sale of assets to smooth out consumption expenditure—to the detriment of future welfare.

Population growth also had an impact on poverty reduction. Appleton and Ssewanyana (2003) conclude that food crop production may not have kept pace with population growth between 1999/2000 and 2002/03. Specifically, food consumption per capita fell by 3 per cent in nominal terms during that period, when poverty also increased.

Poverty in the north was persistently higher than in other regions because of the civil strife. However, even this region experienced poverty reduction, explained partly by the various humanitarian and other government interventions targeting the region such as the Northern Uganda Social Action Fund.

7. Findings and conclusions

Political commitment to prudent macroeconomic policies over a long period has resulted in high economic growth rates. Moreover, the growth strategies adopted have been clearly pro-poor leading to a significant reduction in income poverty. However, the gains have not been equally distributed across the country as income inequalities have remained persistently high and urban–rural disparities have increased.

Pro-poor growth requires the sectoral pattern of growth to be biased in favour of the poor. In Uganda most of the poor reside in rural areas and are engaged in agricultural activities. The strong growth in the agriculture sector during the 1990s largely explains the poverty reduction trends, with crop agriculture being the most important contributor to poverty reduction. As noted above, Uganda experienced pro-poor growth during those periods when agriculture, the major employer, performed well.

Ugandan experience reaffirms the view that growth is a necessary but not sufficient condition for poverty reduction. Although income poverty trends have been impressive, quality of life indicators such as the MDGs paint a mixed picture. Effective integration of poverty efforts into national budgets and programmes is imperative. Where progress has been achieved in quality of life indicators this has usually been a result of targeted public sector expenditure. Direct measures to enhance sectoral growth and structural change for pro-poor growth must be complemented by public spending which targets the poor.

Measuring poverty in Uganda has been based on an absolute poverty line that has been robust enough to demonstrate national trends in poverty reduction to policy makers. However, there is a need to complement this measure with qualitative information to facilitate interpretation of the findings. The PPAs were instrumental in complementing household survey data so as to capture the multi-dimensional nature of poverty. They also helped provide explanations for some of the observed trends in income poverty.

11

Statistics Reform

E. S. K. Muwanga-Zake[1]

1. Institutional history of statistics development

Statistics development in Uganda can be divided into five periods: the Colonial and Obote I periods (before 1971); the Amin era (1971–9); the post Amin and Obote II era (1979–86); the rehabilitation of the Statistics Department (1986–98); and the Uganda Bureau of Statistics (from 1998).

1.1 *The Colonial and Obote I periods*

The collection of official statistics in Uganda started in 1948 with the creation of the East African High Commission by the colonial governments of East Africa to coordinate selected economic and development activities throughout the region. The main office of the East African Statistical Department (EASD) was in Nairobi, Kenya with units located in Entebbe, Uganda and Dar es Salaam, Tanganyika (now Tanzania). The primary responsibility of the Department was to compile traditional statistics on selected aspects of the economies of the three member colonies, including trade, agriculture, migration, labour, and population. The Commission controlled the staff establishment from Nairobi and senior staff could be transferred among the three countries.

After the independence of the three states, EASD was split into territorial departments under the control of their respective national governments, with a reduced EASD under the newly established East African Common Services Organization (EACSO). EASD retained the role of compiling statistics falling under the purview of EACSO departments, including Income Tax, Customs and Excise, Posts and Communications, Meteorological, East African Airways,

[1] Helpful comments from Peter Hodgkinson, Margaret Kakande, and Lynn Macdonald are gratefully acknowledged.

Railways and Harbours. In 1967 the East African Community replaced EACSO: however, this did not change the role of EASD.

At Independence in Uganda a statistics office was established under the Statistics Act 1961. Apart from a brief period under the President's office during the Amin era, for most of the period until 1998 the statistics function came under the Ministry of Planning and Economic Development. Though small, it was efficient and compiled, for example, the data used in drawing up the First and Second Five Year Development Plans.

1.2 The Amin era

The EASD was dismantled with the break-up of the East African Community in 1976 and responsibility for the work previously carried out by EASD was devolved to the individual territorial departments. Inevitably, the work of these departments increased in scope, coverage, and complexity. In Uganda the compilation and dissemination of basic external trade data was taken over by the statistics section of the Customs and Excise Department, but using electronic data processing facilities in Mombasa, Kenya. However, the deteriorating political and economic conditions effectively undermined the devolution of responsibility to the Ugandan department. Ugandan statisticians serving with EASD were reluctant to return to Uganda to join the Statistics Department; most opted to look for jobs elsewhere. As a result, the Uganda Statistics Department found itself in a uniquely difficult position.

Like most government institutions, the Statistics Department declined during the Amin era. The main problem was the lack of investment in statistics production; the Department lacked resources and could not effectively carry out its role as the central coordinating body for statistics within government, let alone for the country as a whole. The Department lacked essential facilities: buildings became derelict; there was only one roadworthy vehicle; and there were no computers, so all statistics had to be manually tabulated and simple desk calculators used for calculations. Other agencies progressively took over aspects of the Department's data gathering and processing responsibilities. Inevitably, there was considerable overlap in some important statistics activities, such as price collection, estimation of GDP, and statistics on central government revenue and expenditure. Any published data had lost credibility.

Annual surveys eventually stopped and, as a result, the publication of statistics was not maintained. The last comprehensive Statistical Abstract was published in 1977 in respect to 1974. Later, during the 1978–9 war to remove the Amin government, the Department's offices were looted. Finally, as real salaries plummeted, the Department lost most of its senior and experienced professional staff.

1.3 *The post Amin and Obote II era*

Attempts to revive the Statistics Department started immediately after Amin's overthrow in 1979, with a number of international missions including a Commonwealth Team of Experts (1979), Colecraft (1979), Martin (1980), and Pillai (1982). A sub-regional workshop was also organized by the Makerere University Institute of Statistics and Applied Economics (1980).

The main recommendations from these missions and workshops included: (1) setting up an autonomous and self-accounting central statistics office with a permanent field presence, including regional and district offices; (2) implementing the UN sponsored National Household Survey Capability Programme as an integrated system for collecting multi-subject information on a continuing basis; (3) funding the resumption of surveys of national importance, such as agricultural and industrial production, as well as fertility and health; and (4) drafting a work plan to guide activities. However, with continuing political instability and negligible funding, little progress was made in reviving and rehabilitating Uganda's statistical services during the Obote II era.

1.4 *Rehabilitation of the Statistics Department*

When the National Resistance Movement took over government in 1986 President Museveni attached high priority to economic planning (see Chapter 6). Timely and reliable statistics were recognized as critical for economic management and planning. The Ministry of Planning and Economic Development made the rehabilitation of the Statistics Department (under the Ministry) a major priority, therefore. As the ministry responsible for negotiating grant aid it was in a good position to address the critical bottleneck hampering previous attempts to revive statistics: the lack of funding. From 1988 progress in rehabilitating the statistics function was largely the result of a series of donor-funded projects. These addressed two dimensions of rehabilitation: reviving technical statistical activities; and reorganizing the Statistics Department.

The Rehabilitation of Statistics Project commenced in 1988 with the objective of restoring the Department's capability in data collection, processing, and distribution, as well as building up its coordination role. The project revived several key economic statistics indices including national accounts, external trade, industrial production, and consumer prices. A parallel national household survey programme also commenced in 1988. Both projects were funded by the World Bank and executed by UNDP.

Initial activities of the projects included rehabilitation of the office premises and purchase of new vehicles, computers, and furniture. Given the collapse in public service salaries (see Chapter 4), a critical success factor for both projects was the introduction of 'incentive' payments to all Statistics Department staff, along similar lines to those given elsewhere in the Ministry (see Box 2.1).

Together with the improved working environment, these incentives transformed attendance, staff morale, and performance.

1.5 Uganda Bureau of Statistics

Many of the above reviews of the Statistics Department recommended that it should have semi-autonomous status, for two main reasons. First, autonomy was expected to provide protection from possible political interference and enhance the objectivity of the data produced. Second, given the collapse in public service salaries, such a body was seen as the only way of providing sufficiently attractive terms of service to recruit and retain well-qualified staff.

Following the merger of the Ministries of Finance and Planning and Economic Development in 1992, the Ministry of Public Service conducted a study to establish a suitable management structure for the new ministry. The report, which was approved by Cabinet, recommended, *inter alia*, the transformation of the Statistics Department into a semi-autonomous body. In 1994 the new Ministry of Finance and Economic Planning commissioned a consultancy to design an organizational structure for a semi-autonomous national statistics authority, with the appropriate mandate and legal framework to provide an efficient and effective statistics service (Uganda Government 1994).

In 1995 the Statistics Department convened a workshop for major data producers and users to: (1) review the status of statistics in Uganda; (2) identify data gaps and set priorities; (3) review the Department's proposed work plan for 1996–2000; and (4) consider the proposed structure and legislative framework of the future National Statistical System.

The outcome of this process was a major overhaul of statistics legislation, with the enactment of the Uganda Bureau of Statistics Act No. 2, 1998. The Act provided for 'the development and maintenance of a National Statistical System which will ensure collection, analysis, and dissemination of integrated, reliable and timely statistical information' (Uganda Government 1998). The Act also established the Uganda Bureau of Statistics (UBoS) as a coordinating, monitoring, and supervisory body for the National Statistical System. In drafting the bill, statistics laws from a number of other African countries were reviewed.

The Act specified the following functions for UBoS:

1) Providing high quality central statistical information services.
2) Promoting standardization in the collection, analysis, and publication of statistics to ensure their uniformity in quality, adequacy of coverage, and reliability.
3) Providing guidance, training, and other assistance to users and providers of statistics.

4) Promoting cooperation, coordination, and rationalization among users and providers of statistics at national and local levels.

The Bureau became operational in late 1998 following the appointment of the Board of Directors and the Executive Director. By 2006 it comprised an executive director and a deputy, eight directors, sixteen principal officers, twenty-four senior officers, thirty-four officers, and sixty semi-professional officers. As discussed below, the Bureau has taken forward the reforms adopted since the late 1980s as well as introducing a number of new initiatives.

2. Major statistical programmes

Since the late 1980s a number of regular data collection activities, surveys, and censuses have been undertaken. These are reviewed in this section, beginning with the major categories of economic statistics and household surveys.

2.1 *Economic statistics*

The Rehabilitation of Statistics Project, which started in 1988, concentrated almost exclusively on economic statistics. The series of household surveys, which were getting under way at the same time, together with the 1991 Census of Population and Housing, were expected to satisfy the principal needs for social statistics.

The obvious starting point for a comprehensive programme of economic statistics was the development of a credible and up-to-date set of National Accounts estimates. The Department was still producing annual estimates of GDP in constant prices but, although these used sound methodology and conformed to the principles of the UN System of National Accounts, they were seriously out of date, being expressed in 1966 prices. There were no current price estimates, and (most seriously of all) the data base on which the estimates were based was almost non-existent. There was therefore no realistic alternative to implementing new statistical collections from scratch.

CONSUMER PRICE INDEX

One of the early successes was the establishment of a comprehensive Consumer Price Index (CPI), initially covering the five major urban centres of Kampala/ Entebbe, Masaka, Mbarara, Jinja, and Mbale. The Department had compiled an index up to 1988, but data was confined to Kampala, and was prepared using weighting from 1961, i.e. it was seriously outdated. Publication of this index had long been abandoned, and the Research Department of the Bank of Uganda (BoU) had taken over responsibility for compiling the only useful measure of inflation. The new CPI produced by the Department formally replaced the BoU index in about 1991. A new feature was the separate compilation of 'headline' and 'underlying' inflation; the latter measure in particular became a key element in the government planning process.

INDEX OF INDUSTRIAL PRODUCTION

An immediate start was also made in constructing an Index of Industrial Production. This was seen as a priority as accurate data were required to monitor progress of the government's plans to resurrect the manufacturing sector, which had virtually collapsed during the 1970s and 1980s.

A comprehensive index was soon established, with monthly data collected each quarter. A publication containing detailed index estimates was first issued in 1989—with 1987 as the reference period. This was the first official publication produced by the Statistics Department for many years and has been produced quarterly ever since. The Index was expanded and reweighted in 1991 based on the results of the 1989 Census of Business Establishments, and again in 2003 based on information gathered in the 2001 Uganda Business Inquiry. It was later complemented by an Index of Major Manufacturing covering fifteen large scale manufacturing establishments, produced monthly to a strict timetable.

CENSUS OF BUSINESS ESTABLISHMENTS

The Census of Business Establishments collected data for the year 1989 from all establishments with five or more employees in all sectors except agriculture, financial intermediation, public administration, education, health, and social work. Large-scale operations in the production of rice, sugar, tea, and tobacco were subsequently added. The census provided much of the basic structural input and output data on formal sector industrial and commercial establishments for National Accounts and input–output tables. It also provided a framework for the establishment of sample surveys to monitor economic developments over time, such as the monthly Industrial Production Survey.

AGRICULTURAL PRODUCTION

Estimation of agricultural production proved to be a major headache in developing National Accounts estimates. The field activities of the Ministry of Agriculture had deteriorated, and the nature of crop production in Uganda (with mixed and successive cropping plus continuous harvesting in very small holdings) made direct estimation of production very difficult. When the 1989 Household Budget Survey was completed, the quality of data reporting appeared to be excellent; it was decided that consumption data represented a superior basis for estimating the contribution of agriculture to GDP over any attempt at direct estimation of production. Moreover, this data source enabled reliable separate estimates of Monetary and Non-monetary GDP (i.e. consumption of own produce) to be made, which was an important consideration.

HEALTH, EDUCATION, AND OTHER SECTORS

Expenditure data from the household surveys have also been used to estimate other sectors in the National Accounts. For example, household expenditure on health and education services has been used to supplement government expenditure data to produce aggregate estimates for the Health and Education sectors, while outlays on public transport are an essential component in estimation of the Transport sector. Modules in the survey programme (1992/93 and 1999/2000) covering household-based economic activities have provided invaluable data for a number of sectors, particularly retail trade, restaurants, and informal manufacturing.

EXTERNAL TRADE

Another major activity was the collaboration with the Customs Department (which was later merged into the Uganda Revenue Authority, URA) to restore the coverage and accuracy of the external trade statistics. After the creation of UBoS a regular committee of senior representatives from BoU, URA, and UBoS was set up. This led to an agreed estimate of total trade (including that not captured by URA statistics) and enabled estimates in the National Accounts and the Balance of Payments (prepared by BoU) to be harmonized. Previously, BoU used statistics on import financing rather than actual recorded imports for the Balance of Payments; the two series were in conflict. Their harmonization represented a major step forward in the planning process.

MIGRATION

Collaboration with the Immigration Department led to reviving the processing of arrival and departure cards at Entebbe International Airport; leading to improved National Accounts estimates in respect of tourism, and providing a basis for estimating expenditure abroad by Ugandans.

NATIONAL ACCOUNTS ESTIMATES

By 1990 the database of economic statistics had been restored to a degree that permitted reliable National Accounts estimates to be compiled and published. The first tabulations were of GDP by industrial sector, in both current and constant (1989) prices, with separate estimates for Monetary and Non-monetary GDP. Data were presented for both calendar years and fiscal years (i.e. 1 July to 30 June). This was followed a year or so later by tabulations of expenditure on GDP, with production and expenditure estimates being harmonized, and pleasingly low statistical discrepancies revealed. The GDP series have subsequently been rebased to 1997/98 and 2002 constant prices.

INPUT–OUTPUT TABLES

Uganda's first ever input–output tables were prepared by the Department, relating to calendar years 1989 and 1992. They were primarily intended to be the basis of economic modelling to be undertaken by the parent ministry, but were not used to the extent originally anticipated.

2.2 Household surveys

PROGRAMME TO ALLEVIATE POVERTY AND THE SOCIAL COSTS OF ADJUSTMENT (PAPSCA)

The Programme to Alleviate Poverty and the Social Costs of Adjustment (1990–5) was designed to provide safety nets for vulnerable groups. It included a Social Dimensions of Adjustment (SDA) component which aimed at enhancing social policy planning by providing: technical support in social research and statistical analysis; a statistical database on the level and evolution of household living conditions; and through designing and implementing actions to address the basic needs of Uganda's most disadvantaged groups (PAPSCA 1995).

The living conditions survey sub-component was to provide data for commissioned policy studies, as well as practical training in statistical analysis. It was linked to two other sub-components: policy studies and institutional capacity building. Technical support was provided by the World Bank and Statistics Norway and was targeted at government ministries, including the Statistics Department, and relevant departments of Makerere University. Training was provided in statistical analysis and use of specialized computer packages, social sector analysis, development management, and human resource management. The Statistics Department also received technical support in sampling design, data collection and processing, and analysis.

The Statistics Department implemented the SDA surveys component through the household surveys discussed below. The objectives of these surveys have been modified and enhanced over time. Data had to be collected in connection with the SDA component and to fill gaps in the socio-economic database, both for monitoring and evaluation and for planning purposes. The specific objectives were to:

1) Provide integrated data sets needed to monitor the effects of economic adjustment programmes at both household and community levels.
2) Provide time series data to measure economic growth and social development.
3) Improve estimates of inputs, outputs, and value added of households and small-scale enterprises, disaggregated at the two-digit industrial classification level.
4) Build a permanent national household survey capability in the Department.

The choice of the type of survey to be conducted mainly depended on the needs of government. At inception the data users, mainly ministries, departments, and some donors, would meet with the Statistics Department to agree on what data was to be collected. The coverage of the surveys also varied with the identified data needs as perceived by different ministries and donors. This illustrates that the statistics produced were demand driven from the start.

Each survey consisted of three components of the main integrated survey. First, it covered socio-economic aspects of the household. Second, it covered small-scale establishments and household enterprises. Third, a community survey module at village level was included. In some cases, there was also a core module.

NATIONAL HOUSEHOLD BUDGET SURVEY, 1989/90

A Household Budget Survey (HBS) was launched in April 1988, alongside the Rehabilitation of Statistics Project. Fieldwork ended in March 1990 while the processing and analysis of data was completed in December 1990. The survey results were used to:

1) Estimate the level and distribution of household expenses at the national and regional level for rural and urban areas.
2) Decide on the composition of the consumption basket and update weights for constructing Consumer Price Indices.
3) Update estimates of National Accounts.
4) Provide, as a by-product, indicative data on some socio-economic aspects of households and activities of household members.

INTEGRATED HOUSEHOLD SURVEY, 1992/93

In order to build a database to monitor and evaluate the economic reforms reviewed in this book, and building on experience from the 1989/90 HBS, it was decided to conduct a baseline national integrated household socio-economic and community survey. Field operations started in March 1992 and ended in March 1993. Data entry, data processing, and analysis were completed in January 1994.

The survey results provided a complete and integrated data set needed to understand the mechanisms and effects of the structural adjustment process at the household and community levels. The results also filled gaps in social data and started the building of time series data relating to the key socio-economic indicators for planning and economic management. Finally, the survey helped to build experience for a permanent national household survey capability in the Statistics Department.

MONITORING HOUSEHOLD SURVEYS

A number of follow up or monitoring household surveys were undertaken; the First, Second, and Third Monitoring Surveys were conducted in 1993/94, 1994/95, and 1995/96 respectively. From 1997 the series was renamed Uganda National Household Surveys (UNHS), with rounds in 1999/2000, 2002/03, and 2005/06.

The core subject matter included in these surveys has generally been comprehensive socio-economic characteristics of households and their members. However, due to the paucity of agricultural statistics, the Second Monitoring Survey added a diagnostic crop survey to explore the possibility of getting reliable estimates of production of major crops by the enquiry method. Then the 1995/96, 1999/2000, and 2005/06 surveys included crop modules. The Third Monitoring Survey, 1995/96 included a labour survey in an attempt to provide labour data, and a pilot mortality survey. Mortality data was required to monitor the HIV and AIDS pandemic.

UGANDA BUSINESS INQUIRY, 2000/01

The 2000 business register exercise and the 2000/01 Uganda Business Inquiry (UBI), had substantial coverage, and included data from all economic sectors apart from agriculture, hunting, forestry, and fisheries. In addition to including all business with more than five employees across mining, manufacturing, construction, trade, banking, and all the service sectors, the survey covered a sample of informal and micro businesses (i.e. fewer than five employees). It also captured data from less traditional sectors such as private schools and private hospitals. Both formal and informal businesses were covered. Response rates were dramatically improved by training a team to extract data from financial statements (where available), thus reducing the burden of form filling for companies.

The UBI was establishment based. To improve coverage further the UNHS 2002/03 facilitated the collection of information from businesses within the household. Data from the UBI and UNHS were adjusted to ensure financial data were comparable for one year (2000/01), and estimates of employment, value added, capital formation, and other economic indicators were aggregated for each sector using data from both surveys. The data from both surveys were then used to rebase the National Accounts. At the same time, the methods to derive the National Accounts were updated to ensure adoption of the 1993 System of National Accounts. The business register and UBI were also used to design a sample frame for subsequent annual business enquiries.

2.3 Population and housing censuses

Population and housing censuses were conducted in Uganda in 1948, 1959, 1969, and 1980. Unfortunately, the data for the 1980 census was never completely analysed as most of it was lost during the war to remove the

Amin government. Only about one third of the districts ended up with full data that could be processed. The 1991 census was therefore the first one to be properly conducted under the rehabilitated Statistics Department, providing much needed data. It was a great success in terms of full coverage. A cartographic unit was set up in 1989 to provide a geographic frame for conducting the census, while a special data centre was also set up to deal exclusively with processing and analysing the data. These were major building blocks for subsequent activities. Another population and housing census was carried out in 2002 without external assistance.

2.4 *District and local government level data*

The decentralization policy announced in 1993 (see Chapter 14) created increased demand for district and other local government data. A number of initiatives were undertaken to meet this demand, with varying degrees of success.

The Statistics Department worked with the Decentralization Secretariat of the Ministry of Local Government to assist districts in building their own databases in 1995/96. A project with Statistics Denmark, which started in the late 1990s, aimed at building capacity to collect socio-economic statistics within District Planning Units in five (out of the then fifty-six) districts. The units were equipped with computers and printers, while staff were trained in data collection methods using sample survey techniques, and in the use of statistical analysis packages. The project contributed substantially to district-based information, providing data on socio-economic characteristics that are not usually generated by administrative records. By the time it ended in 2002 the project had expanded to fourteen more districts.

The Community Based Management Information System is a programme aimed at empowering community leaders at village level, by improving their managerial skills, to plan for their societies. It uses participatory methods of collecting, recording, updating, and utilizing information (mainly in the health sector) for decision-making at village level. It covers forty districts, but only a few parishes are covered within each district because of budgetary constraints. The programme is one of the first to attempt to build capacity at the village level and is important in providing opportunities for the 'voices' of grass-roots people to be heard.

In 2003 the Ministry of Local Government introduced the Local Government Information Communication System aimed at streamlining district level data collection, analysis, and dissemination, as well as enhancing the monitoring and evaluation of district activities.

UBoS established a Directorate of District Statistics, responsible for supporting development of capacity within districts to produce, handle, and utilize statistical data and information. The Directorate coordinates and assists in the generation of district statistics and builds capacity within the districts through technical support. It is responsible for coordinating national exercises undertaken to produce district statistics.

Unfortunately, the various initiatives to strengthen district statistics have not been harmonized, and have created 'stand alone' management information systems that are largely sector based. Efforts to meet local government data needs have been uncoordinated and sometimes poorly managed, leading to production of unreliable data. The 2003 Data Needs Assessment Study showed that lack of coordination and capacity in data management is a major problem hampering district statistics (UBoS 2003b).

2.5 Food and agricultural statistics

As noted above, due to the paucity of food and agricultural statistics, an agricultural module was included in the UNHS programme. An agricultural module was also included in the 2002 Population and Housing Census. The data generated from the census included: the number of crop plots planted during the first agricultural season of 2002; the type of crop stand; livestock and poultry numbers (by local and exotic/improved breed); and information about fish farming.

Other activities that have provided food and agricultural statistics include: the 2003 Pilot Census of Agriculture, which aimed to test methodology and instruments; the 2004 Pilot Permanent Agricultural Statistics System, which collected data on crop areas and production, livestock numbers and crop utilization; and the Informal Cross Border Trade Surveys, which, *inter alia*, collected data on cross border agricultural trade between Uganda and neighbouring Kenya, Tanzania, Rwanda, Democratic Republic of Congo, and Sudan. A livestock census was carried out in February 2008 to be followed by a census of agriculture during 2008/09.

In addition to the Statistics Department, the Ministry of Agriculture, Animal Industry, and Fisheries collected agricultural statistics through a number of instruments: the Census of Agriculture 1963/1965; follow-up surveys in 1967/68 and 1968; the National Census of Agriculture and Livestock, 1990/91; and follow-up sample surveys in 1991/92 and 1992/93. However, there is still no system for regular collection of annual agricultural statistics.

2.6 Labour statistics

Labour force data has been produced infrequently, and little of it has been useful in terms of informing policy makers about employment issues. While labour force information is scanty, attempts have been made to provide information on employment status. These include the National Manpower Survey of 1988 and the 1991 and 2002 population and housing censuses, which provided some labour force data. As noted above, a pilot labour force survey was conducted with the 1995/96 Third Monitoring Survey as a prelude to conducting a full-scale survey later. The survey provided information on the size and structure of the labour force and was used to up-date unemployment indicators. The 2002/03 and 2005/06 UNHS rounds also included labour force modules. However, labour statistics still has major gaps.

2.7 Demographic and Health Surveys

Demographic and Health Surveys (DHS) were carried out in 1988/89, 1995, 2000/01, and 2006 to provide inter-censal demographic data on maternal and child health, including family planning. Although the 1988/89 DHS was conducted by consultants, all subsequent ones were conducted by the Statistics Department or UBoS. The primary purpose of a DHS is to furnish detailed information on fertility; family planning; infant, child, adult, and maternal mortality; maternal and child health; nutrition; knowledge of HIV and AIDS and other sexually transmitted infections.

2.8 Data from other agencies

While national surveys and censuses are the responsibility of UBoS, ministries, departments, and agencies also collect and report administrative data. UBoS' role is to coordinate the collection of this data and to publish it. Many of these arrangements are formalized through Memoranda of Understanding. Examples of this data include:

1) Banking, monetary, and balance of payments data from the Bank of Uganda.
2) External trade data from the Uganda Revenue Authority.
3) Macroeconomic, accounting, and aid data from the Ministry of Finance, Planning and Economic Development (MoFPED).
4) Production information on crops, livestock, and fisheries from the Ministry of Agriculture, Animal Industry, and Fisheries.
5) Education data from the Ministry of Education.
6) Health data from the Ministry of Health.
7) Gender statistics from the ministry responsible for gender.
8) Migration statistics from the Immigration Department.

Other government entities include the Meteorology Department; Ministry of Public Service; Ministry of Works, Transport, and Communications; Uganda Railways; Civil Aviation Authority; Uganda Telecommunications; Criminal Investigation Department (Uganda Police); and Uganda Prisons.

2.9 Use of statistical data for poverty monitoring

Despite rapid economic growth during the first half of the 1990s, by 1995 there were increasing complaints that growth was having little impact on poverty. Statistical analysis of the 1992 UNHS data found that 56 per cent of Ugandans could not meet their basic requirements. This prompted the government to develop the Poverty Eradication Action Plan (PEAP, see Chapter 7) in 1997. Considerable importance was attached to the systematic monitoring of poverty to assess progress in PEAP implementation. A Poverty Monitoring and Evaluation Strategy was drawn up between the Statistics Department, MoFPED and other stakeholders to monitor poverty at all levels, ranging from inputs, processes, outputs, outcomes, to impact. Subsequent household surveys showed poverty dropping to 38 per cent in 2003 and 31 per cent in 2006 (see Chapter 10).

3. Institutional arrangements

3.1 Legal framework

The first statistics legislation in Uganda was the Statistics Act 1961 which led to the setting up of the Statistics Department under the Ministry for Planning following Independence in 1962. There were a number of subsequent amendments to the 1961 Act, mainly regulations to carry out specific surveys and censuses. Apart from a brief period under the President's office during the Amin era, for most of the period up to the establishment of UBoS the statistics function came under the Ministry of Planning and Economic Development. As noted above, in 1998 there was a major overhaul of statistics legislation with the enactment of the Uganda Bureau of Statistics Act No. 2, 1998.

3.2 User–producer consultations

User–producer consultations have been conducted on various statistical issues since the early 1980s. Workshops were conducted with data users at the design stage. Key stakeholders were invited to comment on the scope and priority issues for data collection. Draft questionnaires prepared by the Statistics Department were presented, priorities were discussed and agreed upon with users, and the department would then redesign the questionnaires to accommodate the agreed data needs.

By the late 1990s these consultations had extended to cover the preparation of reports and publications; presentation, dissemination, and interpretation of results; the use of information and further analysis of data for policy purposes. These contacts led to increased use of the statistics and later also included other data producers such as ministries. A producer–producer committee that included major data producers was formed in 2002. A 'Compendium of Statistical Concepts and Definitions used in Uganda Statistical System and Services' was prepared by UBoS in collaboration with data users, to be used as a coordinating tool for standardization of statistical production (UBoS 2001).

The main objectives of these committees were to minimize duplication of effort and ensure optimal use of scarce resources, strengthen linkages in production of statistical data, ensure standardization and thereby quality control, share best practices, and enhance capacity building. UBoS provided the overall coordination role.

3.3 Statistical awareness

The 18th November was set aside by the African Ministers responsible for planning in 1992 to be celebrated each year as Africa Statistics Day in order to create greater awareness about the importance of statistics to society. In 2000 Uganda decided to celebrate for a week, rather than a day. Statistics Week is celebrated with a series of statistical activities involving both statisticians and statistics customers. This has helped increase statistical awareness, particularly among data users and policy makers.

3.4 Financing statistical work

Donor funding has been critical in building the statistics function since the late 1980s, beginning with the Rehabilitation of Statistics Project and the 1989/90 Household Budget Survey. The main donors have included the World Bank, DANIDA, DFID, ILO, NORAD, Sida, UNICEF, UNDP, UNFPA, USAID, Government of Japan, Nordic Development Fund, Statistics Canada, Statistics New Zealand, Statistics Denmark, and Statistics Norway. While most funding focused on strengthening capacity for data collection, analysis, and dissemination, the most visible donor output was World Bank funding for the construction of a modern Statistics House adjoining MoFPED. This facilitated the transfer of UBoS offices from Entebbe to Kampala in 2006, which has greatly improved the Bureau's visibility and proximity to its major users.

Excessive reliance on direct donor funding carries the risk of building systems which are too expensive to be sustainable. As the fiscal situation improved during the 1990s, external funding became less important and the government gradually increased its share of funding of statistical activities. This reached 30 per cent by 2002 (excluding the Population and Housing Census) and 58 per cent by 2005.

3.5 Timing of release of statistics

The Ministry of Planning and Economic Development placed great emphasis on the timeliness of statistics, and the Statistics Department work programme was planned so as to provide the most up-to-date economic data possible. As a first step in meeting the Ministry's requirements, the Department took over full responsibility for preparation of the Statistical Supplement to 'Background to the Budget',[2] and progressively expanded this as more statistical series were developed. This became a major source of economic statistics. For instance, from 1992 onwards, a full set of National Accounts estimates was incorporated, for both calendar and fiscal years, and the fiscal year estimates for the current year were presented in May/June (i.e. at Budget time). Appearing some six weeks before the end of the period to which they related, they clearly contained a significant degree of projection. This was criticized in some quarters as leading to an undesirable amount of subsequent revision, as later information became available. However, in practice revisions were generally only minor, and the advantage of having up-to-date statistics as a basis for the Budget outweighed the disadvantage of having to make revisions.

Strict rules were put in place to ensure that statistics were released on time. From 1991 results of the new CPI were always circulated to key users on or before the last day of the relevant month. Monthly data for the Index of Industrial Production was always circulated before the end of the following quarter, and projections for the fiscal year were made available in time for consideration in the Budget in May.

One of the considerations in giving UBoS a degree of autonomy from government was that autonomy would reduce the danger of political interference in the publication of statistics. In practice, this has never been a problem since 1986. All stakeholders receive UBoS data at the same time, without any influence by government.

Consideration was given early in the statistics rehabilitation process to reviving publication of the annual Statistical Abstract, which had not appeared since 1977. However the Ministry strongly preferred to have a more frequent publication of key indicators that change on a regular basis, so a comprehensive quarterly publication 'Key Economic Indicators' commenced in 1991. Publication of the Statistical Abstract finally resumed in 1996.

3.6 *Analytical capacity and dissemination of results*

The number of statistics publications increased steadily as a result of the above reforms. By the mid 1990s the following publications were being issued regularly:

1) Consumer Price Index (monthly).
2) Index of Major Manufacturing (monthly).

---

[2] The 'Background to the Budget' document is presented to Parliament along with the Draft Estimates of Revenue and Expenditure.

3) Index of Industrial Production (quarterly).
4) Input–Output tables.
5) Poverty and the social impact of economic reforms reports.
6) National Accounts, Migration, and External Trade statistics were published as a supplement to 'Background to the Budget' by MoFPED.
7) 'Key Economic Indicators' (quarterly).

The number of publications has continued to increase. UBoS produces a series of monthly, quarterly, and annual publications, as well as specific survey and census reports.

The results of the national HBS 1989/90 and the three subsequent Monitoring Surveys were published in extensive reports, covering methodological issues and the main results, both nationally and by region. The Monitoring Surveys were each produced in two volumes. The first volumes covered technical aspects and basic tables on demographic particulars and household consumption expenditure. The second volumes presented tables on socio-economic characteristics of the household, comprising education, health, economic activity, housing, migration, and household income. However, there was little analysis of the results. The bulk of the reports comprised tables with no explanations, while the conclusions focused on future survey plans rather than on policy implications of the survey findings. Dissemination of the reports was largely confined to the Ministry of Finance and Economic Planning and academic users.

Beginning with the 1999/2000 Household Survey, a conscious attempt was made to produce reports with text that interpreted tables in user-friendly ways and to disseminate the reports to a wider audience through workshops, briefing papers and, more recently, the UBoS web site and CD-ROMs.

An example is UgandaInfo. Uganda has a wealth of socio-economic data from different sources. However, access to that data is not easy because it is scattered across different ministries and organizations with no overview of what data exists or where to find it. Furthermore, although comprehensive data is collected, only a portion of it is published, with much remaining within ministries. To address this problem, in collaboration with ministries, UBoS established UgandaInfo in 2003. UgandaInfo is a socio-economic database system consisting of key indicators for monitoring progress towards poverty eradication and social development in general. It provides updated time series of key indicators as well as data from various sources, disaggregated data from national level down to the district/sub-county level, by sex and urban/rural strata wherever these are available. Currently, most of the data available is at the national and district levels.

Over time, the Statistics Department and UBoS has graduated from producing simple descriptive statistical reports to more in-depth analytical reports. Data analysis and report writing is increasingly carried out in collaboration with local and international research institutions, which has enhanced the analytical and report writing skills of UBoS staff. A good example is the poverty maps pictorially showing poverty across the country. The nature of dissemination has also gradually changed—from producing extensive tabulation reports with detailed methodological information but little comment, to more diverse methods where results are analytically commented upon and policy implications spelt out. To reach a wider audience, information is packaged differently for different audiences.

4. Conclusions

This chapter has shown how the statistics function in Uganda has not only recovered from the damage inflicted in the 1970s and early 1980s, but has developed into a modern, professional operation. UBoS is currently regarded as one of the strongest central statistics offices in Africa. Critical to this progress was the importance attached to timely and accurate statistics by the Ministry of Planning and Economic Development and its successors since the late 1980s, for both economic management and poverty monitoring. Donors were strongly encouraged to help rebuild statistics capacity and much of the progress noted above was donor funded. However, as the fiscal situation has improved, government has steadily increased its share of UBoS funding. The reforms discussed here now look to be firmly entrenched.

12

Debt Management and Debt Relief

Damoni Kitabire[1]

1. Introduction

Uganda borrowed substantially after Independence in 1962 to finance large scale investment programmes. The external debt stock rose steadily but was generally perceived to be sustainable given the country's strong economic growth at the time. Between 1971 and 1979, however, relatively little borrowing took place, as the international community had blacklisted the country because of the political brutality and economic mismanagement of the Idi Amin government. The ensuing foreign exchange shortages coupled with a severe economic recession led to rapid accumulation of arrears as the government defaulted on its debt service obligations.

A brief return to normal economic and political relations with the international community in the early 1980s caused a renewed inflow of aid. New loans for reconstruction and development were signed with the World Bank and three Standby Arrangements, and Compensatory Financing Facilities, were made available by the IMF for stabilization and recovery programmes. However, owing to continuing foreign exchange shortages over this period, the government decided only to service new debt leading to further accumulation of external payments arrears on old debt.

Between 1986 and 1991 the debt stock and debt service burden grew considerably, largely because of the willingness of the international community to make large sums of credit available to the new NRM government. Loans for reconstruction, recovery programmes, and new infrastructure were contracted in the absence of an effective debt management strategy and often on non-concessional terms.

As at the end of June 1991 Uganda's debt stock stood at USD2.6 billion (83 per cent of GDP), of which 63 per cent was owed to multilateral institutions.

[1] Helpful comments from Tony Burdon are gratefully acknowledged.

The government was also accruing external payments arrears that attracted high penalty interest as a result of failure to pay supply contracts because of budget shortfalls and foreign exchange shortages. At the same time, influential individuals in the private sector often obtained investment finance through government guaranteed loans; their subsequent failure to service these loans further increased government's liabilities.

By the late 1980s Uganda faced a debt crisis. The crisis peaked in 1990 when, following a sharp decline in the terms of trade, the government ran out of foreign exchange to service its external debt obligations. The decline in the terms of trade was caused by the fall in international coffee prices from an average of USD2.80 to USD1 per kilogram between 1986 and 1990 in response to increased production in Brazil. At the time, coffee accounted for close to 90 per cent of total exports. Consequently coffee production in Uganda, which had risen dramatically between 1986 and 1989, fell sharply bringing about a steep decline in export earnings and the country's capacity to service its debt. Debt service falling due alone, excluding arrears, was equivalent to over 60 per cent of export earnings. Moreover, foreign exchange reserves amounted to only two weeks of import cover. Drastic action was therefore necessary to reverse the collapse in the balance of payments, prompting the development of Uganda's first integrated debt management strategy in 1991.

This chapter discusses the 1991 Debt Strategy and analyses its impact. This is followed by a discussion of the 1995 Enhanced Debt Strategy and its evolution. The chapter then looks at Uganda's role in the Heavily Indebted Poor Country (HIPC) Debt Relief Initiative and at how Uganda benefited from debt relief. This is followed by a short discussion of the Poverty Action Fund through which debt relief was ring-fenced for spending on social services.

2. The 1991 Debt Strategy[2]

In response to the debt crisis, the government embarked on the preparation of a comprehensive debt strategy in 1991 intended both to overcome the immediate crisis and to develop mechanisms to ensure that it did not reoccur. A team of international financial advisors was recruited to carry out a thorough debt audit based on the government's existing records and information on claims against the government requested from creditors. By June 1991 a summary of outstanding loans was completed, relatively accurate estimates of the country's debt stock and projections for debt service were known, and a new strategy had been formulated.

---

[2] For a more detailed description of the evolution of Uganda's debt from Independence to the late 1990s see Austrian Development Cooperation (1999).

The 1991 Debt Strategy had five main objectives. The first objective of the Strategy was to provide an immediate solution to Uganda's cash flow problem through extensive restructuring of its debt portfolio as the country could not generate sufficient foreign exchange to service its debt obligations. This necessitated clearing arrears, halting further accumulation of penalty and late interest charges, and reducing annual contractual debt service to levels consistent with Uganda's ability to pay.

The second objective was to improve debt management structures by implementing a new borrowing policy and enhancing internal government coordination. Line ministries were required to work with the Aid Coordination Unit in the Ministry of Finance (MoF) in securing external funds and with four government committees, which had responsibility for overseeing and monitoring debt issues. The Balance of Payments Committee brought together officials from the Central Bank, the Ministry of Finance, and the Ministry of Planning and Economic Development[3] to analyse the sustainability of external debt. The Cash Flow Committee (see Chapter 3) provided a forum for discussing debt issues in the context of the macroeconomic framework, as well as short-term revenue implications of debt service and its impact on other sectors of the economy. The Development Committee (see Chapter 6) identified priority projects and their sources of financing, recommending new loans only when necessary and in line with the Debt Strategy. The External Debt Committee coordinated the external debt repayment process among all key stakeholders and ensured that payments were made on the due date and consistent with the government's repayment policy.

The third objective was to limit new borrowing. The strategy placed strict limits on new borrowing, with a requirement to exhaust all sources of grant financing before considering any new loans. Moreover, new loans were only to be accepted on highly concessional terms, i.e. with a grant element of at least 78 per cent, which was comparable to World Bank IDA terms at the time.

The fourth objective was debt restructuring under the Paris Club arrangements.[4] The scope of Uganda's debt reduction under Paris Club rescheduling operations was limited by an early cut off date of July 1981, the time Uganda received its first Paris Club deal. At the time of the 1992 agreement, most outstanding Paris Club debt was contracted on non-concessional terms. Only half of the USD279 million outstanding had been contracted before the cut off date, leaving USD118 million in the post cut off debt category that was not eligible for rescheduling. By 1991 Uganda had already had four restructuring operations within the framework of the Paris Club—in 1981, 1982, 1987, and 1989. These were not sufficient to ease the debt overhang, for two reasons. First,

---

[3] The two Ministries were merged in 1992.
[4] The Paris Club is an informal group of creditor governments mainly from OECD countries that has met in Paris since 1956 to reschedule bilateral debts.

the first three Paris Club negotiations had covered only debt falling due in the consolidation period[5] of between twelve to eighteen months. This was later expanded to multi-year rescheduling and debt stock reduction under Toronto terms in 1989, enhanced Toronto terms in 1992, Naples terms in 1995, Lyon terms (HIPC I) in 1998, and Cologne terms (HIPC II) in 2000. Second, in the first seven Paris Club arrangements, only pre-cut off debt (accounting for just 4 per cent of the total debt stock) was eligible for debt relief. Moreover, the *demini-mus*[6] clause excluded loans with outstanding amounts of less than Special Drawing Rights (SDR)[7] 500,000 from rescheduling. This condition was only dropped later in Paris Club 8 (HIPC II). Post-cut off debt was considered for restructuring for the first time in the Paris Club 7 and HIPC arrangements.

During the preparation of the debt strategy, it was envisaged that Uganda would immediately seek a rescheduling of the 1991/92 maturities from the Paris Club. However, agreement was not reached until June 1992.

The fifth objective of the Strategy was to buy back and restructure unsecured commercial debt. Although commercial debt accounted for just over 9 per cent of the total debt stock in 1992, 90 per cent of it was already in arrears, with mounting penalty interest charges. Legal action pursued by some creditors (sometimes followed by hefty awards) was giving the country negative publicity and was a burden to the budget. With assistance from the World Bank, the government embarked upon a debt buy-back strategy to reduce its uninsured commercial debt amounting to USD170 million. The offer price was fixed at 12 cents per US dollar and offer documents were issued in December 1992. The buy-back was largely successful, with commercial debt totalling USD153 million being bought back at a steep discount. This represented 6 per cent of the total debt stock (or one third of total arrears or three quarters of all commercial debt) as at December 1992.

Another debt buy-back operation was concluded for the verified portion of Uganda's debt arrears to the government of Tanzania, at 15 cents for each US dollar, with funding from the government of Austria and the Uganda government's own resources. A similar operation was conducted with the government of Burundi on similar terms with the government using its own resources to settle the agreed amount of the buy-back. However, because the government did not service the commercial debt that was not bought back, it continued to be on the receiving end of law-suits by creditors.

---

[5] This is the period in which debt service payments to be rescheduled have fallen or will fall due.

[6] This refers to minor creditors that are exempted from debt restructuring to simplify implementation of the Paris Club rescheduling agreements, with the exposure limit defined in each Agreed Minute. Their claims are payable in full.

[7] The SDR serves as the unit of account of the IMF and some other international organizations. Its value is based on a basket of key international currencies.

3. Impact of the 1991 Debt Strategy

The 1991 Debt Strategy was successful in meeting most of its objectives. It established clear procedures for negotiating new loans and strengthened debt management. It also facilitated an increase in the proportion of payments made on time, thus significantly reducing the accumulation of arrears and penalty interest charges. A number of successful debt restructuring operations took place, reducing commercial debt by 64 per cent and debt service from 66 per cent of exports in 1991 to 24 per cent in 1995. Consequently, the debt stock increased at a much slower rate than GDP and the debt to GDP ratio fell from 83 per cent in 1991 to 64 per cent in 1995 (Ministry of Finance and Economic Planning, various years).

In addition to reducing the level of arrears, the Paris Club rescheduling and commercial debt buy-back reshaped the composition of Uganda's debt stock. While the stock of arrears fell from 15 per cent in 1991 to 7 per cent in 1993, the share of multilateral debt increased from 61 per cent to 75 per cent over the same period. This put the country in a difficult position because no debt reduction or rescheduling efforts at the time covered multilateral debt. Paris Club rescheduling only reduced the debt stock by 1 per cent up-front and debt service by USD10 million per year because Paris Club debt relief only applied to debt contracted before July 1981 (the cut-off date). The debt service ratio was still far too high, crowding out spending in general and social service expenditure in particular. Government attempts to negotiate debt reduction with non-OECD and multilateral creditors met with little success, which necessitated a rethink of the strategy.

4. The 1995 Enhanced Debt Strategy

Despite the progress made, the 1991 Strategy did not make Uganda's debt sustainable mainly because there was insufficient reduction in long-term multilateral debt (which accounted for 75 per cent of the total debt stock by 1993). There was no consensus in the boards of both the IMF and World Bank to provide multilateral debt relief; it was seen as moral hazard too far. Moreover, Uganda continued to require large amounts of new financing to support the economic reform programme, particularly poverty reducing expenditure and investment in infrastructure. The concessionality of much of the new borrowing was below the 78 per cent grant element target as most creditors apart from IDA and the African Development Fund (ADF) were either unwilling or unable to provide financing on such terms. In addition, there remained problems with debt management structures, particularly in the area of coordination and information flows among government departments. As a result, the government continued to regularly incur late payment fees and penalty interest, albeit in lower amounts.

A lasting solution to Uganda's long term debt therefore called for revisiting the 1991 Debt Strategy, reinforcing the institutional framework for debt management, and a commitment by the international community to deal properly with multilateral debt. A comprehensive review of the strategy was carried out in 1995, leading to the adoption of the Enhanced Debt Strategy. The 1995 strategy had four main elements: establishing a Government of Uganda–Donor Debt Committee; building capacity for improved debt management; developing a new borrowing strategy; and setting up a Multilateral Debt Fund.

4.1 Government–Donor Debt Committee

In an attempt to foster greater cooperation and coordination between the government and donors on debt policy, a Government–Donor Debt Committee was set up in 1995/96 and met quarterly to evaluate the country's economic performance and debt reduction efforts. Chaired by the Permanent Secretary/Secretary to the Treasury, it included representatives from all relevant government departments involved in debt management, donors providing support to debt relief to Uganda, the World Bank, the IMF, and UNDP. The committee greatly improved the flow of information, and the overall relationship, between the government and donors. Moreover, it provided a forum to talk about the allocation of public expenditures and funding for social services.

Over time the committee focused increasingly on issues of multilateral debt and how the (largely bilateral) debt relief that Uganda had received to date was being undermined by multilateral debt obligations. The government used this forum to illustrate the point that debt service was taking away critical resources that could otherwise be used for social service spending and to demand debt relief from all creditors—including multilaterals. The committee discussed the possibility of funding social services and pro-poor expenditure from debt relief savings. This forum was later expanded to include civil society organizations (CSOs), which were proving increasingly effective in lobbying for debt relief (both locally and through their international networks and governments) and pro-poor public expenditure. The committee played a critical role in what eventually became the HIPC Initiative. A number of participants, including donors and CSOs, became strong advocates in international fora for multilateral debt relief. Ministry of Finance officials were invited to international meetings to demonstrate the impact of the multilateral debt service on social spending.

4.2 Capacity building for improved debt management

The Enhanced Debt Strategy also led to the creation of a National Debt Management Committee comprising all institutions, departments, and agencies involved in debt management issues. Skills gaps, especially in loan negotiation and debt recording and analysis, were identified and filled through a series of training courses.

4.3 New borrowing strategy

The 1995 Enhanced Debt Strategy placed increased emphasis on seeking grant financing and avoiding contracting new loans altogether. Where loan finance was the only available and viable option then borrowing would only be allowed on highly concessional terms, as in the 1991 strategy. This 'grants before loans' policy was meant to help check the tendency to seek quick finance, regardless of the terms and purpose for which it was being offered.

Another important change to the borrowing policy was introduced in the 1995 Constitution which required all public debt (including guarantees) to be approved by a resolution of Parliament (Government of Uganda 1995: Article 59). Thus all powers for approving new loans were now vested with Parliament.

4.4 Multilateral Debt Fund

As noted above, until 1995 debt reduction efforts concentrated on bilateral debt, despite the fact that multilateral debt constituted about 75 per cent of the total debt stock. Meaningful debt reduction could not be achieved without considering multilateral debt. Consequently, in 1995 the government established the Multilateral Debt Fund (MDF) to receive contributions from donors earmarked for servicing Uganda's multilateral debt. The fund attracted contributions of USD135 million between 1995 and 1998 from Austria, Denmark, Netherlands, Norway, Sweden, Switzerland, and USA, which were used to service debt owed to the IMF, World Bank (IDA), African Development Bank, and ADF. This led to a reduction in multilateral debt service payments by over USD40 million for each of the three years of the Fund's existence. Most of the donors contributing to the fund demanded that debt service savings be spent on pro-poor public expenditure such as health and education.

4.5 Impact of the Enhanced Debt Strategy

The Enhanced Debt Strategy had a significant impact in building institutional debt management capacity and streamlining procedures for contracting new loans. The MDF and the Government–Donor Debt Committee increased awareness among donors of the problems of non-concessional borrowing, thus giving credence to the government policy of highly concessional borrowing at IDA comparable terms. The MDF and the committee also led to closer ties with the donors, many of whom lobbied for multilateral debt relief on behalf of Uganda. Uganda became the 'poster boy' for the HIPC Debt Relief Initiative, arising from its good economic management and linking of debt relief with pro-poor social expenditures in the context of the Poverty Eradication Action Plan (see Chapter 7).

5. HIPC Debt Relief Initiative

The dialogue in the MDF and the Government–Donor Debt Committee clearly demonstrated to the international development community the inadequacy of piecemeal rescheduling without addressing multilateral debt; at the time multilateral debt was considered immune to debt relief and just had to be repaid. Until the HIPC Initiative, multilateral debt was non-reschedulable, and failure to repay would have threatened donor aid. As noted, the Government–Donor Debt Committee, working together with CSOs, played a seminal role in the international campaign to find a lasting solution to multilateral debt which eventually led to the HIPC Initiative, and ultimately to the Multilateral Debt Relief Initiative (MDRI). Uganda's example, showing both clear evidence of the impact of high levels of multilateral debt service on undermining social sector spending, coupled with sound macroeconomic management, and a clear commitment to use debt relief for poverty reduction provided a powerful and convincing case for multilateral debt relief. The case was reinforced by strong leadership in the Ministry of Finance, and an international CSO campaign— Jubilee 2000.

The HIPC Initiative was launched in 1996 by the international community with the aim of ensuring that no poor country faces a debt burden it cannot manage (Boote and Kamau 1997; Andrews et al. 1999). The Initiative entailed coordinated action by the international financial community, including multilateral organizations and governments, to reduce to sustainable levels the external debt burdens of the most heavily indebted poor countries.

In April 1998 Uganda became the first country to benefit from the HIPC Debt Relief Initiative. The speed with which Uganda qualified, without having to go through a standard qualifying period (initially six years), which was a requirement when the Initiative was first set up, reflected both the country's exemplary track record of macroeconomic reform and its clear commitment to poverty reduction as set out in the Poverty Eradication Action Plan (PEAP).[8] The Poverty Action Fund (see below) also played a crucial role in reassuring donors that debt relief savings would be channelled to poverty reduction (Mallaby 2004).

---

[8] The international community was so impressed by the PEAP that production of a 'Poverty Reduction Strategy Paper' (modelled on the PEAP) was made a requirement for countries wishing to access HIPC debt relief.

Prior to receiving HIPC debt relief, the nominal value of Uganda's external debt stock was USD3.5 billion and the Net Present Value (NPV) of debt to exports ratio was 294 per cent.[9] Under the initial HIPC Initiative (this was later topped up under the Enhanced HIPC Initiative) Uganda received debt relief amounting to USD347 million in NPV terms. Of this amount, USD274 million (79 per cent) was from multilateral creditors, meaning that for the first time debt relief had a large multilateral component. This was supposed to reduce Uganda's NPV of debt to exports ratio to 196 per cent, which was six percentage points lower than the threshold ratio of 202 per cent considered sustainable under the initial HIPC Initiative.

Despite this HIPC relief, by 1999 Uganda's NPV of debt to exports ratio again exceeded the 202 per cent threshold, mainly on account of the *El Nino* weather phenomenon, which severely affected export performance that year.

Following a comprehensive review of the scheme in 1999, a number of modifications were made to provide faster, deeper, and broader debt relief and to strengthen the links between debt relief, poverty reduction, and social policies. The new scheme was referred to as the Enhanced HIPC Initiative or HIPC II. Broadly, the new scheme aimed to reduce the time period before a country formally became eligible for debt relief to less than three years and to reduce the restrictive standards in order to allow more countries to obtain more relief. The scheme also aimed at providing greater debt service relief between the time the country became eligible for the scheme and the point that lenders were expected to provide full debt relief.

To be considered for relief under this initiative, a country had to meet four criteria:

- Be IDA-only and eligible for an IMF Poverty Reduction and Growth Facility.
- Face an unsustainable debt burden, after exhausting available debt relief mechanisms.
- Establish a track record of reform and sound economic performance through IMF and World Bank supported programmes.
- Have developed a Poverty Reduction Strategy Paper (PRSP) through a broad-based participatory process.

Once a country made sufficient progress in meeting these criteria, the Boards of the IMF and World Bank formally decided on its eligibility for debt relief, and the international community committed to reducing debt to the agreed sustainability threshold. This was called the decision point. Once a country reached decision point, it would immediately begin receiving interim relief on its debt

---

[9] The NPV is the discounted sum of all future debt-service obligations (interest and principal) on existing debt. The discount rates used for HIPC calculations reflected market interest rates. The NPV of debt-to-exports ratio is the NPV of debt as a percentage of exports of goods and services.

service falling due. However, in order to receive the full and irrevocable reduction in debt available under HIPC II, the country would have to: (i) establish a further track record of good performance under IMF and World Bank supported programmes; (ii) implement satisfactorily key reforms agreed at decision point; and (iii) adopt and implement the PRSP for at least one year (including demonstrating that debt relief was being applied to pro-poor expenditures as identified in the PRSP). Once a country met these criteria, it could then reach completion point, at which time lenders were expected to provide the full debt relief committed at decision point (Andrews et al. 1999).

In May 2000, Uganda qualified for further relief under HIPC II. The nominal value of Uganda's external debt stock had grown to USD3.6 billion as at June 1999. In NPV terms, this amounted to USD1.8 billion and the NPV of debt to exports ratio was 243 per cent. Total relief under HIPC II was expected to amount to an additional USD656 million in NPV terms, with multilateral creditors contributing 83 per cent. This brought the total relief extended to Uganda under the HIPC initiatives to over USD1 billion in NPV terms. Given this additional relief at the Enhanced HIPC 'completion point', Uganda's NPV of debt to exports ratio was projected at 150 per cent, which was the threshold level targeted by HIPC II. The combined relief under HIPC I and II was intended to ensure that Uganda remained on a sustainable debt path as measured by a continuing NPV of debt to exports ratio of 150 per cent or less, thus providing a permanent exit from debt rescheduling.

The Enhanced HIPC Initiative demanded that savings from debt relief be applied to pro-poor public expenditure. Uganda had already commenced on this path through the MDF and the Government–Donor Debt Coordination Committee and had by now developed the PEAP, which identified priorities for pro-poor public spending. This was followed by the creation of the Poverty Action Fund, through which debt relief savings were channelled and spent on pro-poor areas of the budget.

6. Multilateral Debt Relief Initiative

In June 2005 the G8 group of major industrial countries launched the Multilateral Debt Relief Initiative (MDRI). This proposed that the IMF, the International Development Association of the World Bank, and the African Development Fund cancel 100 per cent of their debt to countries that reach completion point under HIPC II. All countries that reach completion point under HIPC II and those with per capita income below USD380 and outstanding debt to the Fund at end 2004 were eligible for the MDRI (IMF 2008b).

Table 12.1 illustrates the combined impact on Uganda's debt service of the four debt relief initiatives discussed above (MDF, HIPC I and II, and MDRI) since 1995/96. It compares the debt service that would have been payable (in dollars

Table 12.1 Uganda's Debt Service, 1995/96–2006/07 (pre- and post-debt relief)

Initiative	Year	Pre-debt relief debt service		Post-debt relief debt service		Savings
		Debt Service USD (m)	% of total government expenditure	Debt Service USD (m)	% of total government expenditure	as a result of debt relief initiatives
	1995/96	142.2	14.2	97.3	9.7	44.9
MDF	1996/97	155.9	13.5	94.5	8.2	61.4
	1997/98	154.6	13.8	95.6	8.5	59.0
HIPC I	1998/99	163.7	14.0	104.2	8.9	59.5
	1999/00	133.4	10.1	90.0	6.8	43.4
	2000/01	146.1	12.3	39.9	3.4	106.2
HIPC I	2001/02	133.6	9.3	33.9	2.4	99.7
HIPC II	2002/03	145.9	10.3	39.4	2.8	106.5
	2003/04	167.8	10.9	54.2	3.5	113.6
	2004/05	192.7	10.2	80.0	4.2	112.7
HIPC I	2005/06	194.8	10.2	98.4	5.1	96.4
HIPC II, MDRI	2006/07	184.8	7.6	60.7	2.5	124.1

Source: Ministry of Finance, Planning and Economic Development.

and as a proportion of total government expenditure) in the absence of debt relief with the debt service actually paid following the debt relief initiatives. The last column shows the annual savings resulting from debt relief. The cumulative savings amounted to just over USD1 billion between 1995/96 and 2006/07, substantially increasing the resources available to the government for pro-poor expenditure. Debt relief has been one of the main factors contributing to the expansion in public services since the mid 1990s (see Chapter 9).

7. Poverty Action Fund

Uganda was the first country to benefit from HIPC largely because it was able to demonstrate that the savings from debt service were applied to pro-poor expenditure, such as primary education, primary health care, and water and sanitation. Debt relief savings were channelled through the Poverty Action Fund (PAF, see Chapter 13) in support of the social service sectors prioritized in the PEAP.

Following the HIPC Initiative, Uganda's debt relief savings have been explicitly channelled to social sector spending via the PAF. The PAF was created in 1998 to ensure that the budgetary savings from HIPC debt relief were ring-fenced for spending on poverty reduction and to reassure the donor community that debt relief savings were being spent in full on poverty reducing areas of the budget.[10] The PAF mechanism has helped mobilize additional resources from donors (on top of debt relief), as the government has been able to demonstrate the direct impact of debt relief on poverty. For programmes to be funded from the PAF, government and donors agreed that they had to be in the PEAP, be directly poverty reducing, deliver a service to the poor, and have a well developed plan.

A recent study concluded that the PAF has been an effective mechanism for drawing donor resources into the budget over and above debt relief (Kitabire et al. 2007). The creation of the PAF has contributed to major increases in expenditure on pro-poor areas and has protected them from within year budget cuts. The share of the budget (excluding donor projects) allocated to expenditures in the PAF progressively increased from 17 per cent in 1997/98 to 35.3 per cent in 2006/07. The PAF has provided a clear and monitorable way of demonstrating a link between debt relief and increased social spending, providing justification for increased support and an accounting framework for debt relief savings. Not surprisingly, similar schemes have subsequently been adopted by a number of other countries benefiting from HIPC and MDRI.

---

[10] The PAF also ensured that the Nordic donors that had been providing funding to the MDF had a mechanism to justify continued support, after debt repayments become sustainable under HIPC.

275

8. Conclusions

Uganda's struggle, as one of the poorest countries in the world emerging from conflict, to win substantial debt relief shows the value of challenging orthodox thought with imagination—alongside a serious commitment to good governance. The slow progression in the attitudes of international creditors from Paris Club rescheduling, to HIPC I, HIPC II, and finally MDRI and complete debt cancellation, took over a decade. Uganda played a major part in setting the framework for these initiatives. The international community, through debt relief, rewarded sound economic policies, a responsible debt strategy, transparent management, and a clear commitment to poverty reduction. The productive partnership between government, CSOs, and donors yielded as much as USD1 billion since 1995/96 in additional resources for the fight against poverty.

13

Aligning Aid with Government Fiscal Objectives

Martin Brownbridge

1. Introduction

Donor aid has comprised a large share of Uganda's budget resource envelope for the last decade and a half.[1] In the sixteen fiscal years from 1991/92 to 2006/07, gross receipts of donor aid (grants plus loan disbursements) to the central government budget, in the form of budget support (including grants for debt relief) and project aid, averaged 52 per cent of total government expenditure and net lending. The heavy dependence of the budget on aid was mainly attributable to the weak capacity for domestic revenue mobilization. Domestic revenues averaged only 10.6 per cent of GDP in this period and, despite major reforms to tax policy and tax administration (see Chapter 5), have increased only slowly since the mid-1990s. Moreover, the government could not mobilize significant budgetary resources through commercial borrowing, because of the shallowness of domestic financial markets and the country's very limited access to international credit markets.

Given such heavy dependence of the budget on aid, donor decisions pertaining to the size and composition of their aid, as well as to any conditions attached to that aid, inevitably have a profound impact on public finances and the wider economy. From the government's standpoint, while aid was necessary to supplement domestic budgetary resources, it also posed problems and challenges for economic and budgetary management. The key challenges included: how to ensure that aid and the expenditures which it funds were consistent with government macro/fiscal objectives (e.g. the level of total expenditure and

---

[1] This chapter only deals with aid to the government budget. There are other categories of donor aid that are usually disbursed outside of the government budget, such as humanitarian assistance.

revenues, government debt, and the fiscal deficit); how to ensure that aid did not distort the composition of budget expenditures away from government expenditure priorities; how to minimize the burden of absorbing and managing aid on overstrained administrative capacities; and how to ensure that the policy conditions attached to the various aid programmes were consistent with government policy preferences as well as with each other.

Since the mid-1990s the government of Uganda has encouraged donors to shift the composition of aid away from project aid and towards budget support so that the use of aid could be better aligned with its own priorities at the macro/fiscal, sectoral, and intra-sectoral levels. This policy has been quite successful, with the share of budget support increasing from an average of a third of gross aid in the second half of the 1990s to just over half in the first seven fiscal years of the 2000s.

This chapter examines the rationale for, and implementation of, this policy. It is organized as follows. Sections 2 and 3 provide some definitions of the variables in the fiscal data and some basic data on the trends in aid to the government budget. Section 4 looks in detail at the shift towards budget support. There were three main types of budget support received by Uganda—general budget support, sector budget support, and budget support for the Poverty Action Fund (PAF, see below)—and each posed different challenges for the government in terms of aligning aid with its fiscal objectives. Section 5 briefly discusses the difficulties involved in integrating donor-funded projects into the budget (policies towards donor-funded projects are dealt with in more detail in Chapter 6). Section 6 examines the aligning of aggregate aid flows with government's macro/fiscal objectives. The large rise in aid which occurred at the end of the 1990s and the early 2000s posed problems for macroeconomic management as well as raising the external debt burden and increasing the aid dependency of the budget. This prompted the government to embark on a medium term strategy of fiscal consolidation to scale back the fiscal deficit excluding grants. Section 7 concludes by examining the lessons that can be learned from Uganda's experience with managing large aid inflows.

2. A note on aid data

There are two main types of aid to government budgets: project aid and budget support.[2] Until the end of the 1990s, most aid received by Uganda was in the form of project aid. The problems associated with project aid in the developing world are well known: projects are often expensive; reflect the priorities of

---

[2] Technical assistance (TA) is sometimes regarded as a third type of aid to the budget. However, in Uganda, almost all TA is provided in the form of project aid and is recorded as such in fiscal data.

donors rather than recipient governments; often require complex and burden-some administrative, accounting, and reporting mechanisms which are separate from those of the main government budget; cannot be properly operated and maintained by the government's own budget when donor-funding has ended; and fragment government budget's between current and capital expenditures. However, they usually do not require policy conditionalities, because they constitute entirely targeted spending.

Budget support, on the other hand, is channelled directly into the main government budget, where it contributes to the pool of resources available to fund all government expenditures. It is not earmarked to fund specific pre-determined expenditures. Aid through budget support is usually regarded as preferable to project aid because, in principle, it is much easier than project aid to align with the recipient government's budgetary objectives as it gives government much more flexibility in terms of the volume and composition of the expenditures which it funds. However, it usually carries with it policy conditionalities and may be earmarked to certain budgetary expenditures, either strictly or notionally. In addition, predictability is essential. Significant shortfalls in budget support relative to projections, unless purely temporary, can either lead to an increase in government borrowing from the banking system and a run down in central bank reserves, or force government to make budget cuts.

Until around the late 1990s in Uganda, budget support was termed 'import support' and labelled as such in fiscal data. This was because the main purpose of this type of aid was to provide foreign exchange to close a projected external financing gap in the balance of payments (BoP). Its name was eventually changed to budget support, reflecting a number of developments. With the adoption of a flexible exchange rate regime in 1993, the improvement in the BoP in the mid 1990s, and the government's desire to expand its budget to meet key social objectives (as set out in the 1997 Poverty Eradication Action Plan, PEAP), the rationale for providing import/budget support shifted from funding a BoP deficit to funding the government budget.

However, apart from the name, budget support is effectively the same thing as import support and has exactly the same economic impact on the government budget and the BoP. Import/budget support consists of financial resources disbursed by donors in the form of foreign exchange. This is deposited in the central bank, the Bank of Uganda (BoU), which then credits the government's main treasury account, termed the Uganda Consolidated Fund (UCF) with the equivalent in Uganda Shillings. All payments under the Government of Uganda (GoU) budget, which constitutes all government expenditures other than the external development projects (which are funded by project aid), are made from the UCF. Hence import/budget support enhances the budget resource envelope for the GoU budget.

The budget support recorded in the fiscal data excludes disbursements from the IMF programmes. This is because these credits are liabilities of the central bank rather than of the central government and are not directly included in the government's budget resource envelope.[3] The recorded budget support includes the flow of resources received by government for external debt relief under the HIPC and Enhanced HIPC debt relief initiatives (see Chapter 12) in the form of the grants made through the HIPC Trust Fund for funding the debt relief applicable to IDA and IMF loans.[4] Because all budget support is deposited in the BoU, or is used to fund scheduled external debt service payments, it is straightforward to compile data on this type of aid.

It is much more difficult to compile accurate data on project aid. Project aid is not disbursed through a centralized agency but is instead disbursed to a multitude of different project implementing agencies. Moreover, project donors often make payments themselves directly to contractors, sometimes offshore, so even the implementing agency may not be fully aware of the value of project aid disbursements. There are also problems with defining what exactly constitutes project aid to the central government, because many projects are administered by public enterprises and other public agencies. The procedures for recording project aid disbursements, especially grants, were also not very effective in Uganda because many project administration units did not report data to the Ministry of Finance, Planning and Economic Development (MoFPED) in a timely manner. This problem was compounded by the fact that, up to 2005, project bank accounts were held in commercial banks, rather than the BoU, and reporting of bank account data to the Treasury in MoFPED was limited. Information on disbursements of project loans is reported to the BoU but there is no such reporting for project grants. As a result the accuracy of project grant aid data is nowhere near as reliable as that of budget support data.

To remedy this, MoFPED adopted a new methodology for recording project aid disbursements in the early 2000s, which utilizes data from both donors and project implementing agencies. In the fiscal data, expenditures funded from project aid are recorded as external development expenditures. These are measured as the total inflow of project aid, from both grants and loans, minus (plus) any increase (decrease) in project deposits in the banking system. Many donor-funded projects require the government to provide counterpart funding from the budget (see Chapter 6). Counterpart funding is recorded under domestic development expenditures.

---

[3] This can be misleading because IMF credits can indirectly support the government's budget resource envelope. If government domestic borrowing (which is a component of the budget resource envelope) is determined as a residual in a monetary programme—which includes targets for broad money growth, foreign exchange reserves, and private sector credit—an inflow of IMF credit, which boosts the foreign exchange reserves, creates room for government to increase its net borrowing from the domestic banking system without violating the targets for broad money and private sector credit.

[4] These resources are not actually disbursed to government; instead they are netted off external debt repayments.

3. Aid flows to Uganda

Table 13.1 sets out the main fiscal aggregates for the central government budget from 1991/92–2006/07. It includes data on aid disbursements, disaggregated into grants and loans, as well as budget support and project aid. Table 13.2 shows the disbursements of budget support and project aid in US dollars and as percentages of GDP. Aid is shown in gross terms, with no deduction for loan repayments. The project aid data in Tables 13.1 and 13.2 are taken from IMF documents (for the 1990s) and the MoFPED database for 2000/01 onwards.

The aid data in Table 13.2 show that gross aid averaged just under USD500 million per annum during the 1990s. This figure, however, fluctuated between USD400 million and USD500 million, with slightly higher levels in the second half of the decade than in the first.[5] Aid subsequently began to rise in 1999/2000, climbing above USD840 million per annum by 2004/05 before falling back in the following year and then jumping to USD1.2 billion in 2006/07.[6]

Data on aid disbursements from the OECD DAC, however, indicate much higher levels of aid, even after excluding emergency aid and food aid, by an average of about USD250 million a year (OECD 2006: 180).[7] The difference between the two estimates of aid is mainly attributable to project aid, which was not disbursed to the budget but instead to public enterprises, local governments, or non-governmental organizations, as well as to disbursements of IMF credits.

Import/budget support accounts for most of the variations in aid disbursements during this period. In the first half of the 1990s the economy faced severe BoP problems and defaulted on external debt servicing. Once the government had begun to implement macroeconomic policies to tackle the economic crisis, donors provided large levels of import support to fund the BoP. Between 1992/93 and 1994/95, import support inflows averaged around USD200 million per annum. As the BoP improved in the mid 1990s, helped by the boom in coffee prices, support for the BoP was no longer required and hence import support was reduced in the next two fiscal years to around USD150 million per annum.

---

[5] Aid disbursements in 1991/92 were exceptionally low because of economic problems in that year.

[6] The large rise in aid disbursements in 2006/07 is attributable to three factors. First, the disbursement of a World Bank PRSC grant, which had originally been scheduled for disbursement in 2005/06, was delayed until 2006/07; hence both a PRSC grant and a PRSC loan, together totalling USD263 million, were disbursed in 2006/07. Second, a USD80 million World Bank loan for thermal energy was disbursed in 2006/07. Both the double disbursement of PRSC funds and the thermal energy loan were one-off events confined to 2006/07, so budget support disbursements in 2007/08 fell back sharply. The third factor was a jump of about USD 100 million in project loan disbursements: it is not yet clear whether this increase will be sustained.

[7] The OECD DAC data show average annual total aid to Uganda, excluding emergency aid and food aid, of USD857 million between 1994 and 2004 (OECD 2006: 180), compared to the average of USD603 million between 1993/94 and 2003/04 in Table 13.2.

Table 13.1 Fiscal Aggregates (% GDP), 1991/92–2006/07

	1991/92	1992/93	1993/94	1994/95	1995/96	1996/97	1997/98	1998/99	1999/2000	2000/01	2001/02	2002/03	2003/04	2004/05	2005/06	2006/07
Total Revenue and Grants	12.4	14.3	12.8	14.1	14.2	15.3	15.3	16.1	17.1	18.1	18.0	17.6	20.1	19.3	17.7	19.2
Recurrent revenue	6.8	7.3	8.3	9.8	10.2	10.9	10.2	11.3	10.9	10.5	11.5	11.5	11.9	11.9	12.7	13.0
Grants	5.6	7.0	4.5	4.3	4.0	4.4	5.1	4.8	6.1	7.6	6.6	6.1	8.2	7.3	4.9	6.2
Budget support	2.6	3.5	1.9	1.7	1.4	1.9	2.5	1.9	2.8	3.5	3.3	3.7	5.8	5.1	2.7	3.5
Project grants	3.0	3.5	2.6	2.7	2.6	2.5	2.6	2.9	3.4	4.1	3.2	2.4	2.4	2.2	2.3	2.7
Expenditure and Net Lending	21.6	16.8	15.5	16.9	16.4	18.3	16.5	18.8	21.5	20.4	23.1	21.4	21.4	20.4	19.5	21.0
Current Expenditures	11.8	8.0	8.8	9.2	9.0	10.0	9.3	10.3	10.6	10.9	13.0	12.8	13.5	12.4	12.3	11.6
Interest payments	3.3	1.4	1.3	1.0	1.0	0.9	1.0	0.9	1.0	1.1	1.3	1.4	1.9	1.5	1.4	1.1
Development Expenditures	9.2	8.7	6.7	7.3	7.0	7.9	6.6	7.1	8.4	8.5	8.9	8.3	7.5	7.7	6.9	8.1
External	7.8	7.7	5.8	6.0	5.8	6.3	5.4	5.4	5.5	5.2	4.8	4.6	4.3	4.6	4.1	4.7
Domestic	1.3	0.9	0.9	1.3	1.1	1.6	1.1	1.7	2.8	3.2	4.2	3.7	3.2	3.1	2.9	3.4
Net lending	0.3	0.0	0.1	0.2	0.1	0.0	0.0	0.0	0.1	-0.3	0.0	-0.1	0.0	0.0	-0.2	0.5
Domestic arrears repayments	0.3	0.1	0.0	0.2	0.4	0.4	0.6	1.4	1.5	1.3	1.1	0.4	0.3	0.4	0.5	0.7
Overall balance including grants	-9.2	-2.5	-2.7	-2.8	-2.2	-3.0	-1.2	-2.8	-4.5	-2.2	-5.0	-3.8	-1.3	-1.1	-1.9	-1.8
Overall balance excluding grants	-14.8	-9.5	-7.2	-7.1	-6.3	-7.4	-6.3	-7.6	-10.6	-9.9	-11.6	-9.8	-9.5	-8.5	-6.8	-8.0
External Financing (net)	8.9	4.5	3.0	4.4	3.2	3.9	2.7	2.4	2.2	2.9	4.2	3.8	2.2	0.8	1.5	3.6
Loan Disbursements	5.4	6.9	6.2	5.4	4.0	4.5	3.5	3.6	3.2	3.5	4.9	4.6	3.1	1.8	2.6	4.3
Budget support	2.4	2.6	3.0	2.2	0.8	0.7	0.6	1.1	0.6	1.4	3.2	2.9	0.4	0.1	0.4	2.2
Project loans	3.0	4.3	3.2	3.3	3.2	3.8	2.8	2.5	2.5	2.0	1.7	1.7	2.7	1.7	2.1	2.1
Domestic Financing (net)	1.9	-3.7	0.5	-2.0	-0.9	-0.8	-1.5	0.1	2.1	-0.7	0.8	0.0	-0.9	0.4	0.4	-1.8

Source: Ministry of Finance, Planning and Economic Development.

Table 13.2. Aid to the Central Government Budget (in USD million and % GDP), 1991/92–2006/07

	1991/ 92	1992/ 93	1993/ 94	1994/ 95	1995/ 96	1996/ 97	1997/ 98	1998/ 99	1999/ 2000	2000/ 01	2001/ 02	2002/ 03	2003/ 04	2004/ 05	2005/ 06	2006/ 07
USD (m)																
Gross Aid (grants plus loans)	252.9	443.4	423.7	565.0	491.6	565.0	581.0	520.6	568.0	647.2	709.1	708.0	813.8	841.4	747.2	1225.3
Budget support	116.6	195.3	194.6	220.2	136.2	164.7	212.1	185.3	207.5	290.6	406.1	433.7	450.0	476.8	307.2	670.2
Project aid	136.3	248.1	229.1	344.9	355.5	400.3	368.8	335.3	360.5	356.6	303.0	274.4	363.8	364.5	440.0	555.1
% GDP																
Gross Aid (grants plus loans)	11.0	13.8	10.7	9.8	8.1	8.9	8.5	8.4	9.3	11.1	11.4	10.7	11.3	9.1	7.5	10.5
Budget support	5.1	6.1	4.9	3.8	2.2	2.6	3.1	3.0	3.4	5.0	6.5	6.6	6.2	5.2	3.1	5.7
Project aid	6.0	7.7	5.8	6.0	5.8	6.3	5.4	5.4	5.9	6.1	4.9	4.2	5.0	4.0	4.4	4.7

Source: Ministry of Finance, Planning and Economic Development.

Now termed budget support, it began to climb back up again in 1997/98, to around USD200 million and, beginning in 2000/01, rose sharply to reach USD450 million in 2003/04. Uganda was one of the first countries to receive budget support and it is one of the largest recipients of budget support in the world.

This increase in budget support was driven by three factors. First, the reforms implemented by the government in the 1990s had established credibility in the quality of its macroeconomic and budget management which gave donors confidence that budget support could be used efficiently in Uganda to meet poverty reduction objectives. Second, both multilateral and bilateral donors began to provide more funds directly to the government budget to support the expansion of core public services, such as primary education. Budget support was the most suitable modality for supporting this expansion in public services because it involved expenditures, such as teachers salaries, which could not easily be funded through projects. Third, Uganda received debt relief in the form of grants from donors to fund scheduled debt service payments, which freed up budget resources for other uses: these grants are classified as a form of budget support. Debt relief was provided by Multilateral Debt Fund grants between 1995 and 1998, before Uganda qualified for external debt relief under the HIPC and Enhanced HIPC initiatives in 1998 and 2000 respectively. HIPC grants averaged US$65 million a year in the 2000s (see Chapter 12).

Table 13.3 provides data on the budget support disbursed between 2000/01 and 2006/07, broken down into three main categories: general budget support, sector budget support, and PAF support. General budget support is intended to provide resources to the government budget without reference to any specific sectors or groups of expenditures, though with policy conditionalities often attached. Sector budget support provides budget resources for specific sectors within the government budget. PAF budget support provides budget resources for a set of identified poverty reducing expenditures grouped together in a 'virtual fund' within the government budget. The PAF includes funds from both the debt relief provided through the HIPC and Enhanced HIPC initiatives, as well as PAF grants from bilateral donors. As can be seen in Table 13.3, both general budget support and PAF budget support doubled in terms of US dollar values between 2000/01 and 2004/05, whereas sector budget support fell sharply. The 2005/06 and 2006/07 fiscal years were both somewhat anomalous because of the delayed disbursement of a large World Bank budget support grant from 2005/06 to 2006/07 and the inclusion in the latter year of a large World Bank thermal energy loan which is classified as sector budget support but is a one-off disbursement and hence will not affect longer term trends.

By 2004/05, general and PAF budget support each accounted for almost half of total budget support; sector budget support comprised only a very small share.

Table 13.3. Breakdown of Budget Support Disbursements (in USD million), 2000/01–2005/06

	2000/01	2001/02	2002/03	2003/04	2004/05	2005/06
General Budget Support	117.7	218.9	236.6	239.0	239.6	121.1
Sector Budget Support	51.6	37.2	46.6	14.0	13.1	15.2
Poverty Action Fund	121.3	150.0	150.4	197.0	224.1	170.9
PAF Grants	66.9	90.3	82.0	135.4	159.4	89.3
Debt Relief	54.4	59.7	68.4	61.7	64.7	81.5
MDRI Debt Relief						26.0
Total Budget Support	290.6	406.1	433.7	450.0	476.8	333.2

Source: Ministry of Finance, Planning and Economic Development.

General budget support was boosted by Poverty Reduction Support Credits (PRSC), which the World Bank piloted in Uganda and which accounted for around two thirds of general budget support in each of the four years from 2001/02 to 2004/05. The reasons behind the increase in PAF budget support were more complex. PAF grants are seen by many bilateral donors as easier to justify than general budget support because of the PAF's poverty focus; hence donors can argue that their aid directly supports poverty reduction. While several sector budget support donors wanted to move away from this type of budget support, they were not prepared to move fully into general budget support. Rather, this aid was switched into the PAF as a compromise. During this time, some bilateral donors also switched their aid from general budget support into PAF because of concerns about the level of military expenditure.

Project aid inflows were more stable between 1991/92 and 2005/06 (if the project grant data provide an accurate guide). They increased during the first half of the 1990s but, after reaching almost USD350 million in 1994/95, subsequently fluctuated around this level for the next ten years. Project aid rose in 2005/06 and then to USD550 million in the following year, but it is not clear whether this simply reflects a bunching of disbursements or a change in the trend.

The distribution of aid between the two aid modalities has altered markedly. In the early 1990s there was a roughly equal split between import support and project aid. In the mid 1990s the share of project aid in total aid rose to around two thirds as import support declined, but from 2001/02 onwards the strong increase in budget support made it the dominant aid modality, with an average share in total aid of 55 per cent.

4. The shift towards budget support

4.1 *Why has budget support been the government's preferred aid modality?*

There are several important public finance reasons for governments to prefer budget support to project aid. First, from the standpoint of maximizing the utility of expenditures, it is optimal to pool together all budgetary resources, including domestic revenues and aid, before allocating these resources. Competing expenditures can then be considered upon their relative social rates of return (if these are known), and how well they accord with government priorities. Earmarking budgetary resources for specific expenditures, as is the case with project aid, distorts optimal expenditure allocations. These expenditures are accorded a privileged status by virtue of their being linked to the availability of a specific budget resource. Hence, expenditures can be undertaken, funded by project aid, which are regarded by government as being of a lower priority than other expenditures, which cannot be accommodated within the budget resource envelope.[8] Even if donors and government were to have the same expenditure preferences, it would still be sub-optimal to divide the budget resource envelope into two, with the allocation of project aid expenditures divorced from that of all other expenditures. In reality, of course, government and donors do not always share the same expenditure preferences, and so project aid distorts expenditure allocations away from the former's preferences and towards the latter's.

Second, project aid tends to bias expenditure allocations towards capital rather than current expenditures. (The exception is where project aid is a relatively minor share of the overall budget resource envelope.) Hence capital projects are undertaken even if the equivalent value of expenditure in the current budget offers potentially higher social rates of return. Moreover, the rates of return on capital projects are often depressed because there are insufficient funds in the current budget to operate and maintain them once the construction phase, paid for from project aid, is completed.

Third, the reality of budgeting in countries such as Uganda is that there is very little flexibility in the budget to reallocate funds to meet strategic expenditure priorities or to accommodate fiscal shocks (such as emergency spending pressures or revenue shortfalls). The lack of flexibility in the budget is due to a large share of the budget constituting expenditures over which government has either no discretion (e.g. statutory expenditures such as interest payments and civil servants' pensions) or only very limited discretion (such as the wage bill). By expanding the budget resource envelope, budget support increases allocative discretion and enhances the flexibility in the budget. Project support, on the

---

[8] The same principle applies to hypothecated taxes; i.e. taxes which are earmarked for specific expenditures.

other hand, does not enhance the flexibility of the budget—and can actually reduce it—because it involves earmarked expenditures and counterpart funds.

Of the three types of budget support received by Uganda—general budget support, sector budget support and PAF budget support—the government's preference has been for general budget support because this provides the greatest degree of flexibility to allocate expenditures according to its own priorities. Budget support to the PAF has been seen as the second best option because it provides flexibility to allocate expenditures between sectors within the PAF. Finally, sector budget support is regarded as the least attractive option because of the potential constraints on inter-sectoral flexibility of the budget that it entails.

From the donor's standpoint, there are two main preconditions for shifting aid from the project modality to budget support. First, if donors are to contribute to a common pool of budgetary resources which funds all government expenditure, they must be reasonably satisfied with the overall allocation of expenditures from this pool; i.e. they must be in general agreement with the government's expenditure priorities. Second, they must be satisfied with the fiduciary standards of the budget. Procedures for budget reporting, accounting and auditing must be strong enough to give budget support donors confidence that budget resources are actually spent on the items for which they have been budgeted and are not misused.

In addition, the difficulty for any budget support donor is that, once funds have been contributed to a common pool, there is no way of distinguishing whether or not its own funds have supported particular expenditures within the government budget which it might not itself approve of, and which might be difficult to explain politically. Such concerns about budget support are in some sense misleading. Any type of aid, including that earmarked for specific expenditures, is potentially fungible and can free up resources for expenditures disapproved of by the donor giving the aid. However there is no doubt that there are potential political pitfalls for donors who provide budget support rather than project aid, if only because the concept of fungibility is not widely understood outside the economics profession.

In Uganda, some bilateral donors have expressed concern about aspects of the composition of the government's budget, notably the level of expenditure on the military and public administration. For these reasons, many of the budget support donors to Uganda have preferred to give sector or PAF budget support rather than general budget support. Both provide an explicit link to types of expenditures, which are easier to justify politically to their own constituents.

4.2 Budget reforms and the Public Expenditure Review

Reforms to budget management implemented from 1992 onwards were instrumental in enhancing donor confidence in the budget and thereby encouraging donors to shift their aid into budget support. In 1997/98 a Medium Term Expenditure Framework (MTEF) was introduced, in which the budget was divided into sectors corresponding to broad functional expenditure classifications (see Chapter 8). This allowed donors and other stakeholders in the budget to understand how the government planned to allocate its budget resource envelope among the major sectors for the coming three years. At the same time, the budget allocations were more clearly linked to the expenditure priorities outlined in the PEAP, with large increases in allocations made to priority poverty reducing expenditures such as the universal primary education programme. Hence, the government explicitly linked the budget to strategic policies, and the reduction of poverty, which donors could share, and signalled its commitment to these allocations through the MTEF. In addition, key sectors, such as Education and Health, established Sector Working Groups (SWGs), led by the relevant line ministry, but which included MoFPED and donor representatives (see Chapter 9). Together, these began to prepare medium-term sector expenditure plans setting out their expenditure priorities.

Donors were provided with several opportunities to participate formally in the budget process and to express their views about the composition of the budget. They were invited, along with other stakeholders, to various budget workshops as well as to the sector expenditure reviews. An important forum for the government to present its budget policies to donors and other stakeholders such as parliamentarians was the annual Public Expenditure Review (PER). Usually a two-day meeting, the PER was held two to three weeks before the presentation of the annual budget to Parliament in mid-June. At the PER MoFPED presented its fiscal strategy, the fiscal framework of the MTEF (i.e. the aggregate fiscal and macroeconomic projections) and the preliminary[9] MTEF sectoral allocations, while some of the line ministries presented their sector plans.

The argument that MoFPED made to the donors at the PER was that they should look at the proposed MTEF as a whole. If donors were broadly in agreement with the fiscal framework and the sectoral allocation of the budget, even if they did not agree with every single allocation within it, they should be prepared to support it and provide the budget support required to fund the resource envelope. They should defer from trying to fund individual expenditure items, which they themselves thought important, outside of the government budget (i.e. through project aid). To assist the donors to understand the budget proposals, MoFPED made a technical presentation to the donors a few days before the PER. The donors then prepared a joint response, which was presented at the PER by the World Bank (as the lead donor), and was generally favourable to the budget proposals.

---

[9] They were preliminary because the budget was still subject to Cabinet and Parliamentary approval.

4.3 *The Poverty Action Fund*

The PAF was set up in the 1998/99 fiscal year to demonstrate that debt relief provided under the HIPC initiative would be used to increase expenditures on public services which directly contribute to poverty reduction.[10] A set of poverty reducing expenditures in the budget was identified and the aggregate level of these expenditures in 1997/98 (the year before PAF was set up) was used as a base from which to determine future PAF-spending levels. In subsequent years, the annual flow of budgetary resources from HIPC debt relief and other PAF grants was added to this base to determine the aggregate level of PAF expenditures in each year. In other words, if A is the total expenditure on PAF expenditure items in 1997/98 and B is PAF budget support in 1998/99, the total budgeted spending on PAF in 1998/99 is A *plus* B. While the PAF is a virtual fund, and its expenditures are an integral part of the budget, it has a privileged status and is protected from within year expenditure cuts.

The PAF encouraged donors to provide budget support by demonstrating that poverty reducing expenditures were being prioritized in the budget. Moreover, providing budget support to the PAF gave donors some degree of certainty that their budget support was directly linked to poverty reducing expenditures rather than to other expenditures which they might have found more difficult to justify to their constituents. Hence, while the PAF began as a vehicle for HIPC debt relief, over time more bilateral donors channelled budget support grants through it. By 2004/05 PAF budget support had risen to USD224 million, although it fell back in the following two years to around USD170 million. PAF budget support comprised almost half of all budget support in 2004/05 and 2005/06 (see Table 13.3).

The PAF has contributed to mobilizing more budget support for Uganda and helped to reduce the transactions costs of coordinating and meeting aid conditionalities. It provided a common set of criteria—comprising of the government's commitment to fund and protect PAF expenditures, together with monitoring and reporting arrangements—to which all donors could adhere and which, therefore, obviated the need for individual PAF donors to impose their own separate conditions for the disbursement of their budget support.

However, the PAF was not without its drawbacks, and in some ways it complicated the task of aligning donor aid with government budgetary objectives—albeit not to the same extent as sector budget support, let alone project aid.[11] The direct link between PAF budget support and additional spending, relative to the 1997/98 base, meant the government lost some flexibility over budget

---

[10] A secondary motive was to provide a vehicle for Nordic donors to continue giving programme aid (originally provided to help meet multilateral debt service payments) after Uganda's debt service became 'sustainable' under HIPC (see Chapter 12).

[11] Williamson and Canagarajah (2003) provide a thorough review of the benefits and drawbacks of the PAF.

allocations. Initially this did not matter very much because the growth of PAF resources corresponded with government's desire to expand poverty reducing expenditures. Following further increases of budget support through the PAF, its share of the government's discretionary budget rose from 17 per cent in 1997/98 to 37 per cent in 2001/02.[12]

The PAF's growth began to reduce the government's flexibility to allocate expenditures optimally, for two reasons. First, the growth of the PAF squeezed the relatively small share of the budget in non-PAF areas, some of which were regarded as high priority by the government even if they were not eligible for inclusion in the PAF.[13] PAF expenditures, alongside statutory expenditures and the wage bill, were protected from within year budget cuts necessitated by fiscal shocks. To ease the pressures on the non-protected parts of the budget, the government's commitment to protect all PAF expenditures from within year cuts was reduced to a commitment to fund a minimum of 95 per cent of budgeted PAF expenditures in 2002/03 and subsequent years.

Second, the PAF biased the allocation of the budget towards direct service delivery for the poor (which qualify as PAF expenditures) because the level of PAF expenditures in the budget was driven by the magnitude of PAF budget support. This bias was at the expense of other priority expenditures, which were not designated as PAF expenditures, such as expenditures to support directly productive activities or new priority areas, for example secondary education to accommodate the graduates from universal primary education (Williamson and Canagarajah 2003). Moreover, from 2002/03 onwards, a key objective of government's fiscal policy became to reverse the widening fiscal deficit before grants, which rendered the direct link between PAF budget support and the level of aggregate PAF expenditures unsustainable. With total government spending constrained by the objective of reducing the fiscal deficit before grants, increasing the size of PAF would inevitably crowd out other non PAF expenditures from the budget. As a result, the government's criteria for determining the magnitude of budgeted PAF expenditures was changed, committing

---

[12] This measure of the PAF share of the budget refers to PAF as a share of discretionary government expenditure; it is defined to exclude interest rates and arrears payments. The PAF share of the budget is about three percentage points lower if the total government budget is used as the denominator.

[13] The categories of expenditure in the government budget that receive *ex ante* protection from within year cuts are wages and salaries, PAF (which includes some wages and salaries), statutory expenditures, and unconditional grants to the districts. These expenditures comprised 65 per cent of the Government's budget in 2004/05, up from 61 per cent in 2000/01, of which the PAF comprised slightly less than half. In practice, some other categories of expenditures are rarely cut, including defence, some parts of public administration, and some counterpart funds for donor funded projects (especially wages for project staff). Hence the share of the government's budget that bore the brunt of any within year expenditure cuts was less than 20 per cent. In 2002/03 these non-protected expenditures suffered cuts of 23 per cent, relative to their budget appropriations, mainly to accommodate supplementary appropriations in other areas.

to hold the PAF share of the budget constant, instead of allowing it to be determined by the value of PAF budget support.

4.4 Sector budget support

The first large scale disbursements of sector budget support to Uganda took place in 1998/99, when USD66 million was disbursed, followed by USD30 million in 1999/2000; almost all of both tranches was for the Education sector (OECD 2006: 197). Sector budget support disbursements during 2000/01 to 2006/07 are shown in Table 13.3. However, the data in Table 13.3 underestimate the amount of sector budget support in one respect. More than half of the PAF budget support grants were also earmarked for specific sectors within PAF, although some of this earmarking was only 'notional'.[14] Sectors that also benefited from sector budget support were Health, Justice/Law and Order, and Agriculture. Sector budget support averaged 25 per cent of total budget support between 1998/99 and 2000/01, but it declined to around 4 per cent in the mid-2000s as donors shifted their aid into either general budget support or budget support for the PAF. As noted in section 3, the jump in sector budget support in 2006/07 was attributable mainly to a one-off disbursement of a thermal energy loan.

Sector budget support was attractive to donors because it enabled them to link their budget support to a more narrowly defined, and politically more acceptable, set of expenditures than would be the case if they were to provide general budget support. Moreover, during this period, the government rapidly expanded the Education sector budget, mainly to meet the requirements of UPE, and therefore the government's budget priorities were compatible with donors providing sector budget support for education.[15]

However, of the three types of budget support, sector budget support is the most difficult to align with government macro/fiscal and inter-sectoral budget priorities. There are strong incentives for each line ministry to negotiate directly with donors, outside of the budget process, to increase its own sector budget support, and then to use this to argue for an increase in its budget allocation on the grounds that donors who give sector budget support expect to see this reflected in a higher sectoral budget allocation. The sectors' line ministries and their donors argue that sector budget support should be 'additional' in full to the budget allocation which the sectors would receive in the absence of any sector support, although how the latter could be determined in practice is not straightforward. Taken to its logical conclusion, such 'additionality' would

[14] Notional earmarking was a term used to denote budget support which was designated to a specific sector but was not intended to affect the overall expenditure allocation to that sector.
[15] Nominal Education sector expenditures in the government's budget almost doubled between 1997/98 and 2000/01, from UGX205 billion to UGX404 billion.

lead to a situation where the size of each sector's budget allocation is determined by how much sector support it can attract from donors. Moreover, how much sector budget support in total each sector receives largely depends on multiple decisions taken by individual donors, and these decisions are driven by many other factors besides the relative funding needs of the various sectors.[16] Such a process, involving decentralized and largely uncoordinated decisions by donors, cannot lead to a rational inter-sectoral allocation of expenditures, let alone one which accords with the government's own budget priorities. Treating sector budget support as 'additional' is not compatible with a centralized inter-sectoral allocation of the budget which accords with the government's overall budget priorities.

The concept of 'additionality' is not the only impediment to aligning sector budget support with government's overall budget priorities. Agreements signed by line ministries and sector support donors link aid disbursements to the meeting of sectoral performance targets, which themselves have budgetary implications, such as the number of teachers employed. This gives the sectors' line ministries and their donors an incentive to agree on sectoral performance targets, which require larger sectoral budgets, and then to use this as an argument for securing an increase in their budget allocations.

During the late 1990s and early 2000s the tensions between the budget implications of sector budget support and the efforts to establish a more rational budget process which could operationalize the government's strategic budget priorities, were relatively mute. This was mainly because the sector which received the bulk of sector budget support, Education, was also the sector which required a major expansion of its expenditure ceiling to accommodate the needs of UPE. However, by 2001/02 the need to control the overall size of the budget and to improve the relative shares of some other sectors meant that these tensions had to be resolved. For this reason, MoFPED resisted efforts by some line ministries and donors to incorporate the concept of additionality into sector budget support funding agreements (usually these were memoranda of understandings). Instead, in 2002 it argued that the size of each sector's budget had to be determined through the annual budget process in line with government's strategic expenditure priorities, but independently of the amount of sector budget support on offer. Hence, any earmarking of budget support to specific sectors could only be regarded as 'notional'. Donors who were concerned that particular sectors deserved higher expenditure ceilings in the MTEF were encouraged to express their views in the appropriate fora of the

---

[16] For example, if donor A decides that it wants to give USD10 million to sector x, the budget for sector x will increase by USD10 million irrespective of whether or not this sector needs an additional USD10 million more than any other sector.

budget process, such as the PER. However, they could not use their sector budget support to lever up the expenditure ceilings for their favoured sectors.[17]

4.5 Poverty reduction support credits and general budget support

During the first half of the 2000s, the PRSC was the World Bank's main instrument for providing budget support to Uganda and the largest single component of budget support from any donor. Disbursements began in 2001/02 and averaged US$156 million per year over that and the next three fiscal years, comprising 35 per cent of total budget support disbursed in this period. The conditionalities pertaining to the approval of the PRSC by the World Bank Board consisted of a series of prior actions, which were set out in the PRSC matrix. These prior actions, plus a larger number of other policy actions in the matrix (which were not conditions for the Board to approve the PRSC) were intended to reflect objectives in the PEAP.

The PRSC offered two important benefits to Uganda in terms of facilitating a better alignment of aid with its own fiscal objectives. First, the large size of the PRSC meant that it led to a marked shift in the composition of aid modalities in favour of general budget support—the government's preferred form of aid. Secondly, to some extent the PRSC facilitated the harmonization of conditionalities attached to budget support from different donors. Bilateral budget support donors accepted the principle of aligning their budget support with the PRSC and participated in the PRSC missions and negotiations. However, this was only partly successful: bilateral donors did not adopt the PRSC matrix as the only conditions governing disbursement of their aid. Rather, many of these donors were concerned about other issues not covered under the PRSC, such as political and governance issues. Some of the bilateral donors even withheld tranches of their own general budget support when the PRSC prior actions had been met and the PRSC disbursed.[18]

The PRSC also imposed heavy transactions costs on the government. PRSC missions were large and frequent, and the documentation required was extensive (Miovic 2004). In addition, the PRSC required the government to undertake a large number of actions that further increased the burden upon itself. There were eleven prior actions in each of the first two PRSCs and nine in the third. Moreover, two of these prior actions entailed the satisfactory completion of Health and Education sector reviews and meant that they effectively required completion of many other actions pertaining to these sectors in advance. In addition to the prior actions, there were forty-six other actions in the matrix

---

[17] This principle was included in the Partnership Principles between the Government of Uganda and its Development Partners, which was signed in 2003 (see Box 9.3).

[18] For example, the UK and other donors withheld some of their budget support when defence expenditures were increased above the budgeted levels in 2003/04.

attached to the first PRSC and seventy attached to the third (OECD 2006: 200). The large number of actions in the matrix reflected the attempt to accommodate the desires of different donors wishing to see their own favoured objectives featured in the matrix. Hence, the effort to use the PRSC to harmonize the conditionalities of all general budget support donors had costs as well as benefits.

While general budget support instruments, such as the PRSC, are attractive to finance ministries which have overall responsibility for managing public finances, for the reasons discussed above, they are not necessarily as attractive for the individual line ministries. For these ministries, which are expected to implement the various conditionalities attached to these instruments, the costs (e.g. of implementing prior actions) are internal while the benefits are external. Budget support boosts the entire budget resource envelope, not their own ministerial budget allocations. Hence, the incentives facing the various government ministries and agencies are not well aligned. The finance ministry has strong incentives for wanting general budget support but does not have direct responsibility for implementing many of the conditions required to obtain it,[19] while line ministries have the responsibility for implementing the conditionalities but fewer incentives to do so. The larger the number of conditions attached to an instrument such as the PRSC, the more difficult it is to align the incentives within government to ensure that the conditionalities are implemented.

5. Integrating donor-funded projects into the MTEF

The efforts in the first half of the 1990s to capture donor funded projects in the Public Investment Plan and integrate them into the budget are addressed in Chapter 6. Here we confine our discussion of donor projects to the situation in the late 1990s and early 2000s when the main concern of MoFPED was aligning donor projects with the broader macroeconomic and budgetary strategies in the PEAP and which were implemented through the MTEF.

As noted in section 2, the shift in the relative shares of budget support and project aid in total aid disbursements occurred without any reduction in the dollar value of project aid, which averaged around USD350 million per annum in the first half of the 2000s, the same level as in the second half of the 1990s. Despite the publicly stated preference of the government, project aid remained attractive to many donors, not least because it is often easier to justify politically to their own constituents. There are also sometimes economic benefits for the

---

[19] The incentives within government are better aligned with an IMF credit, because its conditionalities generally pertain to actions which are under the control of the finance ministry or the central bank, which stand to benefit from the credit.

donor countries, in terms of commercial contracts for construction, consultancy, and other work, while domestic policy in some countries prevents them from providing budget support. In addition there are strong constituencies supporting project aid within donor agencies, especially large ones such as the World Bank, which have a long history of project lending.

It proved very difficult to align donor funded projects with the government's overall fiscal objectives. Although donor projects were shown in the MTEF from 1998/99 onwards,[20] this had little impact on budget planning because the projects were not included in the sectors' expenditure ceilings, which effectively applied only to the GoU budget. Hence a sector (or ministry within a sector) could obtain more resources for expenditures by negotiating directly with donors, thus circumventing the hard budget constraint of the GoU sector ceiling. For this reason project aid remained popular with some line ministries. Indeed, those sectors that are not considered a high priority within the budget have the strongest incentive to seek to boost their expenditures through project aid, which undermines efforts to prioritize expenditures on a sectoral basis. The GoU budget was subject to centralized control and reflected the government's strategic expenditure priorities, at least to some extent given the political and other constraints facing budget planners. In contrast donor projects were not subject to centralized control to anywhere near the same extent, but instead were mainly determined as a result of bilateral negotiations between line ministries and donors. These took place without any coordination with MoFPED's medium term fiscal framework. Projects had to be approved by the Development Committee, but this was not very effective in ensuring that they were in accord with strategic expenditure priorities. It was not able to prevent line ministries and individual donors preparing projects which were not a priority, and which were regarded by MoFPED and even other donors as being highly problematic. MoFPED was a signatory to many of the donor projects, including all those that were funded by loans, but it is very difficult politically for any finance minister to refuse to endorse a project negotiated between one of his cabinet colleagues and a donor, because this would be perceived as turning away 'free money'.

The failure to impose effective control over donor projects and bring them within the MTEF for planning purposes impeded efforts to control aggregate expenditure (and hence the fiscal deficit), align inter sectoral expenditure allocations with strategic priorities, and to align intra sectoral expenditures with sector priorities. Given that line ministries were usually closely involved with negotiating project aid for their sectors, it might be expected that, at the sectoral level, projects would at least be aligned with intra sectoral priorities, but

---

[20] In the MTEF tables, the projects were shown as part of the planned budgets for the next three years under the relevant sectors, but no data on project outturns were included in the MTEF tables because insufficient data were available.

even this was not always the case; several donor projects were accepted which had not been included in the expenditure priorities identified in sector expenditure plans. The main reason for this was that, for most ministries, the attraction of additional projects, which were perceived by them to carry no opportunity costs in terms of having to make cuts elsewhere in their budgets, outweighed the benefits of adhering strictly to their sector strategy. This was especially the case for ministries in sectors which contained multiple ministries (e.g. Public Administration sector and Economic Functions and Social Services sector) where SWGs were very weak; ministries in these sectors had lower government ceilings than they wanted and sought to boost their expenditures through bilateral project negotiations, without having to subject them to the scrutiny of an effective SWG. However, problems of aligning projects with intra sectoral priorities were also evident in some single ministry sectors, notably Roads and Works, and Agriculture.

In the Roads and Works sector, where donor projects accounted for about 55 per cent of total expenditures in the early 2000s, the requirements for counter-part funding and cost overruns on road projects (which often resulted in expenditure arrears being incurred), inevitably squeezed the funds available for road maintenance. The Roads sector also experienced serious delays in implementing donor-funded projects, which suggests that capacity constraints in the sector were acute. The total value of external credits to fund road projects, which were contracted between 1999/2000 and 2001/02, was USD193 million, but, less than a quarter of this amount (USD43 million) had actually been disbursed by the end of 2002/03. Project aid was also used to establish new public institutions (e.g. the National Environment Management Agency) whose running costs would eventually have to be borne by the government budget.

To tackle these problems, MoFPED decided in 2002 to try and integrate donor projects into the MTEF sector ceilings. As a first step, it began compiling a comprehensive data base of all donor funded projects in each sector, which included both *ex post* data on actual disbursements of funding and planned future disbursements. The long-term intention is to establish an overall sector ceiling for each sector in the MTEF which covers both the government budget and the donor funded projects. This overall sector ceiling should act as a hard budget constraint, so that if sectors subsequently negotiate additional donor funding they will suffer a loss in their government budget allocation. Although the overall ceilings for each sector would initially reflect the existing distribu-tion of planned donor funded projects, over time they could be gradually aligned with the inter sectoral priorities of the MTEF and the Long Term Expenditure Framework which was included in the 2004 PEAP.

It is, however, very difficult to implement such a system effectively, not least because of the very strong incentives facing line ministries to try and circum-vent the hard budget constraint. There are also difficulties in imposing an overall hard budget ceiling on sectors which include multiple spending agencies, because each individual agency has an incentive to try and obtain more donor project funding and thereby drive up its own share of the overall sector expenditure ceiling. By mid 2007 it had not been possible to impose a unified expenditure ceiling on any of the sectors, covering both the GoU budget and donor projects. Sectors that suffered a reduction in donor project expenditures were not automatically compensated through an equivalent increase in their GoU budget allocations because of resource constraints. On the other hand, sectors that were able to attract an increase in donor projects did not see their GoU budget ceiling cut by a matching amount.

6. Aligning donor aid with the government's macroeconomic objectives

As discussed in Chapter 3, during the 1990s the priority for fiscal policy was to curb the government's domestic borrowing requirement. Because of the link between government domestic bank borrowing and the monetary aggregates, this was essential to control inflation. The government formulated a target for net domestic financing (NDF),[21] which was determined by the BoU's monetary policy targets, and then constructed the budget to ensure that the target for NDF could be met. The targeted domestic borrowing requirement was negative throughout most of the 1990s to provide the room for the BoU to control money supply growth while simultaneously rebuilding its foreign exchange reserves and allowing for a recovery in private sector credit. Fiscal policy was successful in helping to control inflation, which once it had been brought down from 30 per cent in 1992/93, averaged only 5.7 per cent per annum for the rest of the decade.

Given that the main macroeconomic objective of fiscal policy was to meet a target for NDF, the size of the government budget resource envelope, which determined aggregate spending, was effectively determined by the sum of the available budget resources. These resources were from domestic revenues, donor grants, and loans, less the resources required to service external debt, plus the NDF target. Consequently, at the margin, an increase in donor aid translated directly into higher government expenditure.

As a percentage of GDP, the size of the budget resource envelope was relatively stable between 1992/93 and 1998/99; hence government expenditure was

---

[21] Net domestic financing comprises net bank borrowing, non-bank borrowing and changes in the cheque float. With very shallow domestic financial markets the scope for non-bank financing of the budget was very limited, hence the bulk of NDF comprised net bank borrowing. The NDF does not include privatization receipts, which were held off budget and used to fund the restructuring and privatization costs of the public enterprises.

also relatively stable at around 17 per cent of GDP. The envelope increased sharply with the rise in aid, mainly in the form of budget support, in the late 1990s and early 2000s. With more budgetary resources available, the government was able to expand its budget, especially on expenditure policy priorities such as free universal primary education. In the three years between 1998/99 and 2001/02, government expenditure increased by more than four percentage points of GDP, peaking at 23.1 per cent of GDP in 2001/02. As most of the increase was to be funded by higher external budgetary resources—debt relief and budget support—rather than by domestic revenues, the growth of which was very slow, the fiscal deficit excluding grants widened sharply from 6.3 per cent of GDP in 1997/98 to 11.6 per cent in 2001/02 (see Table 13.1 and Figure 13.1).[22] In fact, the actual (*ex post*) rise in external resources for the budget was lower than the budgeted (*ex ante*) increase because of delays in disbursements of budget support (see Section 6.2). Hence, there was also an increase in government domestic borrowing to bridge the gap between the budgeted and realized inflows of budget support, especially in 1999/2000 and 2001/02.

The rapid expansion of the fiscal stance, reflected in the almost doubling of the fiscal deficit before grants, created problems for macroeconomic management. Furthermore, it prompted the government to revise the link between aid and aggregate government expenditures, a move which was also motivated by concerns to restrain the growth of external debt and the excessive dependency of the budget on donor aid. The problems for macroeconomic management essentially arose from the need to translate a foreign resource (the aid inflow) into domestic expenditures. Concern over the impact of large aid inflows on external debt and aid dependency related to long-term fiscal sustainability and the vulnerability of the budget to fiscal shocks. These issues are examined below, beginning with the impact of higher aid flows on macroeconomic management.[23]

6.1 Impact of aid on macroeconomic management

The large increase in aid flows to the budget created problems for macroeconomic management in two areas: monetary policy and the potential adverse impact on the real effective exchange rate (REER). The most immediate impact was on monetary policy. Fiscal policy has a direct link to monetary policy

---

[22] In countries for which the budget is a large net recipient of aid, and for which external borrowing consists predominantly of concessional loans, the fiscal deficit excluding grants (or before grants) provides a better indicator of the fiscal stance than the fiscal deficit including (or after) grants, which is sometimes referred to as the conventional deficit. An increase in donor grants allows the government to raise expenditures, without having to withdraw spending power from the private sector through taxes, and hence has an expansionary impact on aggregate demand. In terms of the macroeconomic impact, there is no difference between government funding its expenditures from donor grants or concessional loans.

[23] Brownbridge and Mutebile (2007) provide a more detailed analysis of these issues, which are also analysed by Atingi-Ego (2006) and Kitabire (2005).

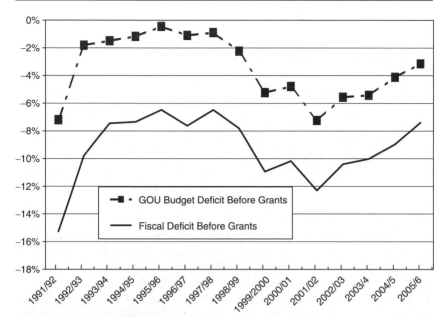

Figure 13.1 Trends in the Fiscal Deficit Before Grants and the Government Budget Deficit Before Grants (% of GDP), 1991/92–2005/06

Source: Ministry of Finance, Planning and Economic Development.

through the base (or reserve) money created by fiscal operations, in particular fiscal operations linked to the GoU budget.[24] GoU budget expenditures in domestic currency (funded from the UCF in the BoU) create base money while the collection of domestic revenues (also in domestic currency) contracts base money. We denote the net creation of base money by fiscal operations as fiscal liquidity creation (FLC); this is the difference between budget expenditures (Egou) and domestic revenues (DR), less the budget expenditures on imports (Eimgou) and external interest payments (Extr), as shown in 1 below.

$$1 \quad FLC = Egou - DR - Eimgou - Extr$$

From the budget identity, budget expenditures (Egou) are equal to the sum of domestic revenues, budget support grants (BSG) and loans (BSL) and net domestic financing (NDF), less repayments (amortization) of external debt (EA), as shown in 2.

---

[24] Disbursements of project aid and project aid expenditures do not directly affect base money unless the project accounts into which these disbursements are paid, and from which project expenditures are made, are held in the central bank. Up until 2004/05 in Uganda, most project accounts were held in commercial banks.

299

$$2 \quad \text{Egou} = \text{DR} + \text{BSG} + \text{BSL} + \text{NDF} - \text{EA}$$

The increase in budget support grants and loans between 1998/99 and 2001/02, plus the provision of external debt relief, expanded the budget resource envelope and enabled GoU expenditures to increase. As most of the expansion of GoU expenditures constituted domestic currency expenditures (such as teachers' wages and salaries), there was a corresponding increase in fiscal liquidity creation. Table 13.4 illustrates these trends.

The GoU budget deficit, excluding grants (defined as GoU budget expenditures less domestic revenues), rose from less than 1 per cent of GDP in 1997/98 to 6.8 per cent of GDP in 2001/02. The widening of the deficit was driven by the increase in budget support and the provision of external debt relief. Hence, there was also an expansion in the net foreign exchange components of the budget; inflows of budget support less external debt servicing and government imports. As a result fiscal liquidity creation, which amounted to less than 1 per cent of GDP in the mid 1990s, rose to 6.4 per cent of GDP in 2001/02. It is worth emphasizing that the increase in fiscal liquidity creation was not caused primarily by an increase in government's domestic borrowing requirement. Although NDF rose, the increase between 1998/99 and 2001/02 was less than 1 per cent of GDP, and was mainly the result of shortfalls of budget support disbursements relative to budgeted levels.[25]

The BoU's monetary policy involved an operating target for base money, derived from its target for broad money and a projection of the money multiplier. As the fiscal deficit before grants widened in the late 1990s and early 2000s, fiscal operations became the main source of base money creation. Fiscal liquidity creation far exceeded the growth of the BoU's base money target. To meet this target, the BoU had to sterilize most of the base money created by fiscal liquidity operations, using a combination of two instruments: the sale of domestic securities, mostly treasury bills, through a weekly securities auction; and sale of foreign exchange to the inter-bank foreign exchange market. This is shown below, where ΔRM denotes the increase in base money, TBs denotes net sales of securities and FX denotes net sales of foreign exchange.[26]

$$3 \quad \Delta \text{RM} = \text{FLC} - \text{TBs} - \text{FX}$$

Sterilizing the liquidity created by the fiscal operations proved difficult for the BoU, especially because both the domestic money market and the foreign exchange market in Uganda were shallow. Initially the BoU planned to put the emphasis, in terms of the balance between the two sterilization instruments, on

---

[25] In 1999/2000, NDF rose to 2.2 per cent of GDP before falling back in the following year. Part of this rise (equivalent to about 1 per cent of GDP) was attributable to government issuing bonds to back the resolution of failed banks.

[26] There were other sources of base money creation, such as the BoU's own operations, but these were relatively small and we ignore them for simplicity.

Table 13.4. Fiscal Liquidity Creation, Sterilization Operations, and Net Domestic Financing (in UGX billion), 1997/98–2005/06

	1997/98	1998/99	1999/2000	2000/01	2001/02	2002/03	2003/04	2004/05	2005/06
GOU Budget Deficit	-67	-183	-468	-478	-741	-654	-715	-625	-545
as % GDP	-0.9	-2.2	-5.2	-4.8	-7.2	-5.6	-5.4	-4.1	-3.1
Net Budgetary Foreign Exchange Receipts	121	9	71	334	518	550	536	469	200
Fiscal Liquidity Creation	63	58	303	484	694	472	485	365	242
Net sales of Foreign Exchange	6	34	177	307	349	465	273	122	287
Net sales of Government Securities	42	46	150	147	266	216	76	284	93
Net Domestic Financing	-121	9	198	-68	88	-5	-124	57	55
NDF as % GDP	-1.6	0.1	2.2	-0.7	0.9	0.0	-0.9	0.4	0.4
Bank financing	-67	1	158	46	21	-92	-206	-260	37
Central Bank	-103	24	86	-42	-190	-208	-175	-359	-234
Commercial banks	36	-24	72	88	212	116	-31	99	271
Non-bank financing	-54	-15	40	-114	67	86	82	317	18
Growth in Private Sector Credit (%)	24.8	33.6	6.2	9.4	4.2	28.2	16.2	14.6	28.7

Source: Ministry of Finance, Planning and Economic Development.

sales of foreign exchange. However, the large volumes of foreign exchange sales needed to meet the base money target threatened to create instability in the exchange rate and damage price incentives for exports. As a result the BoU shifted more of the balance between the two instruments towards sales of securities: net sales of which rose from UGX42 billion in 1997/98 (0.5 per cent of GDP) to UGX266 billion (2.4 per cent of GDP) in 2001/02. In effect, using sales of government securities to sterilize liquidity shifted the distribution of the government domestic borrowing requirement from the central bank to commercial banks. The government accumulated large savings with the BoU but borrowed from commercial banks (see Table 13.4). As a result, commercial bank holdings of government securities as a share of their deposits grew rapidly, from 21 per cent in June 1999 to 41 per cent in June 2002. Government securities competed with private sector credit for the resources available for lending by commercial banks and, as the share of government securities in banks' asset portfolios rose rapidly, the growth of bank loans to the private sector stagnated (see Figure 13.2). Private sector credit increased by only 6.2 per cent in 1999/2000, 9.4 per cent in 2000/01, and 4.2 per cent in 2001/02 (see Table 13.4). Hence, fiscal operations risked crowding out private sector credit, even though the government domestic borrowing requirement (from commercial banks, the central bank, and non-bank sector combined) remained small.

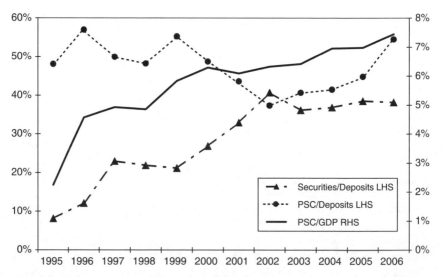

Figure 13.2 Private Sector Credit (PSC) and Bank Holdings of Government Securities (% of Commercial Banks' Deposits, and Private Sector Credit as % of GDP), June 1995–June 2006

Sources: Ministry of Finance, Planning and Economic Development; Bank of Uganda.

The pertinent lesson to be drawn from this experience is that, in countries where the budget is a large net recipient of foreign resources, the size of NDF is not the only constraint with which fiscal policy must comply. Fiscal policy must also take into account the impact on the central bank's monetary policy of the liquidity created by fiscal operations. It is unlikely to be optimal or feasible for the central bank to treat its net sales of foreign exchange as the variable that balances equation 3, irrespective of its impact on the foreign exchange market. But using net sales of treasury bills to balance equation 3 is also not optimal, because of its consequences for private sector credit. Hence, there are limits on the extent to which aid can be used to expand the budget without fiscal policy becoming incompatible with monetary policy, and these limits are tighter the shallower domestic financial and foreign exchange markets are.

In addition to the problems created for monetary policy, the widening of the fiscal deficit before grants, driven by an increase in aid, also had implications for the REER. The expansion of the fiscal stance added about 5.5 per cent of GDP to aggregate demand between 1997/98 and 2001/02.[27] As the bulk of government expenditures consist of non-traded goods, this expansion threatened to drive up the REER and lead to Dutch Disease with the potential to damage the competitiveness of Uganda's exports. Promoting exports, and especially non-traditional exports (NTEs), however, was a government policy priority. Atingi-Ego and Sebudde (2000) found that Uganda's NTEs, as a share of total exports, are sensitive to the level of the REER.

In practice, however, the widening of the fiscal deficit before grants did not bring about an appreciation of the REER, which actually depreciated by about 30 per cent between June 1997 and June 2002. The depreciation was driven by the slump in world coffee prices, which caused a sharp fall in Uganda's external terms of trade. Most of the fall in the REER took place in 1997/98 and 1998/99, and preceded the widening of the fiscal deficit before grants. Given the fall in the external terms of trade, a depreciation of the REER was necessary to restore external competitiveness. Furthermore, as noted above, the BoU shifted the mix of monetary sterilization instruments towards treasury bills and away from foreign exchange sales in 2000/01 and 2001/02 to allow greater depreciation of the exchange rate, though this came at the cost of crowding out private sector borrowers from the credit market.

It could be argued that, at least over the longer term, higher government expenditure funded by aid could counteract any adverse effects on exports through REER appreciation by providing public goods and services which complement private investment, such as transport infrastructure. However, even if this is the case, in the short run the appreciation of the REER is likely

---

[27] The impact on aggregate demand of the fiscal stance is measured as total government expenditure on goods and services, excluding imports and external interest payments, less domestic revenue.

to overshoot its long run level. An overshooting of the REER would have damaging and irreversible effects on export industries, especially NTEs whose profitability is marginal, if these industries do not have the financial resources to withstand a period of reduced competitiveness or if they perceive that the REER appreciation they observe will be permanent and not temporary and so disinvest from the export sector (Adam 2005). In addition, the rapid increase in demand for non-traded goods from the government, especially in the construction sector, drove up costs and undermined quality (Kitabire 2005), which dampened any potentially beneficial effects of higher public investment on the private sector.

6.2 Managing the volatility of budget support disbursements

One of the drawbacks of budget support is that its disbursements tend to be volatile and frequently fall short of budgeted levels (Bulir and Hamann 2003). This was also the case in Uganda. Table 13.5 presents data on programmed budget support and actual disbursements for the five fiscal years 1999/2000 to 2003/04. There were large shortfalls in disbursements relative to programmed amounts in the first three years of this period, mainly because of delays in disbursements (particularly the PRSC). The government avoided having to make within year budget cuts to accommodate these shortfalls by borrowing from the BoU, while the BoU adjusted its foreign exchange reserves downwards to offset the impact on the money supply. In effect the government borrowed from Uganda's foreign exchange reserves. This was only possible because the BoU had built up a substantial holding of foreign exchange reserves, which by 1999/2000 exceeded five months' worth of imports. However, it is obviously not possible to fund permanent shortfalls of budget support in this manner without depleting the foreign exchange reserves. Learning from this experience, and in an attempt to mitigate against shortfalls in disbursements, MoFPED began to apply a discount factor to projected budget support when preparing projections of the medium term budget resource envelope.

Table 13.5. Actual Versus Projected Disbursements of Budget Support (in USD million), 1999/00–2003/04

	1999/00	2000/01	2001/02	2002/03	2003/04
Budgeted disbursements	322	337	567	357	434
Actual disbursements	148	236	155	365	390
Excess/shortfall	−174	−101	−212	8	−44
Excess/shortfall (% GDP)	−2.9	−1.8	−3.6	0.1	−0.6
NDF (% GDP)	2.2	−0.7	0.9	0.0	−0.9

Sources: Budget support data from Atingi-Ego (2006: 356); NDF from Ministry of Finance, Planning and Economic Development.

6.3 *External debt and aid dependency*

The rapid rise in aid in the late 1990s and early 2000s also led to concerns about external debt sustainability and the excessive dependency of the budget on aid. As discussed in Chapter 12, Uganda became eligible for debt relief under the HIPC Initiative in 1998, and for additional debt relief under the enhanced HIPC Initiative in 2000. Debt relief provided under these initiatives reduced the net present value of Uganda's external public and publicly guaranteed (PPG) debt to 150 per cent of its exports, the threshold deemed to be sustainable under the enhanced HIPC Initiative, by 2000. However, Uganda's external PPG debt stock grew rapidly during the next three fiscal years, as almost 40 per cent of the gross aid disbursed during this period took the form of concessional loans. At the same time, export earnings declined because of the slump in world coffee prices; hence the external debt stock climbed far above the sustainability threshold.[28] Only when further debt relief, under the Multilateral Debt Relief Initiative (MDRI) was provided in 2006 was the external PPG debt again brought down below the sustainability threshold.[29]

From the late 1980s Uganda's budget has been heavily dependent on aid, especially for development expenditures. Gross aid inflows funded an average of 50 per cent of the total budget in the 1990s. However, the increase in budget support in the late 1990s and early 2000s made the GoU budget, which constitutes the core of government expenditure (including all those which are non-discretionary, such as statutory expenditures) even more heavily aid dependent. In the mid-1990s, domestic revenues were sufficient to fund more than 80 per cent of GoU budget expenditures and external debt repayments, but this fell to only 59 per cent in 2001/02, the year in which the fiscal deficit before grants peaked.

The heavy reliance on aid was a cause for concern. It increased the vulnerability of the budget to a resource over which government had no direct control, was much more volatile than domestic revenues, and whose long term sustainability could not be guaranteed. While the short-term volatility of budget aid was not necessarily a problem for budget management once Uganda had sufficient foreign exchange reserves to be used as a buffer against temporary disbursement shortfalls as discussed above, the danger of long-term cutbacks in aid created budget vulnerability. Once expenditure increases were implemented, especially if they involved wages or statutory items, it would be difficult to scale them back again. Hence, if the budget became too heavily dependent on aid, any permanent reduction in aid would have either left the budget seriously

---

[28] The NPV value of the debt stock was raised by both new borrowing and a fall in the average level of concessionality (the grant element) of the debt; the latter was caused by a fall in world market interest rates which are used as discount factors in computing the NPV of the debt stock.

[29] The NPV of the external PPG debt was 179 per cent of exports in 2005 but was reduced to 45 per cent after provision of MDRI debt relief in 2006 (IMF 2006: 9).

unbalanced at the expense of expenditure efficiency (e.g. with an excessively large share allocated to wages), or jeopardized macroeconomic stability if the government had borrowed domestically to fund the shortfall in the budget resource envelope. Therefore, reducing fiscal vulnerability, by lowering the dependence of the budget on aid, became an important objective of fiscal policy in the 2000s.

6.4 The medium term strategy of fiscal consolidation

MoFPED adopted a medium term strategy of fiscal consolidation in 2002 and began to implement it in the 2002/03 budget. The objective of the strategy was to cut the fiscal deficit before grants, which had reached 11.6 per cent of GDP in 2001/02, in order to ease the pressures on monetary policy arising from the need to sterilize domestic liquidity created by fiscal operations, to avoid real exchange rate appreciation and to reduce the dependency of the budget on aid. The strategy involved a change in the approach to determining the size of the budget resource envelope. Previously budgeted aggregate expenditure had been determined by the maximum amount of budget resources which were projected to be mobilized, taking account of the target for net domestic borrowing. The new strategy involved explicit targets for reducing the fiscal deficit before grants on a phased schedule to 6.5 per cent of GDP by 2008/09, or reductions of about 0.7 per cent of GDP a year on average. In drawing up the fiscal framework for the MTEF during the budget process, MoFPED and the BoU discussed the size of projected fiscal liquidity creation and how it could be sterilized, in addition to the target for NDF. If projected aid disbursements exceeded the level needed to fund the budget given the target for the fiscal deficit before grants, government would budget to save the excess budgetary resources; i.e. government's NDF would fall and this would be matched by an equivalent increase in the BoU's foreign exchange reserves. As discussed above, setting a target for the fiscal deficit before grants also required de-linking sector budget support from sectoral expenditures and PAF budget support from PAF expenditures. MoFPED presented the rationale for this strategy at a PRSC retreat in 2002 and at the 2002 and 2003 PERs.

The strategy of fiscal consolidation was successful in scaling back the fiscal deficit before grants to 6.8 per cent of GDP in 2005/06, a cut of 4.8 per cent of GDP in four years, which brought substantial benefits for monetary management; the amount of domestic liquidity created by fiscal operations from the GoU budget was cut by 65 per cent over four years, allowing net issues of government securities to be reduced. This created room for a strong recovery in bank lending to the private sector. The annual growth of private sector credit, which had averaged only 6.7 per cent between 1999/2000 and 2001/02, accelerated to an average of 22 per cent in the following four years (see Table 13.4 and Figure 13.2). The dependence of the budget on aid was also reduced, as domestic revenues were able to fund a larger share of the GoU budget and external debt repayments: from 59 per cent in 2001/02 to 81 per cent in 2005/06.

7. Conclusions and lessons

Uganda has made progress in aligning donor aid with its fiscal objectives but the task is not complete. Since the second half of the 1990s, the distribution of aid has shifted towards budget support in accord with the government's preferences. In the first half of the 2000s, more than half of total aid consisted of budget support. Budget support is intrinsically easier to align with government fiscal policies than project aid. Moreover, just over half of all budget support consisted of general budget support, which is the government's preferred form. Among the three main types of budget support, it provides the greatest flexibility in terms of how it is used to fund the budget and is, therefore, more readily aligned with the government's macro/fiscal, inter-sectoral and intra-sectoral budget objectives. In addition, since 2002, sector budget support and PAF budget support are no longer treated as 'additional' in terms of the link between the level of budget support and the level of sector and PAF expenditures, so that these instruments have also become more flexible to incorporate into the budget resource envelope.

On the downside, although many budget support donors have associated themselves with the World Bank's PRSC, this has not led to a streamlining of conditionality. Some bilateral donors have continued to impose their own conditions for disbursement on top of the prior actions in the PRSC matrix, while the PRSC itself entails heavy transactions costs for the government. These are further exacerbated because incentives and responsibilities of large budget support operations are not well aligned for different agents within government. Agencies which have the responsibility for implementing conditionalities often have weak incentives to do so because they do not directly benefit, in terms of larger budget allocations, from the budget support.

The biggest obstacle to aligning aid with fiscal objectives, however, is that donor projects have proved very difficult to properly integrate into the MTEF. Integration, in this context, would mean that each sector has a single overall sector ceiling, covering both the GoU budget and donor projects, which acts as a hard budget constraint. Donor projects have not, in effect, been subject to a hard budget constraint at the sector level. This has given those sectors which are not considered as a priority the incentive to seek to enhance their budget allocations by lobbying donors for project aid, thereby undermining both the macro/fiscal and inter-sectoral objectives of the budget. Furthermore, the large share of project aid in some sectors, notably the Roads and Works sector, distorted intra-sectoral allocations, especially at the expense of funding for essential road maintenance.

What lessons can be learned from Uganda's experience of attempting to align aid with fiscal policies? A number of factors were important for the progress Uganda made. First, as emphasized in Chapter 6, it is necessary to have a strongly centralized budget process, directed by one institution, in most cases the ministry of finance. The budget cannot be fragmented in a manner that allows different spending agencies to negotiate for aid for their own budgets with donors. The concept of 'additionality' for sector budget support is potentially very damaging to a coherent budget allocation because it circumvents centralized control of budget allocations. It prevents an optimal inter-sectoral budget allocation based on the prioritization of competing expenditures within an integrated budget.

Second, the ministry of finance must articulate a clear and coherent strategy for the budget. It must link the medium-term budget allocations with both a sound macroeconomic framework and strategic sectoral expenditure priorities, which can command broad political support. Without this it is unlikely that donors will shift their aid into general budget support. The PER, a public forum organized by MoFPED and held just before the annual budget presentation to Parliament, proved valuable in enabling the government to present its budget strategy to donors and other stakeholders. The message, which MoFPED signalled to the donors at the PER, was that if they could agree with the broad composition of the medium-term budget, they should be prepared to provide general budget support. They should also refrain from trying to force their own favoured projects or programmes into the budget through project aid.

Third, disbursements of budget support are generally volatile, with frequent shortfalls between budgeted and actual disbursements. The government can only avoid having to delay the implementation of expenditures when budget support disbursements are delayed, or avoid cutting the budget in response to shortfalls in budget support, if it has sufficient foreign exchange reserves to act as a buffer. This means countries that rely heavily on budget support to fund the budget must first build up a substantial stock of foreign exchange reserves. Since the end of the 1990s Uganda has held foreign exchange reserves equivalent to at least five months' imports, enabling the country to manage very large shortfalls in budget support disbursements in the early 2000s. However, even a larger buffer of foreign exchange reserves cannot insulate the budget from a permanent fall in budget support. Hence it is prudent fiscal management to ensure that the budget does not become over dependent on donor aid, a budgetary resource over which government has no direct control.

Finally, large aid inflows have implications for macroeconomic management. When the budget is a large net recipient of foreign exchange, a domestic borrowing target is no longer sufficient to ensure that fiscal policy is consistent with monetary policy. This is especially the case if domestic financial and foreign exchange markets are shallow. Sterilizing the domestic liquidity created by fiscal operations requires the central bank selling domestic securities and/or foreign exchange. However, large sales of securities may crowd out private sector credit while large net sales of foreign exchange may destabilize the exchange rate. A large aid funded fiscal deficit may also lead to an appreciation of the real exchange rate, as demand for non-traded goods is driven up by government spending, and could damage incentives for exporters. The damage is likely to be even more serious if the real exchange rate appreciation over-shoots its long run level. Export growth is an important engine of growth in developing countries so it is crucial that fiscal policy does not undermine the competitiveness of the export sector.

The implication for fiscal policy is that governments which are large aid recipients should determine the magnitude of aggregate expenditure and the size of the fiscal deficit before grants independently of the volume of aid which they can expect to mobilize. This may require some of the aid received by the budget to be saved, in the form of lower net domestic financing of the budget and higher foreign exchange reserves, instead of funding higher expenditures. In determining the size of aggregate expenditures and the fiscal deficit before grants it is necessary to take into account a number of factors. These include the impact on aggregate demand and the possible effects on the real exchange rate, the implications for monetary management, the consequences for debt sustainability, and the long run dependency of the budget on donor aid. These considerations motivated MoFPED to implement its medium-term fiscal consolidation strategy, beginning in 2002/03, which has scaled back the fiscal deficit before grants from 11.6 per cent of GDP in 2001/02 to 6.8 per cent in 2005/06 and created room for a strong recovery in bank lending to the private sector.

14

Fiscal Decentralization

Tim Williamson[1]

1. Introduction

Between 1997 and 2007 Uganda saw an unprecedented rapid expansion in the delivery of basic services. This occurred in the context of a new decentralized system of local government responsible for the delivery of those services, which was rolled out from 1993. This chapter discusses how the process of decentralizing service delivery was managed, the achievements, pitfalls, and lessons learned.

Although participatory local democracy was a political priority of the NRM government from 1986, its early focus was on economic and administrative reform at the centre related to structural adjustment. By the mid 1990s the agenda was moving towards addressing poverty more broadly. The rebuilding and expansion of basic service delivery, in particular Universal Primary Education (UPE), was at the centre of the 1997 Poverty Eradication Action Plan (PEAP, see Chapter 7), and high on the President's political agenda. Whilst Sector Wide Approaches (SWAps, see Chapter 9) were developed as mechanisms to oversee the implementation of policies embedded in the PEAP, local governments were chosen as the vehicle for the delivery of basic services.

This chapter starts by describing the evolution of local government in Uganda. It then focuses on the fiscal dimensions of the decentralization process from 1995 to 2005, in the context of the largely centrally driven agenda of expanding the basic services considered pivotal for poverty reduction. The development of planning, budgeting, and financial management systems over the same period is then discussed. The chapter concludes by examining the critical political and technical factors behind the implementation of local government reform, the successes and failures, and the emerging challenges.

[1] The author would like to thank Jesper Steffensen for his comments, and William Ndoleriire for his insights and contribution as the pillar of local government financing in MoFPED.

The process of fiscal decentralization has been one of compromise. The Government's national policy agenda was funded through a rapid expansion of conditional grants earmarked for the delivery of basic services. However, this reduced the incentives for local revenue collection and the fiscal autonomy of local governments, which many consider crucial for strong local democracy and accountability. This chapter attempts to assess whether this compromise was, on balance, a sensible one, or whether it has undermined local service delivery unnecessarily.

2. Evolution of local government

Local governments are not new to Uganda. A de-concentrated system of local government service delivery existed in the colonial era. However, this was centralized soon after independence and local governments were left with only a limited administrative role. By the time the NRM came to power in 1986 the delivery of public services, especially basic services, had long since collapsed. There was substantial leakage in the little funding provided for service delivery and little or no accountability to the intended beneficiaries. There were vast disparities in the level and quality of health, education, and

---

Box 14.1 A SHORT HISTORY OF DECENTRALIZATION IN UGANDA

Throughout the colonial period, the issue of how to govern outlying districts was a source of constant debate. During the 1920s and 1930s a policy known as Indirect Rule was implemented in the kingdom areas, but a more direct form of local administration was implemented in areas that did not have traditional kings or recognized chiefs.

Following Independence in 1962, the Constitution devolved some powers to the kingdoms. However, the 1962 Constitution was abrogated in April 1966 and a new constitution was promulgated in 1967. A new Local Administration Act (1967) was enacted with provisions that totally ignored the significance of local government councils. For example:

• The Minister of Local Government had to approve the budget of local government councils;
• The Ministry of Local Government had to approve local government council by-laws and had the power to revoke them;
• Accountability for resources transferred to local administrations was to the Minister of Local Government and not to the local councils; and
• The Minister had power to fire local councillors and dissolve local government councils.

Local government councils had few powers over their employees. Under the 1967 Act, even the most junior employees in local government had to be appointed by the President. This was the state of affairs until 1986.

Source: Golola (2001)

---

water and sanitation services. The public had to pay for services, whether delivered by the private or public sector.

A key political feature of the early NRM regime was the establishment of Resistance Councils, which oversaw a form of local participatory democracy that coexisted alongside the centralized service delivery. Originally formed by the National Resistance Army when it was fighting the bush war, the Resistance Councils were legalized through the Resistance Council/Committees Statute (Government of Uganda 1987).

As well as increasing popular participation in democracy, a key intention of these reforms was to improve the responsiveness and accountability of service provision to local beneficiaries. However, local governments were not yet responsible for service delivery. A process of administrative and fiscal decentralization was introduced gradually during the 1990s so as to align the public service with these new political structures.

The implementation of political, administrative, and fiscal dimensions of decentralization combined formal legal reforms and pragmatic implementation of the framework provided by those reforms. The development of the legal framework was led by the Ministry of Local Government (MoLG), supported by the Decentralization Secretariat which was largely funded by the Danish Government. Building on the Resistance Council system, the 1993 Local Government Statute introduced formal elements of the administrative and fiscal dimensions of decentralization, and formed the basis for the administrative and fiscal framework that emerged in subsequent legislation. Implementation of the reforms started in phases from 1994, with elements of administrative and fiscal decentralization being introduced over a three-year period. Meanwhile, the legal framework was embedded in the 1995 Constitution and elaborated upon in the 1997 Local Government Act. From 1995 the decentralization process continued to evolve on all three fronts, albeit not always in the direction of increased decentralization of powers.

The legal and policy framework that had been developed by MoLG by 1997 was in principle highly decentralized along political, administrative, and fiscal lines. In terms of functions, local governments were given responsibility for the vast majority of basic service delivery, including primary education, basic health care, agricultural extension, as well as water and sanitation services. In terms of administrative decentralization, district[2] local governments were made responsible for hiring and firing staff, through their district service commissions, which were themselves appointed by the district council. Local governments were given revenue-raising powers, and were responsible for approving their own budgets. The system of grants from central government originally envisaged a high degree of discretion, with most service delivery being funded through unconditional

---

[2] Kampala, the only city council, has similar powers to districts.

Box 14.2 STRUCTURE AND MANDATES OF LOCAL GOVERNMENT

The uppermost tier of local government is the district administration, which includes one city administration (Kampala). The number of districts increased from 39 in 1995 to 80 by 2007. At the next level rural Uganda is divided into 857 sub-county local governments, with an average population of 27,000. Urban areas are divided into 13 municipalities and 69 towns, with an average population of 59,000 and 19,000 respectively. The municipalities and the city are divided into divisions. The sub-counties, towns, and divisions are considered to be lower-level local governments. The next tier comprises 5,225 parishes and wards (the lowest-level administrative unit) and 44,402 villages, cells, and zones. Councillors are elected at the district, sub-county, and village levels in rural areas, and at the city, municipality, town, division, and cell levels of the urban authorities.

Councils exist at three main levels: the district, sub-county, and village. In urban areas councils also exist in municipalities, towns, divisions, and wards. However, the main levels of government are the district and sub-county, municipality, divisions, and towns.

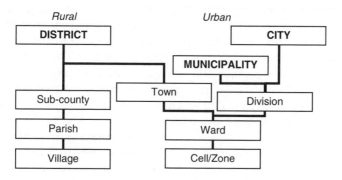

The major services mandated to be delivered by local governments are primary and pre-primary education, district hospital services and primary health care, district and community roads, rural and urban water and sanitation, and agricultural extension and advisory services. Other services include community-based services such as adult literacy, municipal waste management, environment, trade licensing, land administration, and some elements of technical education.

Source: Steffensen et al. (2004)

---

grants, supplemented by equalization grants, and conditional grants for jointly agreed programmes funded by central government. Central government ministries maintained responsibility for setting service delivery policies and standards, and for monitoring the implementation of those policies.

In many respects, the law was implemented in the spirit in which those drafting it intended; districts were given responsibility for the appointment and management of their staff, approval of their budgets and by-laws, and management of their expenditure—crucial aspects of administrative and fiscal decentralization, which had previously required the blessing of the Minister of Local Government. The main tension in the decentralization process arose from the central government policy agenda, spearheaded by the Ministry of Finance, Planning and Economic Development (MoFPED) and sector ministries, to expand basic service delivery in priority areas for poverty reduction. Conditional grants earmarked for those services were used as the main channel for funding this expansion. They were attractive to both line ministries, which were developing sector wide approaches (see Chapter 9), and donors supporting those sectors, as they provided channels through which they could earmark funding towards the achievement of their policy objectives. This, however, limited the degree of fiscal autonomy available to local governments. Given the nature of earmarking, the centre also maintained control over the level of staffing in the major services of education and health through a conditional grant payroll. This limited the degree of administrative decentralization. Whilst within the framework of the law, MoLG and the various local government associations felt that this trend was not consistent with the highly decentralized spirit of that law which they had helped develop.

From the early 2000s, complaints of a retreat from decentralization became louder. The rapid expansion of government grants undermined the incentive for local governments to collect revenue locally, and also made it easier for central government to suspend or limit the scope of local revenue sources such as the Graduated Tax—the largest single local revenue source. Central government started to pay emoluments for the council leadership, which had previously been funded from local revenues. Following central government concern over excessive council interference in the running of local administrations, the appointment of Chief Administrative Officers—the head civil servant in a district—was recentralized prior to the 2006 elections.[3] These factors represented a step back from greater fiscal and administrative autonomy.

There has also been a doubling in the number of districts since 1995, with the number of new districts accelerating as the 2006 presidential elections approached. The government responded positively to demands from some areas to split existing districts. Some have argued that this unduly increased administration costs (Ocwich 2005) and was motivated by local patronage in advance of the elections (Green 2008). It also put back the progress made in building strong district institutions by spreading the capacity that had been established more thinly. The government response has been that creation of new districts brings local government closer to the beneficiaries of services, and is therefore consistent with the spirit of decentralization and local democracy.

---

[3] Local governments still have a say in their appointment, however.

Although there is validity in this argument, little attention was paid to the possibility of strengthening the role of the sub-county level of government in service delivery relative to districts, as a means of bringing services close to the public.

There are inherent ideological and institutional tensions over how best to decentralize service delivery to local governments, and the implementation of the decentralization policy has therefore been one of compromise. The fiscal dimension of decentralization—the focus of this chapter—lies at the heart of these tensions.

3. Financing of local government

The overall framework for financing local governments, including the type, level, and mix of grant transfers and locally raised revenues, has important implications for the ability of local governments to deliver services which are responsive to local needs, and accountable to the local population. It determines whether local governments have adequate resources to carry out their mandates; whether those resources are distributed equitably across local governments; and whether there is sufficient flexibility to facilitate services that are responsive to local priorities. This section describes how, and why, grant transfers to local governments and locally raised revenues have evolved in the way they have, and the implications for local government expenditure.

3.1 *The rise and rise of (conditional) grant transfers*

The legal framework for fiscal transfers was established in the 1995 Constitution and the Local Government Act (1997). As mentioned earlier, the Constitution provides for three types of transfer:

- Unconditional Grants, to fund the decentralized services of local governments, based on the costs of those services;
- Equalization Grants, to support the least developed districts, based on the degree to which their services lag behind other districts; and
- Conditional Grants, to help local governments finance programmes agreed between central government and the local government in line with an agreed set of conditions.

In the legislation there was little detail on how fiscal transfers should work in practice and they have evolved in a very different way to what was envisaged by those drafting the legal framework. Arguably, it was the way central budgets were decentralized by MoFPED that accounts for the nature of the transfer system in operation today.

Table 14.1 Grants to Local Governments, 1995/96–2007/08

Financial Year:	1995/96	1997/98	2002/03	2007/08
Size of Transfers (UGX Billion, 2000 prices)				
Unconditional Grant	50	60	74	90
Conditional Grant	94	189	556	653
Number of Conditional Grants	*4*	*10*	*25*	*37*
Equalization Grant	0	0	4	2
Total	**145**	**249**	**634**	**745**
% of Total Transfers				
Unconditional Grant	34%	24%	12%	12%
Conditional Grant	66%	76%	88%	88%
Equalization Grant	0.0%	0.0%	0.6%	0.3%
% of Total Budget excl. Interest	**22%**	**29%**	**31%**	**34%**

Source: MoFPED Budget Estimates.

Fiscal transfers to local governments started in 1993/94, with the transfer of resources to a first phase of districts. By 1997 all local governments were receiving unconditional and conditional transfers. The bulk of resources were made up of the recurrent budget lines from the ministries for health and education, which were transferred to new district 'votes' as clearly identifiable budget lines—e.g. primary teacher salaries and primary capitation grants for education. These transfers for health and education were, *de facto*, conditional grants. Meanwhile, the unconditional grant was provided to local governments separately from the budget lines that existed for previously centralized services. With one notable exception,[4] this use of conditional grants set the tone for the way in which local governments were funded for their decentralized service delivery mandate thereafter.

The major increases in funding of basic services began in 1997/98. In 1998 Uganda started benefiting from HIPC debt relief (see Chapter 12) and formed the Poverty Action Fund (PAF, see Chapter 13). MoFPED had committed to use debt relief funds to expand basic services in line with PEAP priorities. The obvious way to fund these services, from a central government perspective, was through conditional grants to local governments, as the funding for those services could easily be tracked. This was a pragmatic move, which reassured donors that debt relief funds would not be misdirected. Earmarked grants also fitted well with the budget process based around sector working groups and sector wide approaches (see Chapter 9). At the time there was little complaint from local governments that these funds were conditional, as the volume of funding they were receiving was increasing rapidly. MoFPED was also

---

[4] The local development grant, described below.

committed to releasing budget allocations in full during the financial year. Unsurprisingly, line ministries and donors raised concerns that local governments did not have the capacity to absorb the increased funding. Rather than slow the increase in funding to local governments, 5 per cent of PAF funding was set aside for monitoring and accountability. MoFPED also took procedural measures to enhance the accountability of PAF funding.

The volume of conditional grant funding increased rapidly between 1997/98 and 2007/08 from UGX145 billion to UGX745 billion in real terms (2000 prices), with most of the increase happening in the first four years (see Table 14.1). This ensured that local governments' service delivery mandate was increasingly well funded. As the scope of the PAF increased, funding for new local government programmes was introduced such as water and sanitation, and functional adult literacy. Consequently, the number of conditional grants increased from four in 1995/96 to ten in 1997/98 and thirty-seven in the 2007/08 approved budget. Initially, conditional grants were intended solely for recurrent activities. Subsequently, sector development grants were introduced, first for construction of primary schools and later for primary health care, water, and agriculture.

Allocations to the unconditional grant lagged well behind those for conditional grants, although MoFPED ensured that the Constitutional requirement that such allocations must keep pace with inflation was met. The unconditional grant declined from over a quarter of transfers in 1997 to under an eighth by 2002/03. Subsequently, it increased at a similar pace to conditional grants, in part due to the need to compensate local governments for the suspension of graduated tax. However, in 2007/08 it still only accounted for USD77 million out of a total budget of USD638 million for transfers to local government. This meant that the unconditional grant was only sufficient to cover those salaries of the local administration that were not covered by conditional grants. It was not, therefore, a significant source of discretionary funding. Local governments had few additional resources to fund recurrent administrative costs, whether finance, internal audit or schools inspection. The equalization grant has never received significant allocations either, largely because MoFPED considered that allocations to conditional grants catered for the equalization of services. In 2007/08, at approximately USD2 million, equalization grants were 0.3 per cent of transfers to local governments.

One significant source of discretionary funding has emerged which, ironically, is a conditional grant.[5] In 2000 the local development grant, the central pillar of the Local Government Development Programme (LGDP), was introduced to provide funding for investment to sub-counties and districts in over

---

[5] These conditions do not relate to the sector in which the funds should be spent.

two thirds of districts. This was designed to scale up an earlier pilot programme funded by the UN Capital Development Fund in five districts. Substantial discretion to higher and lower local councils was given by the grant over investment. Meanwhile, the conditions associated with the grant proved a powerful lever for building basic institutional capacity. Although the first LGDP was funded solely by the World Bank, the second LGDP provided a vehicle for harmonizing donor support to local government from 2002, allowing several donors to move away from traditional area based programmes and support local governments via sector budget support. From 2007/08 the World Bank withdrew its earmarked budget support for the local development grant but the government maintained the grant, amounting to USD37 million, representing investments of approximately USD1.40 per capita.

Although line ministries tried to factor some degree of needs/poverty into their criteria for allocating grants between local governments, for most conditional grants this was fairly haphazard (Local Government Finance Commission 2003). By and large, allocations were geographically balanced, although they could have been more equitable. In contrast, the Constitution explicitly stipulated the formula for the unconditional grant as population and land area. In 2003 the Local Government Finance Commission (LGFC) attempted to develop more transparent objective criteria. However some line ministries, most notably the Ministry of Education and Sports, were reluctant to adopt the criteria in full.

3.2 Aid and the funding of local governments

The way donors provided aid in Uganda has had an important effect on the financing framework of local governments and the growth of fiscal transfers. The use of sector and general budget support has meant that transfers have been expanded using government systems. From the outset, donors were willing to take the risk and support the channelling of funds to local governments as conditional grants, whilst the government took actions to address fiduciary concerns. This contrasts with the approach taken by donors in Tanzania, for example, where funding was frequently channelled through common 'basket funds'. As argued below, this use of government systems contributed to the strengthening of local institutions and the systems themselves. Although it tended to undermine local autonomy, it was still a better solution than parallel systems, which are a feature of basket funding (Kizilbash and Williamson 2008).

Why were donors more willing to use government systems in Uganda? While this was partly down to particular individuals in donor agencies who were willing to take risks, the leadership within MoFPED also gave them confidence to do so. In addition, between 1998 and 2001 MoFPED committed to a one to one matching of debt relief and budget support resources to budget lines in the PAF, and to disbursing those budget lines in full during the financial year. The

PAF, combined with the emerging SWAps, made it easier for donors to provide sector budget support; and MoFPED allowed them to earmark budget support to specific local government grants under the PAF. A number of bilateral donors provided funding for specific conditional grants, such as classroom construction and primary health care. Many also provided budget support to the PAF overall. This had a similar impact to earmarked budget support as three quarters of the PAF was channelled to local governments via conditional grants, although the government had significant control over how it was spent.

However, donor funds were and continue to be transferred directly to local governments as project support. An assessment of local government public financial management estimated that project funding represented approximately 16 per cent of local government revenues (Williamson et al. 2006); this makes it the second most important source after central transfers. This support is a mixed bag of multi-sectoral area based programmes direct from donors and sector specific support to local governments channelled via NGO or line ministry projects. However, these funds are far less predictable in budgetary terms than government grants, and are rarely as well integrated within government systems.

3.3 *The gradual, then sudden, decline in locally raised revenues*

While donor funded of fiscal transfers have steadily increased, the trend of local revenues has been largely downwards. These trends are not unrelated. In the late 1990s Kampala commuters were often caught in long traffic queues caused by Kampala City Council staff checking whether people had paid their Graduated Tax, and arresting those who had not. By the start of the 2000s this practice had largely ceased. Why? There were several interrelated factors at play.

In the 1990s the main local revenue source was Graduated Tax. This was a type of poll tax. The amount an individual paid was based on an assessment carried out by the local government. The other major tax, with significant potential in urban areas, was Property Tax. However, until an amendment of the law in 2005 local authorities had to get properties valued by the central government valuer, which lacked manpower and capacity. There was no way property valuations could keep pace with the building boom in urban centres. Local governments were also mandated to collect various other fees and permits, such as business licences, market dues, and parking tickets, which they did to varying degrees. Sub-counties in rural areas and divisions in urban areas were mandated to collect local revenues; they retained 65 per cent and 50 per cent respectively of the revenues they collected locally, transferring the balance to the higher local government.

Different local governments have had vastly different track records in collecting local taxes. For example, in a review of two similarly sized districts:

There was a stark difference in the local revenue collection of Bushenyi and Iganga: Bushenyi had a local revenue of around USD800,000 in 2001/02, whilst Iganga's local revenue collection was only USD90,000, amounting to about 9% and 1% of their total budgets respectively. The political support for taxation in Bushenyi was very evident. (Williamson 2003)

While the relative wealth of different districts clearly affects the potential for local revenue raising, political will has proved a more serious constraint.

Overall, local revenue has fallen dramatically, in both relative and absolute terms (see Table 14.2). It is estimated that between 1997/98 and 2005/06 local revenue declined from UGX143 billion to UGX54 billion in real terms (2000 prices), or from 37 per cent to 4 per cent of local government revenues. Rural local governments have seen the most rapid reduction, with revenues estimated to be less than 1 per cent of total revenues from 2005/06 (Williamson et al. 2006). This is a combined effect of a decline in collections and the withdrawal of some revenue sources.

The rise and rise of central transfers directly undermined the incentives for local councils and local administrations to collect tax. Graduated Tax was unpopular, and the means of enforcement of collection were sometimes crude, with defaulters often tied up and paraded around the streets. Local

---

Box 14.3 LOCAL REVENUE SOURCES

Graduated Tax is a kind of head tax to be paid by everyone aged eighteen and above, who is engaged in gainful employment or business. Central government fixes the maximum rate of the tax. Each local government is responsible for determining the scales, in accordance with the advice of the LGFC, and for carrying out assessments on individuals within its jurisdiction. The total tax proceeds are retained and used by the local government.

Property Tax refers to ground rate and ground rent levied on land and property, as provided for under the Land Decree of 1976. Ground rate is a tax levied on land. The value of the land is based on its area and its location. Ground rent, on the other hand, is a levy assessed on the value of the development on that land. Valuation of the property is based on the actual development made, and takes into account its location. Property tax is particularly important for urban councils, where there is widespread commercial holding of land. In rural areas land is generally held for family tilling and building of owner-occupier homes, rather than for commercial purposes. Each local government sets the ground rate and ground rent for this purpose and is expected to carry out valuation of the land and of the property thereon. Local governments invite central government valuation officers to undertake valuation exercises in their territory. As with graduated tax, local governments retain the full revenue from rates and rents.

User Fees, Permits, and Other Licences. Local governments are allowed to levy charges such as licences, fees, permits, dues, etc. for services they render. These user charges are determined, collected, and appropriated exclusively by the local governments.

Source: Obwona et al. (2000)

Table 14.2 Declining Locally Raised Revenues

UGX Billion, 2000 Prices	1997/98	2001/02	2005/06
Graduated Tax	89	44	0
Property Tax	10	11	6
Market and User Fees	18	20	21
Licences	3	4	10
Other Revenues	23	29	18
Total Locally Raised Revenues	**143**	**107**	**54**

Sources: Mahler (2005); Sarzin (2007).

councillors naturally preferred not to do this to their electorate. By contrast, conditional transfers allowed them to deliver services without having to collect local revenues.

This same factor also made it possible for central government politicians to undermine local revenue with little apparent consequence on service delivery, and so local taxation became politicized. In the lead up to the 2001 presidential elections, the government announced that it was setting the minimum rate of Graduated Tax at UGX3,000 per person, less than USD2. Previously local governments had been free to set their own minimum rates, which tended to be between UGX5,000 and UGX12,000. This was widely misinterpreted as meaning that everyone should pay UGX3,000—which those standing for local council elections were quick to exploit. Local councillors were able to campaign in support of the lower Graduated Tax rate, as the recent increases in conditional grants had reduced the significance of Graduated Tax. It also conveniently enabled local councillors to blame central government for the collapse in local revenues, without making serious efforts to increase revenues from other sources. In 2001/02 Graduated Tax collections were just over half their 1997/98 levels. Although there was some recovery in Graduated Tax and other local revenues from 2001/02, Graduated Tax was suspended completely prior to the 2006 presidential elections. In addition, the scope of property tax was limited, with owner-occupiers excluded from paying the tax. This led to a drop of nearly 40 per cent in local revenues between 2004/05 and 2005/06.

Some used the argument that Graduated Tax was regressive as a justification for its abolition (Bahiigwa et al. 2004). Mahler (2007) concludes that the declining trend in local revenue:

threatens to undermine the very essence of decentralization, which is based on moving the delivery of many services to the local level and having individuals pay sufficient revenue to give them a sense of ownership and a desire to hold their elected and administrative officials accountable for providing the desired services in an efficient (non-corrupt) manner... There is no doubt that in assessing the first decade of implementation of decentralization in

Uganda, the main failure has been the severe weakening of local government revenue collection.

Despite these trends, local governments have received and continue to receive substantial technical support for local revenue collection. The LGFC and MoLG, supported by donor projects, have provided much of this. Policy, technical, and administrative changes to the framework for local revenue have been made. Best practices have been documented and disseminated. However, it is ultimately the political environment that has undermined these technical and administrative efforts to increase locally raised revenues.

3.4 The overall picture of local revenues and the impact on local budgets

Local governments received an unprecedented rise in resources between 1997 and 2007, largely through increases in conditional grant funding financed by debt relief and budget support. Much of this funding was channelled to the salaries of health workers and teachers, as well as to the operational budgets of service providers and to local investments. The fact that donors channelled a major share of their sector budget support via local government grants is important; they thereby supported the use of government systems through the conditional grant system—unlike parallel projects and basket funds. This meant that direct donor funding to districts, though significant, was relatively low.

A negative consequence of the rise and rise in central conditional grant transfers on the one hand and the decline in local revenues on the other is that the discretion local governments have over their budgets has declined significantly (see Table 14.3). Lower local governments, such as sub-counties and divisions, were much more reliant on locally raised revenues. The suspension of Graduated Tax meant that the only significant revenue source available to many lower local governments was the local development grant.[6]

This meant that local expenditures were almost entirely driven by central transfers. Table 14.4 shows a typical sectoral breakdown of expenditure in rural districts. Education is much the largest sector. In 2004/05, per capita expenditure in districts was about USD26. Analysis of expenditure funded by the local development grant in 2003/04 showed that the five largest areas of spending were also the five highest priorities of the PEAP: 37 per cent of spending was on roads and drainage, 25 per cent on education, 15 per cent on health, 12.5 per cent on water and sanitation, and 9 per cent on agriculture (Lister et al. 2006). These areas were also founded by conditional grants, although the high expenditure on roads

---

[6] Some lower local governments received a grant to fund the National Agricultural Advisory Services and Plan for Modernization of Agriculture Non Sectoral Conditional Grants, which had not been rolled out countrywide at the time of writing. Conditional grants have tended to be spent at the district, and not channelled to lower local governments.

Table 14.3 Total Local Government Revenues and the Degree of Flexibility

UGX Billion, 2000 Prices	1997/98	2001/02	2005/06
Transfers from Central Government	249	623	717
of which discretionary transfers	*60*	*111*	*164*
Locally Raised Revenues	143	106	54
Total LG Revenues (excl. donor)	**329**	**719**	**772**
Locally Raised Revenues as % of Total	*43%*	*15%*	*7%*
Discretionary Revenues as % of Total	*62%*	*30%*	*28%*
LG Revenues as % of Total GoU Budget	*31%*	*35%*	*34%*

Note: Excludes donor transfers to local governments.

Sources: Ministry of Finance, Planning and Economic Development (1997–2007); Mahler (2005); Sarzin (2007).

reflects the absence of a development conditional grant for rural roads. This illustrates that central and local priorities were largely consistent.

Another less obvious implication of the relative decline in discretionary resources available to local governments is the negative impact on operational funding for district management functions. As the bulk of discretionary resources were either tied up in salaries or earmarked for investments via the local government development grant, any decline in local revenues directly impacted on operational funding. Prior to the decline in local revenues the contrast was already evident in districts with differing levels of local revenues. Routine funding for activities such as schools inspection or internal audit suffered in local governments with low revenue collection. In addition, non-wage conditional grant funding (which has been squeezed out as a result of increased wage allocations in health and education) has also fallen.

Whilst overall local government expenditure allocations grew by 24% in nominal terms between 2003/04 and 2005/06, non-wage recurrent allocations actually fell by 17%. This trend started because of a relative decline in non-wage recurrent conditional and unconditional transfers from central government, whilst the recent suspension of Graduated Tax has reduced the availability of non-wage recurrent funding still further. (Williamson et al. 2006)

This has the potential to undermine the ability of local governments to deliver improvements in the quality of services in future.

4. Planning, budgeting, and financial management in local government

In this section the evolution of planning, budgeting, and financial management is examined in the context of the framework for financing local governments. As noted above, a key concern from the outset was the capacity of local governments to spend effectively the substantial additional resources being channelled to them. This section describes the attempts to strengthen local government systems in response to these concerns.

Table 14.4 Typical Local Government Revenue and Expenditure in 2005

	USD Per Capita	% Share
Total Revenue	**26.3**	
Local Revenue	0.7	2.5%
Central Grants	21.4	81.3%
Donor Funding	4.3	16.2%
Total Expenditures	**24.8**	
Management and Support Services	2.6	10.4%
Finance and Planning	1.3	5.2%
Production	1.1	4.5%
Health Services	3.9	15.6%
Education	13.3	53.6%
Works and Technical Services	2.0	8.2%
Natural Resources	0.2	0.7%
Community Based Services	0.4	1.7%

Source: Williamson et al. (2006) using data from Tororo, Lira Municipality, Mpigi District, Kasese District, Kabale District.

While there was little elaboration of the framework for fiscal transfers, the 1997 Local Government Act and the 1998 Local Government Financial and Accounting Regulations (Government of Uganda 1998) set out the framework for planning, budgeting, and accounting at the local level in detail. Despite this, the planning and budgeting framework that evolved was not entirely consistent with the spirit of the legal framework.

At the start of the decentralization process, planning, budgeting, and financial management capacity in local governments was particularly weak (Aarnes et al. 2000). The legal framework provided for a three year rolling development plan and an annual budget. However, early development plans were largely 'wish lists', and budgets were unrealistic. The preparation process for development plans and the budget was intended to be consultative. However budgets were usually prepared late, with little consultation, and bearing little relationship to development plans. Books of accounts were rarely maintained, annual accounts rarely produced, and staff poorly skilled and inadequately qualified. Internal audit was generally missing, and external audit weak. There was also little demand for administrations to build financial management capacity, especially from local councils.

4.1 *Measures to improve planning, budgeting, and reporting*

Some of the earliest and most effective interventions in achieving greater accountability and transparency in the new local government system were remarkably simple, and have been replicated elsewhere. For example, since

1997 all financial releases from MoFPED to local governments have been published in the newspapers and schools are required to put up notices showing the funds they have received. Tracking surveys show that the combination of the new decentralized grant framework and improved information meant a greater proportion of resources actually reached the intended beneficiaries (see Box 14.4). Service providers and contractors were increasingly able to deliver what they were meant to deliver.

Early measures to improve the capacity of local governments focused on planning and budgeting. As a mechanism to link development plans to the budget, MoFPED introduced the Local Government Budget Framework Paper (LGBFP) process for the 1998/99 budget. This mirrored the process that had been introduced in central government over the previous two years. Local governments were invited to the National Budget Conference in October, and MoFPED held a series of regional LGBFP workshops with local government staff. In their LGBFPs, districts and municipalities reviewed revenue performance and made revenue projections over the medium term. The importance of the realism of those projections was emphasized by MoFPED. The LGBFPs then reviewed sector performance, and made medium term spending plans based on projected resources. The first LGBFPs were a mixed bag; but they improved over time, as did the guidance provided by MoFPED. Whilst the LGBFP was important in encouraging more strategic thinking at the local level, annual budgets frequently remained unrealistic.

The volume of conditional grant funding was increasing, as were the demands for accountability for those grants from local governments. In 1999 MoFPED introduced a simple monthly financial statement, which districts and municipalities were required to submit to MoFPED and MoLG. Local governments reacted

---

Box 14.4 EFFECTS OF DECENTRALIZATION AND INCREASED TRANSPARENCY ON LEAKAGE OF FUNDS

A 1996 survey of 250 schools revealed that only 13 per cent of capitation grant entitlements, which were transferred by MoLG at that time, actually reached the schools between 1991 and 1995.

In 1997 free Universal Primary Education was launched and the conditional grant for UPE capitation was created. There was a mass communication campaign with publication of releases in newspapers. Schools were required to publish releases on notice boards. In addition, schools became more reliant on the grant for operational funding following the abolition of school fees, so the demand for the grant increased.

A follow up survey of the same schools in 2001 revealed that leakage was reduced to 18 per cent, albeit of a greatly expanded UPE capitation grant, and that information had played a key role in the reduction.

Source: Reinikka and Svensson (2004)

---

angrily to this requirement, saying that they were not accountable to central government but to their local councils, and had no obligation to report to the centre. This issue came to a head at the Education Sector Review in early 2000, where donors demanded that accountability be produced for UPE and threatened to withdraw budget support. The President intervened and directed local governments to submit accountability reports to the centre. They reluctantly obliged.

In 2000/01 MoFPED introduced a framework for accountability for PAF conditional grants (see Box 14.5). This required local governments to prepare annual work plans and quarterly reports for each of the nine non-wage conditional grants included in the PAF. These set out both planned activities and expenditures. If local governments did not report, they would not receive grant funding. Local governments were also required to post public notices at the location of new investments, building on the success of posting notices at primary schools. Line ministries developed their own guidelines for sector grants within the framework prescribed by MoFPED, and 'Letters of Understanding' were signed between those ministries and local governments. This forced line ministries to think about their policies with respect to local governments, and how they should plan for and report on sectoral conditional grants. This led to a more structured relationship between local government and the centre—setting out the responsibilities for both. It countered common misperceptions that line ministries had no responsibility for local services, and that local governments need not be accountable for the funds they received from the centre. At the time, many felt that local governments would not have the capacity to play their part and report regularly on the use of funds. However, with reporting linked to releases, local governments had a strong incentive to do so, and they soon proved themselves able to comply.

In order to disseminate the PAF General Guidelines for conditional grants, representatives from sector departments in local governments and the corresponding sector ministries were involved in the regional LGBFP workshops in early 2000, and in subsequent years. The dialogue at these workshops was often confrontational, with local governments complaining that sector ministries were imposing conditions upon them. Yet, they were an important forum for dialogue with the centre. The PAF system proved an important step in establishing some form of common accountability framework for local governments, and also helped build confidence at the centre that local governments were capable of spending and accounting for money distributed to them. In the second year of PAF reporting, MoFPED required bank reconciliations to be carried out alongside reports for all conditional grants. This provided added discipline to the reporting and accounting process.

Meanwhile, the Local Government Development Programme was establishing strong incentives to improve local capacity in thirty districts. This focused not on imposing new budgeting and reporting requirements, but on putting into operation the legal framework for planning, budgeting, accounting, and

---

Box 14.5 PAF GENERAL GUIDELINES FOR CONDITIONAL GRANTS

The PAF General Guidelines for the Planning and Operation of Conditional Grants were introduced in 2000/01. They set out a uniform framework of reporting and accountability for all non-wage conditional grants under the PAF:

- The preparation of activity based work plans for each grant;
- Quarterly reporting and work plans for each grant;
- Release of grant funds, conditional on the submission of quarterly reports;
- Mandatory public notices and work plans in public places;
- Local government responsibilities for monitoring the use of PAF funds, and also central government activities;
- Technical assistance and sanctions applied to both districts and line ministries for failure to honour their responsibilities; and
- A letter of understanding to be signed by the Chief Administrative Officer of the district and the Permanent Secretary of the respective line ministry.

Source: Ministry of Finance, Planning and Economic Development (2000)

---

transparency, through a combination of incentives and bottom up support to capacity development. The LGDP involved an annual assessment of local governments' administrative performance against minimum conditions and performance measures relating to areas such as planning, budgeting, and financial management (see Box 14.6). Local governments could only access the local development grant if they met several minimum conditions. They were also provided with a discretionary capacity building grant, intended to enable them to meet the assessment criteria. The discretionary development funds were attractive to local councils as they enabled them to deliver visible projects to their electorates. In order to ensure qualification for the grant, local councils paid more attention to building the capacity to perform core tasks such as preparing development plans, budgets, and annual accounts; they began to put in place better qualified staff in areas such as financial management and audit. In 2003 the implementation of the local development grant was rolled out country wide, whilst the assessment framework was broadened to incorporate sectoral issues.

4.2 *Emerging issues*

By 2000 the transfer system and policies of central government had begun to pose problems for local government planning, budgeting, and financial management, and to reduce the discretion of local governments over their resources.

The increases in earmarked transfers focused local governments' attention on conditional grants from the centre rather than on the overall budget, including local revenues approved by councils. Although the PAF guidelines emphasized

---

Box 14.6 LOCAL GOVERNMENT ASSESSMENT AND THE LOCAL
DEVELOPMENT GRANT

All higher local governments can potentially access the discretionary local development grant, which is shared between districts and sub-counties in the ratio 35:65. Access to funds and the level of funding is dependent on an Annual Assessment of Minimum Conditions and Performance Measures of local governments:

- Districts and municipalities are assessed by a team from central government lead by MoLG in five areas: development planning; financial management and internal audit; revenue performance; capacity building; and funds for co-financing investments. Districts and municipalities also carry out an internal assessment of sub-counties and divisions within their jurisdiction, and the team from central government verifies their accuracy on a sample basis. Those local governments which do not meet the minimum conditions do not access the grant.

- Local governments are also assessed against a set of additional performance measures. High performing governments receive a 20 per cent increase in their Local Development Grant, while poor performers get a 20 per cent reduction.

- All local governments receive a capacity building grant, regardless of whether they meet the minimum conditions, to enable them to address capacity constraints and meet the minimum conditions in future.

This framework has provided a strong incentive for local governments to upgrade their corporate performance, especially in terms of the production of plans, budgets, and accounts. Failing to qualify for the local development grant can have serious political consequences, as seen in Mubende:

Several sub-counties failed to reach the minimum standards in the internal assessment of the administrative capacity of sub-counties, conducted by Mubende District Administration. This means that these sub-counties were not able to access the local development grant in the following years. This was widely publicized within the district, and the public did not like it. In the 2001 local government elections, all those leaders of sub-county councils who presided over failing sub-counties were voted out of office. Incentive enough to perform? (Williamson 2003)

Sources: Ministry of Local Government 2002, 2005; Williamson 2003

---

council involvement in the review and approval of work plans and reports, they established vertical lines of accountability from local governments to the centre, and did not pay enough attention to the weaker horizontal accountability relationships between councillors and their constituents. Given the decline in local revenues, there was little to decide upon in the budget process in terms of allocations between departments and services—particularly for the recurrent budget. The only real discretion available to local governments was in the development budget. Under the local development grant, local councils at the district and sub-county levels had flexibility to choose the sector and type of investment (provided it was within the legal mandate of local governments and was consistent with PEAP priorities). Local governments also had some say in the use of conditional grants for the development budget, for example over the location of water points, classrooms, and health centres—although the guidelines stipulated criteria for locating investments. So, despite the increasingly earmarked nature of transfers, councils had some latitude to make investment choices; and this was in the area of the budget—investment—with the most political mileage.

With the increase in the number of earmarked grants, the PAF guidelines led to a proliferation of work plans and quarterly reports. This proved a significant administrative burden on local governments, and also revealed capacity gaps at the centre in terms of line ministries' ability to assimilate the information in reports and monitor the implementation of services. The reports began to gather dust in ministry offices in Kampala. At the local level the effect was to fragment the annual budget; the process of reporting and releasing funds became a largely mechanical 'paper for money' exercise. The number of grants also contributed to the proliferation of bank accounts at the local level; some districts had over 100 accounts. LGBFPs arguably were ineffective in linking local plans and budgets, although they were often useful in consolidating work plans across sectors, and were more realistic than District Development Plans. Approval of budgets was still often delayed, they were still unrealistic and they bore little relationship to development plans.

The nature of the funding framework also meant that local governments faced incentives which encouraged them to prepare unrealistic budgets. The Local Government Act required that the budget for council meetings should not exceed 15 per cent of locally raised revenues; so if local revenue projections were increased councillors could allocate more money to themselves for allowances. The grant framework also encouraged other types of unrealism. For example, if there was insufficient recurrent revenue from central government and locally to cover salaries and pensions, there was an incentive to inflate local revenue estimates to meet the requirement that local governments balance their budgets (conditional grants could not be allocated to these areas). Local governments tended to budget for donor projects in full, whether or not they had received firm commitments, further inflating budget estimates. In summary, the incentives did little to help the local government budget process deliver a realistic budget and meaningful council decision making.

Assessments carried out from as early as 2002 pointed out other systemic weaknesses in local government public financial management, including the accumulation of salary and pension arrears, cash flow management, procurement, and internal audit (Kragh et al. 2003; World Bank 2004; Williamson et al. 2006). Local governments complained that delayed grant releases from the centre were the source of many of their problems, yet ultimately central releases were fairly predictable in terms of both timing (even if they took a long time to arrive via the banking system) and amount over the financial year. Often delays were due to the failure of local governments to report and to plan future cash flows on the basis of the timing of past releases. Procurement was weak, and subject to political interference and corruption, with District

Tender Boards appointed by local councils. While formal accounting and accountability processes had improved, they remained formulaic and lacked bite. Although external audit reports were increasingly timely, District Public Accounts Committees, which were appointed by councils but not made up of councillors, varied in their ability to review audit reports, and their recommendations were rarely considered seriously by councils.

4.3 The Fiscal Decentralization Strategy

Soon after the implementation of the PAF General Guidelines and the introduction of the Local Government Development Programme, concerns over their conflicting approaches to fiscal decentralization emerged, alongside general disquiet from local governments. Donors supporting the decentralization process offered to help MoFPED carry out a review of the framework for intergovernmental fiscal transfers. This was not welcomed on all fronts, with MoLG and LGFC feeling that MoFPED was overstepping its mandate. Some felt that a study was unnecessary since the solution was simple—increase the unconditional grant, not conditional grants, and implement the law as it was originally intended. Nevertheless, a working group was formed to oversee the study and handle the recommendations. It was chaired by MoFPED, made up of representatives from sector ministries, MoLG, the LGFC, local government associations, and the decentralization donor group.

The study acknowledged the political reality of conditional grants and that they were likely to remain the dominant funding modality. It therefore proposed rationalizing the number of recurrent conditional grants to one per sector, and introducing more discretion in development financing through the adoption of LGDP type modalities for all local investments (Government of Uganda/Donor Sub-Group on Decentralization 2001). The working group discussed the proposals in depth. The institutions supporting greater devolution argued for more flexibility in recurrent conditional grants, whist sector ministries demanded that their own sector investment grants be retained. A compromise, accommodating both these demands, was reached and the Fiscal Decentralization Strategy (FDS, see Box 14.7) was drafted. However disagreements between MoLG and MoFPED over how the strategy should be implemented remained. After protracted discussions to resolve these differences, the Ministers of Finance and Local Government met in early 2002 and agreed the contents of the FDS (Ministry of Finance, Planning and Economic Development 2002) and to pilot implementation of the FDS. Cabinet approved the Strategy later in the year.

Implementation of the FDS was problematic. MoFPED led the development of the FDS, but it lacked the institutional capacity to follow through with its implementation. Following changes in staff within MoFPED, it also soon lacked a strong champion. The two committees formed to oversee the implementation of the FDS introduced greater participation in decision making, but also slowed it down. The decision to pilot meant two parallel systems had to be managed, further slowing implementation.

Progress was therefore incremental rather than decisive. Guidelines for Budget Preparation and Implementation, incorporating the principles of the FDS, were developed in 2003. Local governments now prepare comprehensive annual work plans and budgets. This was facilitated by the development of simple computerized tools for the preparation of the BFP and budget, with donor support, whose use is now widespread. An annual process of negotiation of grant conditions has been established between central ministries and local governments, which has increased ownership of the policies embodied in conditional grants. As noted above, a comprehensive set of allocation formulae for conditional grants was developed, but it was not adopted by all sectors. Many sector ministries also opposed the introduction of flexibility to recurrent

---

Box 14.7 OVERVIEW OF THE FISCAL DECENTRALIZATION STRATEGY

The objective of the FDS is:

To strengthen the process of decentralization in Uganda through increasing Local Governments' autonomy, widening local participation in decision making and streamlining of fiscal transfer modalities to Local Governments in order to increase the efficiency and effectiveness of Local Governments to achieve PEAP goals within a transparent and accountable framework.

The focus of the strategy is in two areas:

First, the promotion of local government autonomy and the widening of participation in decision making in order to enhance the efficiency in allocation of resources towards the achievement of PEAP goals in line with local priorities. This will be achieved by:

- Increasing the discretionary powers given to local governments in allocating resources towards both recurrent and development activities;
- Promoting increased participation of all levels of local government in the decision making process;
- Providing direct financial incentives for local governments to increase local revenue, and ensuring that local revenue contributes meaningfully to local development; and
- Harmonizing the central and local government planning and budgeting cycles to ensure that local needs and priorities feed back into the national budget.

Second, improving the effectiveness of local government programmes through strengthening efficiency, transparency, and accountability of local government expenditures. This will be achieved by:

- Streamlining the systems of transferring funds from the centre to local government;
- Developing a strong framework for financial accountability and increasing the focus on book keeping;
- A simple system of reporting on financial and output information;
- Rewarding those local governments which implement programmes well, in adherence to the legal and policy framework, and sanctioning those which do not; and
- A more coordinated, and better-targeted system of monitoring and mentoring local governments by central government.

Source: Ministry of Finance, Planning and Economic Development (2002): 6

---

grant allocations, which allowed local governments to reallocate funding between conditional grants. However, some progress has been made in the use of this flexibility.

There was little progress in two of the most important areas of the FDS—the streamlining of the grants and associated reporting systems. This is because the vertical relationships between line ministries and local governments that the conditional grants introduced proved difficult to dismantle. Although the intention was to move to one conditional grant per sector department in the local government, they remain as separate grants in central government budgets, and have continued to proliferate. The FDS proposed replacing grant-based work plans and reports with a consolidated reporting process based on the local government annual work plan and budget for all local revenues and expenditures. The FDS reporting system was developed, but it did not take off, even in the pilot districts. Many line ministries continued to demand their own work plans and reports from local governments for individual grants. In 2004 systems of cash management and commitment control were developed alongside the reporting requirements under FDS, and incorporated into the budget implementation manuals. However, these have not yet been adequately enforced either and the systemic weaknesses remain. In short, MoFPED failed to implement the accounting and reporting requirements of the FDS as decisively as it did with the PAF.

4.4 *Progress in formal accounting, audit, and capacity development*

There has been significant progress in other areas of financial management beyond the FDS. Bookkeeping improved significantly. The timeliness of local government annual accounts has improved noticeably, and the vast majority of districts have internal audit departments functioning. These trends are, in part, due to the incentives from the Annual Assessment under LGDP. The Integrated Financial Management System (see Chapter 15), which has strong backing from the Accountant General's Office, has been implemented in fourteen local governments (as of 2008). This is expected to improve financial controls. The internal audit function is also being modernized, but again progress has been slow in changing the culture of staff at the local level. As a result of significant political interference in procurement, and to align local practices with central reforms, procurement was made the responsibility of procurement committees, appointed by the Chief Administrative Officer and made up of civil servants. In a related move, to try and put space between local politicians and the administration, the Chief Administrative Officer is now appointed centrally.

The improvements in accounting, in turn, have facilitated better and more timely audit of higher local governments by the Auditor General. However, the auditing of nearly 1,000 sub-county councils has lagged behind, as the Auditor General's office lacks the resources to cover so many institutions. District level

Local Government Public Accounts Committees were weak and had little incentive to be critical of the administration when reviewing audit reports, as they were themselves appointed by the council. In 2001 the Local Government Accounts Committee of Parliament was formed. This committee has added vigour to accountability processes. Parliamentarians, as they were not appointed by the council, were able to provide more robust scrutiny of audit reports. However, it can be argued that this too reinforced accountability to the centre.

Approaches to capacity building have evolved over time. The Second Local Government Development Programme developed standardized training packages for different elements of decentralization, and certified training firms to provide the courses. Meanwhile, USAID supported local governments, through on the job support, in the implementation of the budgeting manual under the FDS. The combination of demand driven capacity building addressing specific local government gaps and supply side support for new systems and guidelines appears to have worked well.

Whilst these changes are important, efforts to introduce and enforce formal decision making processes and rules based financial management systems in local governments are likely to prove challenging. Informal processes are likely to continue. The educated middle class, which dominates the political, business, and local administrative community in most districts, is small and intertwined. Distancing of local administrations' procurement and payment processes from the local political elite will prove difficult in practice. An emphasis on transparency and accountability has been and will continue to be crucial in ensuring effective local governance, and that services are delivered effectively and responsively. However, despite the significant achievements of transparency initiatives during the 1990s and early 2000s, the vigour with which transparency was promoted declined during the 2000s.

4.5 On balance substantial progress, but systemic weaknesses remain

The 2005 Local Government Public Financial Management Assessment concluded that:

Overall . . . there has been substantial progress made in local government public financial management (PFM) since the late 1990s, and that there is little evidence of any deterioration in PFM capacity and performance. However there are signs that there may be a future deterioration in PFM outcomes if several trends, mostly resulting from recent central government actions, are not reversed.

Across the local governments assessed there were significant variations in performance as well as common areas of weakness particularly in terms of the credibility in the budget and the predictability of budget execution in terms of revenue collection cash management and commitment control. (Williamson et al. 2006)

The overall trend over the period assessed was positive, therefore. A combination of explicit incentives for local governments to put in place planning, budgeting, and accounting capacity under the LGDP, the requirements under conditional grants, plus the indirect incentive of the rapidly increasing budgets of local governments, all played their part in building capacity. The fact that the vast majority of local budgets are funded through government grants and local revenues, and donors have used these channels, has contributed to strengthening local systems. The sheer scale of the expansion of local budgets and service delivery meant that local government jobs became more attractive, and they began to attract an improved calibre of staff. However, the collapse in local revenues and indecisiveness in implementing proposals to streamline and introduce more substantial flexibility into the grant system undoubtedly undermined progress significantly.

5. The balance sheet of decentralization

Local governments were responsible for implementing the unprecedented expansion and rebuilding of basic service delivery which has taken place since 1997. Initially, many feared that local governments would not have the capacity to deliver; however, capacity was built as the services were expanded. In 2005 local governments were undeniably far stronger institutions than they were in 1995. This represents a substantial achievement, especially given the state of service delivery and institutions inherited by the NRM government in 1986. Today the main concern is over the quality of the services provided by local governments, highlighted in Chapter 9. Ugandans would still rather send their children to private schools, or use private health practitioners, than use government services—if they can afford it. There is a widespread perception that the level of corruption in local governments is high.[7]

Given the political decisions to expand free basic services, a key question is the extent to which these achievements and problems can be attributed to the way decentralization has been implemented. Was this a pragmatic compromise, or was the way in which the government pursued the decentralization of service delivery flawed?

5.1 On the positive side

A key success factor was the high level of support for the decentralization of service delivery at the national level. First, there was high-level political support. The major decisions to make local governments responsible for approving their own budgets and appointing their own staff were crucial. They

---

[7] Although there is no evidence to suggest the situation is worse than in central government.

made local governments responsible and accountable for the services they were to deliver. In addition, the executive proposed and Parliament approved successive budgets which involved substantial increases in resources to local governments.

Second, there was technical as well as political support from the key central government institutions for this agenda—MoFPED, MoLG, and LGFC. This meant that opposition from sector ministries, which were less enthusiastic about decentralizing services, was overcome. A sound legal framework was developed by MoLG, and supporting regulations provided the detail. When substantial extra resources became available from debt relief and donors, MoFPED proposed that they be channelled to local governments to fund the service delivery agenda and enable local governments to deliver against their mandates. Third, donor support for the PEAP agenda was complemented by a willingness to move towards budget support and have aid channelled via the grant system to local governments. These factors meant that the responsibility for service delivery was decisively shifted to local governments, and funding for local service delivery increased rapidly thereafter.

Conditional grants proved the most convenient mechanism for funding service delivery, and have become predominant. This has enabled central government to track resources for service delivery and gave it a lever to ensure greater accountability from local governments. However, this caused institutional tensions at the centre and concerns that this was undermining local autonomy. Nevertheless, in practical terms local councils were provided with significant discretion—over local investments (such as roads, clinics, and classrooms) and over the hiring, deployment, and firing of staff (albeit within centrally imposed limits). This is arguably where councils were likely to demand autonomy the most; it has provided councils with the autonomy to deliver services responsive to local needs. It can also be argued that conditional grants have helped protect operational allocations to service delivery and thereby service quality. Allocations might otherwise have been squeezed by local councillors spending more on salaries and physical investments.

Meanwhile, substantial capacity has also been built in local institutions. Conventional capacity building activities have been increasingly tailored to the tasks local governments have to perform. This has been balanced between supply and demand driven approaches. Although capacity building support from the centre was important, arguably the use of local systems and the incentives faced by local governments were more significant. Simply increasing the volume of funding going to local governments has by itself attracted higher calibre staff. The demands of the local development grant ensured that local councils sat up and took note of the formal legal requirements for planning, budgeting, and accounting. Capacity followed funding and incentives.

5.2 On the negative side

The most negative feature of the way decentralization has been implemented has been the collapse in local revenue. Increases in transfers undermined the incentives for local governments to raise their own revenues. This was probably unavoidable. Taxes available to local governments have been, and are likely to remain, limited in a poor country like Uganda; most local funding, therefore, is bound to take the form of fiscal transfers from the centre. However, even this limited revenue potential could have had an important role in building local accountability. Yet the politicization of local revenue and the withdrawal of Graduated Tax had the largest detrimental effect on local revenues. These actions by central government could and should have been avoided.

The collapse in local revenue has had two major effects. First, it has undermined the link between the local taxes citizens pay to councils they elect, and the services those councils provide. Local accountability, therefore, is likely to have suffered. Second, this has reduced the operational funding available to local government administrations to manage, monitor, and supervise local service delivery. Although central government made an effort to compensate local governments for the withdrawal of Graduated Tax, it was inadequate.

The framework for fiscal transfers and service delivery has had other more practical negative implications for local administration. The policies, rules, and guidelines of central ministries have not always been consistent. Reporting requirements have increased with the number of conditional grants. This has placed an unnecessary administrative burden on local governments, without significantly improving accountability. Efforts to reduce the number of grants and rationalize planning and reporting requirements, via the FDS, have made slow progress. The vertical relationships between sector ministries and districts have been difficult to dismantle, while local accountability has remained weak.

There are various other areas where central government actions have failed to support strong, accountable local government service delivery. Overall coordination of the interactions between the various central government actors and local governments has proved difficult. The centre gave confusing messages to local governments and contributed to their administrative burden. The politically driven creation of new districts, which accelerated from 2005, has spread the administrative capacity that had been built more thinly across the country. The recentralization of the appointment of the Chief Administrative Officer, also in 2005, has meant that local councils no longer have full control over the appointment of their staff.

6. Conclusion

Access to basic services delivered by local governments increased markedly between 1995 and 2007, although there are major problems with the quality of those services. On balance, however, the decentralization process has been managed pragmatically and innovatively. Without the development of the local government framework, the use of conditional grants to channel resources decisively to local government service delivery, and the establishment of incentives for local capacity and performance, it is hard to see how the rapid expansion of service delivery could have been achieved.

15

Financial Management and Accountability Reform

Gustavio Bwoch and Robert Muwanga[1]

1. Introduction

Public financial management (PFM) in the Ugandan context can broadly be understood to cover the entire infrastructure for the allocation, control, and management of public funds. This includes the processes for planning, budgeting, accounting, auditing, and audit follow-up. The major institutions that are traditionally associated with these processes and form part of the PFM infrastructure include the ministries in charge of planning and management of the national budget and the budget process, the national treasury office,[2] accounting officers,[3] the supreme audit office, and Parliament.

Whilst macroeconomic stability, planning, and budgeting were the focus of reforms in the early 1990s, financial management and accountability have assumed greater prominence over time. Today there are many players in the accountability arena including the media, civil society, and donors. Government institutions such as the office of the Inspectorate of Government and the Ministry of Ethics and Integrity also play a role in promoting accountability.

Of particular concern was the moribund state of many PFM processes and controls. There was lack of timely and accurate financial information for decision making both at central and local government levels. Government entities were not reporting in time for consolidation and audit. Ministries would take

---

[1] The authors gratefully acknowledge the assistance of Paulo Kyama.
[2] In Uganda the national treasury function falls under the Ministry of Finance, Planning and Economic Development (MoFPED).
[3] A person designated accounting officer by the Secretary to the Treasury, in accordance with the Public Finance and Accountability Act 2003, to provide control and accountability to Parliament for expenditures under a ministry or agency funded from the Uganda Consolidated Fund.

up to three months to prepare financial statements and the Treasury would take another month to consolidate the government's accounts. Moreover, the systems in place were inadequate to track the collection and use of public funds.

There was also a backlog of un-reconciled accounts in ministries and local governments. Some bank accounts in ministries and local governments had not been reconciled for a long time. Moreover, there was no uniformity of budget and accounts codes between central and local governments. This made it difficult to consolidate all government accounts to produce information by sector or by activity. As a result, there were endemic budget overruns due to the lack of information regarding actual expenditures and approved budgets. Control of domestic arrears also presented a serious challenge. The combination of these factors and other reform imperatives prompted government to revamp its PFM processes.

2. Pressures to improve financial management and accountability during the 1990s

The political turmoil prior to 1986 severely damaged Uganda's PFM and accountability infrastructure. The legislature was, at best, ineffective in enforcing accountability. Capacity in PFM institutions such as the Ministry of Finance (and the Treasury), and Office of the Auditor General was very weak. For example, as recently as 1998, the entire government had only two professional accountants. Not surprisingly, it was very difficult to produce timely final accounts and audited reports, or even to meet basic standards of accountability.

Between 1986 and the mid 1990s a wide range of economic reforms were implemented aimed at the restoration of macroeconomic stability and overall improvement in the economic, social, and institutional infrastructure. While some aspects of these reforms supported PFM they also created more pressure to improve the fragile infrastructure for financial management and accountability. This section looks at the key policy and structural changes that increased the strain on PFM systems from the early 1990s.

2.1 Constitutional reform

In 1995 the constitutional reform process resulted in the promulgation of a new constitution which sought to promote the principles of democracy and good governance, and to uphold the principles of accountability of the executive to the people of Uganda. These principles were manifested, among others, in the clarity and separation of powers and the role of Parliament and the executive in the control, management, and accountability of public resources. The Constitution established a new legislature with attendant structures (such as a Public Accounts Committee) that were given strong powers to demand accountability from the executive. It also provided a greater role for the national supreme audit institution, the Office of the Auditor General. This prompted the executive to start addressing the weak PFM institutional capacity. However, beyond the Constitution there was little legislative reform relating to PFM in the 1990s. The Public Finance Act (1964) and its supporting regulations, though outdated, continued to provide the basic framework guiding financial management.

2.2 Other public sector reforms

In 1993 the government adopted a new policy of decentralization involving devolution of political and administrative responsibilities to local governments (see Chapter 14). The intention was to allow greater participation of local communities in managing their affairs so as to improve service delivery. While the policy provided greater opportunity for accountability among local communities, it represented a major challenge for formal PFM systems as it increased the number of organizations managing public finances without a corresponding increase in the capacity to do so. Between 1990/91 and 2000/01 the number of recurrent budget votes grew from twenty-five to ninety-three, mainly because of the increasing number of local governments. This placed considerable stress on the Office of the Auditor General and Parliament in their accountability and oversight role.[4]

On the other hand, the creation of the Uganda Revenue Authority (URA) meant that revenue collection was handled by an independent agency (see Chapter 5). This narrowed the core span of PFM processes, allowing the government to focus on expenditure management while holding URA accountable for revenue. The divestiture of public enterprises also helped reduce the scope of PFM (see Chapter 16).

Major public service reforms were undertaken in phases beginning in the early 1990s (see Chapter 4). These helped streamline the public service and strengthen central government's focus on policy management while decentralizing functions to local governments. Overall, the programme of reform had a number of implications for PFM. Greater clarity of PFM roles was achieved as a result of public service restructuring. Further, the ban on recruitment between 1992 and 1998 and the freeze on promotions effectively reduced aggregate staff numbers and kept expenditure within the wage bill ceiling. Yet this had the unintended consequence of stifling the proper functioning of PFM structures. Once the freeze on recruitment and promotions was lifted in 1998, the government was able to fill staff positions for functions within the PFM structures.

---

[4] Commenting on the impact of decentralization, one writer observed that 'The major challenge of decentralization was its political nature which created a large number of autonomous local government units' (Kitunzi 2001).

The reforms to the planning and budget systems during the 1990s (such as the Public Investment Plan, the Poverty Eradication Action Plan, and the Medium Term Expenditure Framework), the rapidly expanding resources available to the government from both domestic and donor sources, and the increasing number of accountable spending institutions (see Chapters 6, 7, 8, 13, and 14) all imposed extra demands on the financial management and accounting systems. Yet throughout the 1990s there was no comprehensive programme to address the weak financial management and accountability processes within government. Local government units were only able to submit accounts for 1996/97 with support from a World Bank project. The backlog of accounts that were not audited in time mounted in the face of expanding government. The PFM infrastructure was increasingly unable to deliver satisfactorily.

2.3 *The donor constituency*

Further pressures emerged from the changing composition and complexity of stakeholder groups. Since the late 1980s donors have played a significant role in the economy, financing about 50 per cent of the national budget. This represents a huge stake in the budgetary process. Donors therefore became a key constituency for accountability. The advent of budget support from the late 1990s (see Chapter 13), with its emphasis on strengthening government systems and the need to reassure taxpayers in donor countries that funds were properly utilized, reinforced donor demands for accountability.

While donors have been key allies in economic reforms, their assistance sometimes caused distortions (World Bank 2004). For example, conditions to deliver agreed targets, or even just to account, often exerted undue demands on existing systems. In some cases *ad hoc* structures, such as project implementation units, were created to cope with these demands. These tended to undermine government capacity by creating parallel reporting systems and paying higher salaries.

3. Challenges faced by financial management and accountability systems in the 1990s

Like most parts of government, the major PFM institutions (accounting, auditing, and inspection) virtually collapsed during the 1970s and 1980s. A low skills base, manual systems, and a consequent weak enforcement of financial controls characterized the system.

3.1 *Low skills base*

The level of skills in the major accounting functions and organizations was very low. The freeze on public service recruitment between 1992 and 1998 made it very difficult to tackle this situation. Following the 1992 restructuring of the public service, and a subsequent review in 1995, only 55 out of 137 approved positions in the Treasury department were filled, and mainly in the lower grades. Even when positions fell vacant, departments were not allowed to recruit. The 2001 World Bank Country Financial Accountability Assessment observed that 'the serious shortage of professionally qualified and experienced accountants and accounting technicians in the accounting units across all levels of Government [raises] considerable fiduciary risk' (World Bank 2001a). In addition, pay levels were very low in comparison to market rates. Despite considerable increases in pay levels since the early 1990s, in 2001 new graduate accountants in government were only earning 33 per cent of the salaries of their counterparts in the private sector (World Bank 2004).

In addition to the recruitment freeze, there was little career progression. There were hardly any promotions and, in many cases, staff acted in higher positions for long periods. Other factors affecting staff motivation included lack of training opportunities and the absence of basic tools including computers. The cumulative effect was a demoralized staff with many technically qualified and competent officers leaving government in search of better opportunities.

3.2 Reliance on manual systems

Financial management and accountability relies heavily on systems, procedures, and controls in addition to the knowledge and skills of staff. Until the late 1990s there were no reforms or improvements in these areas to match the reforms in economic management. The financial operational systems to support the capture, recording, retrieval, reporting, and tracking of financial data were seriously deficient. Documents and reports continued to be compiled manually. Accounting staff at the Treasury did not have access to computers until the late 1990s. Even then, without appropriate training, computers were not optimally deployed or used. The few members of staff that were in place were overwhelmed by the volume of work, yet the demands for accountability kept growing as a result of other reforms. This lack of automated systems slowed the financial management and accountability processes, making it difficult to track and monitor public expenditure transactions and thus increasing the danger of misappropriation and wastage of public resources.

3.3 Weak enforcement of internal controls

Not surprisingly in view of the above institutional weaknesses, there was a significant disregard for financial controls. The internal audit and inspection functions were largely ineffective and there was little awareness of the level of outstanding government commitments. By 1999 the stock of domestic arrears had accumulated to USD70 million (World Bank 2001a).

Efforts were made to address this through the introduction of a manual commitment control system in 1998/99 (World Bank 2004). It had two main objectives: to ensure that expenditures were contained within expenditure limits and cash releases set by MoFPED, and to tackle the problem of domestic arrears.[5] The system required accounting officers to submit a monthly commitment control return to the Director of Accounts, failing which the release of fresh funds would be withheld. While it helped contain the growth in arrears, it could not curb them completely. This was largely due to costs that continued to be incurred by government departments for which resources were not adequately provided under the commitment control system. These included expenditures such as rent, contributions to international organizations, and utilities. It was also possible to by-pass the system, for example by issuing purchase orders that were not reflected in the commitments.

4. Reforms to the policy framework for public financial management

Beginning in the early 1990s, the government implemented a series of reforms to strengthen economic and financial management, using a mix of donor funded projects, in-house capacity building, and technical assistance. The most prominent projects were the two economic and financial management projects funded by the World Bank. However, the initial focus of these interventions was on supporting fiscal discipline, planning, and budget formulation. There was little progress in financial management and accountability reforms until the late 1990s.

There were a number of disparate initiatives focusing on specific PFM problems. However, a major challenge was the lack of a clearly sequenced strategy for reform to strengthen financial management and accountability. In the late 1990s an attempt was made to develop a comprehensive strategy, incorporating legal, institutional, human process, and systems reforms with support from the above World Bank projects. This section looks at the main reforms; it begins with the legal framework before moving on to look at the new institutional framework, and interventions aimed at enhancing human resource capacity and improving coordination. A crucial intervention underpinning many of these reforms was the automation of financial management processes, through the implementation of the Integrated Financial Management System (IFMS); this is looked at in section 5.

---

[5] In 1999 domestic arrears were estimated at about USD70 million and were continuing to grow. This was attributed in part to failure by Accounting Officers to adhere to Accounting Instructions.

4.1 *The legal framework*

The 1995 Constitution defined the principles and overall legal and institutional framework for the control, management, and accountability of public resources. The promulgation of the new Constitution meant that all PFM had to be examined to ensure harmony. Moreover, some new laws were required to make certain provisions of the Constitution operational. Without legislative amendments some PFM reforms could not be implemented as intended. For example, audit practices prescribed by the old legislation were based on manually drawn books and records. Accounts generated from computerized financial management systems could not be audited. Yet much of the Public Finance Act of 1964 remained in force eight years after the new Constitution was adopted.

Significant amendment of PFM legislation only began in 2001, to codify modern requirements for financial management and to capture the changes in the Constitution and the 1997 Local Government Act. There was also a deliberate effort to monitor PFM laws to ensure that they were relevant for emerging PFM needs. In 2002 the Accountant General's Office established a department with specific responsibility for policy and legal aspects of financial management.

Two important pieces of legislation arising from the provisions of the 1995 Constitution were the Budget Act (2001), which elaborated Parliament's role in

---

Box 15.1 PROVISIONS FOR PFM IN THE 1995 CONSTITUTION

The ultimate authority for controlling the generation of public funds and their utilization is vested in Parliament. The government (executive) is mandated to initiate any measures required to raise and use public funds. Moreover, the Constitution establishes a central fund, the Uganda Consolidated Fund, and provides that all public revenues must be paid into that Fund, and that funds may only be disbursed from it under the authority of Parliament.

Article 164 of the Constitution stipulates that the permanent secretary or the 'accounting officer' in charge of a ministry or department shall be accountable to Parliament for the funds in that ministry or department. The same article also provides that any person holding a political or public office who directs or concurs in the use of public funds contrary to existing instructions shall be accountable for any loss arising from that use and shall be required to make good the loss even if he or she has ceased to hold that office. Article 163 establishes the position of Auditor General and mandates the appointee to audit and report on the public accounts of Uganda and of all public offices and any public corporation or other bodies or organizations established by an Act of Parliament. The Auditor General is required to report to Parliament, which has the mandate to consider the audit report and confirm that the funds have been utilized in accordance with the authority and set procedures. To complete the accountability process, the Executive is required to submit a Treasury Memorandum to Parliament indicating how issues raised in the Auditor General's report are being or will be dealt with.

Box 15.2 PUBLIC FINANCE AND ACCOUNTABILITY ACT (2003)

The Public Finance and Accountability Act prescribes the controls and administrative framework for the management and accounting of public funds. It vests authority and responsibility for supervision of the collection and use of public funds in the 'Minister responsible for Finance', who is charged with management of the Uganda Consolidated Fund. However, for accountability and control purposes, the minister is required to seek the authority of Parliament to use funds for specified purposes by submitting an Appropriations Bill. Moreover, following Parliamentary approval, the minister and public officers: (i) may only use the appropriated funds for authorized purposes; (ii) may not incur expenditure in excess of the appropriated funds; and (iii) must use the appropriated funds within the financial year. At the same time, the minister must ensure that a full account for the management of the Consolidated Fund and use of public funds is made to Parliament. To assist in this process, the Act provides for the positions of Secretary to the Treasury, Accountant General, and Accounting Officers.

---

the increasingly sophisticated budget process, and the Public Procurement and Disposal of Public Assets Act (2003), which decentralized the procurement function to spending agencies.

The central piece of legislation which provided the enabling framework for PFM reforms was the 2003 Public Finance and Accountability Act. This replaced the 1964 Public Finance Act and was a response to the new political and constitutional dispensation calling for greater accountability. It was also a response to changing PFM practices and procedures to match modern standards of financial management. The Act aimed at removing restrictions in the legal framework to pave the way for the implementation of the planned automated financial management system.

Following the enactment of the above laws, Uganda had a legal framework which was in harmony with modern financial management practices. This included:

- Streamlined responsibility for budgeting, accounting, internal audit, and reporting resulting in improved government capacity for aggregate fiscal planning and management;
- Improved procurement practices through the introduction of guidelines to prescribe best practice in procurement;
- Adoption of professionally recognized standards; for example, government financial statements prepared in accordance with International Public Sector Accountancy Standards; and
- Clarification of accountability mechanisms within and among key stakeholders.

4.2 Strengthening institutional structures and human resource capacity

In parallel with reforms to the legal framework, a number of measures were taken to strengthen the institutional framework and capacity within government for PFM. Of particular importance was the restructuring in 2002 of the Treasury from a single department into a Directorate with three departments, each headed by a commissioner. Following the enactment of the Public Finance and Accountability Act 2003, the Directorate became the Accountant General's Office with statutory status and with a broadened mandate.

As noted above, the legacy of the 1970s and 1980s combined with unattractive terms and conditions in the public service made it difficult for government to attract and retain good quality staff, particularly in the area of PFM. If meaningful PFM reforms were to be achieved, serious attention needed to be paid to building human resource capacity.

It was only in 2005 that a strategy was developed to bridge the PFM skills gap, focusing on the short to medium term while ensuring sustainability in the longer term. In 2006 the government embarked on a major exercise to fill vacant positions in the accounting, auditing, and IT cadres. It focused particularly on young graduates, who were considered more trainable. Initially, twenty graduates were recruited and assigned to support the IFMS implementation sites. Financial management and IT professionals were recruited from abroad and from the private sector as consultants as an interim measure to fill the skills gaps in these areas. They were expected to support the implementation of PFM reforms and provide knowledge transfer to staff, particularly the new entrants into the Accountant General's Office.

The recruitment drive was accompanied by a rigorous training programme and a state-of-the-art in-house training facility was established. The programme was effective in addressing the skills gaps and motivating and energizing staff. There was a marked rise of interest in professional development, with increased enrolment for professional courses and participation in various reform activities. The recruitment drive and training raised the number of professionally qualified accountants from two in 1998 to ninety-three in 2008, bringing in a wave of new thinking and commitment.

In restructuring the Accountant General's Office it was decided to fill supervisory and management positions on the basis of completion of training and attainment of professional qualifications. This sent a strong message about linking qualifications and knowledge to positions.

Government has invested heavily in capacity building programmes and training which has been translated into greater learning and staff productivity. These interventions have involved all key PFM institutions including the Auditor General.

4.3 Coordination

Coordination of PFM reforms was considered important, in order to minimize duplication and to maximize their overall impact. Furthermore, the importance attached to fiduciary risk by donors (particularly those providing budget support), brought out the need for a framework within which donors could work to support government reforms.

In 1998 MoFPED established the Public Expenditure Management Committee, chaired by the Secretary to the Treasury. The committee's mandate was to provide a framework for improved awareness, coordination, harmonization, and the resourcing and monitoring of central and local government PFM activities. Membership included the permanent secretaries of the Ministry of Public Service and Ministry of Local Government as well as senior representatives from the Auditor General, the Accountant General's Office, the Budget Directorate and later on the Public Procurement and Disposal of Assets Authority. The PFM donor group was also represented.

However the Committee only met sporadically, and was rarely a functional mechanism for coordination of PFM reforms. Between 2000 and 2006 the dialogue around general budget support in the context of the World Bank Poverty Reduction Support Credits was a far more effective forum for strengthening PFM. The use of PFM 'prior actions' put added managerial pressure on different actors to implement reforms (Williamson 2005).

5. Automation of financial management systems

5.1 *Early initiatives*

In the mid 1960s the Ministry of Finance established a data processing department which supported major data processing needs of government using mainframe based technology. This later became Uganda Computer Services (UCS). Processes in other government departments remained largely manual; there was no electronic link between UCS and these departments. All data capture, processing, and report generation had to be done at UCS.

For most of the 1980s and 1990s, UCS supported two main systems relevant to financial accountability, one for the government payroll and the other for cheque processing. UCS systems were exceedingly limited in terms of functionality, especially as demands for accountability expanded. For example, the cheque printing system could not generate accounting reports beyond those relating to cheques. The lack of integration with the budget implementation process meant that some expenditure data was not captured through the cheque printing system. Consequently, it was not captured in the government accounts either—undermining attempts to obtain a comprehensive accounting picture of government expenditure.

In 1988 a strategic financial information systems plan was drawn up by consultants for the development, implementation, and maintenance of an integrated financial management system. However, apart from a few elements such as enhancement to the UCS cheque printing system, it was never implemented due to a lack of both resources and commitment.

The reporting requirements resulting from reforms to the budget system during the 1990s highlighted the inadequacies of the technology and human resources. In the absence of an integrated system, a number of stand-alone solutions were developed in-house in the early 1990s for both recurrent and development (projects) budget management. These aided the capture, reporting and consolidation of budget numbers, as well as:

- Printing the budget book (estimates and approved budget);
- Capturing and reporting virements and supplementary expenditure;
- Managing monthly budget releases and reporting; and
- Strengthening budgetary control and eliminating budget overruns during implementation.

A key contribution of these small applications was increased awareness and a more informed demand for a comprehensive integrated financial management solution.

5.2 Rationale for the integrated financial management system

In 2003 the government finally began to implement computerized financial management systems. This was to be used as an opportunity to embed PFM reforms and provide the capacity to improve the productivity and delivery of the financial management and accountability processes (Bwoch 2002). The IFMS is an information technology based budgeting and accounting system designed to assist government entities to prepare budgets, plan budget requests, spend their budgets, manage and report on their financial activities, as well as deliver services to the public more efficiently, effectively, and economically.

The IFMS was meant to address a wide range of accountability and PFM weaknesses including poor maintenance of ledgers and asset registers, disregard of financial controls, and poor record keeping. Ministries and local governments were constrained by the poor state of financial systems. The 2001 Country Financial Accountability Assessment highlighted the poor state of financial management systems as a common problem affecting service delivery (World Bank 2001a). As a result, many organizations undertook independent initiatives to address their PFM concerns, often supported by donors. There was a proliferation of disparate and disjointed systems, standards, and even charts of accounts.

In addition, local governments had a separate compliance and reporting framework deriving from the Local Government Act. It allowed them to use a separate chart of accounts. Furthermore, some local governments used accounting systems different from those in central government.

The net effect was slow and ineffective national financial management systems. The World Bank summed up the state of the financial management system at the time as follows: 'the accuracy and reliability of accounting and reporting could not be assured' (World Bank 2001a).

IFMS was introduced in order to improve the delivery and credibility of financial management systems overall and to address the following issues in particular:

- Poor financial recording, tracking of budget commitments and expenditure, and reporting;
- Improving the quality and timeliness of reporting;
- Increasing the availability and timeliness of budget and expenditure data to support financial decisions; and
- Harmonizing standards for recording, accounting, and reporting between central and local government.

5.3 IFMS design and implementation

The IFMS that was introduced was based on a centralized database architecture with distributed access and transaction management, and was located at the Treasury, MoFPED. It was designed to provide electronic links to ministries and local governments over a wide area network. This enabled centralized management of the system while allowing agencies to process their financial transactions and reports as they wished. Ministries and departments obtained access to up-to-date financial data and became fully responsible for managing, and processing, commitments and payments, aspects of which were previously managed by MoFPED. Accounting Officers had better financial control and were more proficient in managing their operations. MoFPED was increasingly able to focus on its coordination and monitoring role.

The system was implemented in three phases; design, pilot, and roll out. The initial design took place in 2001/02 by way of a feasibility study. The system was then developed between 2002/03 and 2003/04 using a Central Implementation Team and focus groups.[6] Finally, the system went live in February 2004, covering six ministries and four local governments on six modules of the Oracle Financials. By 2006 the system had been extended to all eighteen ministries and to fourteen local governments. Interface links to the Bank of Uganda and URA enabled faster sharing of financial data, particularly on payments and tax collections respectively.

---

[6] The Central Implementation Team comprised government officers drawn from several ministries and agencies familiar with PFM business. The team reviewed the proposed business processes. The agreed designs were then presented to the focus group, which mainly comprised senior management of the various ministries and agencies.

5.4 Challenges to IFMS implementation

Introducing IFMS was arguably the most complex technical and institutional undertaking ever implemented by the Ugandan government. It faced a number of major challenges:

- *Proliferation of parallel systems*: stand alone systems were already being implemented or were under consideration in a number of ministries and local governments. A single integrated solution across government was seen as critical to fiscal and financial management and control. MoFPED therefore wrote to all ministries and local governments, prior to implementation, informing them about the plans for IFMS and requesting them to halt any parallel investments.

- *Attitudes and perceptions*: acceptance of government-wide systems was never going to be easy (Bwoch 2005b). Some interpreted IFMS as a measure to further centralize control in MoFPED. At a price of about USD20 million, the cost of the investment also raised concern. An intensive change management campaign was therefore necessary. Officers from across government were involved in the design and implementation while open sessions were organized for various groups, including politicians and managers, and information on the proposed systems was widely disseminated.

- *Scale of implementation*: given the limited accounting and information technology skills in government at the time, undertaking a project of this magnitude as an in-house bespoke solution was not an option. After examining the experience of IFMS implementation in Ghana and Tanzania, it was decided to use existing proven off-the-shelf solutions and to work with a single firm on a turnkey basis. This firm was to supply the entire solution and take full responsibility for delivery of all components. The government was responsible for overall supervision of the contract and availing counterpart staff to participate in implementation.

- *Staffing*: even with a turnkey approach, the government still faced large gaps in staffing levels. IFMS implementation required staff to support the training function and assist ministries and local governments in adopting the new systems. It was decided therefore to recruit up to ten local financial management experts (professional accountants), ICT consultants, project management professionals, and forty graduate interns (accountants and IT graduates) to meet these needs (Bwoch 2005a).

5.5 Benefits and lessons from IFMS

Initial results from IFMS implementation were encouraging and point to a number of benefits. An independent assessment considered implementation satisfactory and successful (Bhatt et al. 2004). For the first time in a central government accounting entity, the entire process flow from payment requisition to cheque printing could be completed (electronically) within about five hours. This process used to take at least three days. Many reports that used to take over three months could now be produced in under an hour. Another review established that ministries and local governments covered by IFMS were able to reconcile their accounts within thirty days following month closure, and could generate financial accounts much faster (within three months) and with much more flexibility (Asebe and Mwanje 2007).[7] Expenditure data can now be easily compared with budget data and reported on more accurately. Votes also have enhanced control and the processes are more transparent. Above all, Accounting Officers have better access to financial data, payment processing, and a more flexible reporting mechanism.

A number of lessons can also be drawn:

- *Top management leadership and client ownership*: the success of any reform is greatly dependent on the involvement of those at the top of the organization. The Deputy Secretary to the Treasury was the IFMS Project Sponsor who in turn liaised with the Permanent Secretary/Secretary to the Treasury. There was also consistent stakeholder involvement at all stages (design, formulation, development, and implementation) of the project, promoting ownership across government.

- *Change management*: effective delivery of extensive reform programmes calls for a comprehensive, well-thought out change management and communication strategy. A dedicated change management and communication team, reporting directly to the Accountant General, championed IFMS implementation (Kyama 2005).[8] The team was able to formulate a comprehensive strategy and to analyse and anticipate risks and to design mitigation measures.

- *Creating the right incentives*: given the low level of public service remuneration, building an effective incentive structure was critical to IFMS implementation. A strategy that sought to extend financial rewards to all those involved in IFMS implementation was adopted. An honorarium was paid to officers involved in the IFMS pilot for the period from commencement of implementation to the go-live date. This was a one-off payment designed to create a performance-oriented and motivated team.

- *'Quick wins'*: the order and pace of reform should be designed to show early gains—'quick wins'—to the key players, ensuring the credibility of early stages of reform and creating a basis for the successful development of later

---

[7] The same review also undertook a cost–benefit analysis at four sites. Internal rates of return in the range 20–45 per cent were calculated (Asebe and Mwanje 2007).

[8] A structured and dedicated team devoted to change management was identified as a critical parameter underlying successful system implementation.

stages (Kotter 1996). With this in mind, IFMS implementation involved project sequencing that yielded early visible outputs and benefits for the staff involved. For example, during site preparation many of the sites were equipped with computers and other facilities. A significant 'quick win' was the printing of cheques electronically on the system.

- *Political commitment*: securing the commitment of ministers and senior officials is critical to the success of any major reform. There needs to be a champion who has the motivation, authority, and drive to sustain the process. Unequivocal support from the Minister of Finance, Planning and Economic Development and top management was vital in driving the IFMS project. Leading politicians participated at various stages during the awareness and change management campaigns.

The roll out of IFMS implementation was still on-going in 2008. Only fourteen out of more than eighty local governments were covered. Even at central government level many agencies, including large spending institutions like the police and prisons, were yet to be connected.

The ultimate test will be whether the government is able to sustain IFMS once donor support ends. While donors funded most of the capital costs, government is responsible for recurrent operating costs.[9] Since 2003/04 provisions for IFMS recurrent costs have been included in the budgets of each of the entities implementing IFMS. The other key aspect of sustainability is the retention of skilled staff. A particular challenge for projects like this in poor countries is that staff becomes more marketable as a result of the skills acquired. Given the inflexibility of the public service pay structure, rapid staff turnover is probably unavoidable. This implies a high on-going requirement for training.

6. Overall impact of PFM reforms

The above reforms have had a positive impact in a number of areas, including improved timeliness of accounts, the attraction and retention of large numbers of professional accountants, and the successful deployment of an IFMS. While the timeliness and regularity of accounts reconciliation and the quality and timeliness of in-year budget returns have presented serious challenges (Pretorius 2006), progress has been made. External scrutiny and audit, as well as legislative scrutiny, of the annual budget have improved significantly. Since 2003 the scope and coverage of the Auditor General's work has been extended to cover classified expenditure.

---

[9] Recurrent costs for maintenance and support are about USD30,000 per annum per site. There are additional annual costs of about USD2 million for the data centres, WAN links, and Oracle application support that are managed directly under the Accountant General's Office.

There is a clearly perceptible trend of continuous improvement. For example, the Auditor General's 2006/07 Annual Report, observes that 'Generally there has been an improvement in timely submission' (Government of Uganda 2007). By 2006/07 63 per cent of the 272 votes submitted accounts within the statutory deadline, and most others submitted soon after. This improvement meant that the proportion of accounts the Auditor General was able to include in his reports increased from 63 per cent in 2003/04 to 89 per cent in 2006/07, with all central votes included. The quality of audit reports has also improved over time.

Despite this progress, concern has been expressed that PFM outcomes do not appear to be improving significantly (Pretorius 2006). In this regard, it is important to note that much of what is unfolding is work in progress, and that it takes time for reforms to yield results. The reforms *per se* are not sufficient to deliver the desired outcomes. Rather, it is the combined interplay of well-sequenced strategic interventions that is necessary to achieve the benefits from the reforms (Williamson 2005).

Major achievements in the establishment of PFM can be summarized as follows:

- A clear and comprehensive legal and policy framework;
- An improved institutional set up for PFM through a restructured Accountant General's Office and Office of the Auditor General;
- A stable functional IFMS being rolled out across government; and
- Greatly improved human resource capacity (i.e. increased number of professional accountants) and training infrastructure.

These represent significant achievements. The challenge is to translate this progress into improved PFM outcomes.

7. Conclusions

While financial management and accountability reform started later than economic reform, there is no doubt that significant progress has been made, primarily in the areas of legal, institutional, and system reforms. This can be attributed largely to the following factors:

- *Learning process*: because financial management reforms only began to take off in the late 1990s, several years after the key economic reforms, they were able to build upon the experience gained during the first wave of reforms. A number of officers involved in the economic reforms were now in management positions. They recognized the importance of PFM reform for the consolidation of economic reforms and were able to apply their experience in formulating and implementing reforms.

- *Strong leadership*: both at the political level and within MoFPED, was critical in driving PFM reform. The continuity of this leadership throughout the 1990s and into the 2000s was also important.

- *A critical mass of well-motivated staff was vital*: the implementation of new systems could not have been contemplated with the staff numbers and public service terms and conditions pertaining in the late 1990s. Reforms must be well resourced to ensure implementation.

- *Sequencing of reforms*: there was no conscious sequenced strategy in carrying out the above reforms. However, the constitutional, economic, and structural reforms of the early 1990s laid a good base for financial management reforms. Sequencing makes it possible to match reforms with the institutional capacity to absorb them.

More work remains to be done on PFM reform in Uganda. The biggest challenges include ensuring sustainability of and continued political commitment to changes already introduced. The PFM situation for local governments in particular remains fragile due in part to the continued expansion in their numbers. Progress in PFM is always at risk of being reversed by political decisions.

16

Privatization and Parastatal Reform

Emmanuel Nyirinkindi and Michael Opagi

1. Introduction

Uganda's experience of direct state engagement in commercial activity, through wholly or partially publicly owned enterprises, predates Independence in 1962. In most cases, and specifically those involving large utility and service providers, these government commercial entities took the form of statutory corporations (established by Statute or Act of Parliament). However, public enterprises or parastatals (PEs) were created under different circumstances and took various forms.

Particularly after Independence, the key drivers behind the creation of parastatals were: (i) the need to establish and maintain control over sectors which government perceived as strategic (the 'commanding heights' of the economy); (ii) the unwillingness of the private sector to undertake large investments (this was the basis for the creation of Uganda Development Corporation with a mandate to enter into joint ventures with the private sector); (iii) the perceived need to promote and develop the country's nascent entrepreneurs; and (iv) political and ideological considerations that led to the nationalization of some private companies.

From the mid-1950s and throughout the 1960s, economic policy supported a 'mixed economy', where both the public and private sectors engaged in commercial activity. The public sector was dominant in the provision of infrastructure (electricity, water, railways, telecommunications), and the private sector in commerce, industry, banking, and finance. Many of the large sector based PEs (e.g. crop marketing boards, housing and construction, insurance, dairy processing, commercial banking) were established during the period 1964–68, mainly via joint ventures. While some of these enterprises were set up to achieve certain political and social objectives, resource mobilization was the primary aim.

Although little data is available, the parastatal sector is widely believed to have been relatively well managed prior to 1971 and to have contributed significantly to the strong industrial performance of the economy. In particular, Uganda Development Corporation[1] and its subsidiaries, the crop processing and marketing boards, Uganda Hotels, and Uganda Commercial Bank were all seen as strong performers during this period, as were the infrastructure institutions of the East African Community.

Participation of the state in the economy expanded throughout the 1970s, albeit in a chaotic fashion. Four distinct phases of expansion within the parastatal sector can be identified during the period 1970 to 1976:

i) Acceleration of the nationalization policy following the 1 May 1970 Nakivubo Pronouncements. This followed the Obote administration's policy shift in 1969 described as the 'move to the left'. It resulted in the government nationalizing almost 60 per cent of all companies, industries, and financial institutions (Mutibwa 1992).

ii) The expulsion of the Asian community in 1972 resulted in a large number of enterprises being nationalized. These were mainly large industrial and commercial concerns involved in import substitution production. However, the mismanagement of these and other enterprises under state ownership and control led to a steep decline in industrial output. Acute economic mismanagement, combined with the breakdown of infrastructure, shortages of essential inputs, spare parts, and consumer goods, affected production throughout the economy. This led to the next wave of PEs; a range of enterprises was established with the sole objective of importing and distributing consumer goods such as houseware, machinery, and spare parts.[2]

iii) The collapse of the East African Community in 1976 led to the creation of a number of large public utilities, which had previously been run regionally, mainly in the areas of transport and communications. Being both large-scale and capital-intensive enterprises, they required investment and technology beyond the willingness and capability of the Ugandan private sector.

iv) A number of PEs were also created as subsidiaries, through internal growth and diversification as well as forward and backward linkages, by a number of the marketing boards, trading companies, and industrial enterprises.

All parastatals were affected by the general economic collapse during the Idi Amin regime and the turmoil following his removal from power (1971–79). By 1986 the PE sector had 129 parastatals and approximately 45,000 employees. The industrial parastatals, which accounted for 46 per cent of the industrial

---

[1] Uganda Development Corporation was created to initiate large projects in which the private sector was unwilling to commit large investment resources. It participated through joint ventures with the private sector.

[2] Foods and Beverages, Uganda Hardware, Uganda Motors, Uganda Industrial Machinery, Uganda General Merchandise, Uganda Pharmaceuticals, Transocean (Uganda), and Intra-African Trading Co.

work force, were virtually all operating below 30 per cent of production capacity. Fewer than 30 per cent of PEs made operating surpluses, most relying on direct funding from government. Net financial transfers to parastatals totalled some USD25 million between 1982 and 1986 (Privatization Unit reports). In addition, parastatals accounted for much of the loan portfolio of the government-owned Uganda Commercial Bank and Uganda Development Bank (UDB). These loans later formed a significant proportion of both banks' written-off portfolio in the late 1990s.

When the National Resistance Movement came to power in 1986 it inherited a PE sector that was in fast decline. Buildings and equipment were run down, destroyed, and looted, many records were missing and legal issues unresolved, and the workforce had little motivation to work. The 'performance of these enterprises was characterised by low productivity, high losses, and rising debts, which placed a considerable burden on the banking system, public finances, and the balance of payments' (Collier and Reinikka 2001: 37).

Given the very limited resources at its disposal and the massive financial challenge of rebuilding almost all sectors of the shattered economy, the new government decided to rationalize its PE portfolio and to operate PEs along commercial lines as far as possible.

This chapter discusses the measures adopted by the government of Uganda since 1987 to address the crisis in the PE sector. Section 2 sets out the policy foundations for PE reform and divestiture adopted since 1987. Section 3 looks at changes to the legal framework. Section 4 discusses the implementation of the new policies. Section 5 looks at the proceeds of divestiture and the uses to which they have been applied. Section 6 presents the findings of impact assessments of the programme. Section 7 draws out some of the main lessons from the Ugandan experience. Appendix 16.1 looks at reforms relating specifically to infrastructure utilities.

2. Parastatal policy from 1987

In developing its Economic Recovery Programme in 1987, the new government identified the private sector as the 'engine' of economic growth: it recognized that the PE sector was an obstacle to growth. It decided, therefore, to undertake a comprehensive reform of the sector with a view to reducing its financial and administrative burden.

In 1989 the Ministry of Finance obtained funding from the World Bank for a Public Enterprises Project to support the PE reform process. The project, which was managed by a new Public Enterprise Secretariat based in the ministry, included technical assistance and capacity building to the Secretariat, to the Public Industrial Enterprise Secretariat in the Ministry of Industry and Technology, and to Uganda Development Corporation.

The Public Enterprise Secretariat commissioned a number of studies to prepare for the PE reform programme. Of particular significance was the 1990 Action Plan for Public Enterprise Reform and Divestiture (APPERD). The Action Plan set out the main policy principles, components, and guidelines for divestiture and parastatal reform. The main thrust of the policy was, first, to reduce the size of the PE sector (and correspondingly increase the role of the private sector) and, second, to ensure that those PEs that remained under government ownership and management operated efficiently. The action plan set clear targets for the number of PEs to be rehabilitated, privatized, and liquidated; it also included a package of supporting policies and administrative reforms, and the proposed institutional arrangements. Although elements have been modified over time, APPERD provided the foundation for the parastatal reform and privatization process through to the mid 2000s.

APPERD classified PEs into five categories:

- Class I. These were to remain fully government owned because they operated in strategic or sensitive industries (16 PEs);
- Class II. Government would retain majority ownership as the PEs were considered economically viable, security (politically) sensitive—or they provided essential services (24 PEs);
- Class III. Government would retain minority ownership in some PEs they were considered economically viable and were expected to undertake high cost projects which would only attract private equity and technology if government was a partner (10 PEs);
- Class IV. Economically viable and commercially oriented PEs which were to be fully divested (46 PEs); and
- Class V. Economically non-viable PEs, including defunct and dormant ones, which were to be liquidated (17 PEs).

The list was developed as a guide to direct implementation of the programme in the short term, and did not represent a comprehensive listing of the PE sector. In particular, it excluded PEs in the banking sector, which was to be treated differently. Line ministries participating in APPERD were given the flexibility to reclassify PEs following a more detailed technical evaluation.

The programme was to be implemented in phases. The main focus of the initial five-year phase was the immediate restructuring of Uganda Development Corporation (UDC), with the intention of enabling it to revert to its original role as an investment promotion agency while removing its holding company role. This led to the de-linking from UDC of a number of its subsidiaries, which were then earmarked for divestiture.

2.1 *Divestiture*

Valuation of PEs would be based on market, rather than book, value. Unviable PEs would be liquidated and their assets sold off. Joint venture partners would be allowed to exercise management control without interference. Foreign investment would be considered where there was a need for external equity, management, and/or technology. Government undertook to resolve all legal issues affecting a PE before putting it up for sale, while making clear that no undue advantage or protection would be offered to investors.

To encourage investor interest in divestiture, the government agreed to privatize PEs with attractive investment (profit) potential and to provide access to term finance for rehabilitation of PEs (primarily through the Uganda Development Bank). It also undertook to provide managerial autonomy and control on fully commercial principles and to encourage commercial banks to provide credit.

2.2 *Parastatal reform*

There would be a 'hard budget constraint'[3] and greater financial discipline in the relationship between government and PEs. Government subsidies to commercial PEs would cease, while those to non-commercial PEs would be channelled through the Public Investment Plan (PIP, see Chapter 6) and subject to approved corporate plans. This was important, as PE funding had previously circumvented the requirement that all public investments be subject to the normal annual budgeting process that established public spending and investment priorities. Competition would be promoted by removing restrictions to entry and, in the case of natural monopolies, developing suitable regulatory mechanisms in supervising ministries.

Commercial and non-commercial objectives would be clearly distinguished, with the latter supported through transparent public subsidies from the Treasury to cover losses on non-commercial activities that the government wanted to continue. This represented a break with the widely held view that it was acceptable for PEs to incur perennial losses, borne by government, simply on the basis that they were providing a public service. In most instances, these services were not identified, quantified, or verified to ensure the public was receiving value for money. For example, the Uganda Railways Corporation operated a number of commercially non-viable services, which drained its resources. From 1994, however, the losses on these services were quantified and an explicit subsidy was paid through the budget (see Appendix 16.1).

Government proposed to allow increased managerial autonomy and cede control of operational matters to PE boards and management, while demanding greater accountability from both. An independent and transparent mechanism

---

[3] A hard budget constraint strictly limits PE expenditure to a specific budget approved by government. It aims to address the perennial practice of PE budget overruns.

for selecting experienced and qualified board directors was to be developed. While work commenced on preparation of a database of technically competent and experienced nationals from which government would select board directors, this was abandoned in the mid-1990s. Finally, government intended developing a performance monitoring and evaluation system, as well as an incentive mechanism to reward good, and penalize poor, performance. However, again little progress was made on this front.

3. Legal framework

The APPERD programme was formally adopted by Cabinet in 1991. By August 1993 the divestiture of five enterprises had been completed. However, due to the lack of a legal basis, Parliament suspended the privatization programme pending the enactment of a supporting law. In 1993 the Public Enterprise Reform and Divestiture Statute (PERD Statute) was enacted to provide the legal framework for implementation of the privatization programme. It reflected all the components and policy elements of APPERD. President Museveni was keenly engaged in the intense policy debate in Parliament and was instrumental in ensuring and hastening passage of the Statute.

As well as legalizing the initial APPERD programme and supporting policies, the PERD Statute provided an opportunity to streamline the implementation framework and provide flexibility to adapt to changing circumstances. It sought to: (a) enable the reduction of government equity holding in PEs; (b) promote institutional arrangements, policies, and procedures for ensuring the efficient and successful management of PEs; and (c) support the growth of local entrepreneurship. The PERD Statute was divided into five main parts, supported by four schedules.

3.1 *Institutional framework*

The Statute established the Divestiture and Reform Implementation Committee (DRIC) as the body responsible for the programme, and also specified its membership and functions. The Committee initially had representation from the Parliamentary committees on the National Economy and for Statutory Corporations. This was subsequently revoked in recognition of Parliament's conflict of interest in participating both in the implementation and oversight of the programme.

3.2 *Conduct of PEs*

The Statute provided the operating principles for PEs—allowing for managerial autonomy and control, outlining reporting requirements for monitoring and evaluation, and stressing accountability. This section was subsequently strengthened to reflect a better understanding of the practices that were weakening PEs and to give greater powers to the Ministry of Finance and Economic Planning (MoFEP), relative to parastatal management, to enforce financial discipline and oversight.

3.3 Reform/restructuring

The Statute established principles for financial discipline and criteria for reform and restructuring of PEs.

3.4 Divestiture

The Statute provided principles for the sale and transfer of enterprises, as well as the legal basis for the establishment and operation of a divestiture and a redundancy account. Subsequent amendments to the law brought greater clarity to the process of implementing divestiture and the Divestiture Procedures Manual was integrated into the law.

3.5 Reporting

The Statute required biannual progress reports to be submitted to Parliament; it provided for its own primacy (in situations when it conflicted with any other statute) for purposes of implementation of divestiture; and included provisions regulating any amendment to itself and its supporting schedules.

A number of amendments to the Statute were adopted subsequently. In 1997 Class III (PEs in which government was required to retain a minority shareholding) was eliminated and all Class III PEs were moved to Class IV (full divestment). The Divestiture Guidelines were also revised in 1997.

In 1998 amendments were passed to the Statute that required Parliamentary approval for any PE reclassification. This arose from Parliament's desire to remove DRIC's legal authority to reclassify PEs within the various classes and required the minister in charge of privatization to inform Parliament on reclassification. This amendment mainly arose from concerns about the reclassification of Uganda Commercial Bank (UCB), whose privatization was one of the most contentious in the entire programme.

In 1998 the privatization programme was suspended for a second time, following a Parliamentary resolution, and was investigated by a Select Committee of Parliament.[4] This followed a national outcry regarding perceived political interference and corruption in the privatization of key PEs. As a result, a

---

[4] The Committee's report covered several key divestiture transactions (e.g. UCB, Hima Cement, Uganda Airlines, Transocean, and Uganda Air Cargo). It made several recommendations relating to revision of the PERD Act, standardization of implementation procedures for the divestiture programme, as well as the prosecution of individuals and officials considered to have caused financial loss to government.

comprehensive revision of the PERD Statute was undertaken leading to the PERD Act Amendment of 2000. This streamlined the Act and increased the transparency of the privatization process. It reduced Parliament's direct involvement in programme implementation and introduced a minister responsible for privatization, while subjecting the programme to greater oversight by the legislature.

Additional amendments following the 1998 Parliamentary review included reducing DRIC's role with regard to policy approval (with technical work left to the Privatization Unit) and the introduction of an offences section (providing for fines and jail terms for financial losses caused by PE management and boards). Lastly, procedural guidelines were adopted to further streamline the divestiture process and ensure its transparency.

Box 16.1 outlines the generic steps adopted for a typical privatization transaction.

4. Implementation

Implementation of the privatization and parastatal reform programme can be divided into three broad phases:

Box 16.1 GENERIC STEPS IN TYPICAL PRIVATIZATION TRANSACTIONS

- **Preliminary Matters:** policy approval (Cabinet/ministerial); formation of technical working group; conduct of due diligence studies (financial, legal, and valuations) on PE;
- **Divestiture Action Plan:** DRIC reviews a summary of due diligence information and approves the plan outlining government objectives, mode of privatization, and bidder pre-qualification criteria;
- **Pre-qualification (where relevant):** call for expressions of interest and issuance of pre-qualification terms of reference; short listing of eligible bidders who then proceed to the bidding stage;
- **Bidding:** issuance of bidding documents (request for proposals, information memoranda, sale and purchase agreements), carrying out of investigative due diligence on short listed bidders (including verification of bidder pre-qualification documentation); conduct of pre-bid negotiations on legal agreements—responses and final legal agreements circulated to all bidders; and
- **Selection of bidder:** pre-qualified bidders submit separate technical and financial bid envelopes; financial envelopes for bidders with compliant technical bids are opened and the winning bid is chosen using clear and objective criteria.

The Expressions of Interest, receipt of pre-qualification documents, and submission of final bid documents are conducted in public with the events covered by the media.

PHASE 1: 1987–1994

This spans the period until the suspension and restructuring of the APPERD programme in 1994. Prior to the commencement of privatization sales in 1992, the main divestiture activity was the return of Asian properties (see Box 16.2).

The key objectives during this phase were to define and implement reforms in the PE sector policy and legislative framework while strengthening sector administration and individual enterprise management; to prepare and initiate an overall programme of rehabilitation and rationalization of all PEs; and to begin to implement a programme of rehabilitation, restructuring, divestiture, and liquidation of selected industrial parastatals. The earlier emphasis on publicly financed rehabilitation of PEs prior to divestiture was downgraded by 1993 in recognition of the fact that such programmes had not produced the anticipated results and were often discounted by potential buyers.

From 1987 reforms were led by the Ministry of Finance, initially through its Statutory Corporations Division and from 1989 through the PERD Secretariat. In 1991, with the implementation of the APPERD programme, a minor institutional restructuring took place with the appointment of a coordinator for the PERD Secretariat and the creation of a new entity—the Divestiture Secretariat—to implement the privatization programme. The Public Industrial Enterprise Secretariat focused on industrial PEs, the Public Enterprise Secretariat became

---

Box 16.2 RETURN OF DEPARTED ASIAN PROPERTIES

In one of the most notorious episodes in Ugandan history, in 1972 Idi Amin expelled some 80,000 Asians (many of them citizens) and expropriated their properties and businesses (Mutibwa 1992). After the restoration of civilian government in 1980, the Expropriated Properties Act 1982 vested the properties in the hands of the government, managed by the Departed Asians Property Custodian Board. It allowed 'departed Asians' to apply for repossession of their properties, and empowered the Ministry of Finance to sell off unrepossessed properties and pay their former owners compensation. The Act gave the Asians ninety days within which to apply for repossession. However, although over 10,000 applications were received, only about 300 properties were repossessed between 1983 and 1986, mainly large enterprises such as tea and sugar estates, breweries, tobacco, and textile factories. While this was partly due to the civil war, it also reflected resistance from the significant number of Ugandans who feared the return of Asian dominance of the economy or were renting Asian properties cheaply from the government.

In 1989 the government created a position of Minister of State in charge of Custodian Board under the Ministry of Finance to expedite the disposal of Custodian Board properties. This politically brave act was significant in demonstrating government commitment to private sector development, to the rule of law, and to the reinforcement of property rights. In 1991 the government made a worldwide appeal to 'departed Asians' to repossess their property; this was arguably the start of the privatization programme. Over 3,000 fresh applications were received. By 1997 some 4,000 properties had been returned and a further 1,500 sold off.

---

the focal point for developing and implementing PE reform policies, while UDC continued to manage (and increasingly to hand over for divestiture) its holding companies.

During this period studies were completed which formed the basis for the APPERD policy. Diagnostic studies undertaken in 1991 on the Bank of Uganda, Uganda Commercial Bank, and Uganda Development Bank formed the basis for reforms in the banking sector. A series of management audits formed the basis for restructuring a number of industrial PEs.

Appendix 16.2 lists all divestiture transactions up to June 2007. Fifteen divestitures were completed up to 1994, of which five were undertaken through the sale of assets, four through the sale of shares, four through repossession by previous owners, one through a joint venture, and one (Shell Uganda Ltd) through the transfer of government's shareholding in settlement of debts owed to the buyer. Nine of these divestitures were to foreign firms.

PHASE 2: 1995–1999

In January 1995 the entire privatization programme was overhauled due to concern about the pace of implementation. Implementation was suspended for six months and new staff recruited to manage the programme under a newly appointed Minister of State for Finance for Privatization. The establishment of a ministerial post specifically to manage privatization was in recognition of the programme's high political profile and the need for a full-time political head who could: (a) provide a communication link to Cabinet, Parliament, and the public; (b) exercise operational oversight; and (c) assist the programme's managers in addressing challenges beyond their authority to resolve (such as labour disputes or differences of opinion with sector ministries).

To streamline programme implementation, new operational entities were created under MoFEP to manage the process. A Privatization Unit and a Parastatal Monitoring Unit replaced the Divestiture Secretariat, the Public Industrial Enterprises Secretariat, and the Public Enterprise Secretariat. The role of UDC was changed from that of a manager of PEs to a holding company of a steadily diminishing portfolio as its subsidiaries were divested. The Privatization Unit was given a mandate to implement divestiture of PEs, while the Parastatal Monitoring Unit (PMU) was mandated to record, supervise, and manage financial flows between PEs and the government on behalf of MoFEP. It was also tasked with ensuring adherence to the 'hard budget constraint' determined by government for each PE. The Directors of both Units, while granted extensive operational autonomy, were placed administratively under the Secretary to the Treasury.

The key objectives during this phase were to accelerate the pace and efficiency of the divestiture process, to complement the general policy of economic liberalization and competition, and to increase Ugandan ownership in divested entities.

During this period the first initial public offering (IPO) was issued on the newly formed Uganda Stock Exchange (USE) through the divestiture of government's interest in Uganda Clays Ltd. In addition, the first management buyout transactions of PEs were undertaken.

The pace of implementation accelerated as a result of increasing experience with the technical process of divestiture, as well as the institution of clearer processes and guidelines for transactions. Forty-seven transactions were completed during this period. Fifteen divestitures were undertaken through the sale of assets, fifteen through the sale of shares (including an IPO), six through the auction of assets to the highest bidder, four through the exercise of pre-emptive rights by government's partners in private companies, three through management buyouts, two through concessions, and two through joint venture and repossession. Twenty-nine of these divestitures were to Ugandan firms or individuals and seventeen to foreign firms.

PHASE 3: 1999–2006

The key goals and objectives during this phase were to ensure greater transparency in the transaction process (see Box 16.3), to broaden the distribution of ownership in divested entities, to increase investment in the infrastructure and tourism sectors, and to accelerate infrastructure utility reform.

A Divestiture Procedures Manual was commissioned to detail and streamline the formal processes for divestiture, and guidelines for implementation were passed into law by Parliament. Guidelines for the prioritization and protection of workers' termination benefits were designed and adopted.

In 1999 a Utility Reform Unit was created within the renamed Ministry of Finance, Planning and Economic Development (MoFPED) to coordinate reforms in the infrastructure sector. Following the creation of the Uganda Communications Commission in 1997 as an independent regulatory agency for the telecommunications sector, the establishment of regulatory agencies for the basic infrastructure sectors led to accelerated divestitures. Liberalization and privatization of the telecommunications sector led to a substantial increase in access and quality of service, and to lower prices (Shirley et al. 2002; Byaruhanga 2005). Utility reform is discussed in Appendix 16.1.

During this period a number of long-term (twenty- to fifty-year) and complex transactions were implemented, including:

- Divestiture of Uganda Commercial Bank which enabled greater competition in the commercial banking sector, wider branch networks, and a successful IPO by Stanbic Bank;
- The joint concession of the Kenya–Uganda railway;
- Divestiture of several major hotels (Kampala Sheraton, Nile, and Lake Victoria Hotels); and

---

Box 16.3 BROADENING PARTICIPATION AND TRANSPARENCY

In the early years of the programme, parastatal divestiture and reform was seen as a largely technical process undertaken by the various implementing agencies within the finance ministry. However, this approach was gradually abandoned from 1999 in order to include representatives from sector ministries and other government agencies in the decision-making process leading to a PE's divestiture. Privatization implementation teams were organized around technical working groups, which included representatives from sector ministries, regulatory agencies, and sector PEs. These groups collectively addressed issues vital to the successful implementation of privatization and determined the transaction structures to be implemented. They also participated in the privatization operations (including review of transaction documentation, bid tendering, evaluation, award and subsequent contract negotiations, and closing).

During the overhaul of the privatization programme in 1999, the need to engage with non-traditional partners assumed greater prominence. Major divestiture initiatives only proceeded after consulting with Parliament, organized labour, and concerned business associations. While this was very time consuming, it limited (without eliminating) resistance to controversial elements of divestiture and reform. Nevertheless, organized labour typically continued to press for higher terminal benefits while business operators, in the main, opposed tariff increases on principle.

Recognition of the importance of public communication was one of the reasons a Minister of State in charge of Privatization was appointed in 1995. Several public information campaigns were undertaken through the media from 1999. In 2001 it was decided to abandon the use of external public relations firms and instead an office was created within the Privatization Unit. The Unit was linked more directly to Parliament and other key stakeholders; press relations and communications became more organized and effective.

- Divestitures in the agri-business sector (Kinyara Sugar, Kakira Sugar, Rwenzori Highland Tea, Kyempisi and Kiryana ranches).

This period saw the largest and most complex transactions undertaken throughout the privatization programme, using various transaction methods (asset sales, share sales, pre-emptive rights share sales,[5] concessions, IPOs, and management buy-outs). To ensure broader ownership of nationals in the divested entities contractual commitments to sell shares to the public were written into the divestiture agreements for DFCU Ltd, the Stanbic Bank purchase of UCB, and the electricity and railway concessions. The first two resulted in highly successful IPOs, which helped broaden public ownership.

---

[5] Pre-emptive rights are essentially the legal right (as pre-determined within the Articles of Association) of government's partners to buy the government's shares (and vice versa if necessary) within the co-owned entity should government exercise its right to sell any of its shares.

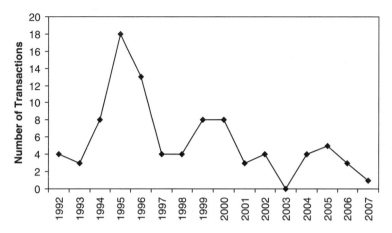

Figure 16.1 Number of Divestitures by Year

Source: Privatization Unit, Ministry of Finance, Planning and Economic Development.

Twenty-nine transactions were completed during the period. Two divestitures were undertaken through the sale of assets, six through the sale of shares, five through the exercise of pre-emptive rights by government's partners in private companies, nine through concessions, four through IPOs, one through a debt for equity swap (sovereign bilateral debt settled through the transfer of a minority shareholding in National Housing and Construction Corporation), and one through a management buy-out. Ten of these divestitures were to Ugandan firms or individuals and fifteen to foreign firms, while the four IPOs were to both.

Figure 16.1 illustrates the number of transactions undertaken each year between 1992 and 2007. It can be seen that the largest number of transactions took place in the mid-1990s.

5. Divestiture proceeds

The proceeds of the divestiture process—their magnitude, accountability, and use—have been the subject of continued public controversy. This stems largely from concerns that public assets were sold for too low a price, that some were never fully paid for, and that the proceeds were not used wisely or in accordance with the law.

With regard to the magnitude of sales proceeds, the public perception that sales values were too low reflected poor understanding of the concept of discounted cash flow valuation. The PERD Statute required that a 'fair' value be obtained for each public entity disposed of; the guidelines accompanying the statute spelt out some valuation methods. Prior to the statute, there were no guidelines in place and valuations tended to be 'more of an art than a science'. Following passage of the statute, valuation practices were continuously refined. By value, the largest divestiture transactions handled by the Privatization Unit were Uganda Telecom Ltd (51 per cent share sale in 2000 at USD33.5 million), Kinyara Sugar Works (51 per cent share sale in 2006 at USD33 million), Uganda Cement Industries, Hima (100 per cent asset sale in 1994 at USD20.5 million), Apolo Hotel Corporation (100 per cent share sale in 2001 at USD18 million), and Stanbic Bank (10 per cent share sale through an IPO in 2007 at UGX31 billion, equivalent to USD17.3 million).

Regarding accountability, the proceeds of divestiture are by law required to be retained with commercial banks and, as with all government accounts, audited by the Office of the Auditor General. These accounts are collectively referred to as the Privatization Unit's Divestiture Account, which was created in 1993.

Table 16.1 Cumulative Divestiture Proceeds to June 2006: Sources and Uses

	UGX million	USD million
Sources of Divestiture Account Funds		
Divestiture/Sales Proceeds	303,027	163
Government Contribution	40,491	22
Other Income (Interest, Debt Settlement Fees, Forex gains)	54,344	29
Total income	**397,862**	**214**
Major Uses of Divestiture Account Funds		
Caretaker costs	47,764	26
Liabilities assumed on behalf of PEs	85,641	46
Professional fees and statutory expenses	71,530	38
Terminal benefits	113,395	61
Arbitration awards	7,903	4
Provision for doubtful debts	72	0
Bad and doubtful debts	29,234	16
Total divestiture costs	**355,539**	**191**
Net Surplus	**42,323**	**23**

Notes:
1. The table shows cumulative sources and uses of divestiture proceeds from 1 September 1993 to 30 June 2006. The Privatization Unit retains several accounts in commercial banks in which are deposited proceeds from the divestiture of PEs, as well as investment income arising from these deposits. These accounts are collectively referred to as the Divestiture Account. Funds for the payment of worker termination settlements are retained in a separate fund financed from divestiture proceeds, which is by law referred to as the Redundancy Account.
2. Since inception, the Privatization Unit has recorded its proceeds in Uganda shillings. All proceeds received in foreign currencies (primarily the US dollar) are translated at the ruling exchange rate and the proceeds recorded in Shillings.
3. The US dollar figures above are purely illustrative. Since an annual breakdown is not available, they have all been converted from the shilling balances at the Bank of Uganda mid-rate as at 30 June 2006, USD1 = UGX1,859.

Source: Office of the Auditor General. Audited Accounts for the Divestiture and Redundancy Accounts for the year ended 30 June 2006.

Since 1995 all disbursements from the account have been pre-audited by the Auditor General, with annual audits undertaken by the big four accounting firms on a rotating basis. In accordance with the PERD Statute, semi-annual reports have been presented to Parliament on the proceeds and uses of these funds as well as on operations of the privatization programme.

Turning to the uses of divestiture proceeds, a key decision in 1996 was that government would assume direct responsibility for settling the terminal benefits of retrenched employees. Even employees retained by the new owners were paid their entitlements so as to avoid a repeat of earlier experiences where workers suffered delayed payment of their benefits, or even missed them completely in the worst case. As a result, worker terminal payments accounted for 30 per cent of all payments from the proceeds of divestiture between 1993 and 2006. Liabilities that were assumed on behalf of divested enterprises, including some that were liquidated and for which proceeds were not collected, accounted for 24 per cent of payments. Professional fees and costs (legal, technical, and accounting) accounted for a further 20 per cent of disbursements up to June 2006 (see Table 16.1).

While the privatization process itself was largely financed from divestiture proceeds, administrative costs (staff and technical assistance) were mainly financed by donors.

6. Impact of the divestiture programme

Until 2004 the Privatization Unit attempted to identify the impact of its programme through conducting enterprise level impact assessments (UMACIS 2000). In 2004 the Unit commissioned a comprehensive impact assessment of privatization in seven sectors (agro-processing, textiles, manufacturing, banking, tourism, transport/oil distribution, and telecom/business services) over the period 1993–2003. The results were mixed and highlighted the difficulty of obtaining sufficient data to draw firm conclusions (Adam Smith International et al. 2005).[6]

The assessment found that privatization had generated positive outcomes for certain enterprises and stakeholder groups. The major beneficiary was the national treasury through: (a) reduced outflows to PEs; (b) increased tax revenues from privatized entities; and (c) increased dividends from PEs in which government had retained a shareholding. In addition, the programme had

---

[6] The report points out the inability to conduct a counterfactual analysis due to the lack of accurate, reliable, and complete pre-privatization data. Data were obtained for only 32 of 65 contacted enterprises. Only 19 of the 32 enterprises that provided data were able to provide at least 3 years of pre- and post-privatization financial data. The other 13 only provided post-privatization data.

created and promoted competition in sectors previously dominated by PEs and had helped attract foreign direct investment not only to privatized enterprises but also to green field projects. Privatization had also led to increases in casual employment, which by then had out-stripped formal employment in privatized enterprises.

The assessment noted that Uganda's privatization proceeds up to 2005 were the eleventh highest of the forty-eight countries for which data were available. However, after accounting for divestiture costs, the Treasury had not received significant direct monetary inflows from the proceeds of divested enterprises. The programme had not generated significant direct formal employment in privatized enterprises, while indirect formal employment was limited. Finally, the report concluded that divestitures up to 2004 had not generated sufficiently broad based ownership among Ugandan business operators and small investors. While Ugandans had bought a significant proportion of divested enterprises in terms of absolute numbers, these were mainly relatively small, low value enterprises, thereby limiting the impact.

6.1 *Subsidies*

A key policy objective of the privatization programme was the reduction of the financial burden imposed by the public sector on the Treasury. Initially, the focus was on the direct financial impact of direct budgetary transfers, as well as on payments guaranteed by government on behalf of PEs. However, by 1995 there was a more nuanced understanding of the magnitude of the problem. Since 1995 the Parastatal Monitoring Unit has prepared an annual report that measures both direct and indirect subsidies to the PE sector.[7] The first report, for fiscal year 1994, found that indirect subsidies that PEs derived purely on the basis of their ownership were several orders of magnitude larger than the direct financial payments. The review highlighted the opportunity cost of government engagement in PEs and identified both the enterprises responsible for the largest subsidies and the key sectors.

Over time, the annual PMU subsidy reports became an increasingly important guide to the privatization drive. Prior to 1997, the selection of PEs to be divested (or restructured) was based on a mix of considerations such as speed and ease of implementation, size of proceeds expected, and spread of shareholding (particularly for IPOs). By 1997 there was a greater appreciation of the need to target those PEs that were the major recipients of subsidies, particularly in the utility and financial services sectors.

---

[7] This report is based on direct measurement of subsidies to a sample of representative PEs that is then extrapolated to the entire sector. As the sector has reduced significantly since 1995, the sample has represented an increasing proportion of the total sector.

An intriguing phenomenon that was often experienced shortly after the completion of divestiture was that, while PE direct subsidies reduced, large indirect subsidies were introduced. For example, balance sheet restruction; pre-diverstiture involved writing off government guaranteed foreign loans from PEs' books. However, the divestiture proceeds were not sufficient to offset these amounts. In some cases, substantial direct subsidies were made to prepare a PE for sale—the largest of which were bonds issued on behalf of UCB in 1997/98.

The reduction of subsidies to the PE sector as a whole, particularly the massive indirect subsidies which dwarfed direct budgetary contributions, was a clear benefit of the divestiture programme. This is illustrated in Figure 16.2. Other African privatization drives have also been characterized by relatively low divestiture proceeds which are enhanced by reduced public financing of inefficiently managed PEs (Berthelemy 2004; Pamacheche and Koma 2007).

6.2 Tax revenue

A key benefit of privatization for government is where private sector led improvements (through increased investment and operational efficiency) result in

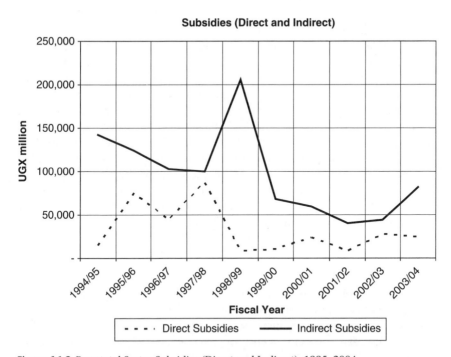

Figure 16.2 Parastatal Sector Subsidies (Direct and Indirect), 1995–2004

Source: Parastatal Monitoring Unit, Ministry of Finance, Planning and Economic Development.

greater tax revenues than would have occurred without privatization. Ugandan privatized enterprises now account for the bulk of all taxes paid to Uganda Revenue Authority (Adam Smith International et al. 2005: 26). Many of the largest taxpayers today are companies that have been divested or created as a result of the reform programme (such as the utilities, tourism concessions, and newly formed entities such as MTN).

6.3 Economic efficiency gains

Due to data limitations, the Impact Assessment limited its analysis to two efficiency indicators—profitability and labour productivity. It found that profitability had increased significantly following privatization in the banking, telecommunications, and oil distribution/transportation sectors, less significantly in agro-processing and had deteriorated in the tourism and textile sectors (Adam Smith International et al. 2005). Labour productivity had increased significantly in telecommunications, agro-processing, and oil distribution/transport. Tourism productivity only increased after the year 2000.

6.4 Investment

The Uganda Investment Authority has identified privatized companies as leading sources of foreign direct investment. Substantial investment has taken place in privatized enterprises in the telecommunications, infrastructure, hotel and tourism, agro-processing, manufacturing, and banking sectors. Investments in divested corporations are expected to substantially increase over the next few years as contractual obligations under several privatization agreements (such as the electricity and railways concessions) are fulfilled. In addition, some downstream investments have been undertaken as a result of greater confidence in the ability of privatized companies to resolve long-standing sector issues. An example is the Bujagali hydro-electric project (costing over USD700 million) which is predicated on the presence of a strong operator for power distribution.

6.5 Developing capital markets

Since the late 1990s Uganda's stock exchange has been one of the strongest performers in Africa in terms of investor returns. All Ugandan stocks traded on the USE are from privatized enterprises. The ability to participate in initial public offerings has been important in ensuring that ownership is spread across a wider proportion of the public than were previously reached through the direct sale share or asset sale methods, which benefited fewer, wealthier local investors.

7. Conclusions

The NRM government inherited a large parastatal sector which dominated much of the formal economy. Its poor performance in the late 1980s was a drag on economic production and a drain on government finances. By the mid 2000s the sector had been transformed, with most parastatals either privatized or closed down. Along with the restoration of political and macroeconomic stability, this has provided a huge boost to private sector activity. Virtually all of significant economic production in Uganda today takes place in the private sector; government's role is confined to the provision of social infrastructure and services. While the impact of many of the later, and more complex, privatizations has yet to be properly assessed, there has been a significant improvement in the operational and financial performance of many former parastatals. They have attracted substantial investment, while government subsidies to the sector have been largely eliminated.

A number of mistakes were made during implementation of the privatization programme. Some reflected the fact that Uganda was a pioneer in the region with no clear precedents to follow, some the lack of technical experience (particularly in the early years), while others reflected poorly designed processes and procedures. These had an adverse impact both on programme implementation and on public confidence in the management of the process. However, in most cases lessons were learnt and revisions made to policy, operating procedures and processes that eventually enabled the programme to be widely regarded as successful.

One lesson stands out above all—and it is completely non-technical. The single most important factor in ensuring a smooth privatization programme is transparency. Privatization is a highly sensitive political issue in most countries. No matter how professionally it is undertaken, failure to clearly explain to the public what is going on at all stages of the process is likely to give rise to suspicions of corruption or that the 'family silver' is being undervalued. The value of broad participation, good public relations and transparency, particularly during the bidding process, cannot be over-emphasized.

UTILITY SECTOR REFORM

While most of the privatization programme was intended to promote private sector involvement in the economy and to reduce the drain on government finances, in the case of a small number of infrastructure parastatals reform was driven more by the importance of reliable infrastructure services to the economy. In 1999, therefore, a Utility Reform Unit was established within the Ministry of Finance, Planning and Economic Development to coordinate and accelerate reforms in the electricity, railway, telecommunications, and water sectors, and to facilitate the involvement of the private sector. The Unit was responsible for the reform and divestiture of the parastatal enterprises in these sectors on behalf of the DRIC, while sector ministries were responsible for other aspects of private sector participation. In the telecommunications sector many of the initial divestiture measures were led by the Privatization Unit and eventually supported by the Utility Reform Unit (particularly regulatory reform), as reforms in this sector preceded the creation of the latter Unit.

Telecommunications

Following the decision to partially privatize the Uganda Posts and Telecommunications Corporation, the Uganda Communications Act was passed in 1997. This provided for: (1) an independent regulatory agency, the Uganda Communication Commission, to oversee the supervision and development of the telecommunications sector; (2) the incorporation of Uganda Telecom Ltd (UTL) as a limited liability company, with a licence to operate a national telecommunications network; and (3) the incorporation of Uganda Post Ltd (UPL) with a mandate to provide national postal services. Both UTL and UPL were incorporated in 1999 as fully owned public enterprises, under the provisions of the PERD Act.

One of government's key objectives for telecommunications sector reform was to foster private sector investment and management, primarily through divestment of its shares in UTL. To promote competition in the sector, government undertook to license an additional operator (to UTL) to operate a national network. In 1997 MTN won the right to build and operate the new network with an offer of USD6 million.

In 2000 51 per cent of UTL shares were divested to a consortium led by Detecon for USD33.5 million. In 2007 they acquired an additional 18 per cent. Government intends divesting its remaining 31 per cent shareholding through an IPO.

Electricity

Power has been one of the most problematic sectors of the Ugandan economy since the 1980s because of the poor performance of the state-owned monopoly, the Uganda

Electricity Board (UEB). Considered a strategic enterprise, UEB was classified as a Class II PE, in which the state should retain a majority shareholding, under the PERD Statute. By the late 1990s, UEB had generation losses of up to 30 per cent, low revenue collection rates, and high accounts receivable. The quality of service was poor, characterized by frequent system breakdowns and load shedding.

Government efforts in the mid 1990s to attract private investment in new generation capacity floundered due to the sector's dismal performance and private sector insistence on large government guarantees. As the government was in the process of seeking debt relief, it was reluctant to contract additional debt on behalf of the inefficiently managed UEB, or to guarantee privately financed projects.

In 1999 the Power Sector Restructuring and Privatization Strategy was adopted. This called for (1) the unbundling of UEB into separate generation, transmission, and distribution companies; (2) the letting of these companies' assets to private companies by way of concessions; and (3) the establishment of an autonomous Electricity Regulatory Authority. These were to be undertaken in accordance with the 1999 Electricity Act and the PERD Act.

It was subsequently decided that: (i) the two main hydropower stations, Nalubaale and Kiira, would be operated by a single concessionaire; (ii) there would be a single distribution concession with a service area defined closely around the existing network, leaving un-served areas open to competing suppliers; and (iii) the transmission company would continue to act as a bulk buyer/supplier of power until it became possible to develop and finance new generation capacity on the basis of an open access transmission system and without government guarantee.

In 2001 the assets, liabilities, and operations of UEB were transferred to separate limited liability companies for generation, transmission, and distribution. These were registered and created in accordance with the Companies Act and the PERD Statute as the Uganda Electricity Distribution Company (UEDC) Ltd; the Uganda Electricity Transmission Company (UETC) Ltd; and the Uganda Electricity Generation Company (UEGC) Ltd.

UEDC owns the grid connected supply infrastructure operating at and below 33kV, and operates the electricity retail business including metering, billing, connections, and supplying reliable power. UEGC operates and maintains the Nalubaale and Kiira power stations under a concession arrangement. UETC owns, operates, and maintains the grid connected electricity supply infrastructure operating at above 33kV. It is responsible for extending the grid nationally, for import and export of power, for bulk power purchase, and for commissioning large power projects to ensure adequate supply to the grid.

UEGC and UEDC were divested under the PERD Statute. In 2003 UEGC leased its generation assets to Eskom Enterprises Africa under a twenty-year concession arrangement memorialized by a Generation License, a Concession and Assignment Agreement, a Power Purchase Agreement, and a Government Support Agreement. In 2004 concession agreements were signed between UEDC and UMEME Ltd comprising a Distribution License, a Supply License, a Lease and Assignment Agreement, and a Government Support Agreement. In addition, government provided certain guarantees in the event of delayed government payments or non-compliance to the tariff approval formula by the regulator.

Both concessions have performed fairly well. Since 2004 improved efficiency and machine reliability, coupled with prudent water and operational management of available plant, have led to increased production and improved reliability of supply. Between

April 2003 and June 2008 UEGC paid approximately UGX59.3 billion in concession fees to government.

The sector's financial and operational performance has improved rather dramatically. Under the concession, UMEME has a contractual obligation to connect 60,000 customers in the first five years of operation and it looks like it will achieve this target. It connected an estimated 35,000 new customers between March 2005 and October 2006. Equally important, the cash collection rate increased from 73 per cent at the time of takeover, to 88 per cent in October 2006. Lastly, since assuming operational control of the distribution network, UMEME has reduced distribution losses significantly.

Railways

On coming into existence in 1977, Uganda Railways Corporation (URC) inherited all the Uganda based assets of the former East African Railways and Harbours Corporation and received substantial financial assistance to rebuild the railway sector. As well as operating commercial services between Kampala, Kenya, and Tanzania, URC operated services to northern and western Uganda, which were financially non-viable. During the early 1990s the finance ministry started providing explicit subsidies for these routes in the budget. However, the calculation and settlement of these payments became a major point of contention between government and URC. By mid 1997 URC was on the point of financial collapse.

In 2001 DRIC commenced efforts to privatize URC via a long-term concession. The Utility Reform Unit undertook a number of studies to prepare the process of awarding a concession. However in 2003, following a meeting between the Presidents of Kenya and Uganda, both countries decided to abandon plans for single country concessions and to pursue a joint concession instead. The URC and Kenya Railways Corporation networks and operations would be concessioned together to a common investor under a common set of contractual agreements. A Joint Steering Committee, which brought together the privatization technical committees from the two countries, was established to implement the joint concession.

Following an extensive procurement process, the Rift Valley Railways consortium assumed control, and commenced operation, of the rail and marine networks of the two countries in 2005. Kenya and Uganda both handed over significant real estate and non-core assets to the residual state owned asset holding companies for management and disposal, primarily for the purpose of settling retrenchment costs and meeting railway worker pension obligations. In addition, both asset-holding authorities assumed responsibility for monitoring technical aspects of the consortium's compliance with the concession agreements.

The joint concession has been plagued by a number of issues and while it has been under operation for less than two years, there have been reported breaches of the concession agreements. It has been reported that the required contractual performance targets related to investment and volume increase have not been attained.

Water

Reforms in the water sector mainly took the form of improved commercial and technical operations, rather than divestiture. The Utility Reform Unit focused on the urban water sector reforms as these were mainly undertaken through the National Water and Sewerage Corporation (NWSC), which was listed under the PERD Statute.

NWSC was responsible for investing in, and operating, water production and distribution for the largest urban centres. From the late 1990s NWSC management undertook a number of innovative short-term initiatives and incentive programmes. Private firms were engaged to provide management services in Kampala, mainly in the form of revenue collection improvements. Investments in the NWSC network were mainly funded through a mix of donor funded capital grants and on-lent loans, government budget funds, and internally generated cash flows.

In August 2000 a three year performance contract was signed between the government and NWSC aimed at ensuring the Corporation's financial and commercial viability. It set out specific targets, both qualitative and quantitative, against which NWSC's performance was to be assessed. Under the initial performance contract, a competent and independent board was appointed and NWSC gained substantial commercial freedom, though with limitations on tariffs, salaries, and borrowing. A government review of the contract found that NWSC had both met its qualitative targets and most quantitative targets.

A second performance contract covered the period 2003–6. Its key features were more realistic targets being set (especially for unaccounted for water in Kampala, the only target to have been missed), acknowledgement of the need for debt restructuring to bring NWSC to profitability, and a commitment by government to pay its arrears and meet all dues on time. The new contract also announced government's intention to establish a new industry structure by the end of 2005, while undertaking to protect NWSC from any additional costs due to the restructuring.

In 2004 NWSC undertook a form of performance contract with its own management and staff. These were called the internally delegated area management contracts. By July 2004 they were in place in all fifteen NWSC service areas. They provided financial incentives for staff and management to achieve and exceed minimum targets and established a good framework for monitoring performance.

A review of the second performance contract found that NWSC's staff costs had declined from 45 per cent of revenues in 2003 to 26 per cent in 2006, while unaccounted for water within the Corporation's network (with the exception of Kampala) dropped from 45 per cent to 27 per cent. This was accompanied by a rise in collection efficiency to 95 per cent, an increase in the number of metered connections to 94 per cent of all connections, and an increase of 76 per cent in the Corporation's annual income.

APPENDIX 16.2

Public Enterprises Divested, 1992–2006

	Enterprise	% Divested	Buyer	Year of Divestiture	Method used
1	East African Distilleries	51	International Distillers & Vintners	1992	Share Sale
2	Nile Breweries Ltd	100	Nile Breweries Limited on a/c of Madhvani Group	1992	Repossession
3	Shell (U) Ltd	50	Shell International Petroleum Co. Ltd	1992	Debt/Equity Swap
4	Uganda American Insurance Company	Repossession	American Life Insurance Company	1992	Repossession
5	Agricultural Enterprises Ltd	Debt/Equity Swap	Commonwealth Development Corp and James Finlay plc	1993	Joint Venture
6	Lake Victoria Bottling Co. Ltd	100	Crown Bottlers Ltd	1993	Share Sale
7	Uganda Securiko Ltd	Repossession	Securiko (U) Ltd	1993	Repossession
8	Blenders (U) Ltd	100	Unilever Overseas Holding BVC	1994	Share Sale
9	Hotel Margherita	100	Reco Industries Ltd	1994	Asset Sale
10	Mt. Moroto Hotel	100	Kodet International Ltd	1994	Asset Sale
11	Rock Hotel	100	Swisa Industries Ltd	1994	Asset Sale
12	TUMPECO	100	GM Company Ltd	1994	Share Sale
13	Uganda Cement Industry — Hima	100	Rawals Group of Industries	1994	Asset Sale
14	Uganda Tea Corporation Ltd	51	ABM investment Company (Mehta group)	1994	Repossession
15	White Horse Inn	100	Kabale Development Company Ltd.	1994	Asset Sale
16	Acholi Inn	100	Ms Laoo Ltd	1995	Asset Sale
17	Hilltop Hotel	—	Three Links Ltd	1995	Asset Sale
18	Kampala Auto Centre (Gomba Motors Ltd)	100	Management	1995	Auction
19	Lake Victoria Hotel Ltd (Phase 1)	51	Windsor Ltd	1995	Share Sale
20	Lira Hotel	100	Showa Trade Company Ltd	1995	Asset Sale

No.	Company	%	Buyer	Year	Method
21	Mt. Elgon Hotel	100	Bugisu Cooperative Union	1995	Asset Sale
22	Mweya Safari Lodge	Concession	Muljibhai Madhvani & Co. Ltd	1995	Concession
23	Republic Motors	100	Rafiki Trading Company (Hussein Mohamed)	1995	Auction
24	Soroti Hotel	100	Speedbird Aviation Services Ltd	1995	Asset Sale
25	Uganda Cement Industry — Tororo	100	Corrugated Sheets Ltd	1995	Asset Sale
26	Uganda Fisheries Enterprises	100	Nordic-African Fisheries Co. Ltd	1995	Share Sale
27	Uganda Hardware Ltd	100	Management (Justin Nkrunziza)	1995	Management Buy Out
28	Uganda Hire Purchase Co	100	Tadeo Kisekka	1995	Auction
29	Uganda Leather and Tanning Industry	100	Leather industries of Uganda Ltd	1995	Asset Sale
30	Uganda Meat Packers Ltd (Kampala Plant)	100	Uganda Meat Industries Ltd	1995	Asset Sale
31	Uganda Motors Ltd	100	Management (A.A Motors Ltd)	1995	Management Buy Out
32	White Rhino Hotel	100	Dolma Associates Ltd	1995	Asset Sale
33	Winits (U) Ltd	100	EMCO Works Ltd	1995	Auction
34	African Ceramics Co	100	Muhindo Enterprises Ltd	1996	Asset Sale
35	African Textile Mills	51	Ranchhodobhai Shivabhai Patel Ltd	1996	Share Sale
36	Agip (U) Ltd	50	Agip Petroli International BV	1996	Share Sale
37	Foods & Beverages Ltd	100	James Mbabazi	1996	Auction
38	Fresh Foods Ltd	100	Eddie & Sophie Enterprises Ltd	1996	Auction
39	ITV Sales	100	ROKO Construction Ltd	1996	Asset Sale
40	Kibimba Rice Co. Ltd	100	Tilda Holdings (Africa) Ltd	1996	Share Sale
41	Motorcraft and Sales Ltd	100	Andami Works Ltd. on a/c of the Management	1996	Management Buy Out
42	NYTIL	100	NYTIL Picfare Ltd	1996	Asset Sale

(Continued)

(Continued)

	Enterprise	% Divested	Buyer	Year of Divestiture	Method used
43	Stanbic Bank (U) Ltd	49	SBIC Africa Holdings Ltd	1996	Share Sale
44	Total (U) Ltd	50	Total Outre Mer	1996	Share Sale
45	Uganda Grain Milling Co. (PHASE 1)	51	Calebs International Ltd	1996	Share Sale
46	Uganda Pharmaceuticals Ltd	100	Vivi Enterprise Ltd	1996	Share Sale
47	Comrade Cycles (U) Ltd	100	Uganda Motors Ltd	1997	Share Sale
48	Uganda Crane Estates Ltd	100	Buganda Kingdom	1997	Repossession
49	Uganda Industrial Machinery Ltd	100	F.B. Lukoma	1997	Share Sale
50	Uganda Meat Packers Ltd — Soroti	100	Teso Agro-Industries Co Ltd	1997	Asset Sale
51	Barclays Bank of Uganda Ltd	49	Barclays Bank Plc	1998	Shares/Pre-emptive rights
52	Entebbe Handling Services (ENHAS)	50	Efforte Corp Ltd, Global Airlinks Ltd & Sabena S. A.N.V	1998	Shares/Pre-emptive rights
53	Lango Dev. Co	99.78	Sunset International Ltd	1998	Share Sale
54	Second National Operator	—	MTN Uganda Ltd	1998	Concession
55	Bank of Baroda	49	Bank of Baroda (India)	1999	Shares/Pre-emptive rights
56	BAT Uganda (PHASE 1)	20	BAT Investments Ltd	1999	Shares/Pre-emptive rights
57	NEC Pharmaceuticals Ltd	60	Heinz Haupt, Chem.—Pharm. Fabrik GMBH & Co.KG	1999	Joint Venture
58	PAPCO Industries Ltd	26	Praful Chandulal Patel (Authorised Agent of Late CK Patel Family)	1999	Share Sale
59	SAIMMCO	100	Steel Rolling Mills Ltd	1999	Share Sale
60	Uganda Clays Ltd	75	Various	1999	Initial Public Offering

No.	Company		Buyer	Year	Method
61	Uganda Consolidated Properties Ltd (PHASE 1)	100	Government of Uganda	1999	Asset Sale
62	Uganda Spinning Mills, Lira	Court Sale	Guostar Enterprises (U) Limited	1999	Asset Sale
63	BAT Uganda (PHASE 2)	10	Various	2000	Initial Public Offering
64	Central Purchasing Company Ltd	100	Management and Employees	2000	Management Buy Out
65	Kakira Sugar Works	30	East African Holdings Ltd	2000	Shares/Pre-emptive rights
66	Lake Victoria Hotel Ltd (Phase 2)	49	Windsor Ltd	2000	Shares/Pre-emptive rights
67	Masindi Hotel	100	Ottoman Engineering Ltd	2000	Asset Sale
68	Steel Corporation of East Africa Ltd	25.78	Muljibhai Madhvani & Co. Ltd	2000	Shares/Pre-emptive rights
69	Uganda Garment Industries Ltd	100	Phoenix Logistics Uganda Ltd	2000	Asset Sale
70	Uganda Telecom Ltd	51	UCOM Ltd	2000	Share Sale
71	Apolo Hotel Corporation Ltd	100	MIDROC Ethiopia PVT Ltd Co	2001	Share Sale
72	Associated Match company Ltd	0.003	Muljibhai Madhvani & Co. Ltd	2001	Shares/Pre-emptive rights
73	Transocean 1998 (U) Ltd	100	Coin Ltd	2001	Share Sale
74	Kiryana Ranch	—	Ziwa Ranchers Ltd	2002	Concession
75	Rwenzori Highland Tea Company Ltd	6.885	Rwenzori Tea Investments Ltd a/c of Finlay	2002	Shares/Pre-emptive rights
76	Uganda Commercial Bank	80	Stanbic Bank	2002	Share Sale
77	Uganda Electricity Generation Co. Ltd	Concession	Eskom Enterprises	2002	Concession
78	DFCU	18.5	Various	2004	Initial Public Offering

(Continued)

(Continued)

	Enterprise	% Divested	Buyer	Year of Divestiture	Method used
79	New Vision Printing and Publishing Co Ltd	20	Various	2004	Initial Public Offering
80	Nile Hotel International Ltd	Concession	TPS (U) Limited on a/c of Serena Tourism Promotion Services	2004	Concession
81	Uganda Electricity Distribution Co Ltd	Concession	Umeme Uganda Ltd	2004	Concession
82	Kyempisi Ranch	Concession	Royal Ranches Limited	2005	Concession
83	National Housing	49	Government of Libya	2005	Debt/Equity Swap
84	National Insurance Corporation Limited	60	Corporate Holdings Ltd	2005	Share Sale
85	Uganda Seeds (Kasese)	Concession	Nyakatonzi Cooperative Union	2005	Concession
86	Uganda Seeds (Masindi and Kisindi)	Concession	Farm Inputs Care Centre	2005	Concession
87	Dairy Corporation	Management Contract	Sameer Investments Group	2006	Concession
88	Kinyara Sugar	51	RAI Group	2006	Share Sale
89	Uganda Railways Corporation	Concession	Sheltam Rail Company	2006	Concession
90	Stanbic Bank (U) Ltd (merged with UCB)	10	Various	2007	Initial Public Offering

Source: Privatization Unit, Ministry of Finance, Planning and Economic Development.

Bibliography

Chapter 1

Adam Smith International, Ernst and Young, and Economic Policy Research Centre (2005). 'Uganda Privatisation Impact Assessment Report' (mimeo).

Akiyama, T. (2001). 'Coffee Market Liberalisation since 1990' in T. Akiyama, J. Baffes, D. Larsen, and P. Varangis (eds), *Commodity Market Reforms: Lessons from Two Decades. Regional and Sectoral Studies*. Washington, DC: World Bank.

Collier, P. and Reinikka, R. (2001). 'Reconstruction and Liberalization: An Overview' in R. Reinikka and P. Collier (eds), *Uganda's Recovery*. Washington, DC: World Bank, 15–47.

Kitabire, D. and Oumo, P. (2005). Debt Sustainability Project Country Study: Uganda. Ministry of Finance, Planning and Economic Development (mimeo).

MIGA (Multilateral Investment Guarantee Agency) (2004). Competing for FDI. Investment in Development Series. Washington, DC: MIGA: 47–76.

OECD (Organisation for Economic Cooperation and Development) (2006). 'Joint Evaluation of General Budget Support 1994–2004: Uganda Country Report'. Paris: OECD.

Robinson, M. (2006). 'The Political Economy of Governance Reforms in Uganda'. IDS Discussion Paper 386. Brighton: Institute of Development Studies.

Selassie, A. (2008). 'Beyond Macroeconomic Stability: the Quest for Industrialisation in Uganda'. *IMF Working Paper* WP/08/231. Washington, DC: International Monetary Fund.

UBoS (Uganda Bureau of Statistics) (2008). 2008 Statistical Abstract. Kampala: UBoS.

UNDP (United Nations Development Programme) (2007). *Millennium Development Goals: Uganda's Progress Report 2007*. Kampala: UNDP.

World Bank (1991). 'Public Choices for Private Initiatives'. Report 920-UG, Washington, DC: World Bank.

Chapter 2

GBRW Limited and Denton Wilde Sapte (2002). Evaluation of the Resolution of Uganda Commercial Bank Ltd (mimeo).

Government of Uganda (1992). 'The Way Forward I. Macroeconomic Strategy, 1990–1995'. Ministry of Planning and Economic Development. Kampala.

—— (1995). Constitution of the Republic of Uganda. Kampala.

—— (2002). National Planning Authority Act, Number 15. Kampala.

Bibliography

Henstridge, M. and Kasekende, L. (2001). 'Exchange Reforms, Stabilisation, and Fiscal Management' in R. Reinikka and P. Collier (eds). *Uganda's Recovery: The Role of Farms, Firms and Government*. Washington, DC: World Bank.

IDRC (International Development Research Centre) (1986). Economic Adjustment and Longer Term Development in Uganda. Report by the Uganda Economic Study Team. Vol. 1 (mimeo).

Museveni, Y. (2008). Speech to the Ninth Summit of the African Peer Review Forum. Sharm el Sheikh, Egypt. 26 June.

Mallaby, S. (2004). *The World's Banker*. New York: Penguin Press.

Chapter 3

Adam, C. and Bevan, D. (1997). 'Fiscal Restraint and the Cash Budget in Zambia'. Centre for the Study of African Economies, University of Oxford (mimeo).

—— O'Connell, S., Buffie, E., and Pattillo, C. (2007). 'Monetary Policy Rules for Managing Aid Surges in Africa'. IMF Working Paper, WP/07/180. Washington, DC, (forthcoming in *Journal of Development Economics*, 2009).

Appleton, S. (2001). 'Changes in Poverty and Inequality' in: R. Reinikka and P. Collier (eds). *Uganda's Recovery: The Role of Farms, Firms, and Government*. Washington, DC: World Bank.

Bevan, D. (1998). 'Uganda Public Expenditure Review: Macroeconomic Options in the Medium Term'. St. John's College, University of Oxford (mimeo).

—— Collier, P., and Gunning, J. (1989). *Peasants and Governments: An Economic Analysis*. Oxford: Clarendon Press.

—— (1990). *Controlled Open Economies: A Neoclassical Approach to Structuralism*. Oxford: Clarendon Press.

Brownbridge, M. and Tumusiime-Mutebile, E. (2006). 'Aid and Fiscal Deficits: Lessons from Uganda on the Implications for Macroeconomic Management and Fiscal Sustainability', *Development Policy Review*, Vol. 25(2): 193–213.

Buffie, E., Adam, C., O'Connell, S., and Pattillo, C. (2008). 'Riding the Wave: Monetary Responses to Aid Surges in Low-Income Countries', *European Economic Review*, 52: 1378–95.

Collier, P. and Gunning, J. (1996). 'Policy towards Commodity Shocks in Developing Countries'. IMF Working Paper, 96/84. Washington, DC: International Monetary Fund.

Dinh, H., Adugna, A., and Myers, B. (2002). 'The Impact of Cash Budgets on Poverty Reduction in Zambia—A Case Study of the Conflict between Well-Intentioned Macroeconomic Policy and Service Delivery to the Poor', Policy Research Working Paper, WPS2914. Washington, DC: World Bank.

Henstridge, M. (1997). 'Implementing Fiscal Adjustment: Uganda's Cashflow', Centre for the Study of African Economies, University of Oxford.

—— and Kasekende, L. (2001). 'Exchange Reforms, Stabilisation, and Fiscal Management' in R. Reinikka and P. Collier (eds), *Uganda's Recovery: The Role of Farms, Firms and Government*. Washington, DC: World Bank.

International Monetary Fund (2000). 'Uganda: Letter of Intent for 2000/01, and Memorandum of Economic and Financial Policies of the Government of Uganda for 2000/01',

21 August. Washington, DC: IMF. (http://www.imf.org/external/np/loi/2000/uga/01/index.htm)

—— (2005). 'Uganda: Fifth Review under the Three-Year Arrangement under the Poverty Reduction and Growth Facility, Request for Waiver of Performance Criterion, and Extension of Arrangement', 23 June. Washington, DC: IMF. (www.imf.org)

—— (2006). 'Uganda: Staff Report for the 2006 Article IV Consultation, First Review of the Policy Support Instrument, Request for Waiver of Assessment Criteria, and Request for a Three-Year Policy Support Instrument', 1 December. Washington, DC: IMF. (www.imf.org)

—— (2008). 'Uganda: IMF Staff Report for the Third Review under the Policy Support Instrument and Request for Waiver and Modification of Assessment Criteria', 25 June. Washington, DC: IMF. (www.imf.org)

Katarikawe, M. and Sebudde, R. (1999). 'Is the Reserve Money program still a Useful Operating Framework for the Conduct of Monetary Policy in Uganda?' Bank of Uganda Staff Papers, 1(1). Kampala.

Kasekende, L. and Malik, M. (1994). 'Dual Exchange Regimes, Unification and Development: The Case of Uganda', Paper presented to a conference on adjustment and poverty in Sub-Saharan Africa, Accra, Ghana.

—— Kitabire, D., and Martin, M. (1996). 'Capital Inflows and Macroeconomic Policy in Sub-Saharan Africa', International Monetary and Financial Issues for the 1990s, Vol. 8. New York: United Nations: 58–82.

—— and Ssemogerere, G. (1994). 'Exchange Rate Unification and Economic Development: the Case of Uganda, 1987–92', World Development, 22(8): 1183–98.

Kharas, H. and Pinto, B. (1989). 'Exchange Rate Rules, Black Market Premia and Fiscal Deficits: the Bolivian Hyperinflation', Review of Economic Studies, 56(3): 435–47.

Lizondo, J. (1987). 'Unification of Dual Exchange Markets', Journal of International Economics, 22: 57–77.

MoFPED (Ministry of Finance, Planning and Economic Development) (Various years). Background to the Budget. Kampala.

Moon, A. (1997). 'Uganda's Budget Framework: Presentation to the Parliament of Uganda' Uganda: Public Expenditure Review 197/98. Washington, DC: World Bank (mimeo).

Morris, S. (1989a). 'Macroeconomic Features of the Uganda Economy and Some Policy Implications. Part One: The relationship between money prices and the parallel market exchange rate'. MoPED Discussion Paper No. 1. Kampala: Ministry of Planning and Economic Development.

—— (1989b). 'Macroeconomic Features of the Uganda Economy and Some Policy Implications. Part Two: The impact of official exchange rate devaluation on Uganda'. MoPED Discussion Paper No. 2. Kampala: Ministry of Planning and Economic Development.

—— (1995). 'Inflation Dynamics and the Parallel Market for Foreign Exchange', Journal of Development Economics, 46: 295–316.

Obbo, S. and Waswa, J. (1992). 'Budget Aims at 15% Inflation', The New Vision, 2 July, 7(154): 1.

Pinto, B. (1988). 'Black Markets for Foreign Exchange, Real Exchange Rates, and Inflation: Overnight versus Gradual Reform'. Policy Research Working Paper 84. Development Research Group, Washington, DC: World Bank.

Pinto, B. (1989). 'Black Market Premia, Exchange Rate Unification, and Inflation in Sub-Saharan Africa', *World Bank Economic Review*, 3(3): 321–38.

Reinikka, R. and Collier, P. (eds) (2001). 'Uganda's Recovery: The Role of Farms, Firms, and Government'. Washington, DC: World Bank.

Republic of Uganda (1992). 'The Way Forward I. Macroeconomic Strategy, 1990–1995'. Ministry of Planning and Economic Development. Kampala.

—— (2000). 'Poverty Eradication Action Plan'. Ministry of Finance, Planning and Economic Development. Kampala.

—— (Various years). 'Statistical Abstract'. Uganda Bureau of Statistics, Kampala.

Stasavage, D. and Moyo, D. (1999). 'Are Cash Budgets a Cure for Excess Fiscal Deficits (and at what cost)?' CSAE Working Paper 99.11. Centre for the Study of African Economies, University of Oxford.

UBoS (Uganda Bureau of Statistics) (2008). 2008 Statistical Abstract. Kampala.

Chapter 4

Constitution of the Republic of Uganda (1995). Kampala.

High Court of Uganda (1998). Civil Suit No. 1029 of 1998, 'Charles Abola, Silvester Agwaru, and A. Kasirivu as representatives of 63339 ex-civil servants retrenched in 1992 versus The Attorney General, Consent Judgment.' Kampala.

Kiragu, K. and Mukandala, R. (2005). *Politics and Tactics in Public Sector Reforms: The Dynamics of Public Service Pay in Africa*. Dar es Salaam: Dar es Salaam University Press.

Langseth, P. (1996). 'The Civil Service Reform Programme' in P. Langseth and J. Mugaju (eds). *Post Conflict Uganda: Towards an Effective Civil Service*. Kampala: Fountain Publishers.

Ministry of Finance, Planning and Economic Development (Various years). Approved Estimates of Revenue and Expenditure, 1997/98 to 2004/05. Kampala: Government Printer.

Ministry of Public Service (Various years). Circular Standing Instructions on the salary structures for 1989–2005. Kampala.

—— (1989). Circular Standing Instruction No.11 of 1989. Integrated Establishment, Staffing, and Payroll Control. Kampala.

—— (1990). Report of the Public Service Review and Reorganization Commission. Kampala.

—— (1994a). Circular Standing Instruction No.9. Abolition of Group Employees Scheme and Introduction of the Support Staff Cadre. Kampala.

—— (1994b). Management of Change: Context, Vision, Objectives, Strategy, and Plan of the Civil Service Reform. Kampala.

—— (1994c). Circular Letter on Public Service Housing Scheme, Guidelines, and Procedures on Sale of Government Pool Houses. Kampala.

—— (1995). Uganda Civil Service Reform Programme Status Report 6. Kampala.

—— (1996a). Circular Letter on Recruitment Freeze. Kampala.

—— (1996b). Circular Standing Instruction No.3. Monetization of Benefits. Kampala.

—— (1997a). Circular Standing Instruction No.1. Special Voluntary Retirement Scheme for Support Staff. Kampala.

—— (1997b). Public Service Reform Programme 1997–2002. Kampala.

—— (1998a). Circular Standing Instruction No.4. Special Voluntary Retirement Scheme. Kampala.

—— (1998b). Establishment Notice No. 2. Lifting of the Recruitment Freeze. Kampala.

—— (2002). Pay Reform Strategy. Kampala.

—— (2003). Study of Cost Efficiency and Effectiveness of Human Resource Deployment in Social Sectors. Kampala.

OECD (Organisation for Economic Cooperation and Development) (2005). Paris Declaration on Aid Effectiveness. Paris: OECD.

Pensions (Amendment) Statute (1994). Kampala.

Robinson, M. (2006). The Political Economy of Governance Reforms in Uganda. IDS Discussion Paper 386. Brighton: Institute of Development Studies.

Chapter 5

Chen, D., Matovu, J., and Reinikka, R. (2001). 'A Quest for Revenue and Tax Incidence', in R. Reinikka and P. Collier (eds), *Uganda's Recovery*. Washington, DC: World Bank, 271–317.

Coopers and Lybrand (1991). 'Planning for a Revenue Authority for Uganda'. Kampala.

Ebrill, L., Keen, M., Bodin, J-P., and Summers, V. (2001). The Modern VAT. Washington, DC: International Monetary Fund.

—— (2002). 'The Allure of the Value Added Tax', *Finance and Development*, 39(2): 44–7.

Ghura, D. (1998). 'Tax Revenue in Sub-Saharan Africa: Effects of Economic Policies and Corruption'. IMF Working Paper, 98/135. Washington, DC: International Monetary Fund.

Government of Uganda (1991a). Uganda Revenue Authority Statute, No. 6. Kampala.

—— (1991b). The Investment Code 1991. Kampala.

—— (1996). The Value Added Tax Act 1996. Kampala.

—— (1997). The Income Tax Act 1997. Kampala.

IMF (International Monetary Fund) (1995). *Tax Policy Handbook*. Washington, DC: IMF.

—— (2006). World Economic Trends in Africa (World Economic Outlook/Economic Trends in Africa). Washington, DC: IMF.

Lortie, J. (1999). Uganda Revenue Authority—Information Systems and Technology Strategy. Kampala.

Therkildsen, O. (2003). 'Revenue Authority Autonomy in sub-Saharan Africa: The Case of Uganda', a paper for the Norwegian Association for Development Research conference on 'Poverty and Politics', Oslo.

World Bank (1995). *The Challenge of Growth and Poverty Reduction*. Washington, DC: World Bank.

—— (2006). African Indicators database.

WTO (World Trade Organization) (2001). *Uganda—Trade Policy Review*. Geneva: WTO.

Zake, J. (1995). 'Creating an Enabling Environment for the Development of Small-scale Enterprise through Tax Reform: The Case of Uganda, 1986–1993', in P. English and G. Hénault (eds), *Agents of Change: Studies on the Policy Environment for Small Enterprise in Africa*. Ottawa: IDRC/ITDG Publishing.

Bibliography

Chapter 6

Ministry of Finance and Economic Planning (Various years). Estimates of Revenue and Expenditure. Kampala: Government Printer.
—— (1994). Public Investment Plan, 1994/95–1996/97. Kampala: Government Printer.
—— (1995). Public Investment Plan, 1995/96–1997/98. Kampala: Government Printer.
Ministry of Planning and Economic Development. Rehabilitation and Development Plans, 1987/88–1990/91, 1988/89–1991/92, 1990/91–1993/94, 1991/92–1994/95, and 1993/94–1995/96. Kampala: Government Printer.
Museveni, Y. (1992). Procedures for Soliciting Foreign Aid. Presidential Directive. Entebbe: Government of Uganda.
Reinikka, R. and Svensson, J. (2006). 'Using Micro-Surveys to Measure and Explain Corruption', World Development, 34(2): 359–70.
World Bank (1991). Public Choices for Private Initiatives: Prioritizing Public Expenditure for Sustainable and Equitable Growth in Uganda. Washington, DC: World Bank.
—— (1995). Uganda: The Challenge of Growth and Poverty Reduction. Washington, DC: World Bank.
—— (2004). http://www-wds.worldbank.org/servlet/WDS_IBank_Servlet?pcont= details &eid=000012009_20040331092212

Chapter 7

Canagarajah, S. and van Diesen, A. (2006). 'The Poverty Reduction Strategy Approach Six Years On: An examination of Principles and Practice in Uganda', Development Policy Review, 24(6): 647–67. London: Overseas Development Institute.
Goodwin-Groen, R., Bruett, T., and Latortue, A. (2004). 'Uganda Microfinance Sector Effectiveness Review', Report prepared for the Private Sector Donor Group, Kampala.
Hauge, A. (2001). Strengthening Capacity for Monitoring and Evaluation in Uganda: A Results Based Management Perspective. World Bank Operations Evaluation Department Working Paper Series No. 8. Washington, DC: World Bank.
Isooba, M. (2005). Civil Society Participation in Uganda's PRS Process: Opportunities and Dilemmas. Kampala.
Ministry of Finance, Planning and Economic Development (1996). Background to the Budget. Kampala.
—— (1997). Poverty Eradication Action Plan. Kampala.
—— (2000a). Plan for Modernization of Agriculture. Kampala.
—— (2000b). Poverty Eradication Action Plan. Kampala.
—— (2001). Poverty Eradication Action Plan, Volume 3: Building Partnership to Implement the PEAP. Kampala.
—— (2003). PEAP Revision Guide. Kampala.
—— (2004). Poverty Eradication Action Plan, 2004/05–2007/08. Kampala.
OECD (Organization for Economic Cooperation and Development) (2005). Paris Declaration on Aid Effectiveness. Paris: OECD.

OPM (Office of the Prime Minister) (2006). Plan for the Annual PEAP Implementation Review, Kampala.

Sewakiryanga, R. (2005). 'The Politics of Revising the PEAP/PRSP in Uganda', presentation made at the International Conference on Political Dimensions of Poverty Reduction, Lusaka.

Tumusiime-Mutebile, E. (1999). 'Making Partnerships Work on the Ground—Experience in Uganda', presentation made in Stockholm.

Williamson, T. and Ndungu, M. (2002). 'Financing Poverty Eradication in Uganda'. Kampala.

—— and Canagarajah, S. (2003). 'Is there a place for virtual poverty funds in pro-poor public spending reform? Lessons from Uganda's PAF'. *Development Policy Review*, 21(4): 449–80, London: Overseas Development Institute.

Chapter 8

Ahmad, E., Brosio, G., and Gonzalez, M. (2006). 'Uganda: Managing More Effective Decentralisation', *IMF Working Paper* WP/06/279. Washington, DC: International Monetary Fund.

Bevan, D. and Palomba, G. (2000). 'Uganda: the Budget and Medium Term Expenditure Framework set in a wider context' (mimeo).

Foster, M. and Mijumbi, P. (2002) 'How, When and Why does Poverty get Budget Priority?' Working Paper 163. London: Overseas Development Institute.

Le Houerou, P. and Taliercio, R. (2002). 'Medium Term Expenditure Frameworks: from Concept to Practice. Preliminary Lessons from Africa'. Working Paper Series. Washington, DC: World Bank.

MoFPED (2001a). 'Poverty Status Report 2000'. Ministry of Finance, Planning and Economic Development. Kampala.

—— (2001b). 'Background to the Budget, 2001/02'. Ministry of Finance, Planning and Economic Development. Kampala.

—— (2004). 'Poverty Eradication Action Plan 2004/05–2007/08'. Ministry of Finance, Planning and Economic Development. Kampala.

—— (2006). 'Budget Speech, 2006/07'. Ministry of Finance, Planning and Economic Development. Kampala.

Williamson, T. and Canagarajah, S. (2003). 'Is there a place for Virtual Poverty Funds in Pro-poor Public Spending Reform? Lessons from Uganda's PAF', *Development Policy Review*, 21(4): 449–80.

World Bank (2004). 'The Republic of Uganda: Country Integrated Fiduciary Assessment'. Report 29377–UG. Washington, DC: World Bank.

Chapter 9

Lister, S., Williamson, T., Steffensen, J., and Barayabanoha, W. (2006). Joint Evaluation of General Budget Support 1994–2004: Uganda Country Report. Paris: Organization for Economic Cooperation and Development.

Ministry of Education and Sports (1998). Education Sector Investment Plan. Kampala.

—— (2004). Education Sector Annual Performance Report 2003/04. Kampala.

Bibliography

Ministry of Finance, Planning and Economic Development (1997). Poverty Eradication Action Plan. Kampala.

—— (1998–2007b). Budget speeches. Published annually. Kampala.

—— (1998–2007c). Estimates of Revenue and Expenditure. Published annually. Kampala.

—— (1998–2007d). Budget Framework Papers. Kampala.

—— (2000a). Poverty Eradication Action Plan. Kampala.

—— (2000b). Plan for Modernization of Agriculture. Kampala.

—— (2001). Poverty Eradication Action Plan, Volume III: Building Partnership to Implement the PEAP. Kampala.

—— (2003). Partnership Principles between Government of Uganda and its Development Partners. Kampala.

—— (2004). Poverty Eradication Action Plan, 2004/05–07/08. Kampala.

Ministry of Health (2007). Health Sector Annual Performance Report. Kampala.

Ministry of Works, Housing and Communications (1996). Road Sector Development Plan. Kampala.

Overseas Development Institute (2007). Uganda Development Partner Division of Labour Exercise Interim Report. London: ODI.

Ward, M., Penny, A., and Read, T. (2006). Education Reform in Uganda—1997 to 2004: Reflections on Policy, Partnership, Strategy and Implementation. London: DFID.

Williamson, T. (2003). Targets and Results in Public Sector Management: Uganda Case Study. ODI Working Paper 205. London: Overseas Development Institute.

Chapter 10

Appleton, S. (1998). Changes in Poverty in Uganda, 1992–96: A Report to the World Bank (mimeo).

—— (1999). Changes in Poverty and Inequality in Uganda, 1992–97 (mimeo).

—— (2001). 'Changes in Poverty and Inequality', in P. Collier and R. Reinikka (eds), *Uganda's Recovery: The Role of Farms, Firms and Government*. Washington, DC: World Bank.

—— and Ssewanyana, S. (2003). Poverty Analysis in Uganda, 2002/03. Economic Policy Research Centre (mimeo).

Bird, K. and Booth, D. (2000). Explaining the Differences in Poverty Trends between Quantitative Survey Data and the PPA. London: Overseas Development Institute.

Deininger, K. and Okidi, J. (2003). Growth and Poverty Reduction in Uganda, 1992–2000: Panel Data Evidence (mimeo).

Kappel, R., Lay, J., and Steiner, S. (2005). 'Uganda: No More Pro-Poor Growth?' *Development Policy Review*, 23(1): 27–53.

Ministry of Finance, Planning and Economic Development (2002a). Poverty Monitoring and Evaluation Strategy. Kampala: Gem Connection.

—— (2002b). Criteria for Budget Allocations: Is it Poverty Focused? (mimeo).

—— (2002c). Discussion Paper 5: Challenges and Prospects for Poverty Reduction in Northern Uganda. Kampala: Monitor Publications Ltd.

—— (2002d). Discussion Paper 6: Infant Mortality in Uganda: Why the Non-Improvement? Kampala: GEM Connection.

—— (2004). Infant and Maternal Mortality in Uganda: Causes, Interventions, and Strategy. Kampala.

—— (2007). PMAU Briefing Paper 5: Wage Determination and Gender Discrimination in Uganda. Kampala.

Norton A., Bird, B., Brook, K., Kakande, M., and Turk, C. (2001). *A Rough Guide to PPAs: Participatory Poverty Assessments: An Introduction to Theory and Practice.* London: Overseas Development Institute.

Okidi, J., Ssewanyana, S., Bategeka, L., and Muhumuza, F. (2005). Distributional and Poverty Impacts of Uganda's growth 1992–2003. *Research Series* No. 46. Kampala: Economic Policy Research Centre.

Okware, S., Opio, A., Musinguzi, J., and Waibale, P. (2001). Fighting HIV/AIDS: Is Success Possible? Bulletin of the World Health Organization. Geneva: WHO.

Uganda Bureau of Statistics and Macro International Inc. (1996). Uganda Demographic and Health Survey 1995. Kampala.

Uganda Bureau of Statistics and ORC Macro (2001). Uganda Demographic and Health Survey 2000–01. Kampala.

Uganda Bureau of Statistics and Macro International Inc. (2007). Uganda Demographic and Health Survey 2006. Kampala.

Uganda Bureau of Statistics (2004). 2004 Statistical Abstract. Kampala: NicePrint.

—— (2006a). Uganda National Household Survey 2005/2006: Report on the Socio-Economic Module. Kampala.

—— (2006b). Uganda Participatory Poverty Assessment Process: Uganda National Household Survey 2005/06: Qualitative Module. Kampala: New Vision Printing and Publishing Corporation.

United Nations Development Programme (1997). Human Development Report. New York: Oxford University Press.

UNDP (United Nations Development Programme) (2007). Millennium Development Goals: Uganda's Progress Report 2007. Kampala: UNDP.

West, C. (1987). Food Composition Table. Department of Human Nutrition, Wageningen Agricultural University: De Grejien (mimeo).

Chapter 11

Colecraft, E. (1979). 'Report on a Mission to the Republic of Uganda'.

Commonwealth Team of Experts (1979). 'The Rehabilitation of the Economy of Uganda', Volume 2, Paper 31.

Institute of Statistics and Applied Economics (1980). 'Report on the Sub-Regional Workshop on the Development of an Integrated Statistical System for a Developing Country (with Uganda as a Special Case)'. Makerere University: Kampala.

Martin, C. (1980). 'Report on the Organization of the Uganda Statistical Department with Proposals for the Improvement of its Functions, Structure, and Staffing'. World Bank.

Ministry of Finance, Planning and Economic Development (1998). 'Poverty Trends in Uganda, 1992–1996'. Discussion Paper No.2. Kampala.

Ministry of Planning and Economic Development (1991). 'Report on the Uganda National Household Budget Survey (1989–90)'. Statistics Department. Kampala.

Bibliography

Ministry of Finance and Economic Planning (1993). 'Report on the Uganda National Integrated Household Survey 1992–93; Volumes 1–3'. Statistics Department. Kampala.

—— (1995). 'Report on the Uganda National Household Survey 1993–94 (First Monitoring Survey)—Volumes 1–2'. Statistics Department. Kampala.

PAPSCA Coordination Unit (1995). 'PAPSCA Final Evaluation Report'.

Pillai, K. (1982). 'Report on a Mission to Uganda', Economic Commission for Africa.

Singh, P. (1992). 'Rehabilitation of the Statistics Department, Ministry of Planning and Economic Development'. Commonwealth Secretariat.

Uganda Bureau of Statistics (UBoS) (2001). 'Compendium of Statistical Concepts and Definitions Used in Uganda Statistical System and Services'. Kampala.

—— (2002). 'Uganda Bureau of Statistics: Corporate Plan 2002–2007'. Kampala.

—— (2003a). 'Uganda National Household Survey 2002/2003: Report on the Socio-Economic Survey'. Kampala.

—— (2003b). 'The District Data Needs Assessment Study'. Kampala.

Uganda Government (1994). 'Transforming the Statistics Department into a Semi-Autonomous Body'. Report prepared by Development Consultants International, mimeo.

—— (1998). Uganda Bureau of Statistics Act 1998. Entebbe: Government Printer.

Chapter 12

Andrews, D., Boote, A., Rizavi, S., and Singh S. (1999). Debt Relief for Low-income Countries: The Enhanced HIPC Initiative. Pamphlet No.51. Washington, DC: International Monetary Fund.

Austrian Development Cooperation (1999). Uganda's External Debt Management, Restructuring, and the HIPC Initiatives: a Case Study. Kampala.

Boote, A. and Kamau T. (1997). Debt Relief for Low-income Countries: The HIPC Initiative. Pamphlet No.51. Washington, DC: International Monetary Fund.

Government of Uganda (1995). Constitution of the Republic of Uganda. Kampala.

International Monetary Fund (2008a). Debt Relief under the Heavily Indebted Poor Countries Initiative. Fact sheet. Washington, DC.

—— (2008b). The Multilateral Debt Relief Initiative. Fact sheet. Washington, DC.

Kitabire, D., Kabanda, M., and Zigiti, Z. (2007). Recent Debt Relief Initiatives and Social Service Delivery in Africa: Uganda's Experience. Kampala.

Mallaby, S. (2004). *The World's Banker.* New York: Penguin Press.

Ministry of Finance and Economic Planning (Various years). Background to the Budget. Kampala.

Chapter 13

Adam, C. (2005). 'Exogenous Inflows and Real Exchange Rates: Theoretical Quirk or Empirical Reality?' Paper presented at the IMF Seminar on Foreign Aid and Macroeconomic Management, Maputo.

Atingi-Ego, M. (2006). 'Budget Support, Aid Dependency and Dutch Disease: the Case of Uganda', in Stefan Koeberle, Zoran Stavreski, and Jan Walliser (eds), *Budget Support as More Effective Aid: Recent Experiences and Emerging Lessons*. Washington, DC: World Bank, 353–69.

—— and Sebudde, R. (2000). 'Uganda's Equilibrium Real Exchange Rate and its Implications for Non-traditional Export Performance', *Bank of Uganda Staff Papers*, 2(1): 1–43.

Brownbridge, M. and Tumusiime-Mutebile, E. (2007). 'Aid and Fiscal Deficits: Lessons from Uganda on the Implications for Macroeconomic Management and Fiscal Sustainability', *Development Policy Review*, 25(2): 193–213.

Bulir, A. and Hamann, A. (2003). 'Aid Volatility: an Empirical Assessment', *International Monetary Fund Staff Papers*, 50(1): 64–89.

International Monetary Fund (2006). 'Uganda: Sixth Review under the Three Year Arrangement under the Poverty Reduction and Growth Facility, Request for Waiver of Performance Criteria and Request for Policy Support Instrument', *IMF Country Report No. 06/43*.

Kitabire, D. (2005). 'Implications of Substantially Increased Development Aid: the Case of Uganda', *IDS Bulletin*, 36(3): 40–4.

Miovic, P. (2004). 'Poverty Reduction Support Credits in Uganda: Results of a Stocktaking Study', mimeo 29602, World Bank.

OECD (Organization for Economic Cooperation and Development) (2006). Joint Evaluation of General Budget Support 1994–2004: Uganda Country Report. Paris: OECD.

Williamson, T. and Canagarajah, S. (2003). 'Is there a place for Virtual Poverty Funds in Pro-poor Public Spending Reform? Lessons from Uganda's PAF', *Development Policy Review*, 21(4): 449–80.

Chapter 14

Aarnes, D., Sjolander, S., and Steffensen, J. (2000). Public Financial Management Issues in Uganda—A Joint Review. Study commissioned by NORAD, DANIDA, and SIDA.

Bahiigwa, G., Ellis, F., Fjeldstad, O., and Iversen V. (2004). Rural Taxation in Uganda: Implications for Growth, Income Distribution, Local Government Revenue and Poverty Reduction. *Research Series* No. 35. Kampala: Economic Policy Research Centre.

Golola, M. (2001). Reforms, Rural Bureaucracies, and Service Delivery in Uganda. United Nations University World Institute for Development Economics Research. Discussion Paper No. 2001/115. Helsinki: WIDER.

Government of Uganda (1987). Resistance Council/Committees Statute No. 9 of 1987. Kampala.

—— (1995), Constitution of the Republic of Uganda, Kampala.

—— (1997), Local Government Act, Kampala.

—— (1998), Local Government Finance and Accounting Regulations, Kampala.

Government of Uganda/Donor Sub-Group on Decentralization (2001). Fiscal Decentralization in Uganda—The Way Forward, Final Report. Kampala.

Bibliography

Green, E. (2008). District Creation and Decentralization in Uganda, *Crisis States Working Paper* No. 24, London: Development Studies Institute, London School of Economics and Political Science.

Kizilbash, Z. and Williamson, T. (2008). Common Funds for Sector Support. Building Blocks or Stumbling Blocks? *ODI Briefing Paper* 36. London: Overseas Development Institute.

Kragh, O., Steffensen, J., Williamson, T., and Baryabanoha, W. (2003). Design of the Financial Management, Accountability and Reporting Systems under Fiscal Decentralization Strategy and Issues on Local Government Financial Management, Background paper for Public Expenditure Review.

Lister, S., Williamson, T., Steffensen, J., and Barayabanoha, W. (2006). Joint Evaluation of General Budget Support: Uganda Country Report. Paris: OECD.

Local Government Finance Commission (2003). Allocation Principles, Formulae, Modalities and Flow of Central Government Transfers. Kampala.

Mahler, W. (2005). Options for Financing Local Governments in the Ugandan Context. Duke Center for International Development.

Ministry of Finance, Planning and Economic Development (1998–2007). Budget Speeches. Published Annually. Kampala.

—— (2000). Poverty Action Fund: General Guidelines for the Planning and Operation of Conditional Grants. Kampala.

—— (2002). Fiscal Decentralization in Uganda—Draft Strategy Paper. Kampala.

Ministry of Local Government (2002). Preparation of Local Government Development Programme Phase II. Kampala.

—— (2005). Annual Assessment of Minimum Conditions and Performance Measures for Local Governments 2004. Final National Synthesis Report. Kampala.

Obwona, M., J. Steffensen, S., Trollegaad, Y., Mwanga, F., Luwangwa, B., Twodo, A., Ojoo, F., and Seguya, F. (2000). 'Fiscal Decentralization and Sub-National Government in Relation to Infrastructure Provision in Uganda'. 'Fiscal Decentralization and Sub-National Finance in Africa'. Copenhagen: National Association of Local Authorities in Denmark.

Ocwich, D. (2005). Can Uganda's Economy Support More Districts? *New Vision*, Kampala, 8 August.

Reinikka, R. and Svensson, J. (2004). Local Capture: Evidence from a Central Government Transfer Program in Uganda. *The Quarterly Journal of Economics*, 119(2): 679–706.

Sarzin, Z. (2007). Local Government Revenue Policies and their Impacts: A Model For Tanzania and Uganda. Washington, DC: World Bank.

Steffensen, J., Tidemand, P., and Ssewankambo. E. (2004). A Comparative Analysis of Decentralization in Kenya, Uganda and Tanzania: Final Synthesis Report. Washington, DC: World Bank.

Williamson, T. (2003). Targets and Results in Public Sector Management: Uganda Case Study. *ODI Working Paper* 205. London: Overseas Development Institute.

—— Mugerwa, C., Smith, G., Mubaale Kafuko, P., and Baryabanoha, W. (2006). Local Government Public Financial Management Assessment, 2005. London: Overseas Development Institute.

World Bank (2004). Uganda Country Integrated Fiduciary Assessment—Volume IV, Local Government Integrated Fiduciary Risk Assessment. Washington, DC: World Bank.

Chapter 15

Asebe, E. and Mwanje, D. (2007). Cost Benefit Analysis Report: The Integrated Financial Management System Implementation in Uganda, Report prepared for the World Bank and Ministry of Finance, Planning and Economic Development.

Bhatt, H., Kianpour, D., and Murphy, P. (2004). Integrated Financial Management System: Pilot Evaluation Report. Kampala.

Bwoch, G. (2002). 'Financial Management Reforms in Uganda: The Uganda Experience'. Paper delivered at the Integrated Financial Management System Launch Workshop, Entebbe.

—— (2005a). 'Public Sector Accounting Issues and Challenges in Eastern Africa', Paper presented at the Eastern Africa Convention for ACCA members and other accountants. Nairobi.

—— (2005b). 'The IFMS and its Implications'. Paper presented at the fifth Government/Donor Water and Sanitation Joint Review, Speke Resort, Munyonyo.

Government of Uganda (1997). Local Government Act. Kampala.

—— (1999). Improving Public Procurement in Uganda: Report of the Task Force on Public Procurement in Uganda. Kampala.

—— (2001). Budget Act. Kampala.

—— (2003a). Public Finance and Accountability Act. Kampala.

—— (2003b). Public Procurement and Disposal of Public Assets Act. Kampala.

—— (2006a). Annual Report of the Auditor General. Volume 2: Central Government.

—— (2006b). Public Financial Management Performance Report and Update of CIFA Action Plan 2005.

—— (2007). Annual Report of the Auditor General. Volume 2: Central Government.

Kitunzi, A. (2001). 'Decentralization in Uganda: An Analytical Overview of the Intergovernmental Fiscal Systems'. Report for the World Bank.

Kotter, J. (1996). *Leading Change.* Boston: Harvard Business School Press.

Kyama, P. (2005). 'Change Management for System Implementation: Issues and Challenges'. Paper delivered at the Ministry of Water, Lands and Environment Organizational Development Workshop, Nile Resort Hotel, Jinja.

Pretorius, C. (2006). Public Financial Management Performance Report and Update of CIFA Action Plan 2005. Kampala.

Williamson, T. (2005). 'General Budget Support and Public Financial Management Reform: Emerging lessons from Tanzania and Uganda'. Paper based on a presentation made at the Centre for Aid and Public Expenditure Conference on Budgets and Accountability held at the Overseas Development Institute, London.

World Bank (1995). Republic of Uganda: Staff Appraisal Report (Institutional Capacity Building Project). Report No. 13610–UG. Washington, DC: World Bank.

—— (2001a). Uganda Country Financial Accountability Assessment. Washington, DC: World Bank.

—— (2001b). Uganda Country Procurement Assessment Report. Washington, DC: World Bank.

—— (2004). Uganda Country Integrated Fiduciary Assessment. Washington, DC: World Bank.

Chapter 16

Adam Smith International, Ernst & Young, and Economic Policy Research Centre. (2005). Uganda Privatization Impact Assessment Report, Prepared for Privatization and Utility Sector Reform Project (mimeo).

Berthelemy, J. (2004). *Privatisation in Sub-Saharan Africa: Where Do We Stand?* Paris: OECD Publishing.

Byaruhanga, C. (2005). 'Managing Investment Climate Reform: Case Study of Uganda Telecommunications' (mimeo).

Collier, P. and Reinikka, R. (2001). 'Reconstruction and Liberalization: An Overview' in R. Reinikka and P. Collier (eds), *Uganda's Recovery.* Washington, DC: World Bank, 15–47.

Gokgur, N. (2004). 'Assessing Trends and Outcomes of Private Participation in Infrastructure in Sub-Saharan Africa'. Paper presented at World Bank Conference on Private Participation in Sub-Saharan Africa, Johannesburg.

Mutibwa, P. (1992). *Uganda since Independence—A Story of Unfulfilled Hopes.* London: C. Hurst & Co. Publishers.

Orono, O. (2001). 'Privatization: The Ugandan Experience'. Paper for Privatization Unit.

Pamacheche, F. and Koma, B. (2007). Privatisation in Sub-Saharan Africa—An Essential Route to Poverty Alleviation, *African Integration Review*, Vol. 1, No. 2.

Public Enterprise Reform and Divestiture Statute No. 9 of 1993.

Public Enterprise Reform and Divestiture Act 1 of 2000.

Shirley, M., Tusubira, F., Gebreab, F., and Haggarty, L. (2002). Telecommunications Reform in Uganda. *Policy Research Working Paper* 2864. Washington, DC: World Bank.

UMACIS Ltd. (2000). 'Impact Assessment of the Uganda Privatization Programme'. Kampala.

World Bank. (2000). 'Enterprise Development Project Implementation Completion Report'. Washington.

Internal Documents and Reports from the Privatization and Utility Reform Units, Ministry of Finance, Planning and Economic Development

BMB Consultants. (1990). 'Public Sector Administration Reform and Planning Study'. Study for Enterprise Development Project, Ministry of Finance.

Divestiture and Reform Implementation Committee. (1991). 'Action Plan for Public Enterprise Reform and Divestiture'. Paper DRIC/2/91.

Internal Privatization and Utility Sector Reform Progress Reports

Privatization and Utility Sector Reform Project. (2003). 'Update of Key Performance Indicators for Various Privatized Firms'. Internal working document.

Henry Schroeder & Wagg Co Ltd. (1990). 'Uganda Divestiture Design Study' for Enterprise Development Project, Ministry of Finance.

Statutory Reports (bi-annual) for the Privatization and Utility Sector Reform Programmes, 1999–2004.

Utility Reform Unit. (2008). 'Summary Report on Reforms and Various Activities of URU'. Internal working document, Ministry of Finance, Planning and Economic Development.

Waweru, R. (2005). 'Technical Evaluation and Assessment of Privatization and Utility Sector Reform Project'.

Index